Illustrated by Atsushi Suzumi

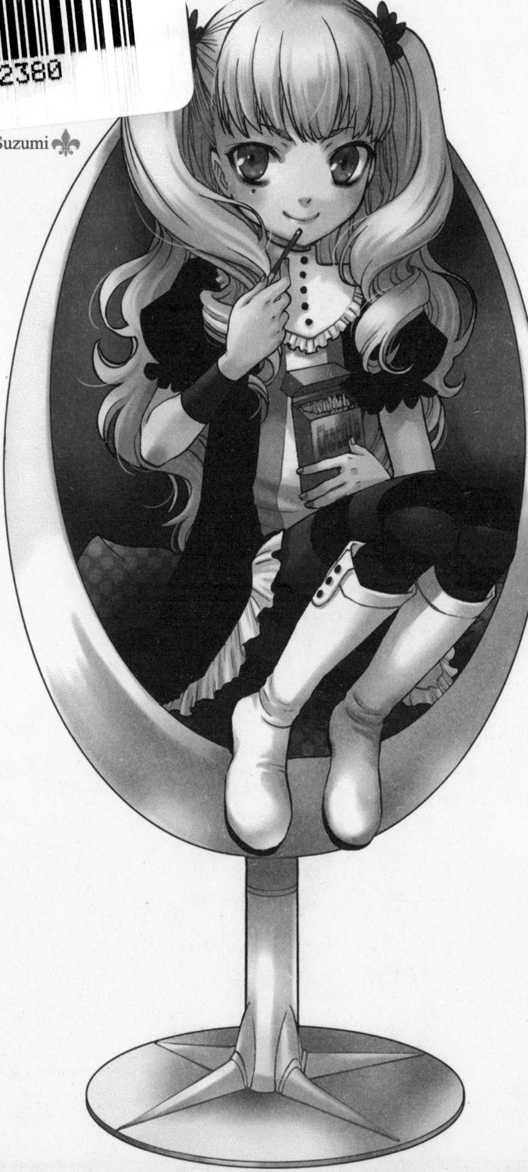

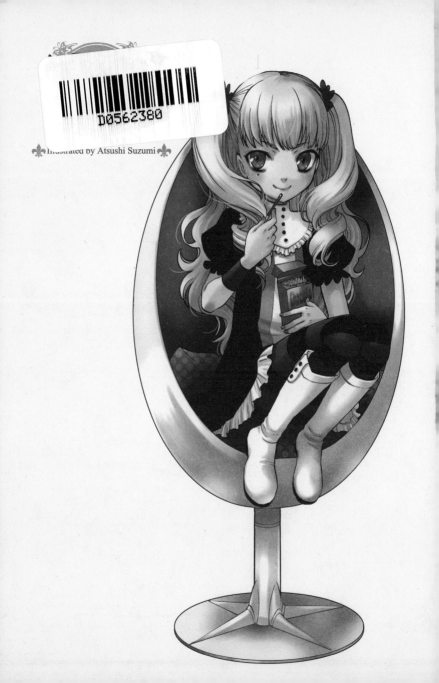

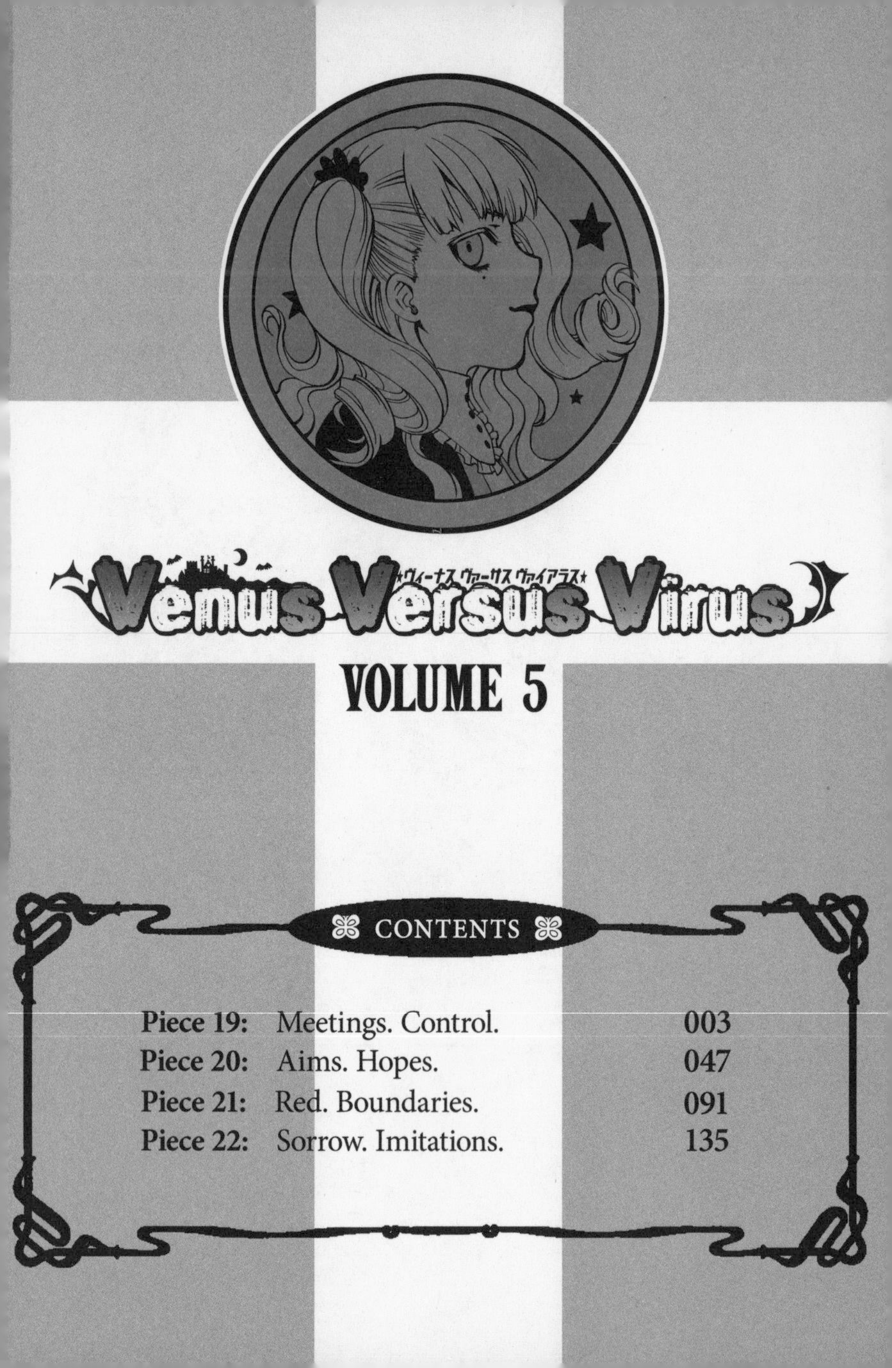

Venus Versus Virus

ヴィーナス ヴァーサス ヴァイアラス

VOLUME 5

CONTENTS

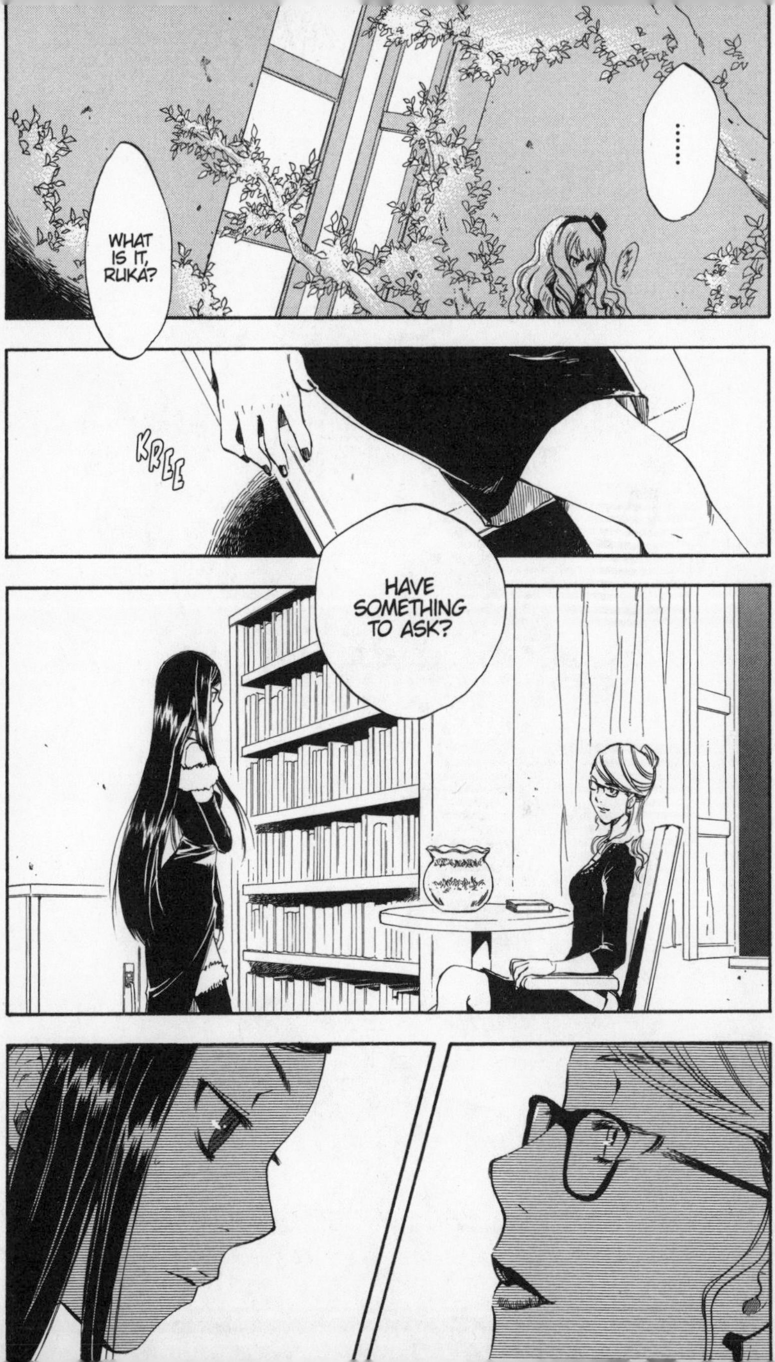
......
WHAT IS IT, RUKA?
KREE
HAVE SOMETHING TO ASK?

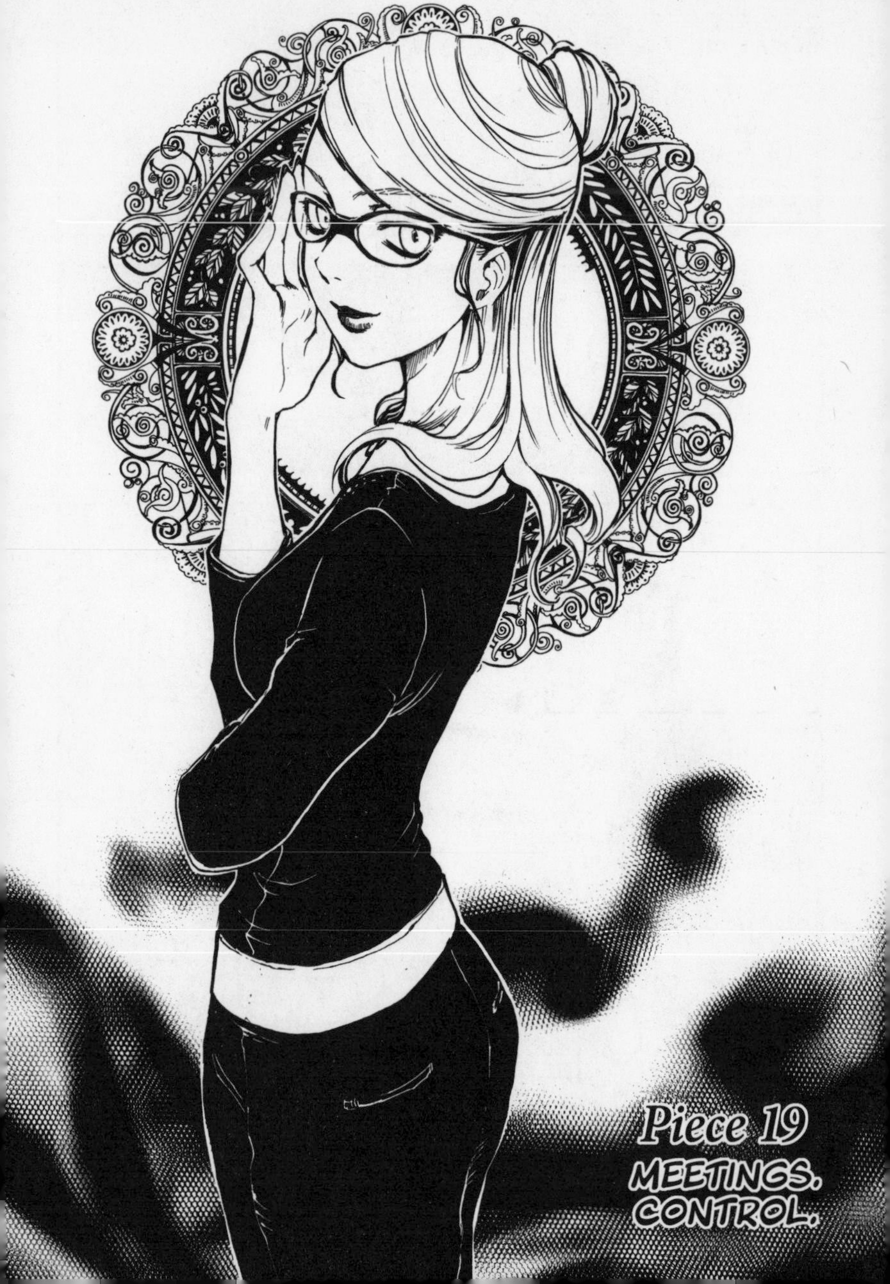
Piece 19
MEETINGS.
CONTROL.

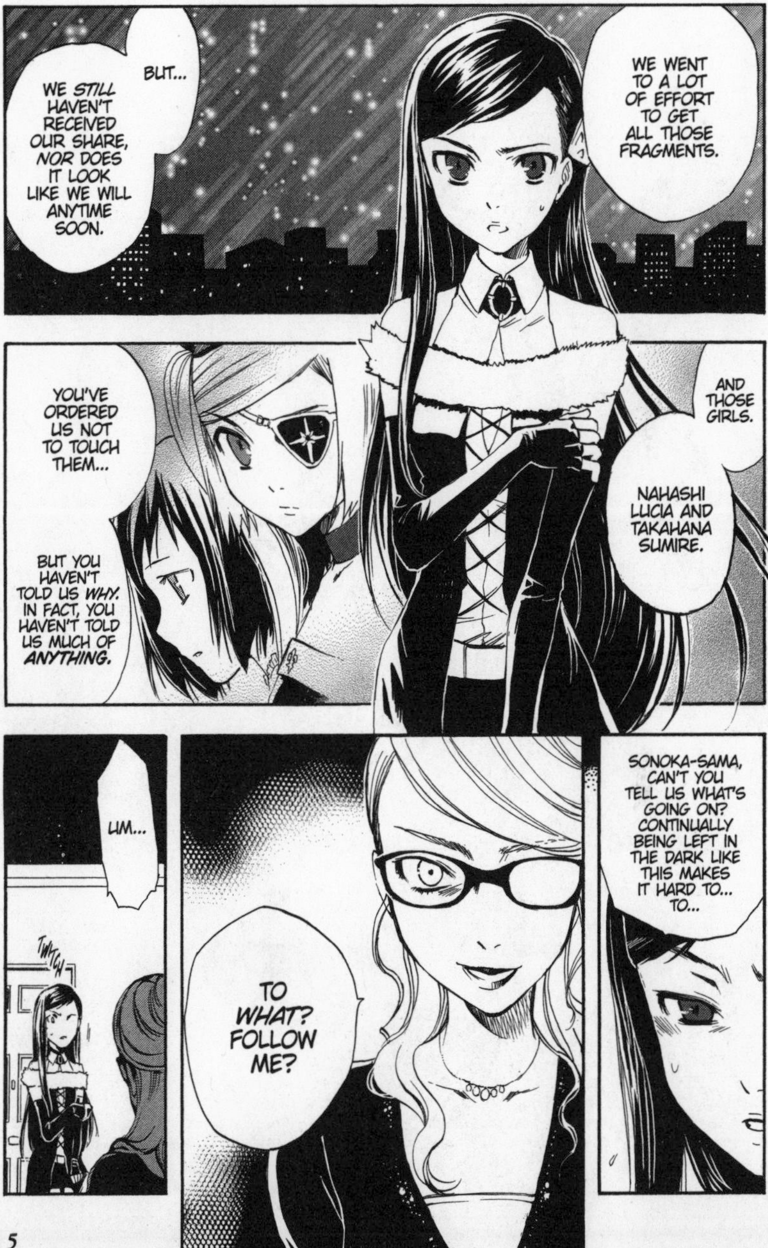
WE WENT TO A LOT OF EFFORT TO GET ALL THOSE FRAGMENTS.
BUT...
WE *STILL* HAVEN'T RECEIVED OUR SHARE, *NOR* DOES IT LOOK LIKE WE WILL ANYTIME SOON.
AND THOSE GIRLS.
NAHASHI LUCIA AND TAKAHANA SUMIRE.
YOU'VE ORDERED US NOT TO TOUCH THEM...
BUT YOU HAVEN'T TOLD US *WHY.* IN FACT, YOU HAVEN'T TOLD US MUCH OF ***ANYTHING.***
SONOKA-SAMA, CAN'T YOU TELL US WHAT'S GOING ON? CONTINUALLY BEING LEFT IN THE DARK LIKE THIS MAKES IT HARD TO... TO...
TO *WHAT?* FOLLOW ME?
UM...
TWITCH

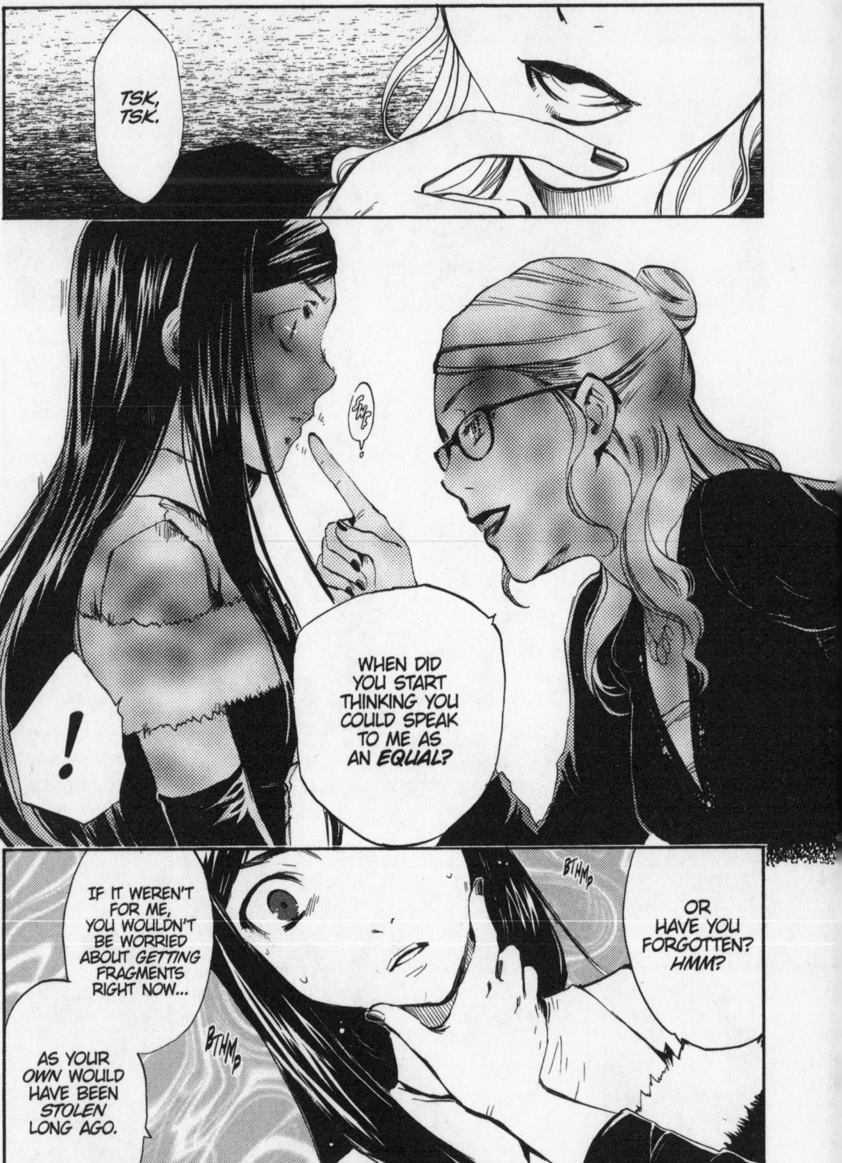
TSK, TSK.
WHEN DID YOU START THINKING YOU COULD SPEAK TO ME AS AN *EQUAL?*
!
OR HAVE YOU FORGOTTEN? *HMM?*
BTHMP
IF IT WEREN'T FOR ME, YOU WOULDN'T BE WORRIED ABOUT *GETTING* FRAGMENTS RIGHT NOW...
BTHMP
AS YOUR *OWN* WOULD HAVE BEEN *STOLEN* LONG AGO.

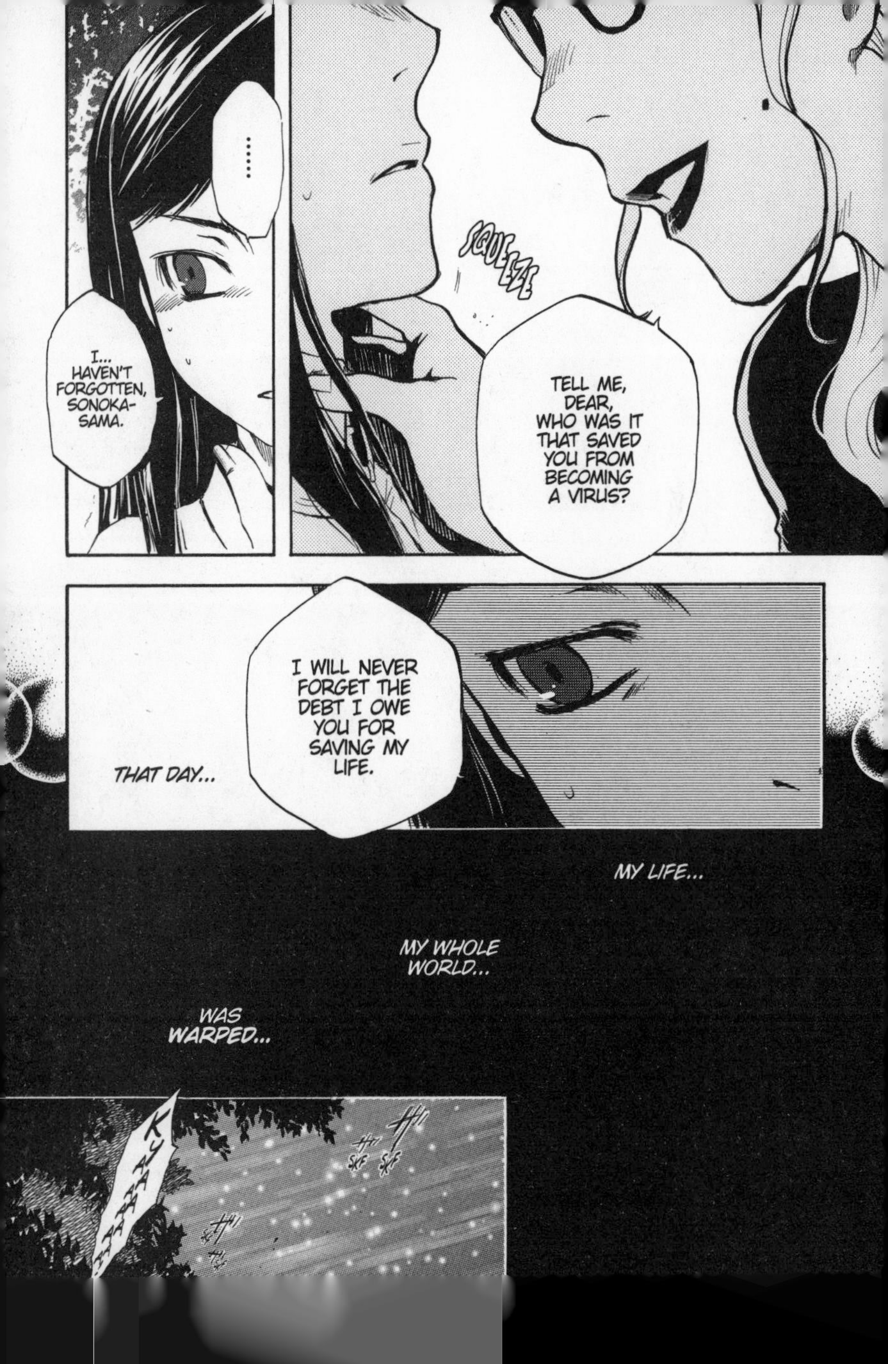
SQUEEZE
TELL ME, DEAR, WHO WAS IT THAT SAVED YOU FROM BECOMING A VIRUS?
......
I... HAVEN'T FORGOTTEN, SONOKA-SAMA.
I WILL NEVER FORGET THE DEBT I OWE YOU FOR SAVING MY LIFE.
THAT DAY...
MY LIFE...
MY WHOLE WORLD...
WAS WARPED...
SKF
SKF
KYAAAAA

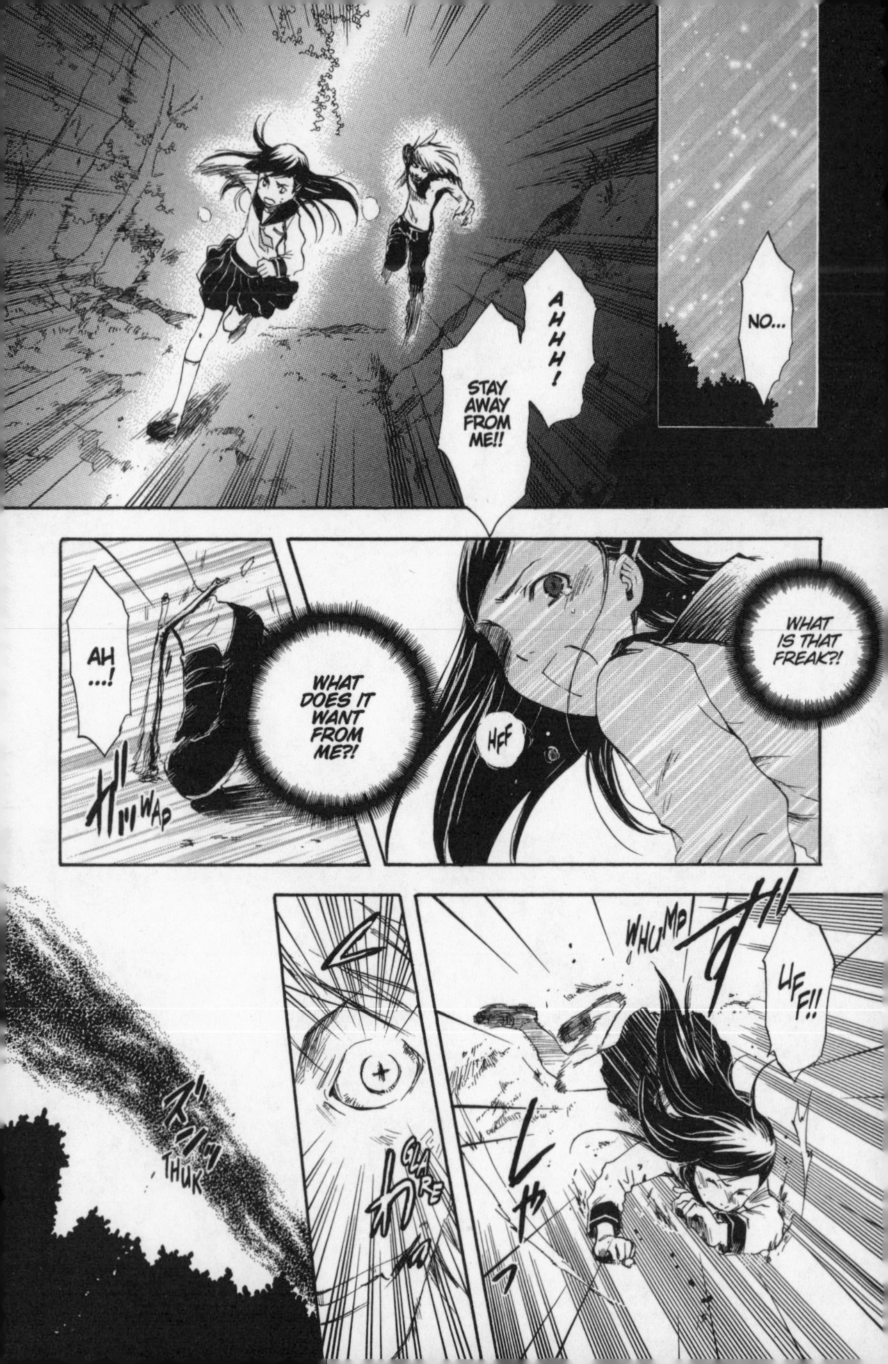
NO...
AHHH!
STAY AWAY FROM ME!!
WHAT IS THAT FREAK?!
HFF
WHAT DOES IT WANT FROM ME?!
AH ...!
WAP
WHUMP
UFF!!
GLARE
THUK

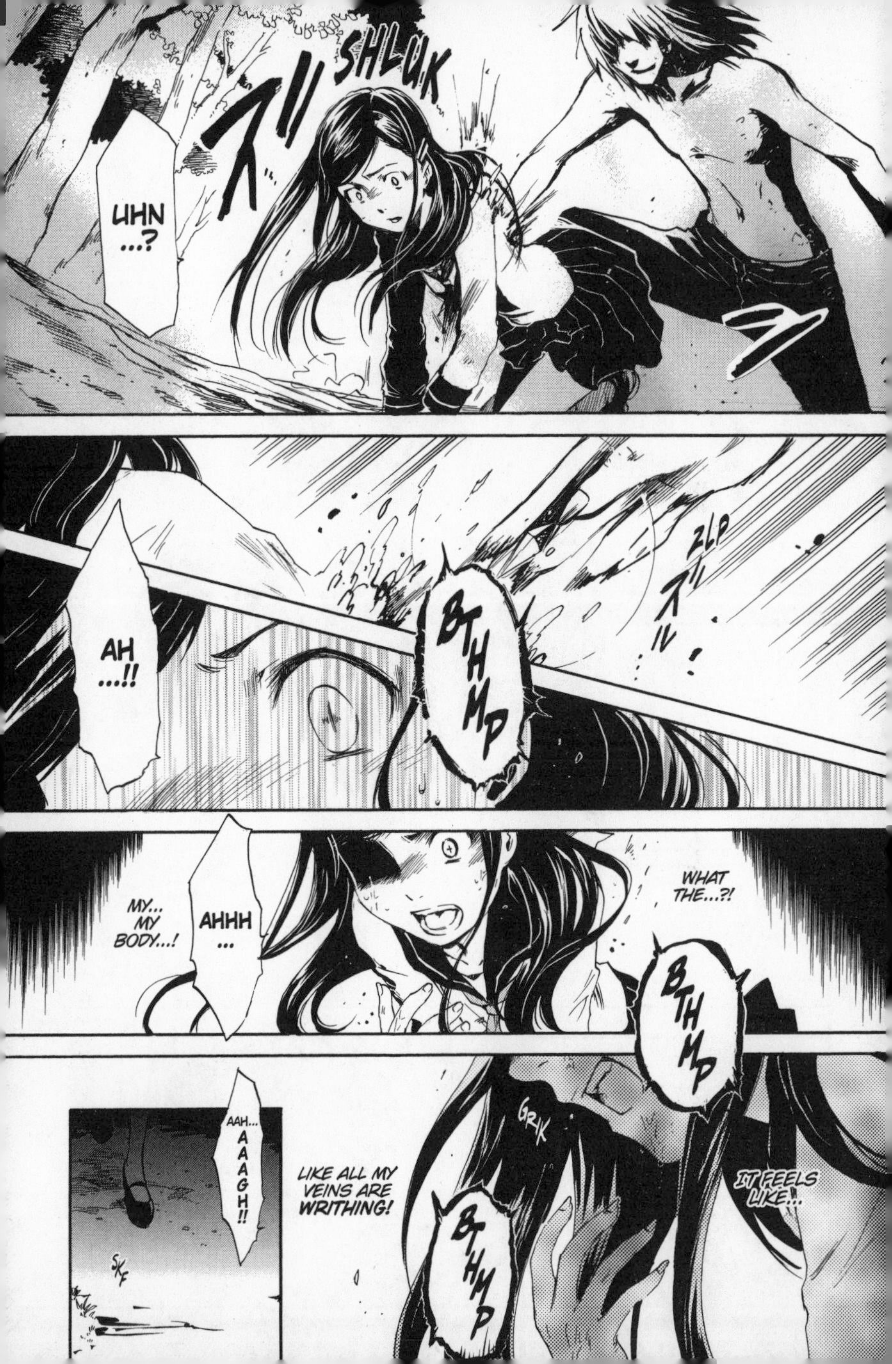
SHLUK
UHN ...?
ZLP
BTHMP
AH ...!!
WHAT THE...?!
BTHMP
AHHH ...
MY... MY BODY...!
IT FEELS LIKE...
GRIK
BTHMP
LIKE ALL MY VEINS ARE WRITHING!
AAH... AAAAGH!!
SKF

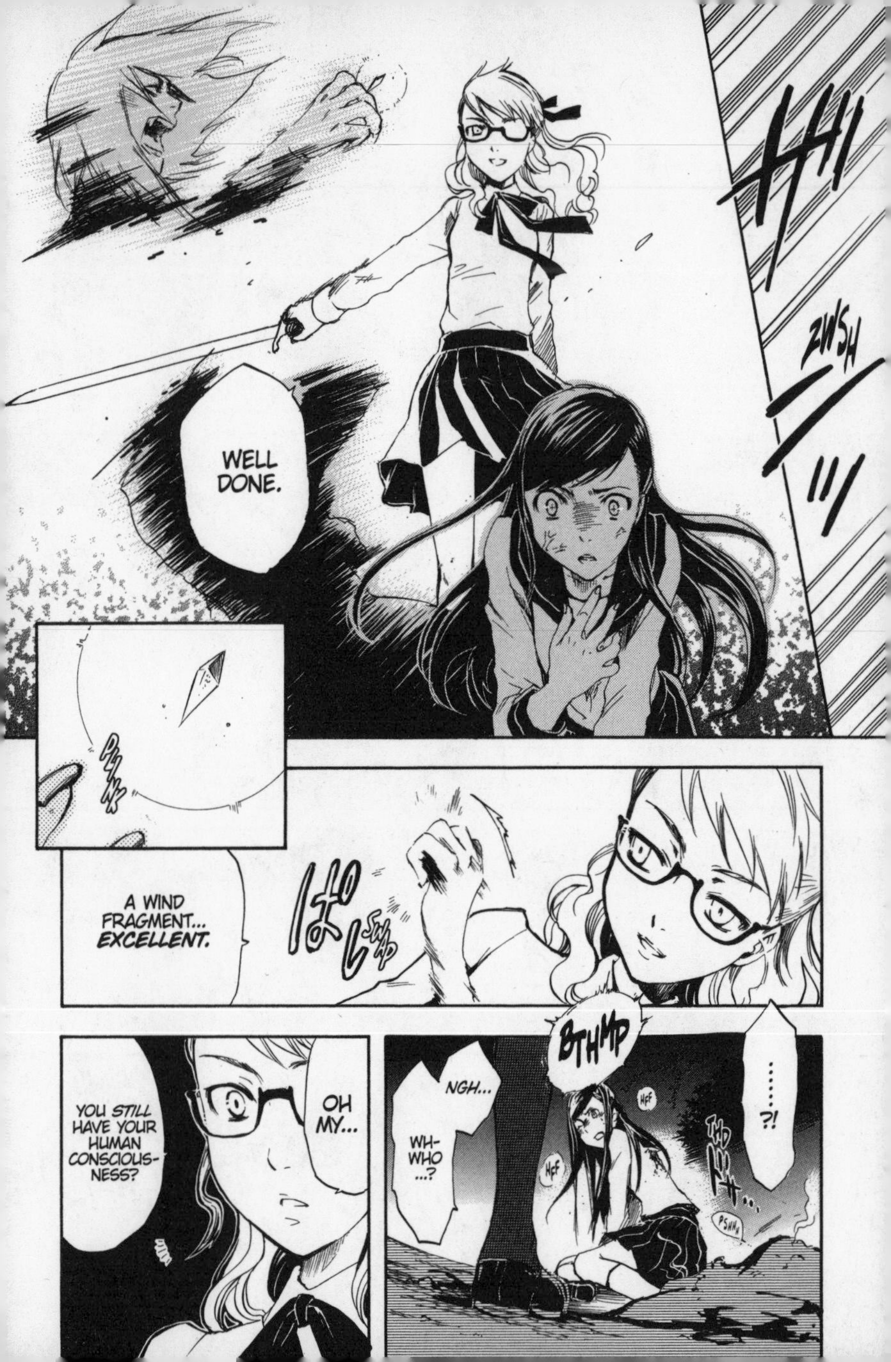
ZWSH
WELL DONE.
PLINK
SWP
A WIND FRAGMENT... *EXCELLENT.*
BTHMP
......?!
THD
PSHHH
NGH...
HFF
HFF
WH-WHO ...?
OH MY...
YOU *STILL* HAVE YOUR HUMAN CONSCIOUS-NESS?

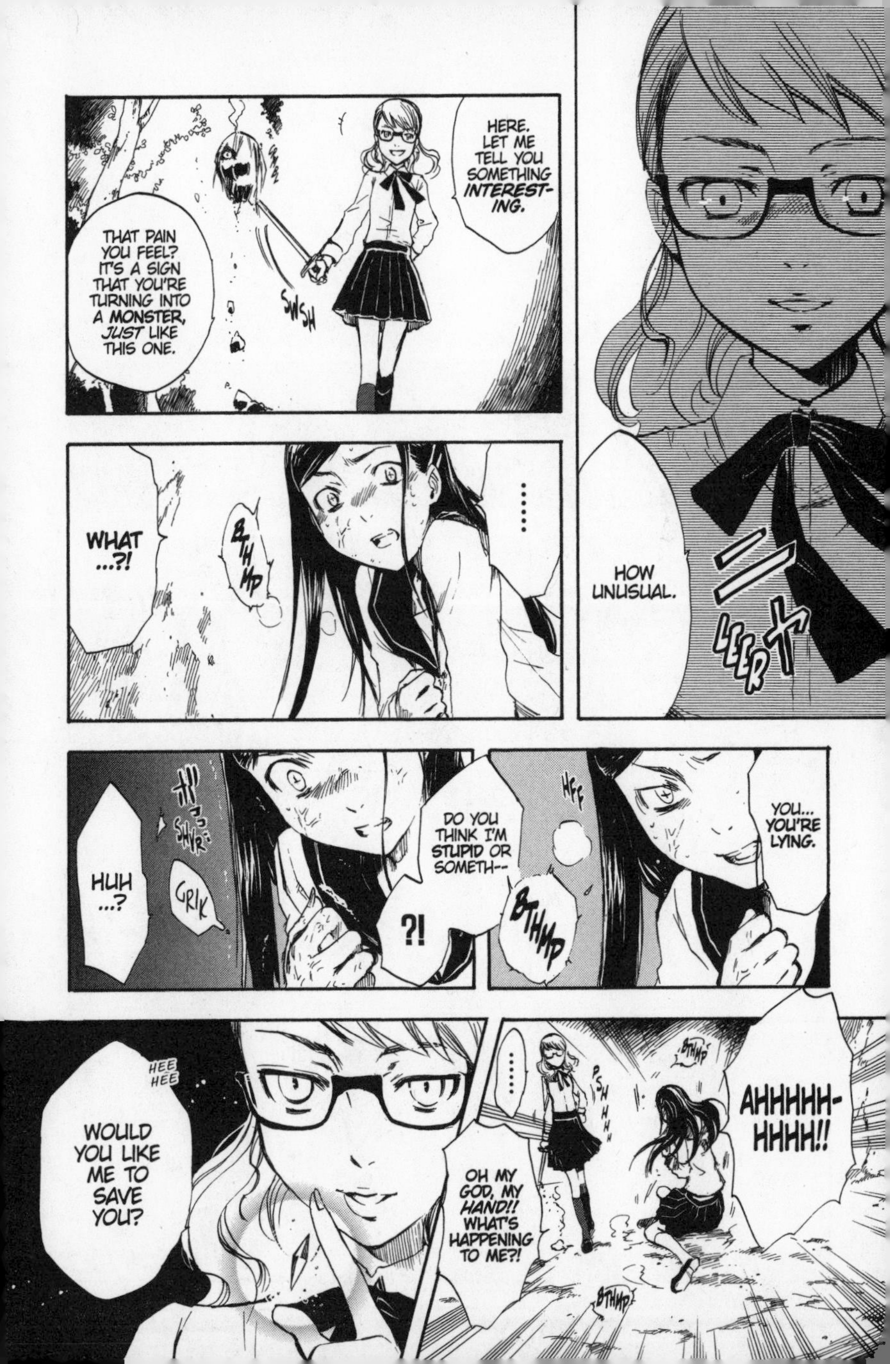
HOW UNUSUAL.
LEER
HERE. LET ME TELL YOU SOMETHING *INTERESTING.*
THAT PAIN YOU FEEL? IT'S A SIGN THAT YOU'RE TURNING INTO A **MONSTER**, *JUST* LIKE THIS ONE.
SWSH
......
BTHMP
WHAT ...?!
YOU... YOU'RE LYING.
HFF
BTHMP
DO YOU THINK I'M STUPID OR SOMETH--
?!
GRIK
SHVR
HUH ...?
AHHHHH-HHHH!!
BTHMP
PSHHHH
......
OH MY GOD, MY *HAND!!* WHAT'S HAPPENING TO ME?!
BTHMP
HEE HEE
WOULD YOU LIKE ME TO SAVE YOU?

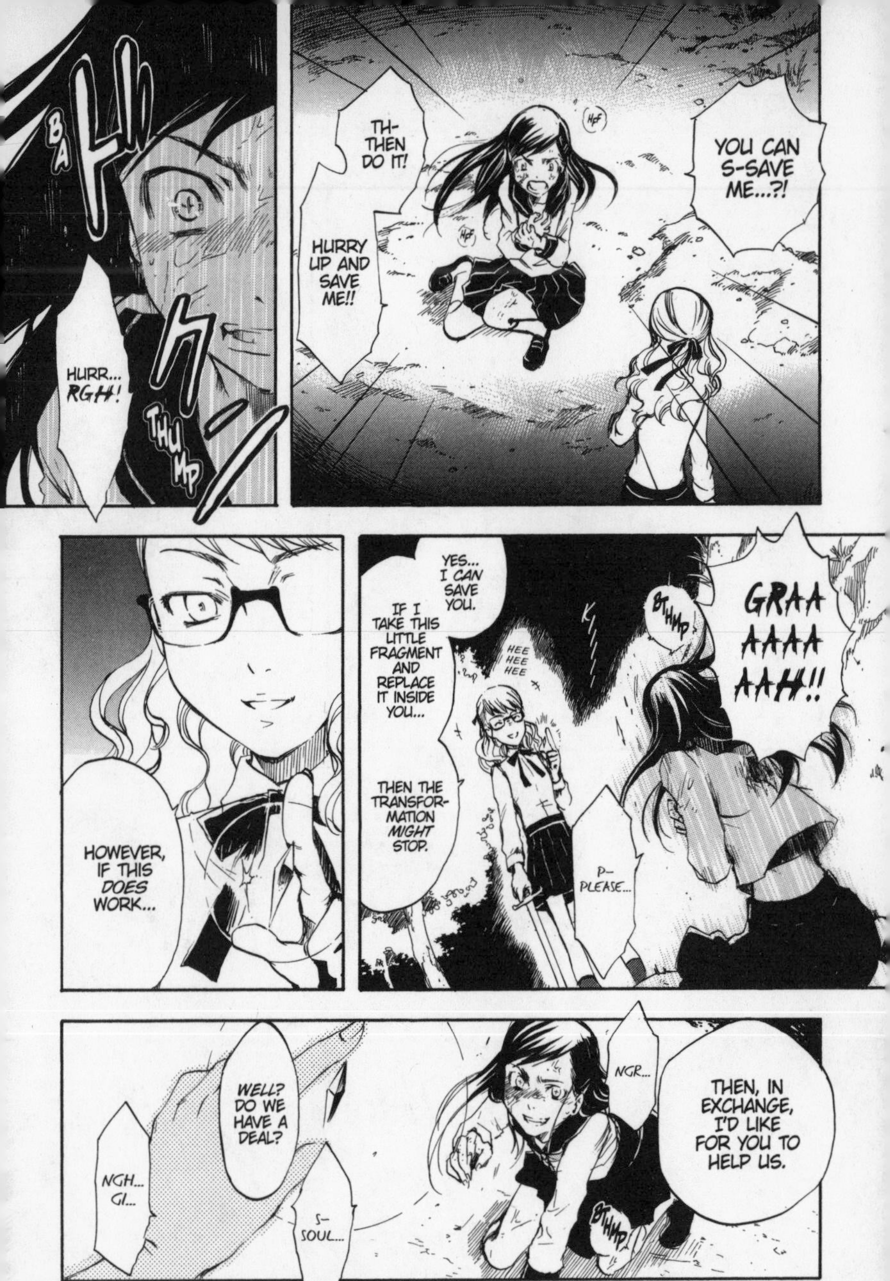
YOU CAN S-SAVE ME...?!
TH-THEN DO IT!
HURRY UP AND SAVE ME!!
BA
HURR... *RGH*!
THUMP
GRAA AAAA *AAH*!!
BTHMP
YES... I *CAN* SAVE YOU.
IF I TAKE THIS LITTLE FRAGMENT AND REPLACE IT INSIDE YOU...
HEE HEE HEE
THEN THE TRANSFORMATION *MIGHT* STOP.
P-PLEASE...
HOWEVER, IF THIS *DOES* WORK...
THEN, IN EXCHANGE, I'D LIKE FOR YOU TO HELP US.
NGR...
BTHMP
WELL? DO WE HAVE A DEAL?
S-SOUL...
NGH... GI...

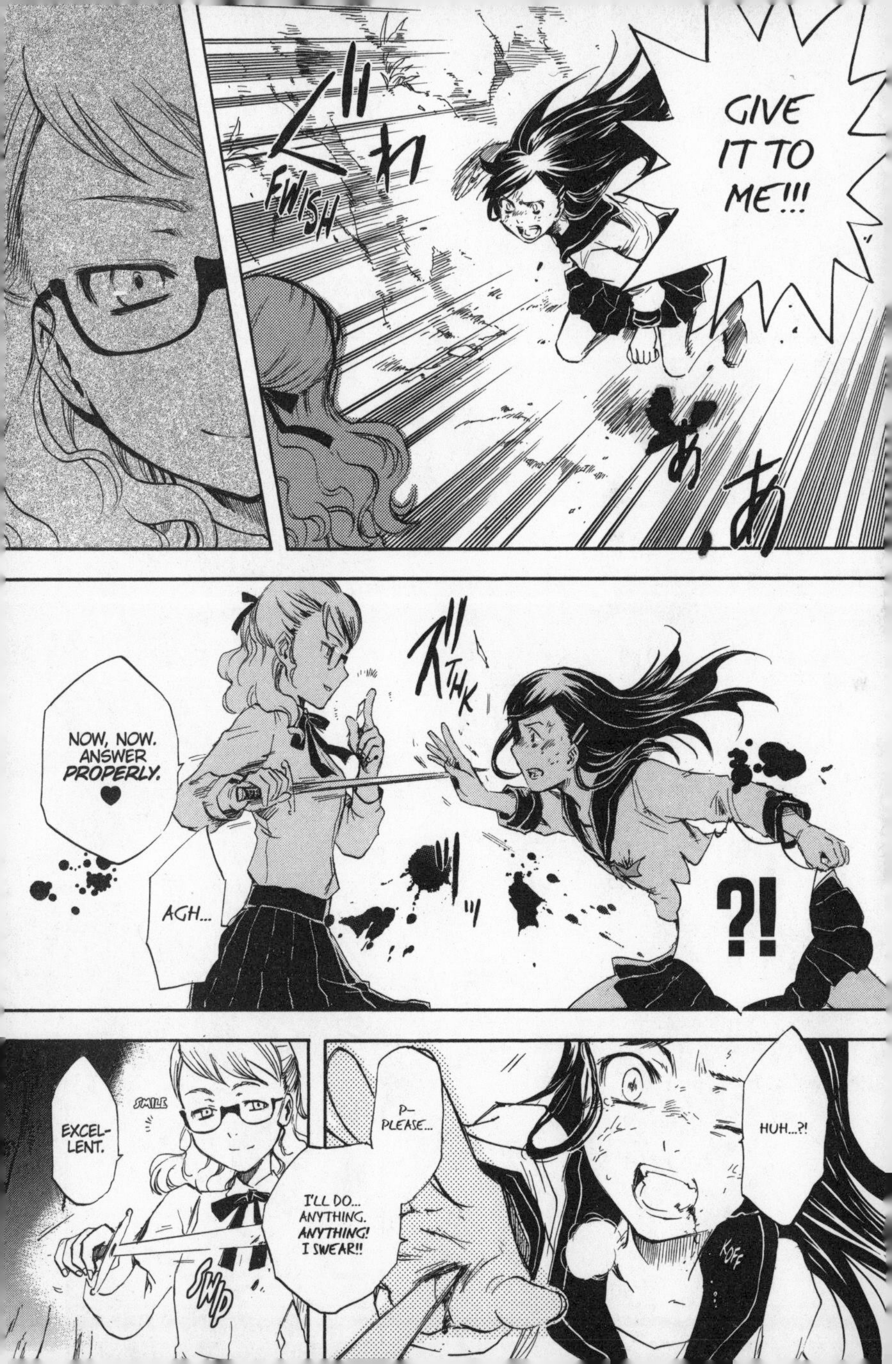
GIVE IT TO ME!!!
FWISH
THK
?!
NOW, NOW. ANSWER PROPERLY. ♥
AGH...
HUH...?!
KOFF
P-PLEASE...
I'LL DO... ANYTHING. ANYTHING! I SWEAR!!
SMILE
EXCEL-LENT.
SWIP

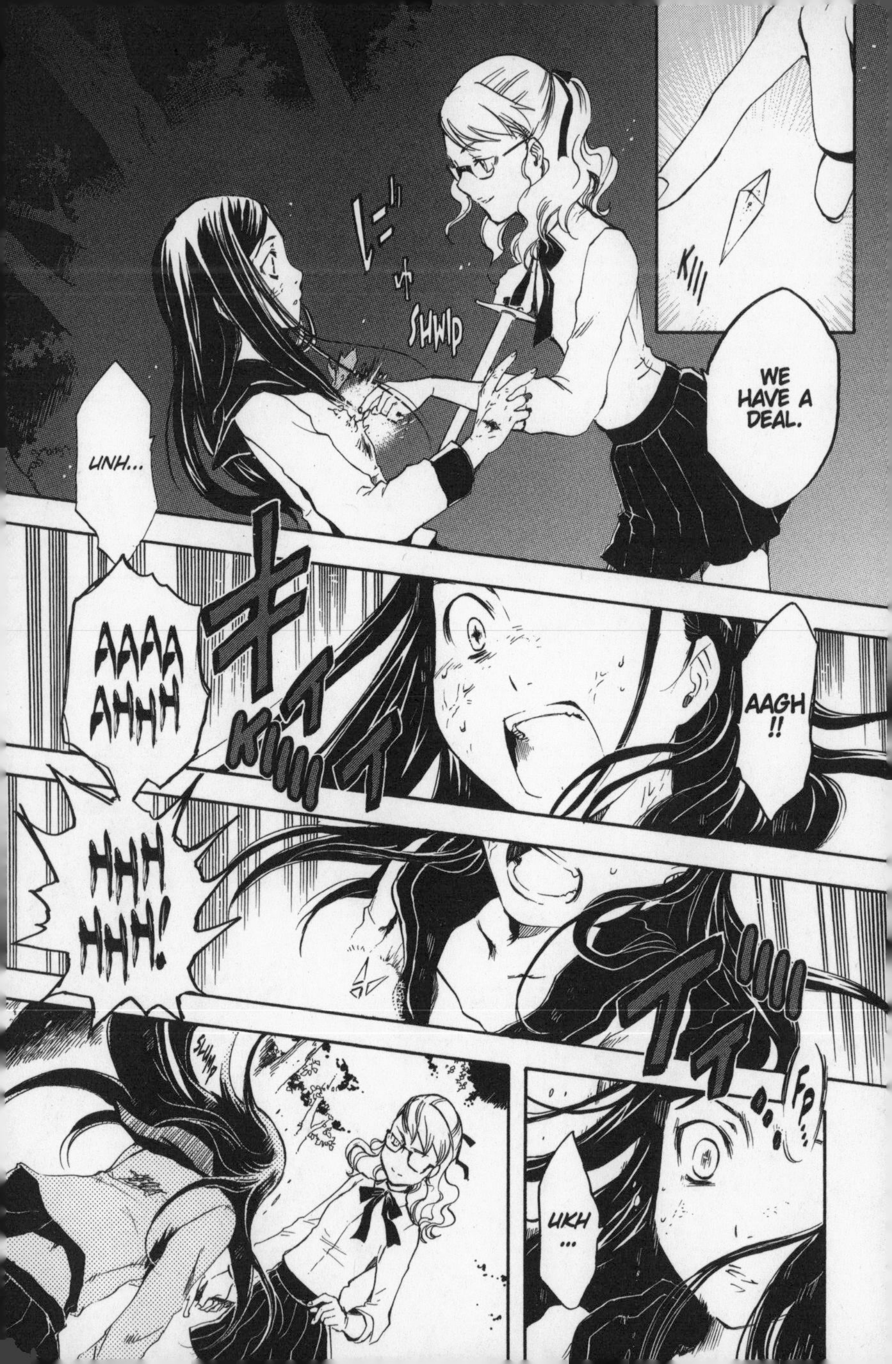
KIII
WE HAVE A DEAL.
SHWIP
UNH...
AAGH!!
KIIII
AAAA AHHH
HHH HHH!
FP...
UKH ...
SLUMP

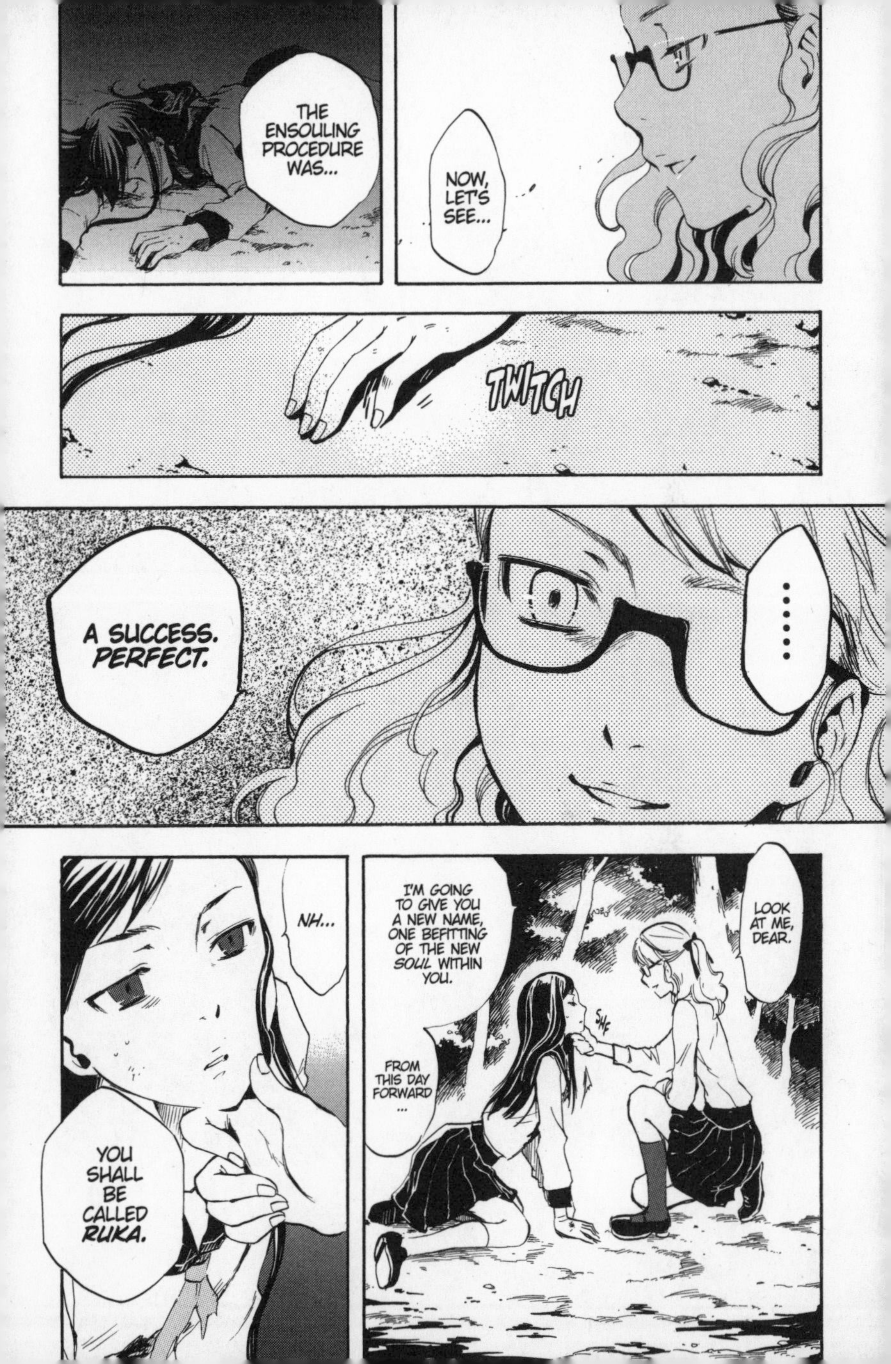
NOW, LET'S SEE...
THE ENSOULING PROCEDURE WAS...
TWITCH
......
A SUCCESS. PERFECT.
LOOK AT ME, DEAR.
I'M GOING TO GIVE YOU A NEW NAME, ONE BEFITTING OF THE NEW *SOUL* WITHIN YOU.
FROM THIS DAY FORWARD ...
NH...
YOU SHALL BE CALLED *RUKA*.

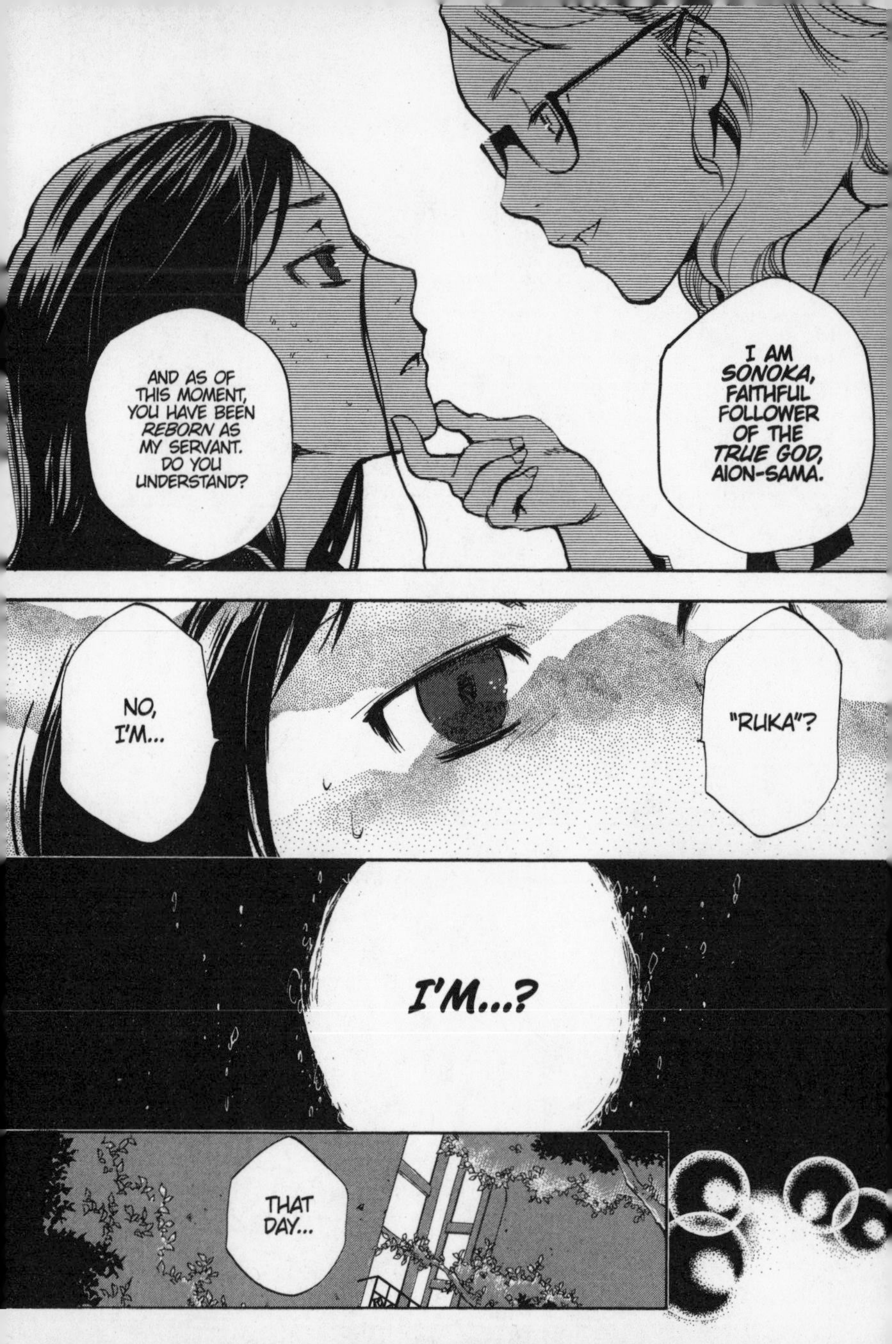
I AM SONOKA, FAITHFUL FOLLOWER OF THE TRUE GOD, AION-SAMA.
AND AS OF THIS MOMENT, YOU HAVE BEEN REBORN AS MY SERVANT. DO YOU UNDERSTAND?
"RUKA"?
NO, I'M...
I'M...?
THAT DAY...

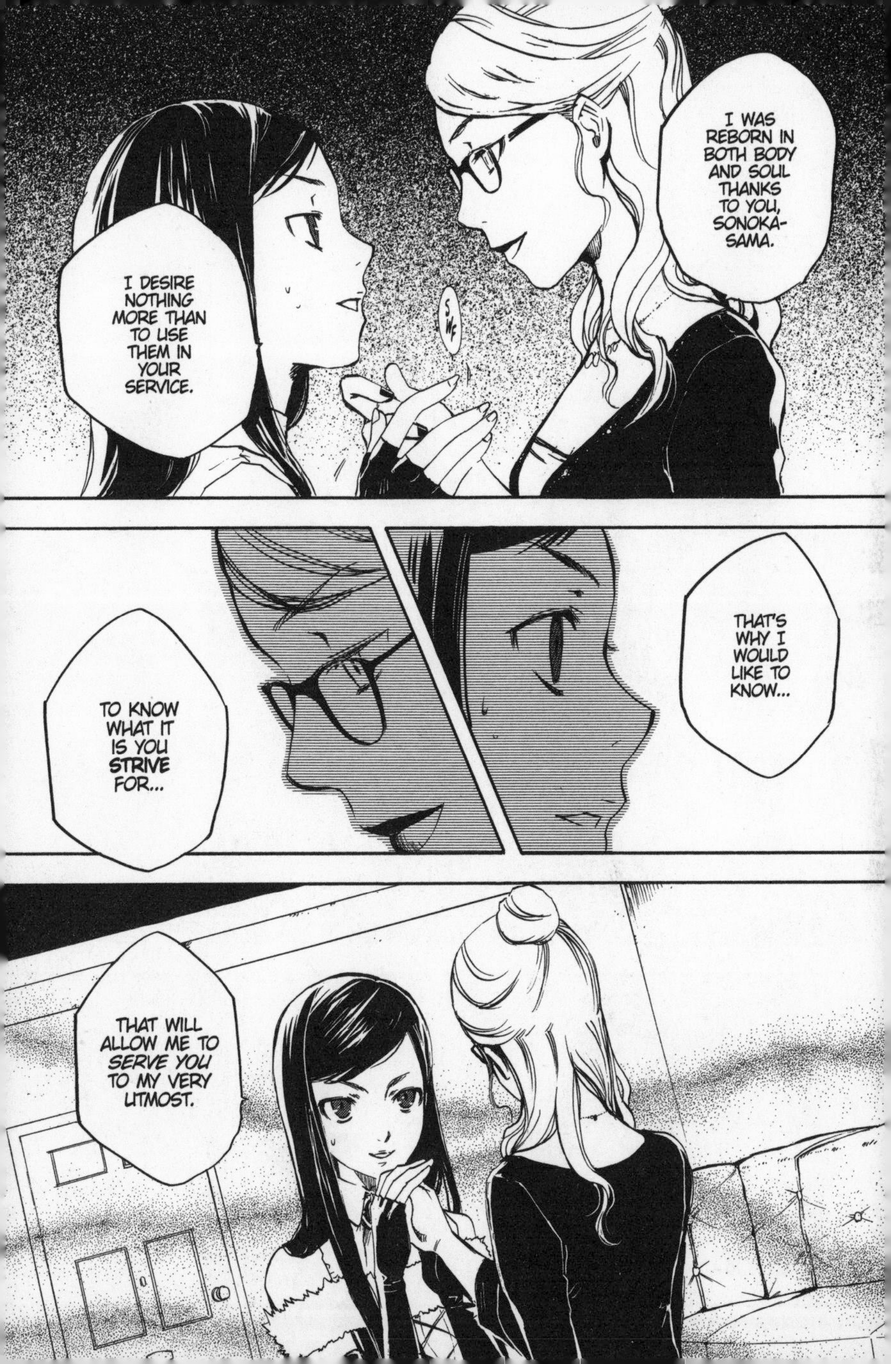
I WAS REBORN IN BOTH BODY AND SOUL THANKS TO YOU, SONOKA-SAMA.
SWF
I DESIRE NOTHING MORE THAN TO USE THEM IN YOUR SERVICE.
THAT'S WHY I WOULD LIKE TO KNOW...
TO KNOW WHAT IT IS YOU STRIVE FOR...
THAT WILL ALLOW ME TO SERVE YOU TO MY VERY UTMOST.

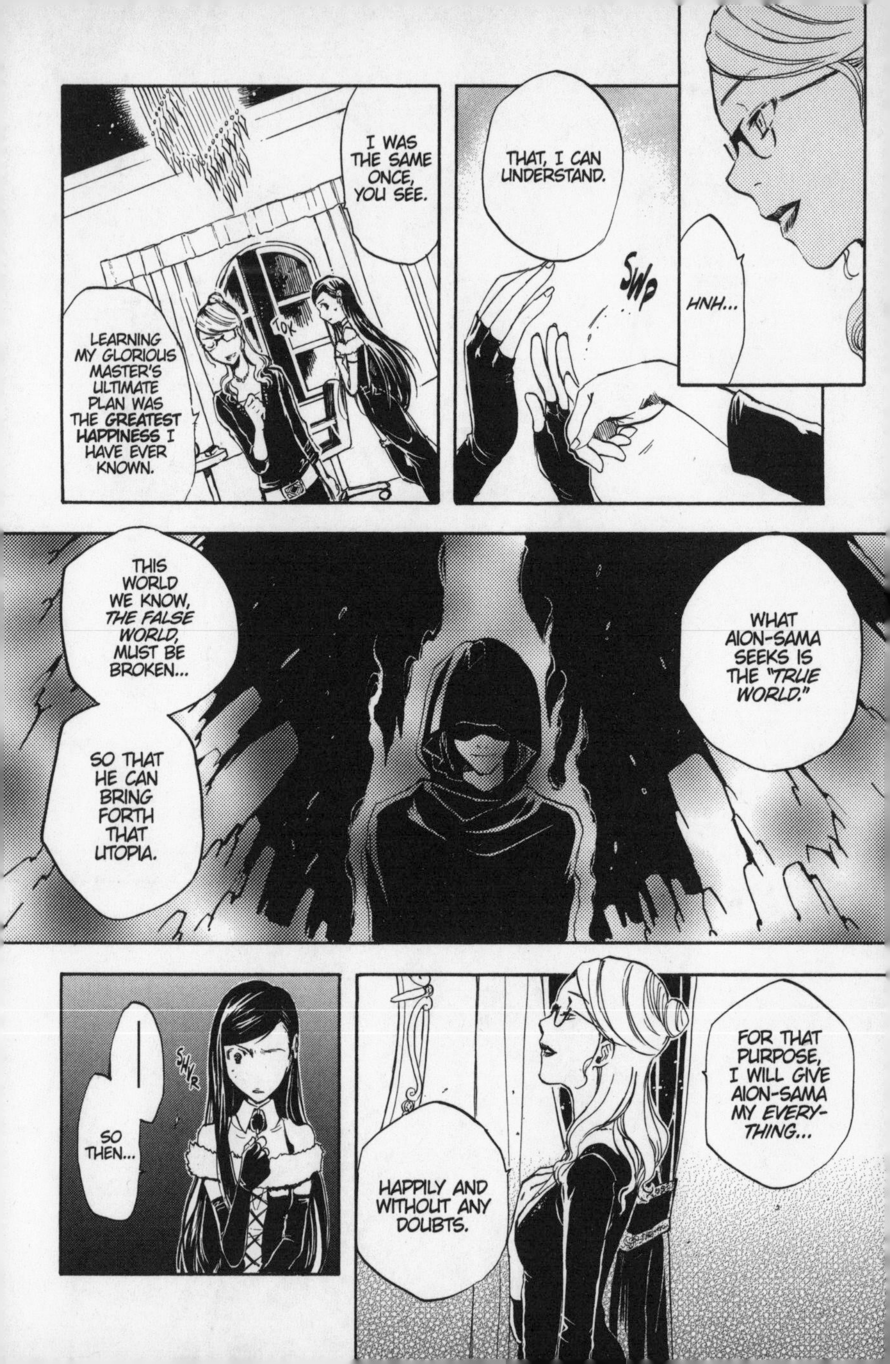
HNH...
THAT, I CAN UNDERSTAND.
SWP
I WAS THE SAME ONCE, YOU SEE.
TOK
LEARNING MY GLORIOUS MASTER'S ULTIMATE PLAN WAS THE GREATEST HAPPINESS I HAVE EVER KNOWN.
WHAT AION-SAMA SEEKS IS THE "TRUE WORLD."
THIS WORLD WE KNOW, THE FALSE WORLD, MUST BE BROKEN...
SO THAT HE CAN BRING FORTH THAT UTOPIA.
FOR THAT PURPOSE, I WILL GIVE AION-SAMA MY EVERY-THING...
HAPPILY AND WITHOUT ANY DOUBTS.
SHYR
SO THEN...

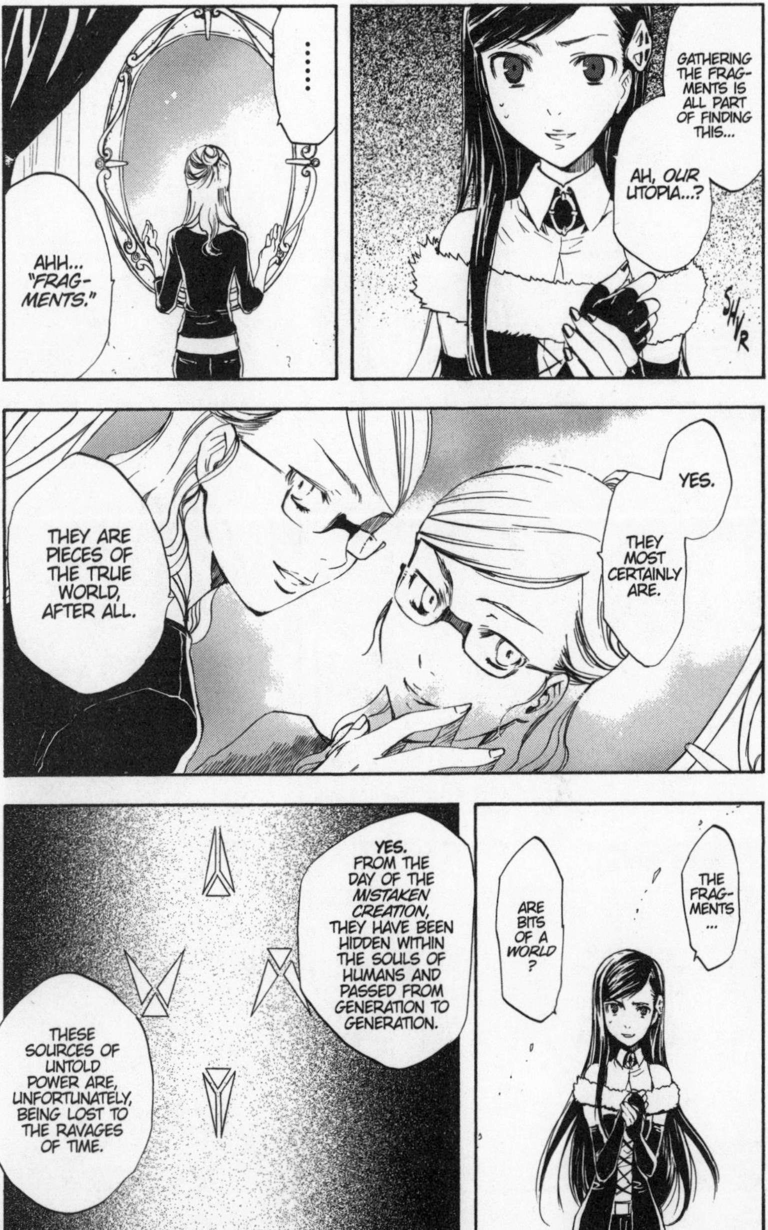
GATHERING THE FRAGMENTS IS ALL PART OF FINDING THIS...
AH, *OUR* UTOPIA...?
SHVR
......
AHH... *"FRAGMENTS."*
YES.
THEY MOST CERTAINLY ARE.
THEY ARE PIECES OF THE TRUE WORLD, AFTER ALL.
THE FRAGMENTS...
ARE BITS OF A *WORLD*?
YES. FROM THE DAY OF THE *MISTAKEN CREATION*, THEY HAVE BEEN HIDDEN WITHIN THE SOULS OF HUMANS AND PASSED FROM GENERATION TO GENERATION.
THESE SOURCES OF UNTOLD POWER ARE, UNFORTUNATELY, BEING LOST TO THE RAVAGES OF TIME.

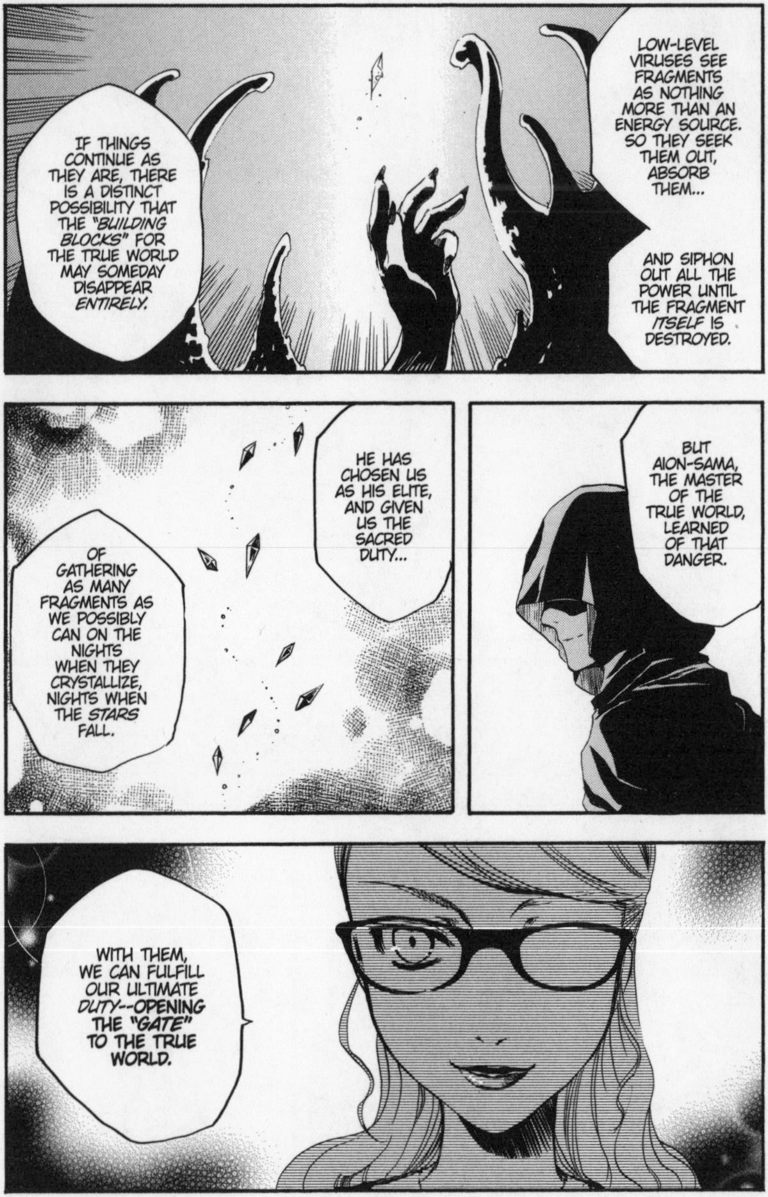
LOW-LEVEL VIRUSES SEE FRAGMENTS AS NOTHING MORE THAN AN ENERGY SOURCE. SO THEY SEEK THEM OUT, ABSORB THEM...
AND SIPHON OUT ALL THE POWER UNTIL THE FRAGMENT *ITSELF* IS DESTROYED.
IF THINGS CONTINUE AS THEY ARE, THERE IS A DISTINCT POSSIBILITY THAT THE "*BUILDING BLOCKS*" FOR THE TRUE WORLD MAY SOMEDAY DISAPPEAR *ENTIRELY.*
BUT AION-SAMA, THE MASTER OF THE TRUE WORLD, LEARNED OF THAT DANGER.
HE HAS CHOSEN US AS HIS ELITE, AND GIVEN US THE SACRED DUTY...
OF GATHERING AS MANY FRAGMENTS AS WE POSSIBLY CAN ON THE NIGHTS WHEN THEY CRYSTALLIZE, NIGHTS WHEN THE *STARS* FALL.
WITH THEM, WE CAN FULFILL OUR ULTIMATE *DUTY*--OPENING THE "*GATE*" TO THE TRUE WORLD.

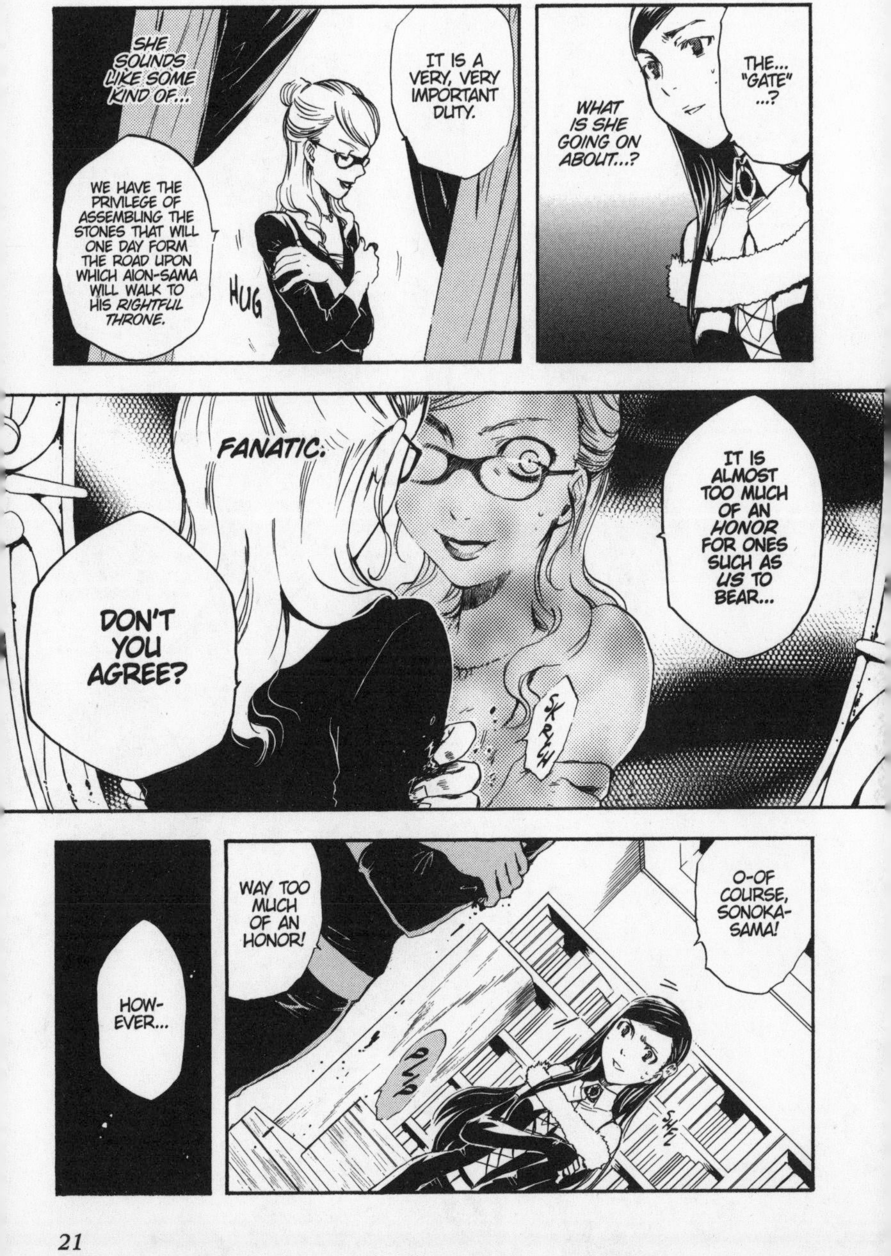

THE... "GATE" ...?
WHAT IS SHE GOING ON ABOUT...?
IT IS A VERY, VERY IMPORTANT DUTY.
SHE SOUNDS LIKE SOME KIND OF...
WE HAVE THE PRIVILEGE OF ASSEMBLING THE STONES THAT WILL ONE DAY FORM THE ROAD UPON WHICH AION-SAMA WILL WALK TO HIS *RIGHTFUL* THRONE.
HUG
IT IS ALMOST TOO MUCH OF AN *HONOR* FOR ONES SUCH AS *US* TO BEAR...
FANATIC.
DON'T YOU AGREE?
SKRCH
O-OF COURSE, SONOKA-SAMA!
WAY TOO MUCH OF AN HONOR!
HOW-EVER...

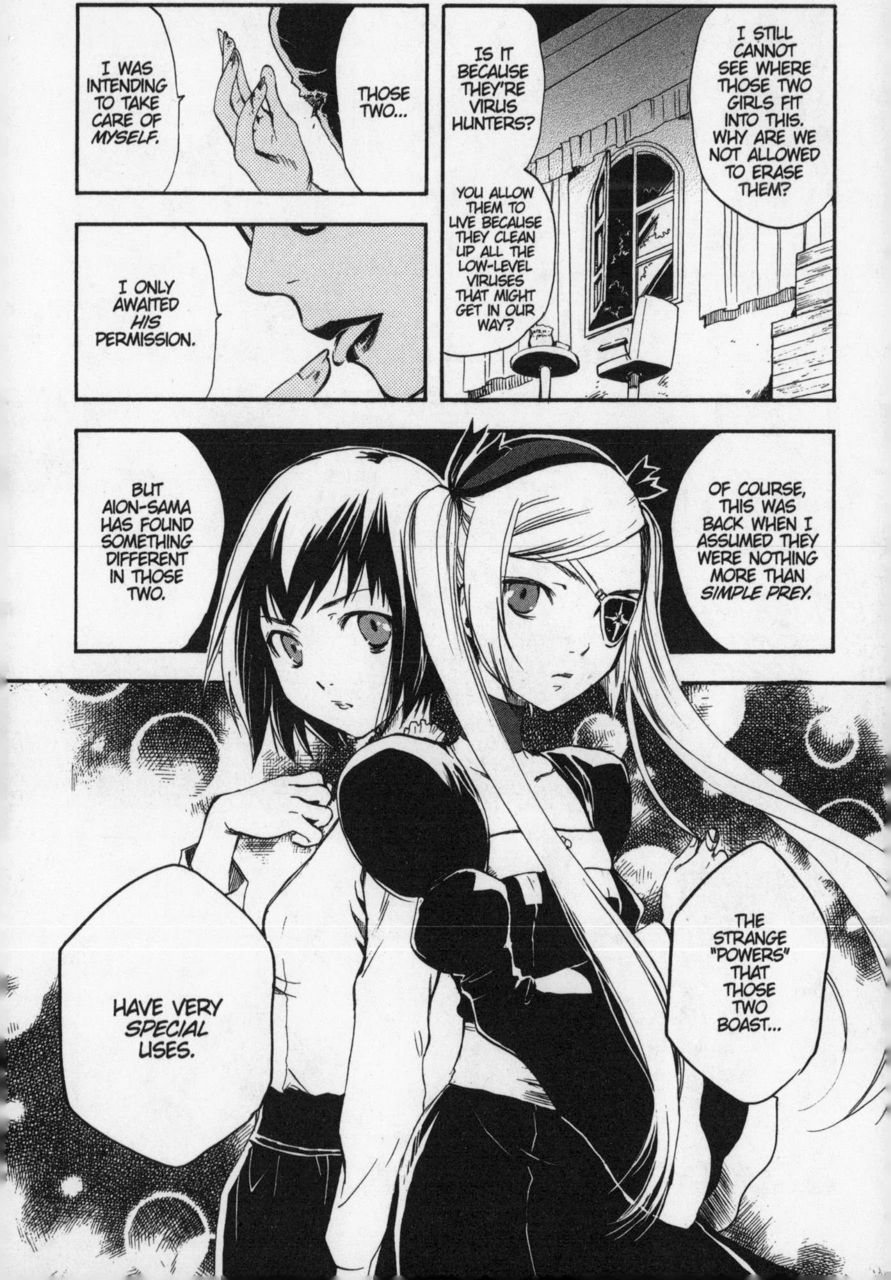
I STILL CANNOT SEE WHERE THOSE TWO GIRLS FIT INTO THIS. WHY ARE WE NOT ALLOWED TO ERASE THEM?
IS IT BECAUSE THEY'RE VIRUS HUNTERS?
YOU ALLOW THEM TO LIVE BECAUSE THEY CLEAN UP ALL THE LOW-LEVEL VIRUSES THAT MIGHT GET IN OUR WAY?
THOSE TWO...
I WAS INTENDING TO TAKE CARE OF *MYSELF.*
I ONLY AWAITED *HIS* PERMISSION.
OF COURSE, THIS WAS BACK WHEN I ASSUMED THEY WERE NOTHING MORE THAN *SIMPLE PREY.*
BUT AION-SAMA HAS FOUND SOMETHING DIFFERENT IN THOSE TWO.
THE STRANGE "POWERS" THAT THOSE TWO BOAST...
HAVE VERY *SPECIAL* USES.

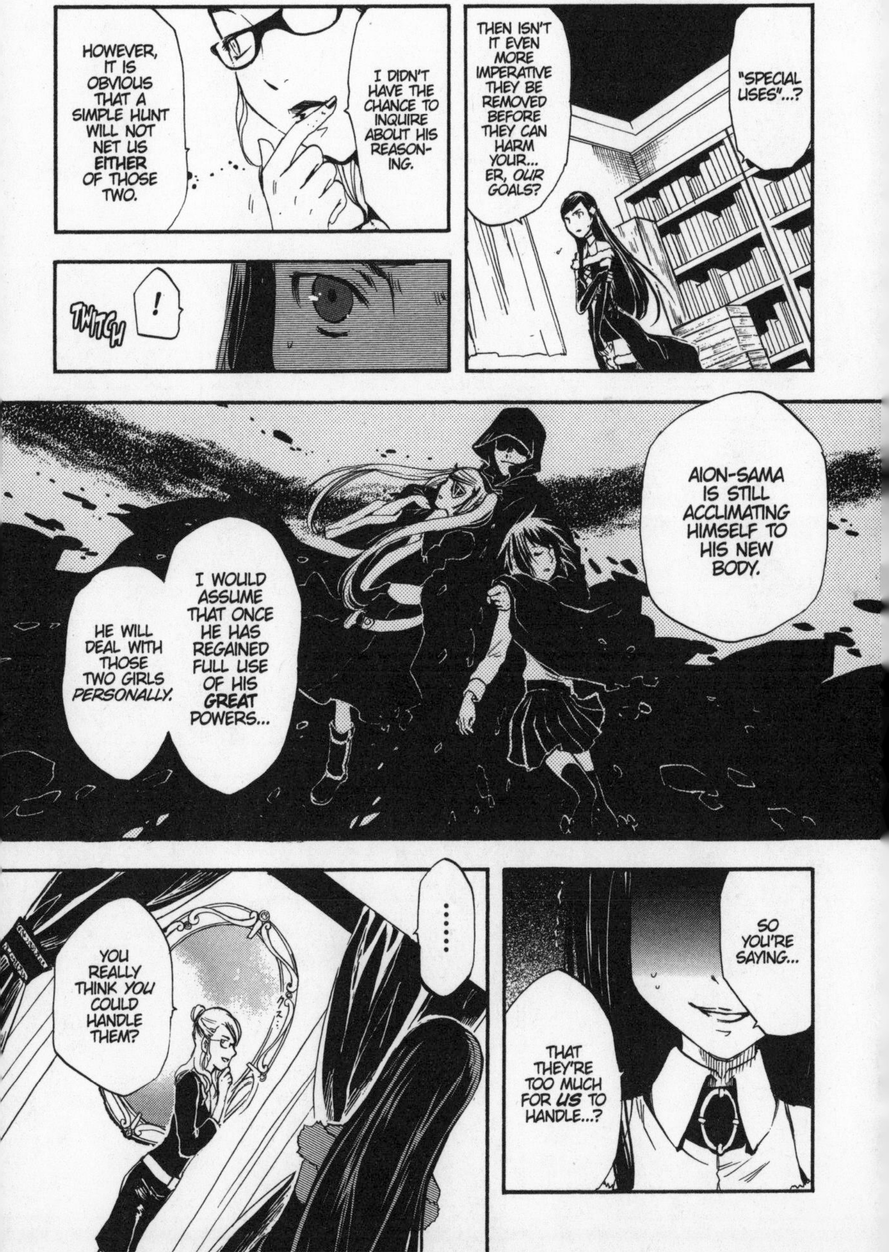
"SPECIAL USES"...?
THEN ISN'T IT EVEN MORE IMPERATIVE THEY BE REMOVED BEFORE THEY CAN HARM YOUR... ER, *OUR* GOALS?
I DIDN'T HAVE THE CHANCE TO INQUIRE ABOUT HIS REASONING.
HOWEVER, IT IS OBVIOUS THAT A SIMPLE HUNT WILL NOT NET US EITHER OF THOSE TWO.
!
TWITCH
AION-SAMA IS STILL ACCLIMATING HIMSELF TO HIS NEW BODY.
I WOULD ASSUME THAT ONCE HE HAS REGAINED FULL USE OF HIS **GREAT** POWERS...
HE WILL DEAL WITH THOSE TWO GIRLS *PERSONALLY.*
SO YOU'RE SAYING...
THAT THEY'RE TOO MUCH FOR ***US*** TO HANDLE...?
......
YOU REALLY THINK *YOU* COULD HANDLE THEM?

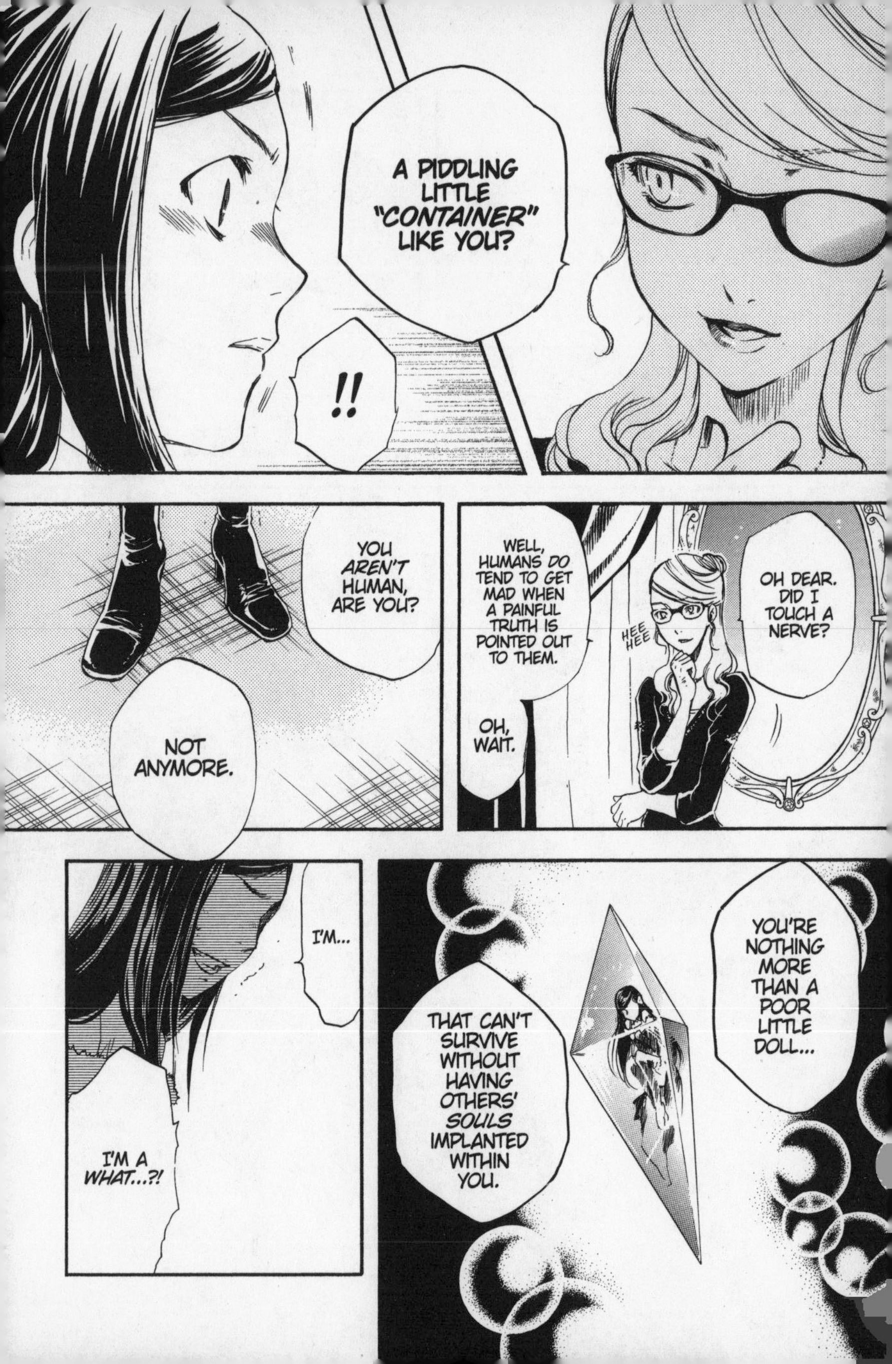
A PIDDLING LITTLE "CONTAINER" LIKE YOU?
!!
OH DEAR. DID I TOUCH A NERVE?
HEE HEE
WELL, HUMANS DO TEND TO GET MAD WHEN A PAINFUL TRUTH IS POINTED OUT TO THEM.
OH, WAIT.
YOU AREN'T HUMAN, ARE YOU?
NOT ANYMORE.
YOU'RE NOTHING MORE THAN A POOR LITTLE DOLL...
THAT CAN'T SURVIVE WITHOUT HAVING OTHERS' SOULS IMPLANTED WITHIN YOU.
I'M...
I'M A WHAT...?!

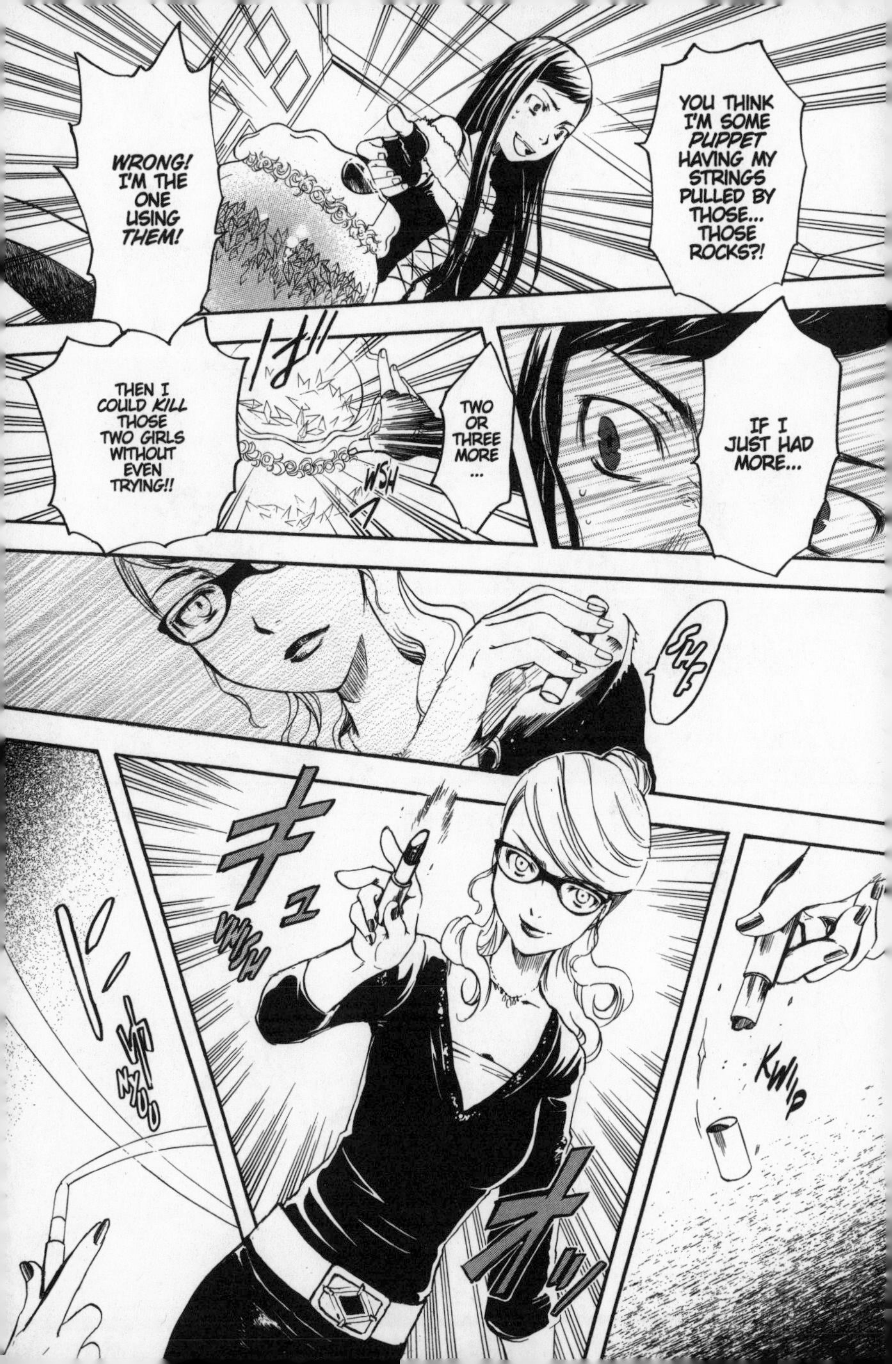
YOU THINK I'M SOME *PUPPET* HAVING MY STRINGS PULLED BY THOSE... THOSE ROCKS?!
WRONG! I'M THE ONE USING *THEM!*
IF I JUST HAD MORE...
TWO OR THREE MORE ...
WSH
THEN I COULD *KILL* THOSE TWO GIRLS WITHOUT EVEN TRYING!!
VWISH

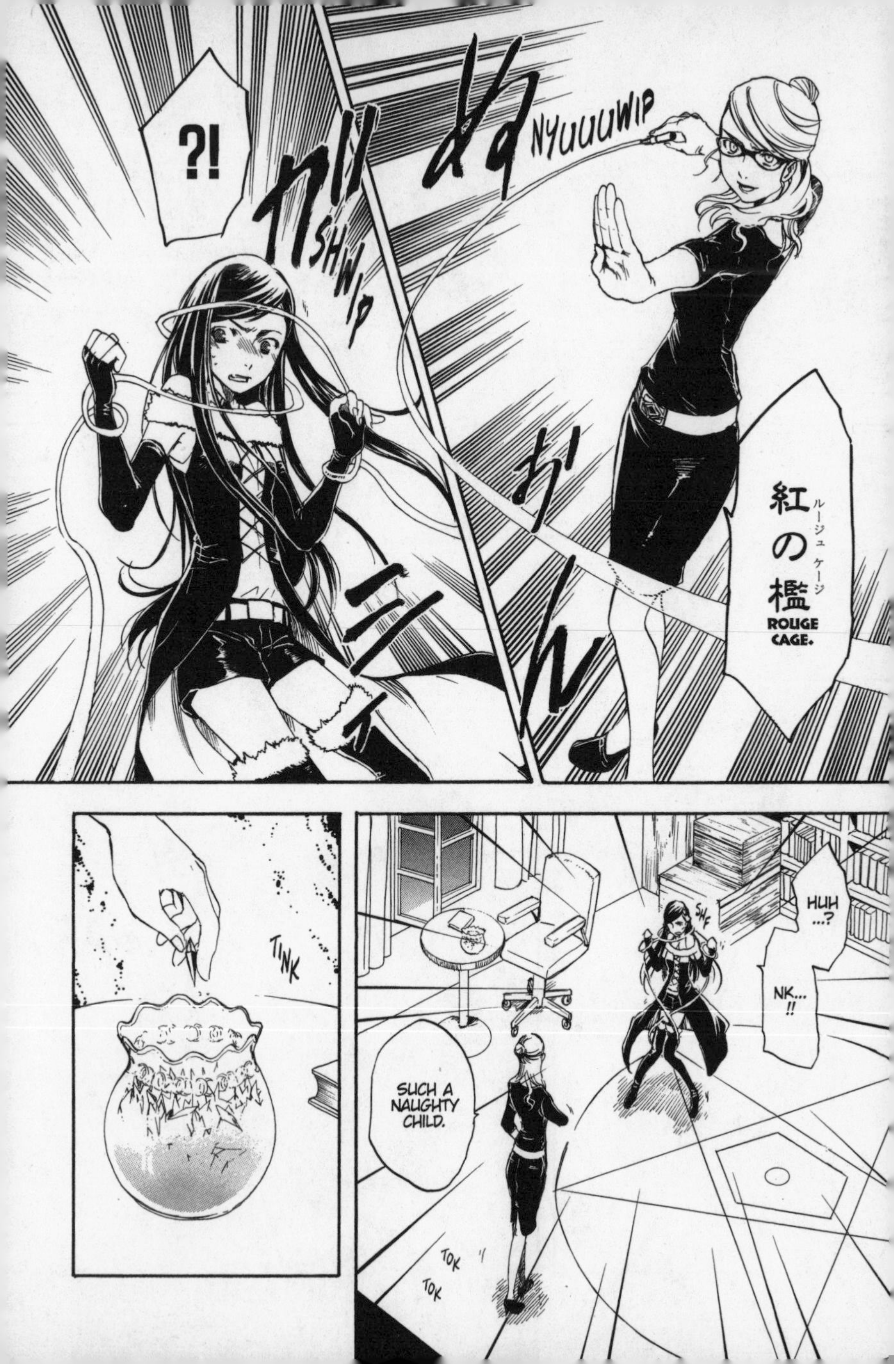
NYUUUWIP
紅の檻
ルージュ ケージ
ROUGE CAGE.
?!
SHWIP
HUH ...?
SHF
NK... !!
SUCH A NAUGHTY CHILD.
TOK
TOK
TINK

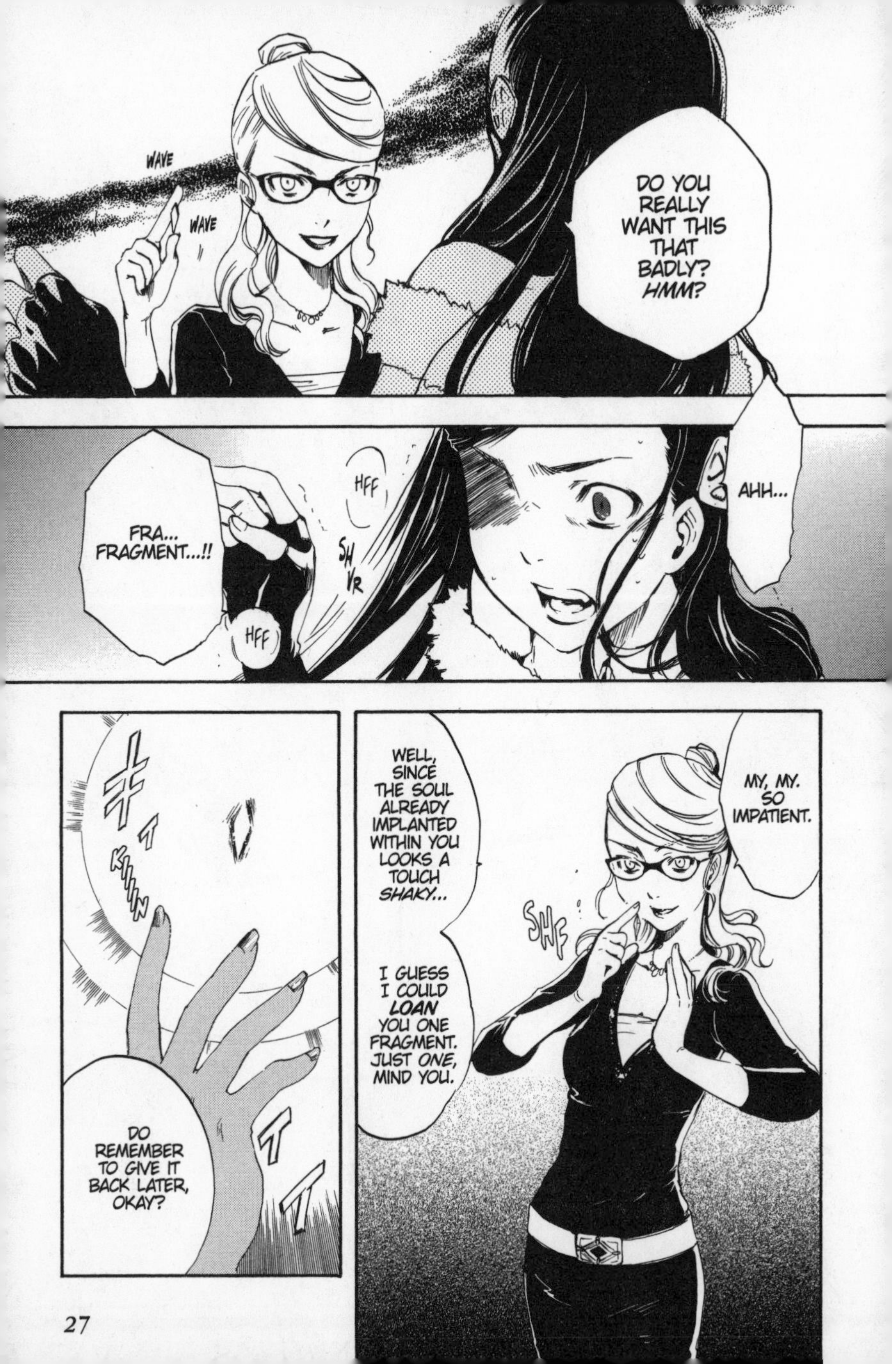
DO YOU REALLY WANT THIS THAT BADLY? *HMM?*
WAVE
WAVE
AHH...
SHVR
HFF
FRA... FRAGMENT...!!
HFF
MY, MY. SO IMPATIENT.
WELL, SINCE THE SOUL ALREADY IMPLANTED WITHIN YOU LOOKS A TOUCH *SHAKY...*
SHF
I GUESS I COULD **LOAN** YOU ONE FRAGMENT. JUST *ONE*, MIND YOU.
KIIIN
DO REMEMBER TO GIVE IT BACK LATER, OKAY?

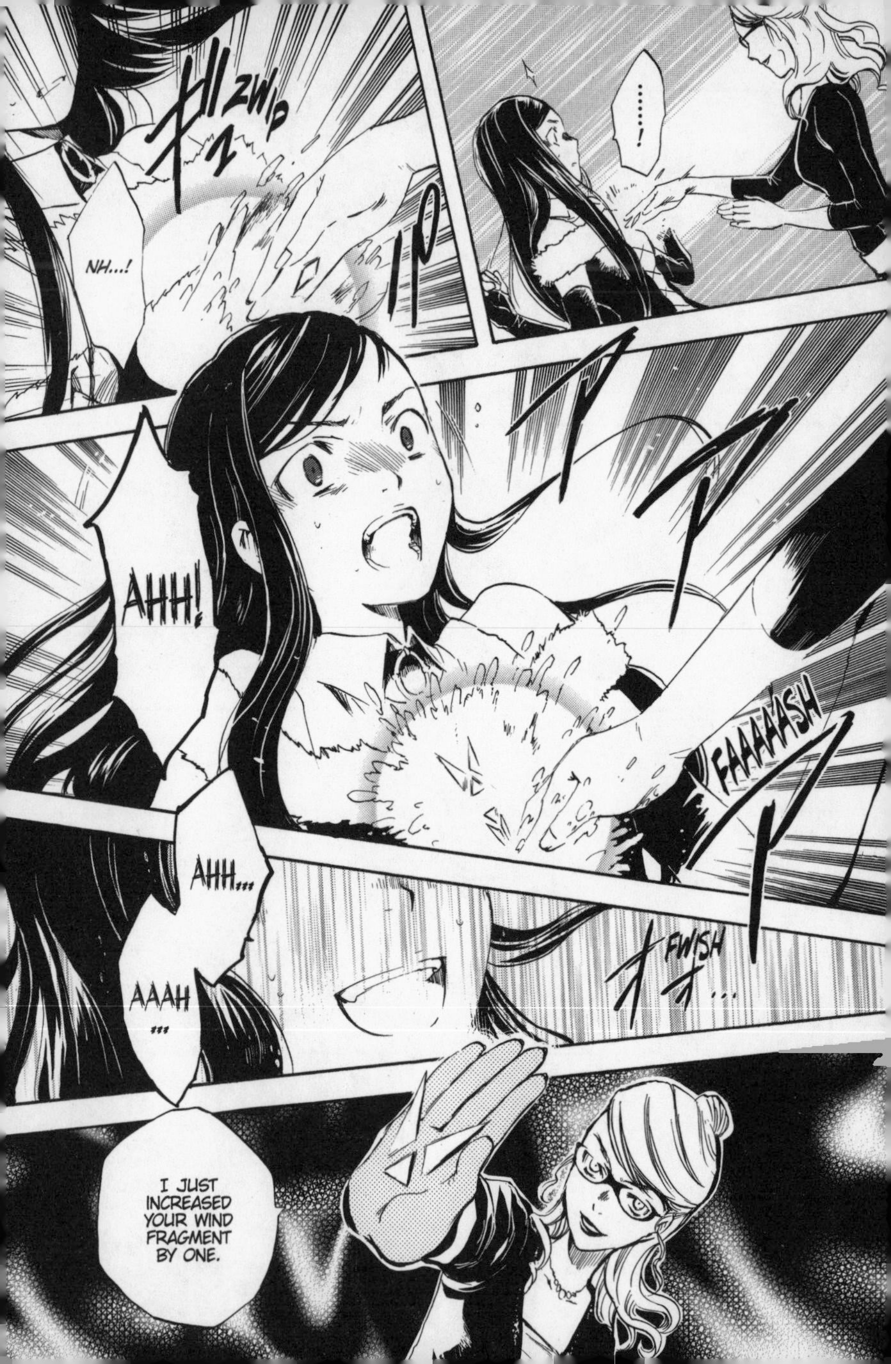
......!
ZWIP
NH...!
FAAAAASH
AHH!
FWISH...
AHH...
AAAH...
I JUST INCREASED YOUR WIND FRAGMENT BY ONE.

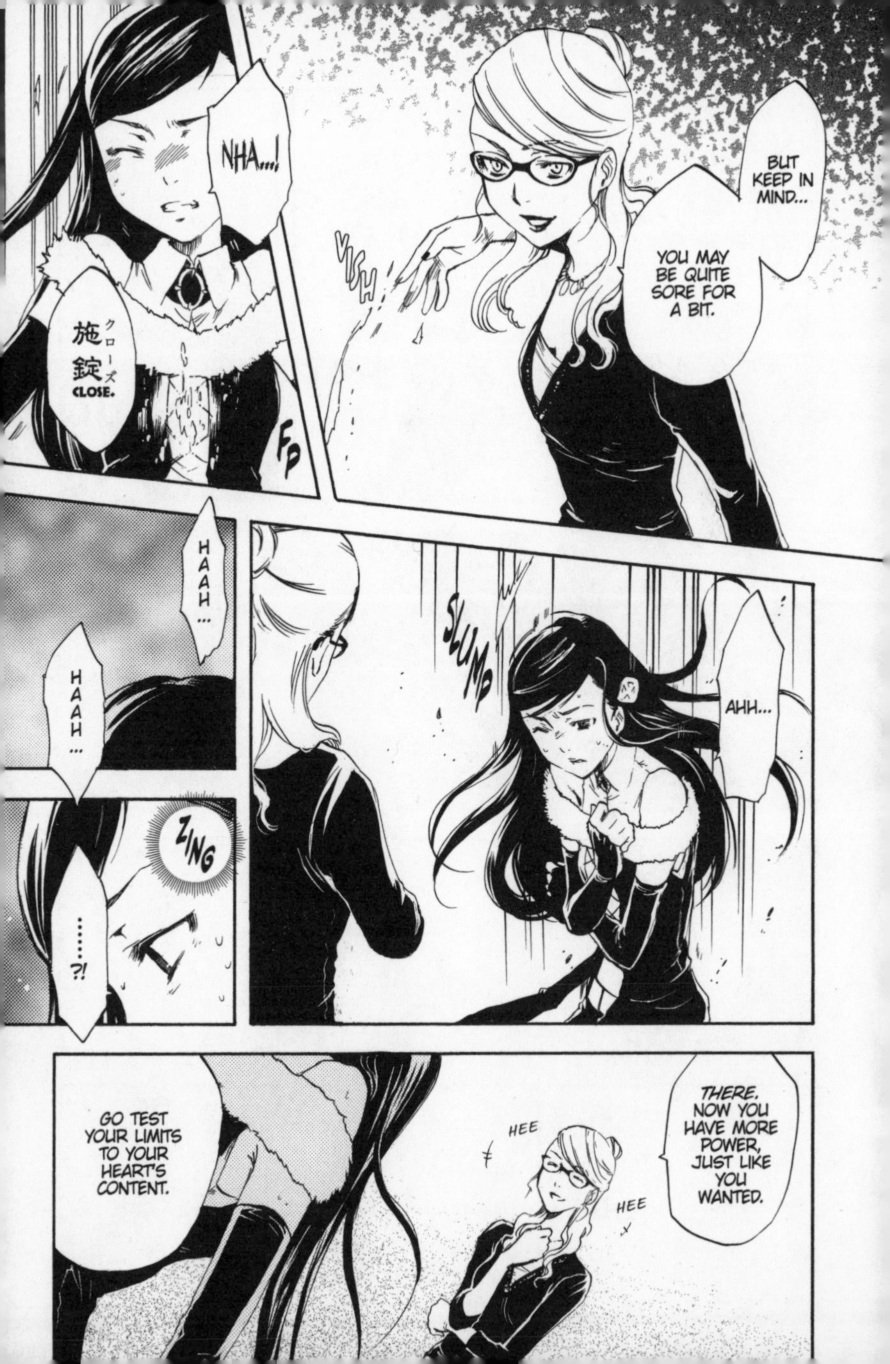
BUT KEEP IN MIND...
YOU MAY BE QUITE SORE FOR A BIT.
VISH
NHA...!
施錠 (クローズ)
CLOSE.
FP
SLUMP
AHH...
HAAH...
HAAH...
ZING
......?!
THERE. NOW YOU HAVE MORE POWER, JUST LIKE YOU WANTED.
HEE
HEE
GO TEST YOUR LIMITS TO YOUR HEART'S CONTENT.

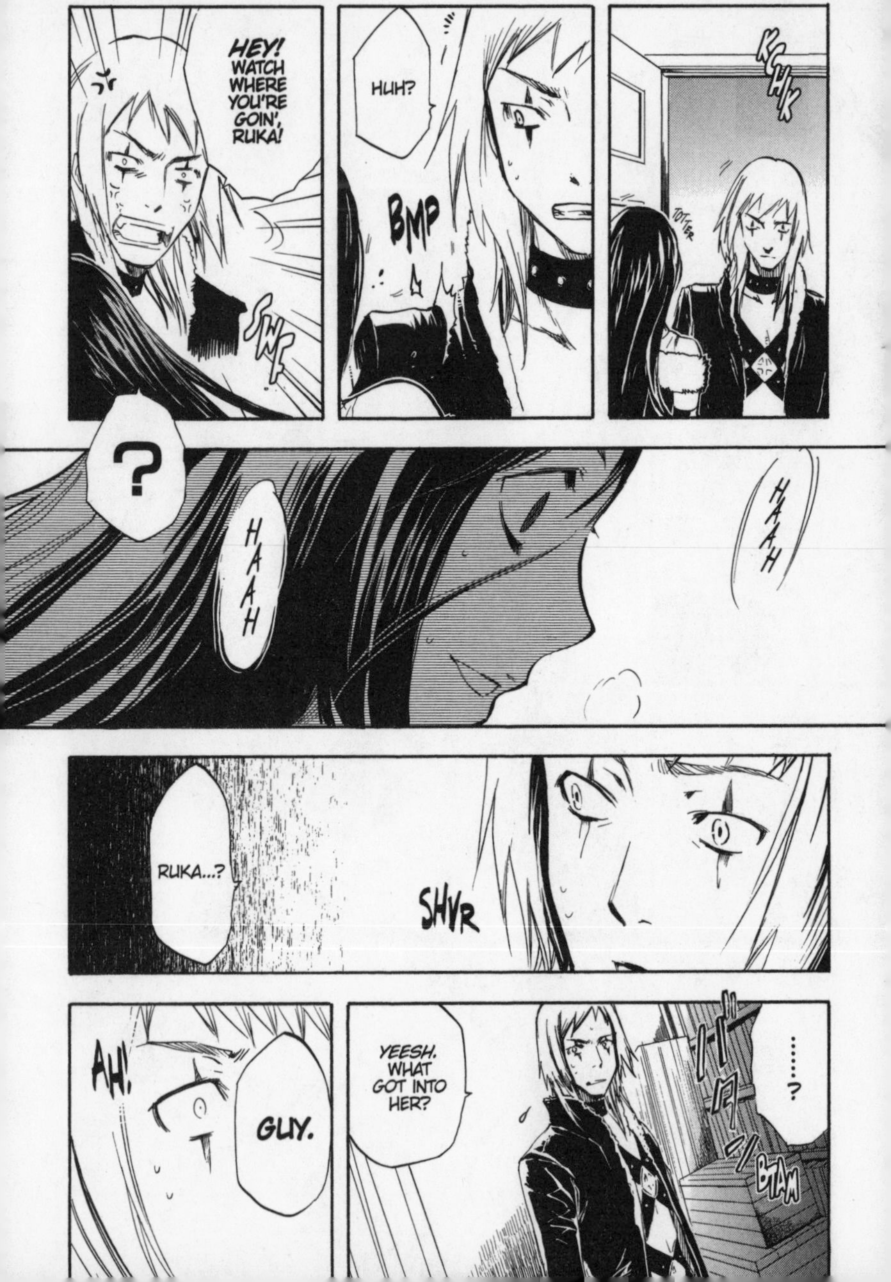
KCHK
TOTTER
HUH?
BMP
HEY! WATCH WHERE YOU'RE GOIN', RUKA!
SWF
HAAH
?
HAAH
SHVR
RUKA...?
......?
BTAM
YEESH. WHAT GOT INTO HER?
GUY.
AH!

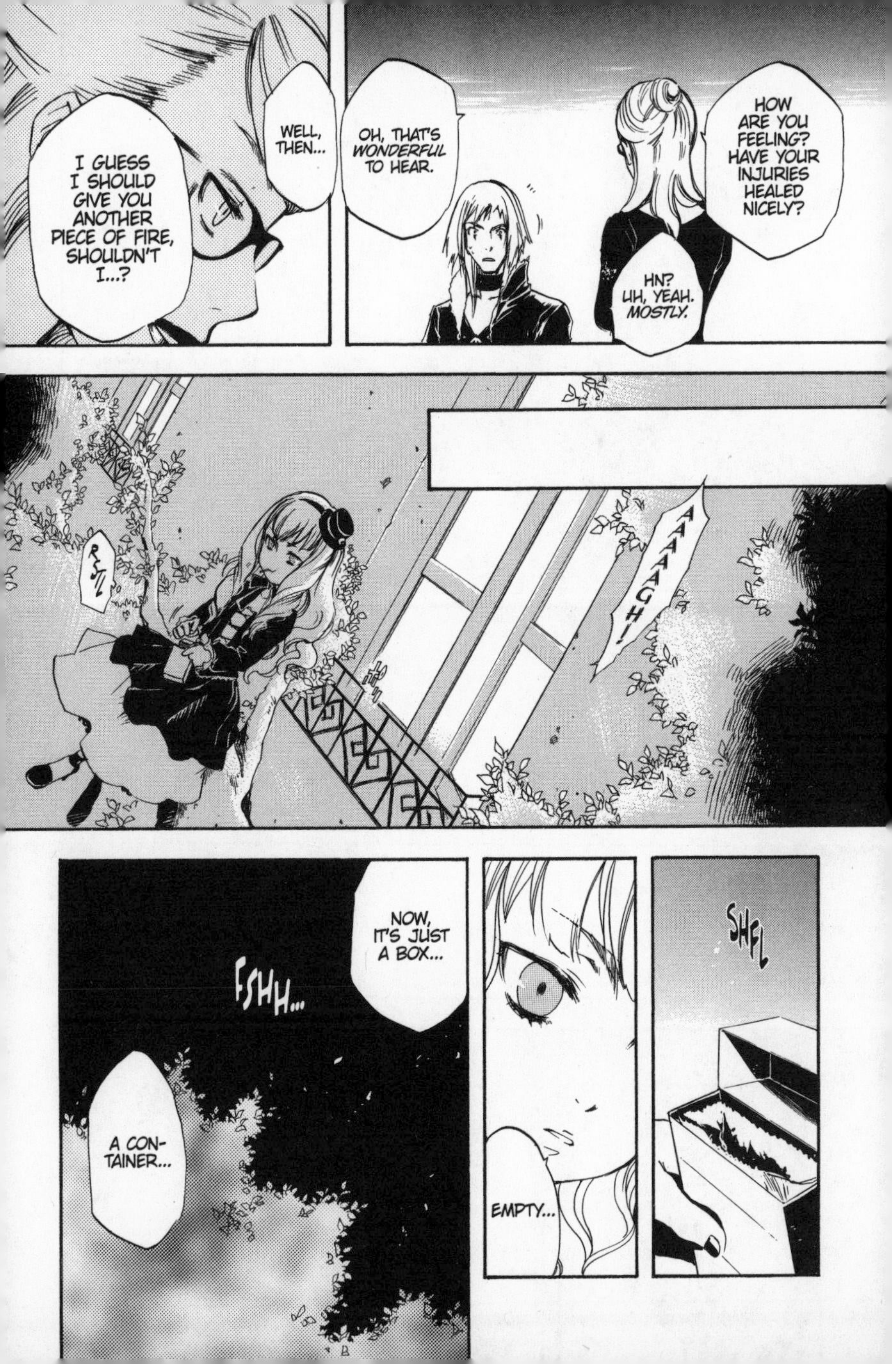

HOW ARE YOU FEELING? HAVE YOUR INJURIES HEALED NICELY?
HN? UH, YEAH. *MOSTLY.*
OH, THAT'S *WONDERFUL* TO HEAR.
WELL, THEN...
I GUESS I SHOULD GIVE YOU ANOTHER PIECE OF FIRE, SHOULDN'T I...?
AAAAAGH!
RSTL
SHFL
EMPTY...
NOW, IT'S JUST A BOX...
FSHH...
A CON-TAINER...

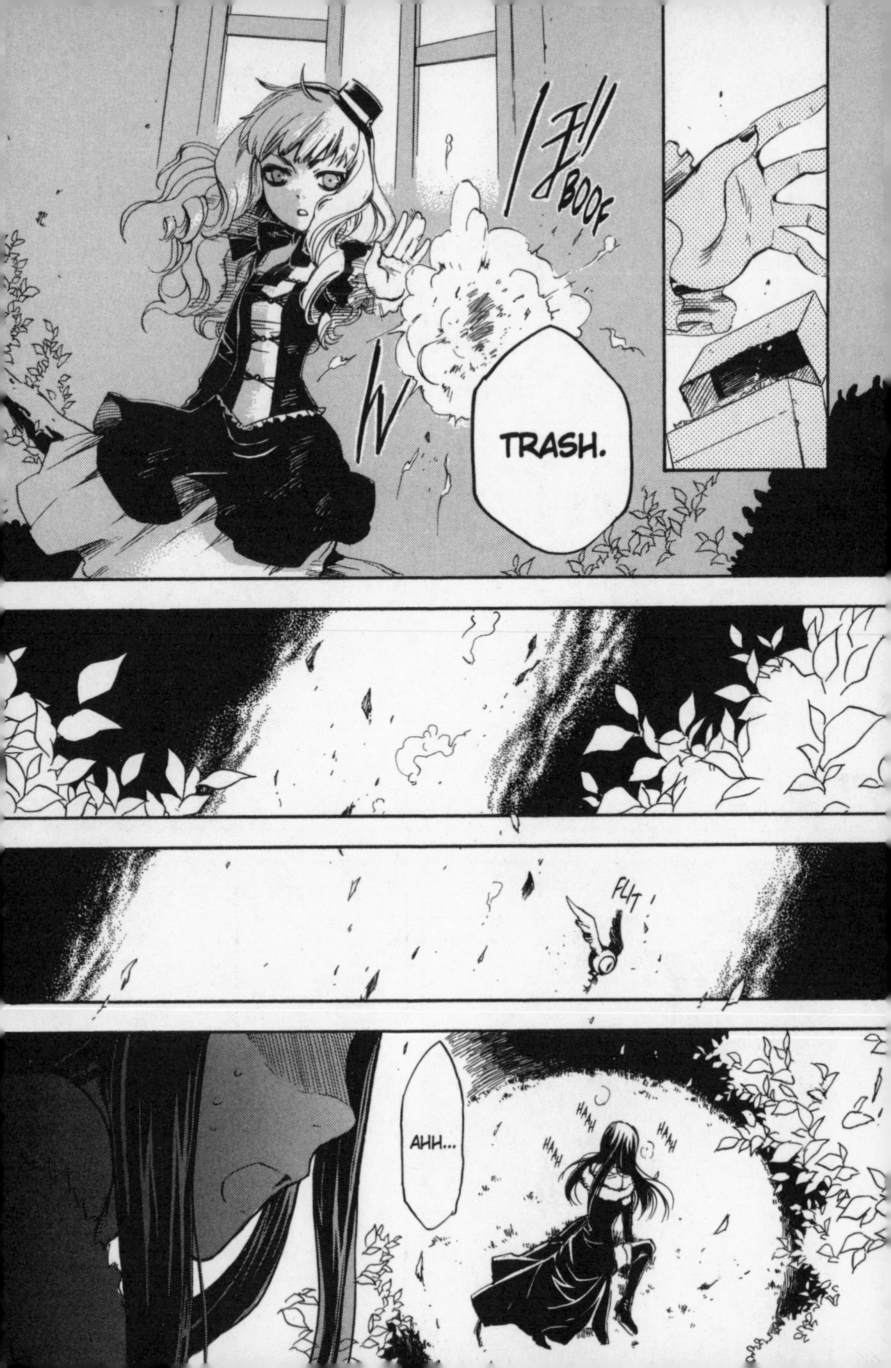
BOOF
TRASH.
FLIT
HAAH
HAAH
AHH...
HAAH

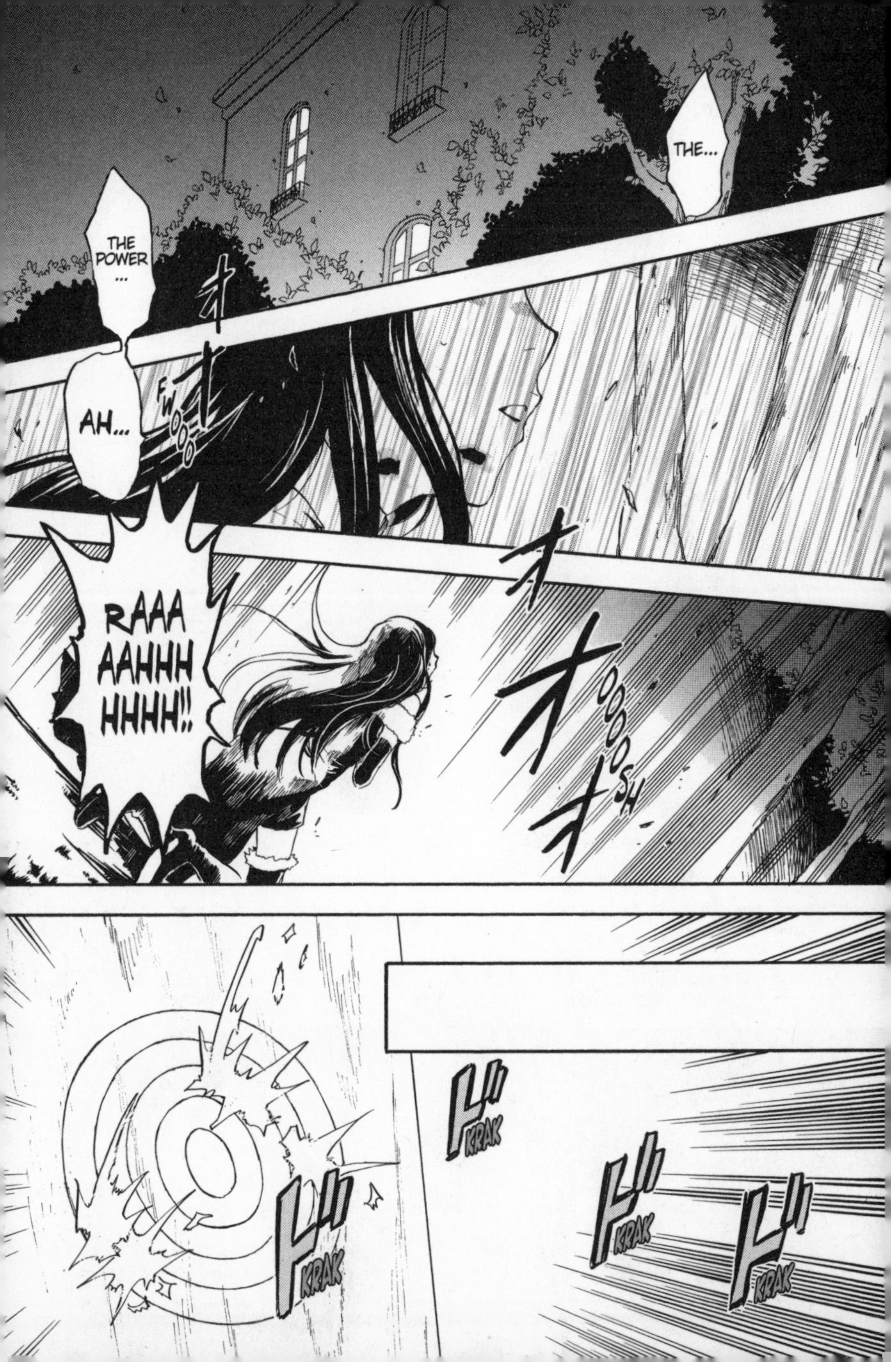

THE...
THE POWER ...
AH...
FWOOO
RAAA AAHHH HHHH!!
OOOOSH
KRAK
KRAK
KRAK
KRAK

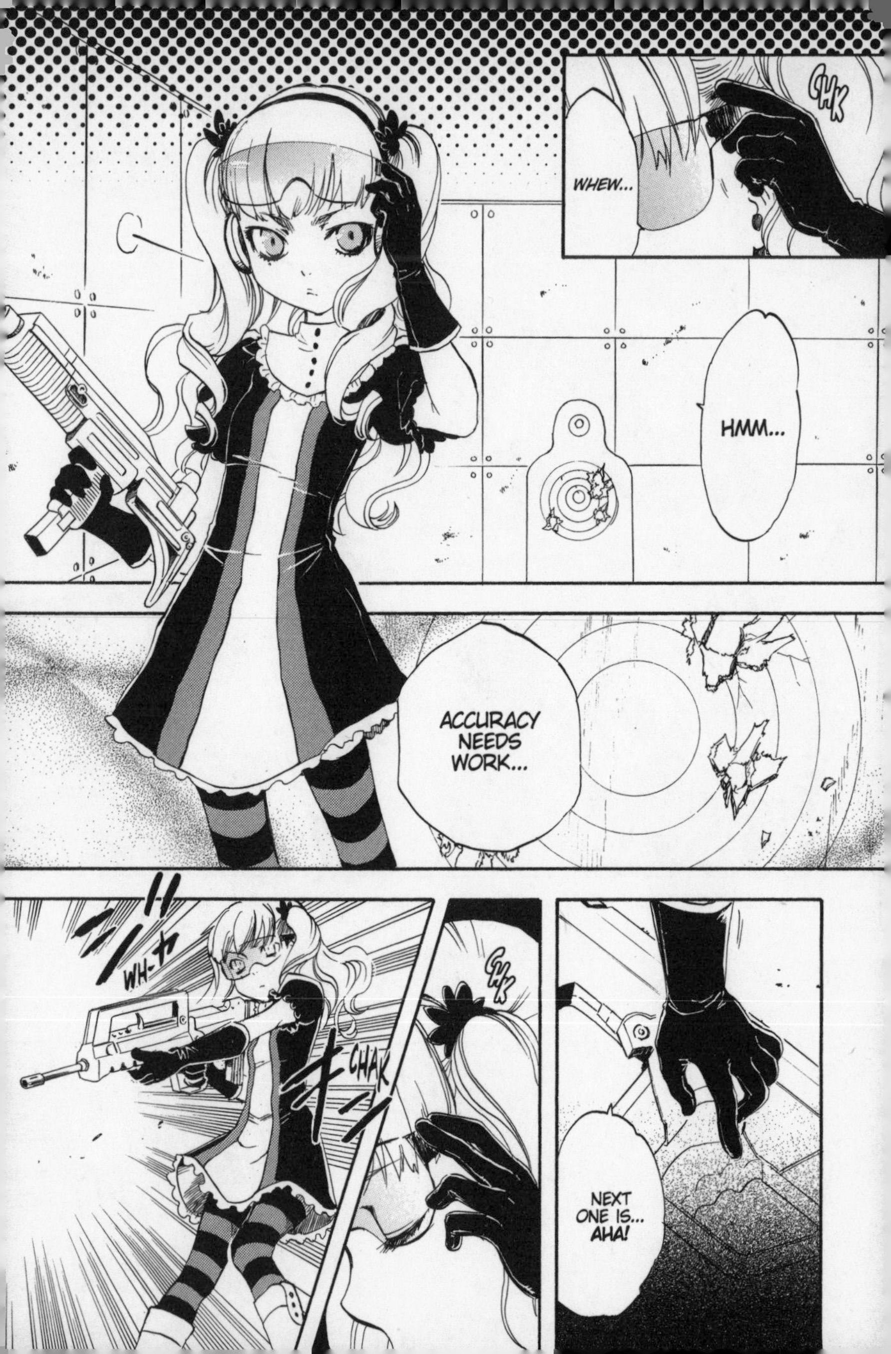
CHK
WHEW...
HMM...
ACCURACY NEEDS WORK...
NEXT ONE IS... AHA!
CHK
CHAK
WH-

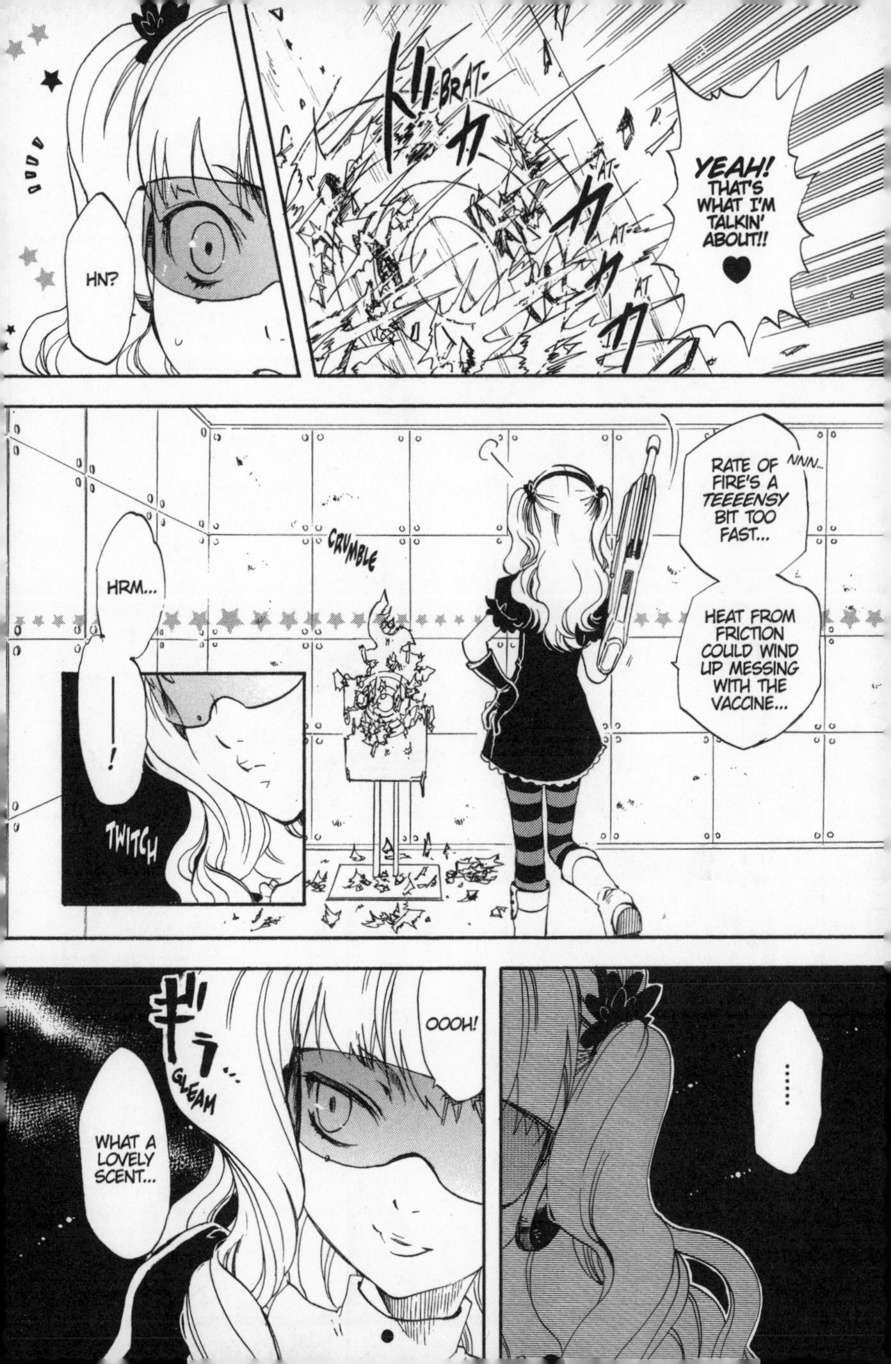
BRAT-
AT-
AT-
AT
YEAH! THAT'S WHAT I'M TALKIN' ABOUT!! ♥
HN?
NNN...
RATE OF FIRE'S A TEEEENSY BIT TOO FAST...
HEAT FROM FRICTION COULD WIND UP MESSING WITH THE VACCINE...
CRUMBLE
HRM...
!
TWITCH
......
OOOH!
GLEAM
WHAT A LOVELY SCENT...

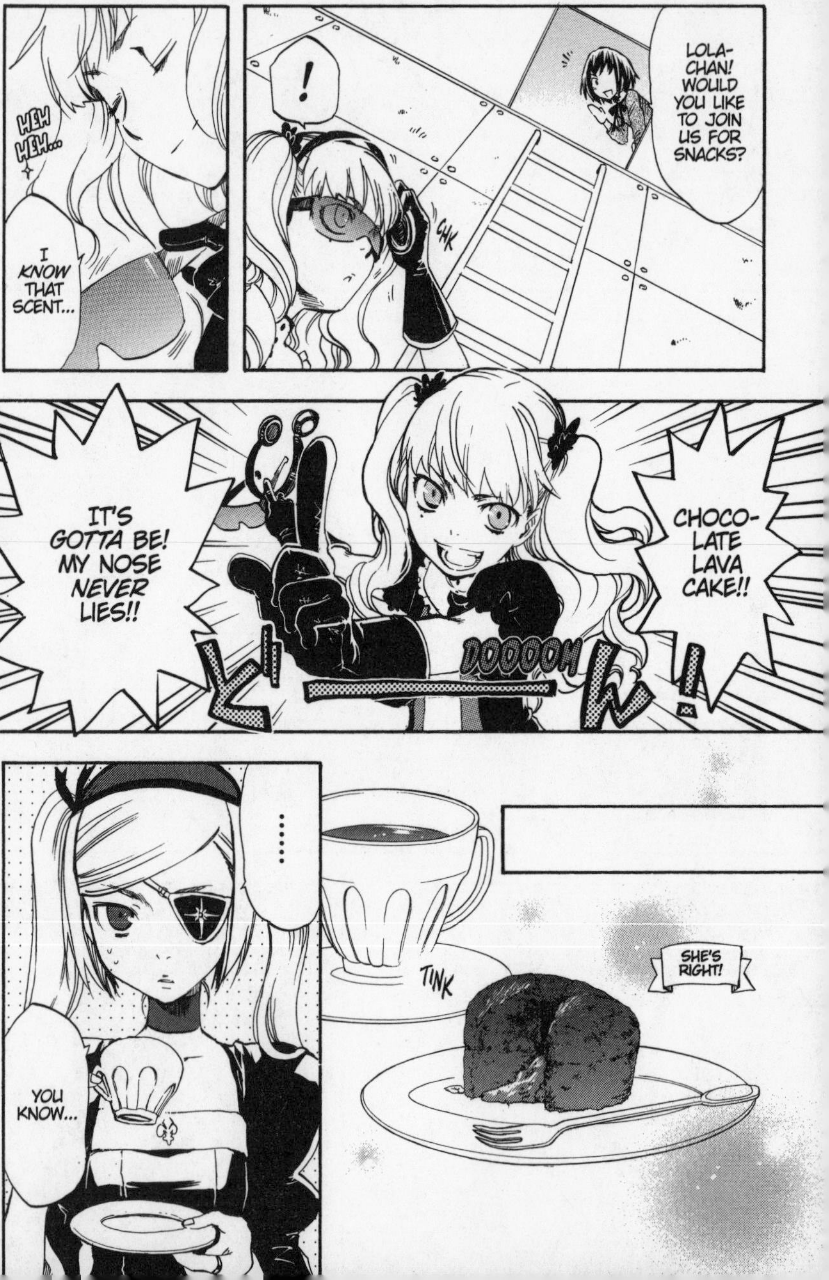
LOLA-CHAN! WOULD YOU LIKE TO JOIN US FOR SNACKS?
!
CHK
HEH HEH...
I KNOW THAT SCENT...
CHOCO-LATE LAVA CAKE!!
DOOOOH
IT'S GOTTA BE! MY NOSE NEVER LIES!!
SHE'S RIGHT!
TINK
......
YOU KNOW...

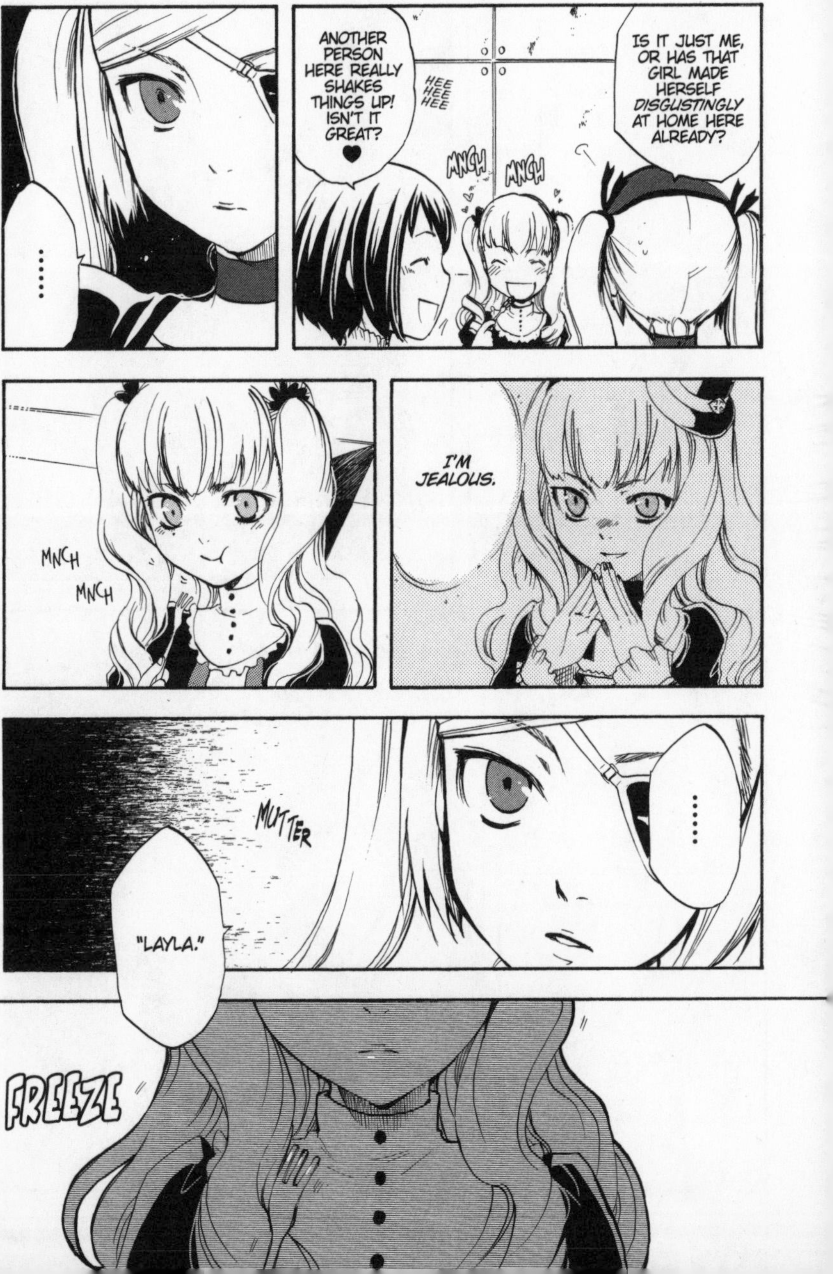
IS IT JUST ME, OR HAS THAT GIRL MADE HERSELF DISGUSTINGLY AT HOME HERE ALREADY?
HEE HEE HEE
MNCH MNCH
ANOTHER PERSON HERE REALLY SHAKES THINGS UP! ISN'T IT GREAT? ♥
......
I'M JEALOUS.
MNCH MNCH
......
MUTTER
"LAYLA."
FREEZE

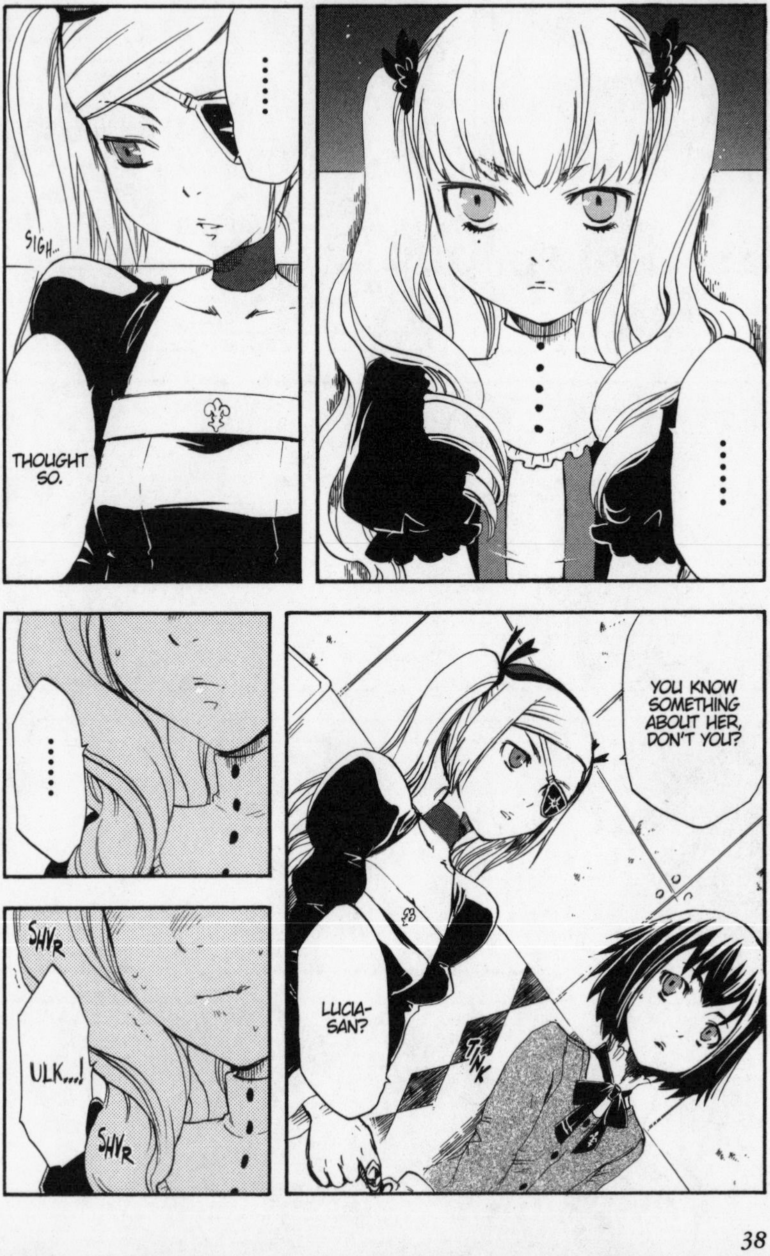
……
……
SIGH…
THOUGHT SO.
YOU KNOW SOMETHING ABOUT HER, DON'T YOU?
LUCIA-SAN?
TINK
……
SHVR
ULK…!
SHVR

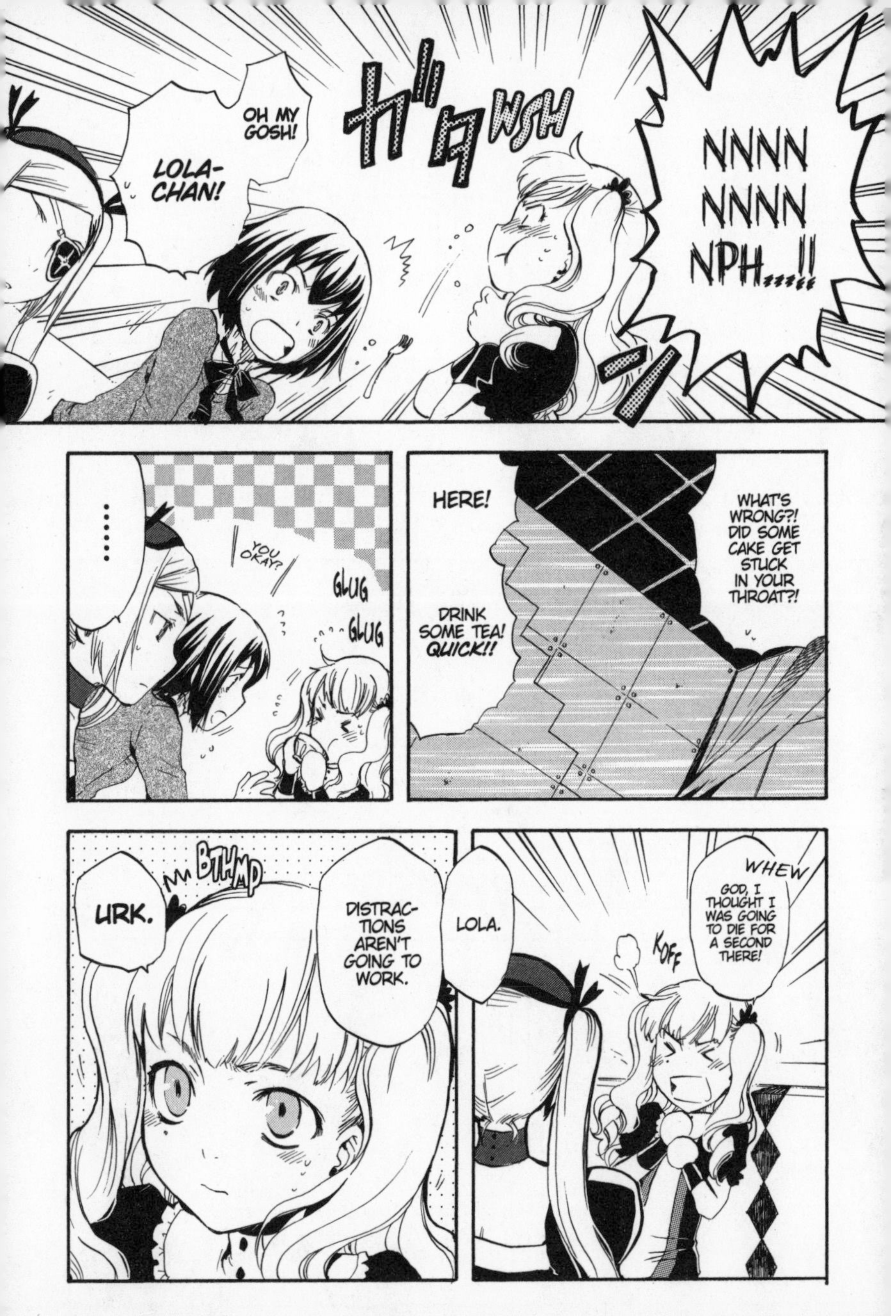
NNNN NNNN NPH...!!
ガタWSH
OH MY GOSH!
LOLA-CHAN!
WHAT'S WRONG?! DID SOME CAKE GET STUCK IN YOUR THROAT?!
HERE!
DRINK SOME TEA! QUICK!!
GLUG
GLUG
YOU OKAY?
......
WHEW
GOD, I THOUGHT I WAS GOING TO DIE FOR A SECOND THERE!
KOFF
LOLA.
DISTRACTIONS AREN'T GOING TO WORK.
BTHMP
URK.

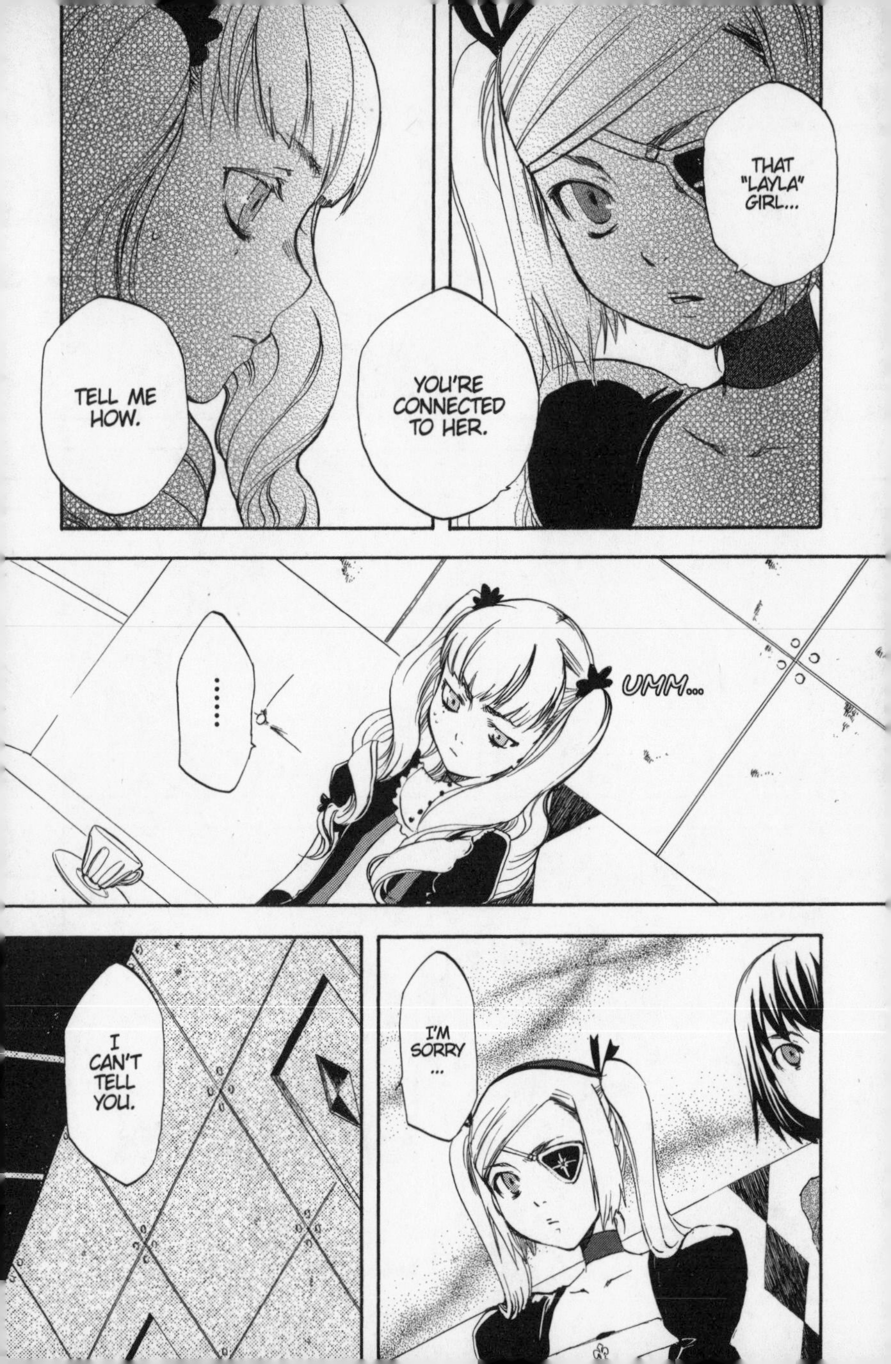
THAT "LAYLA" GIRL...
YOU'RE CONNECTED TO HER.
TELL ME HOW.
UMM...
......
I'M SORRY ...
I CAN'T TELL YOU.

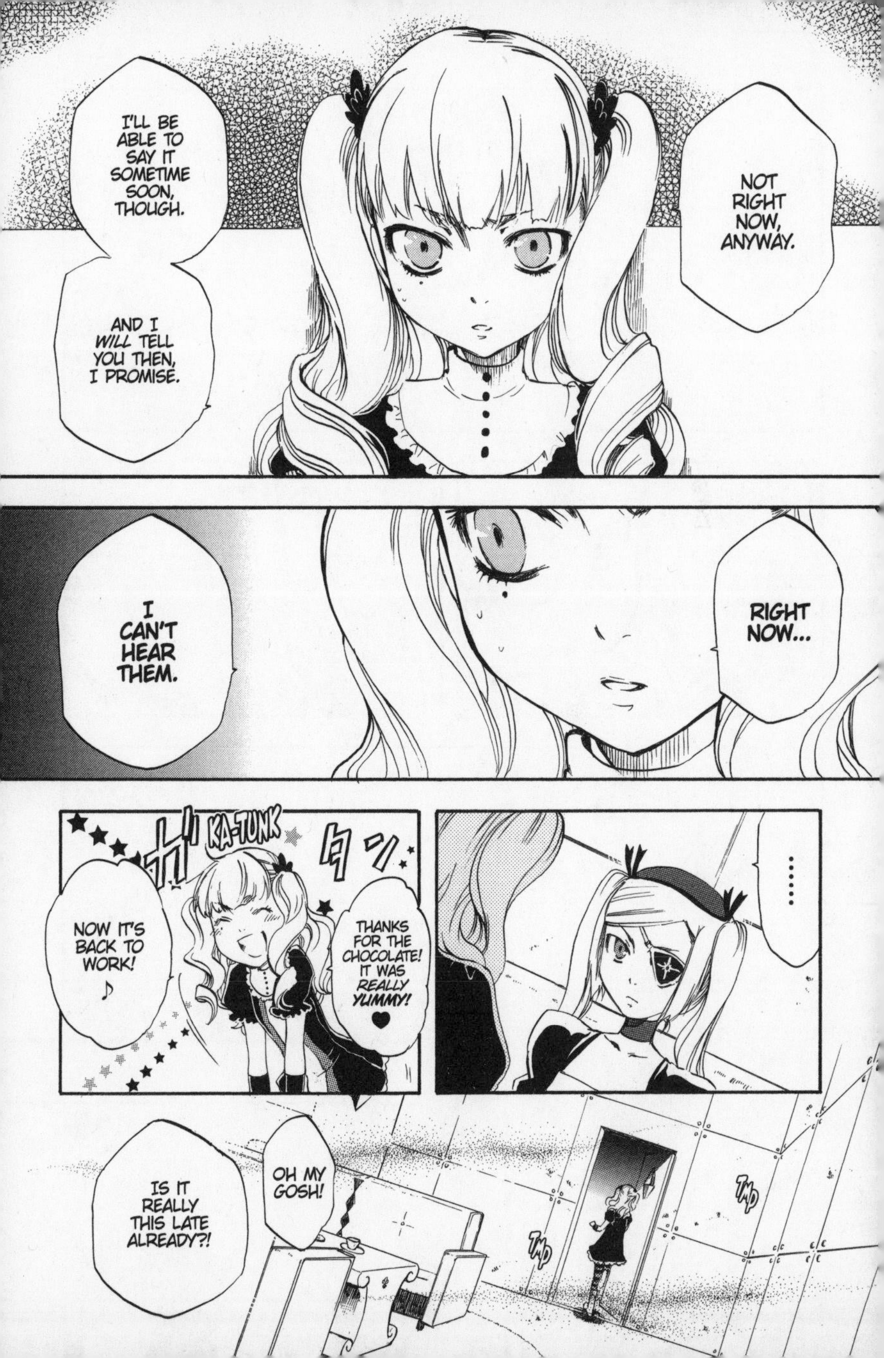
NOT RIGHT NOW, ANYWAY.
I'LL BE ABLE TO SAY IT SOMETIME SOON, THOUGH.
AND I *WILL* TELL YOU THEN, I PROMISE.
RIGHT NOW...
I CAN'T HEAR THEM.
......
KA-TUNK
THANKS FOR THE CHOCOLATE! IT WAS *REALLY YUMMY!* ♥
NOW IT'S BACK TO WORK! ♪
TMP
TMP
OH MY GOSH!
IS IT REALLY THIS LATE ALREADY?!

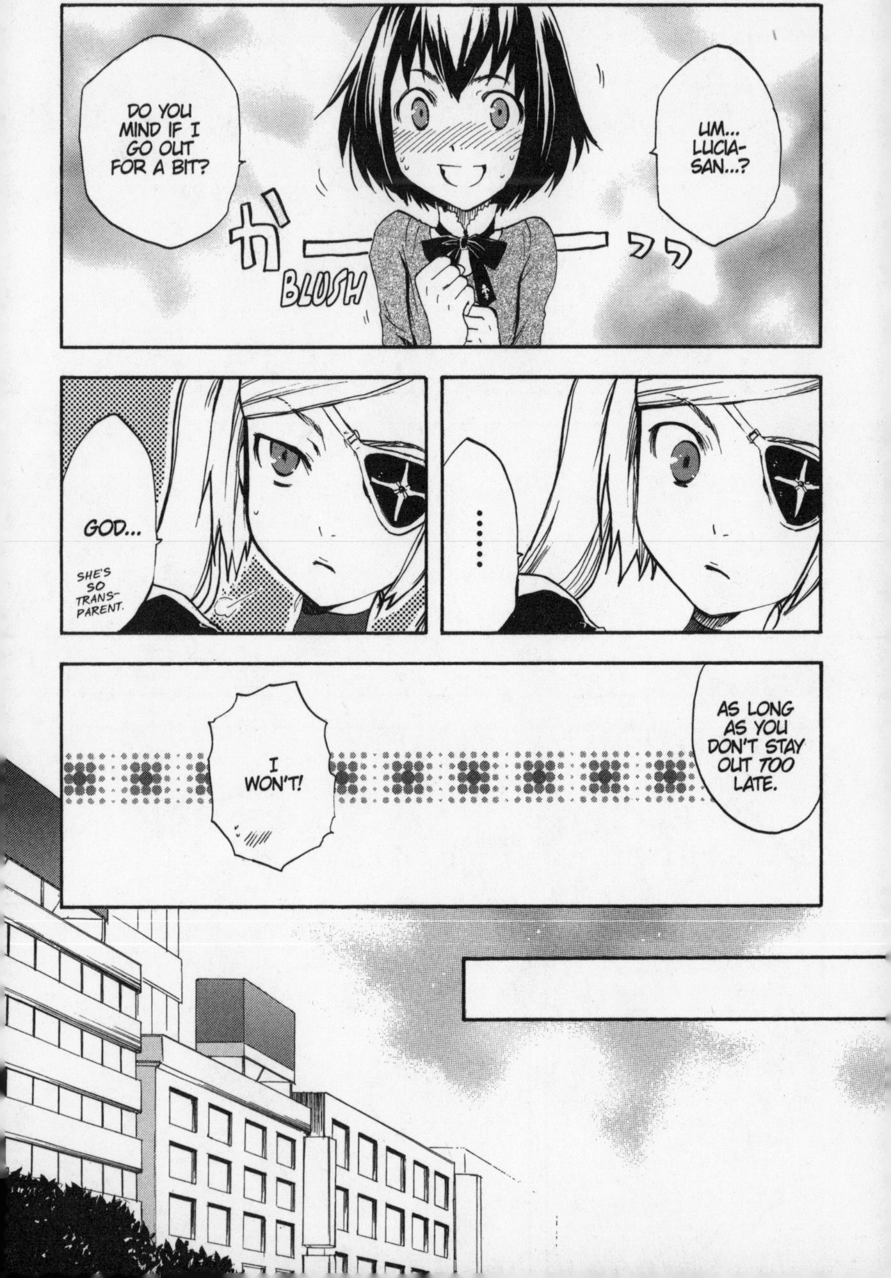

UM... LUCIA-SAN...?
DO YOU MIND IF I GO OUT FOR A BIT?
かーっっ
BLUSH
......
GOD...
SHE'S SO TRANSPARENT.
AS LONG AS YOU DON'T STAY OUT *TOO* LATE.
I WON'T!

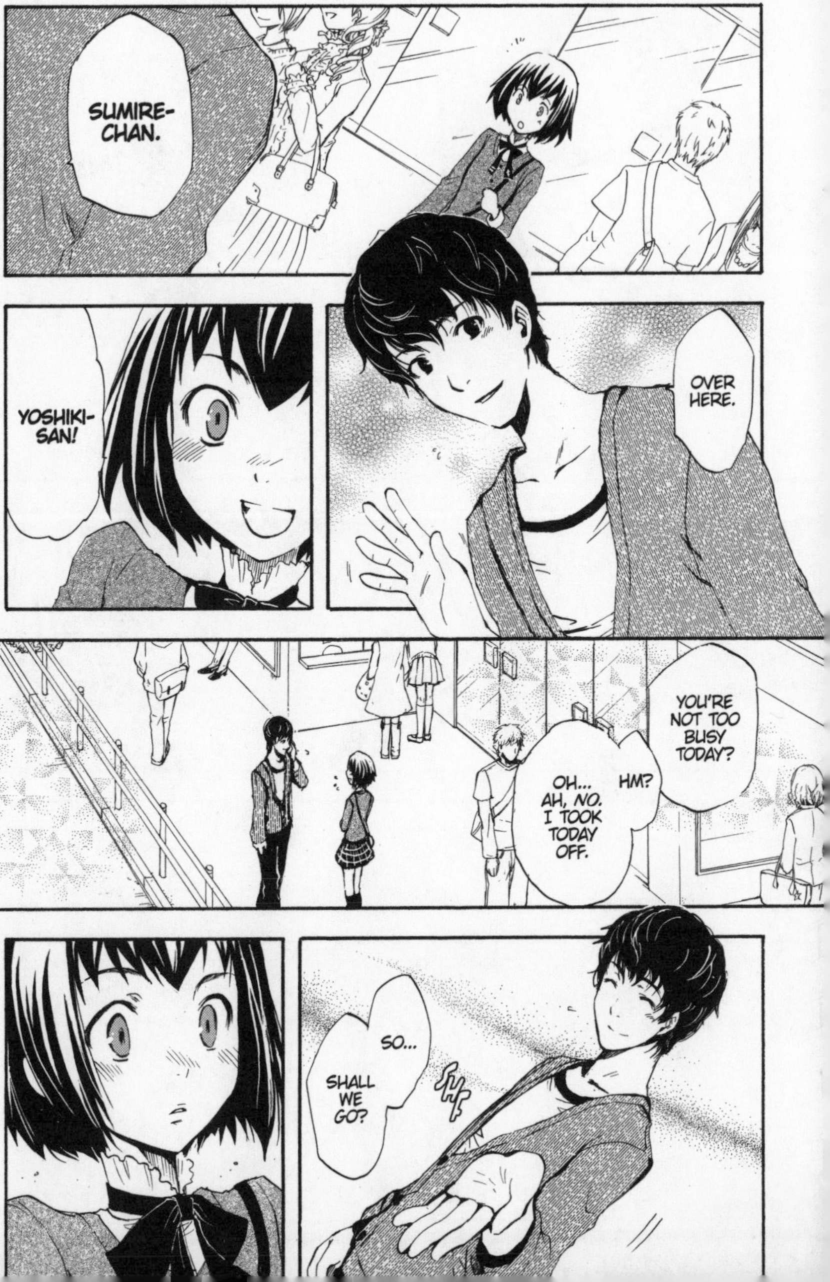
SUMIRE-CHAN.
OVER HERE.
YOSHIKI-SAN!
YOU'RE NOT TOO BUSY TODAY?
HM?
OH... AH, NO. I TOOK TODAY OFF.
SO...
SHALL WE GO?

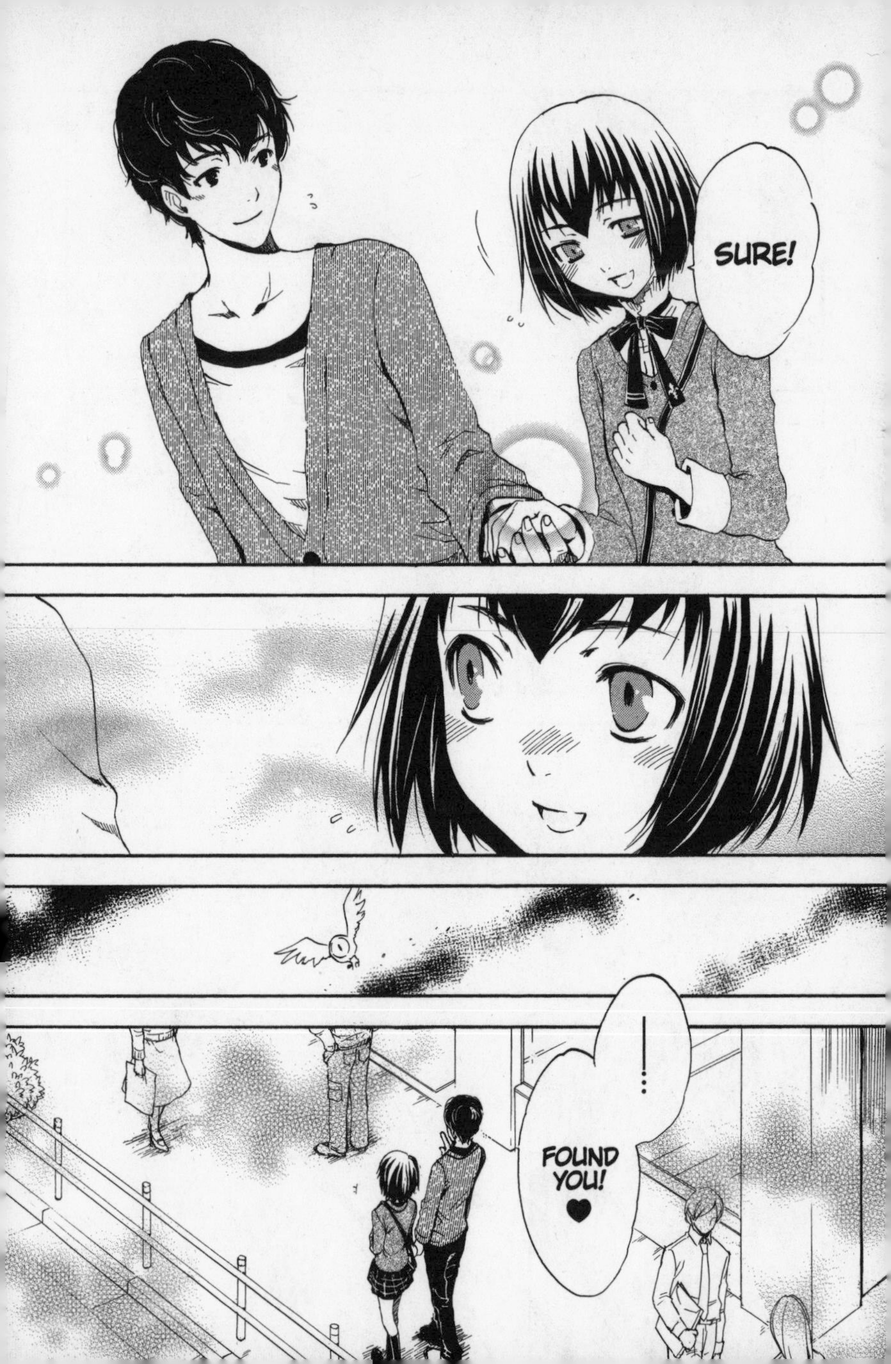
SURE!
...!
FOUND YOU! ♥

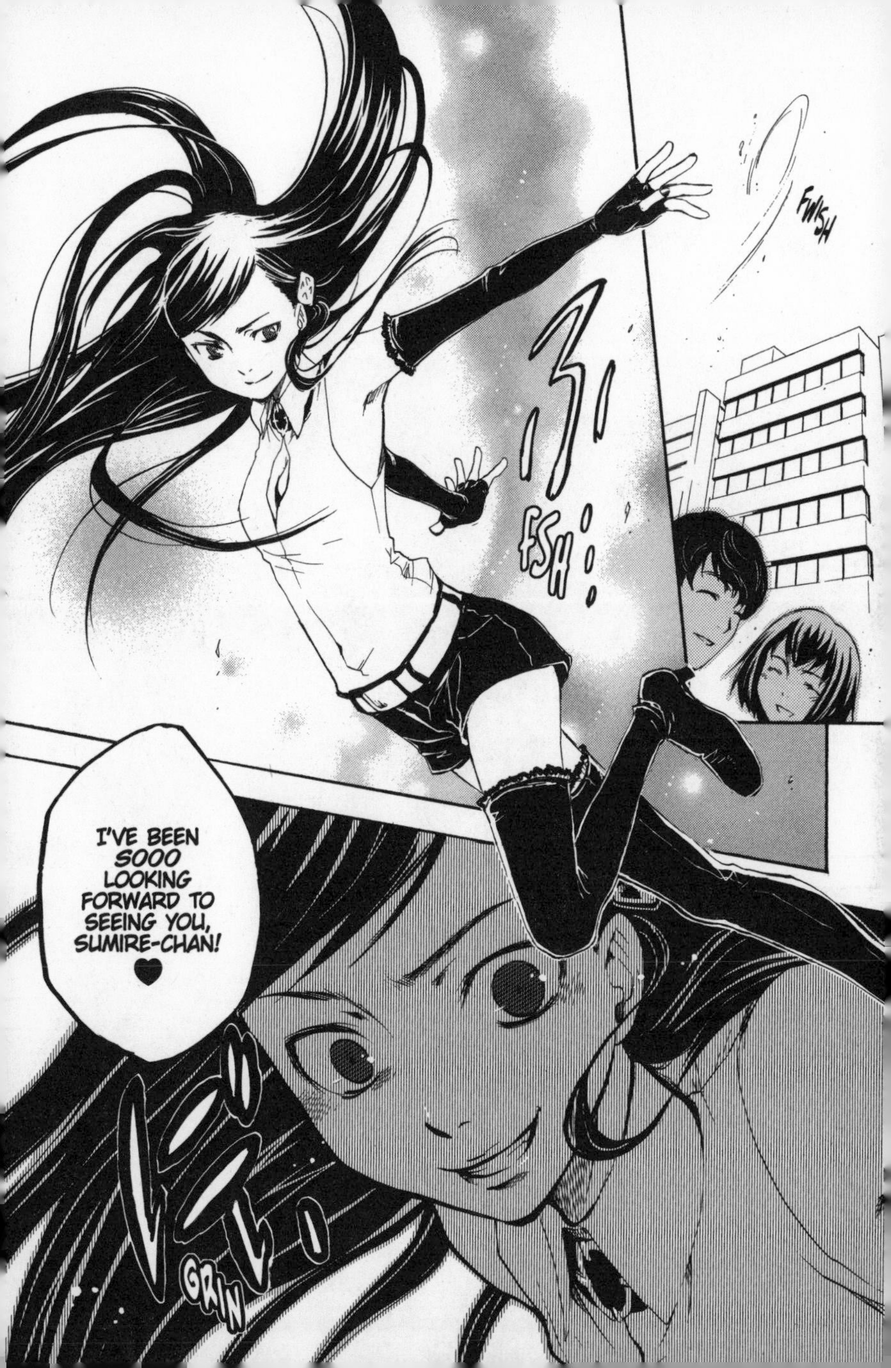
FWISH
FSH
I'VE BEEN SOOO LOOKING FORWARD TO SEEING YOU, SUMIRE-CHAN! ♥
GRIN

Jewelry
and
Clothes

Venus Vangard

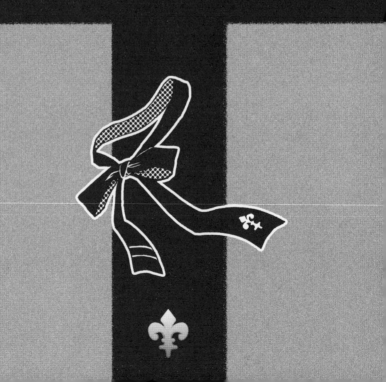

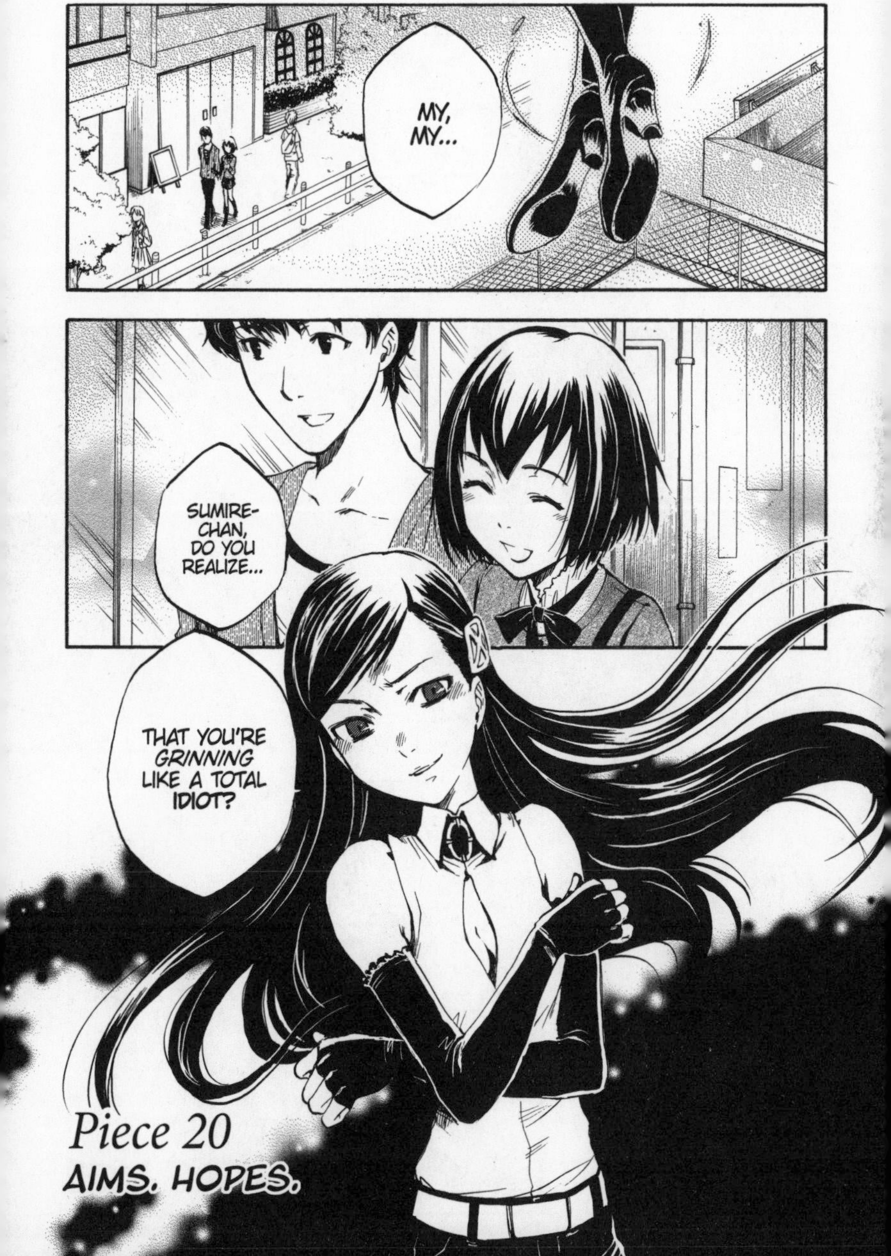
MY, MY...
SUMIRE-CHAN, DO YOU REALIZE...
THAT YOU'RE *GRINNING* LIKE A TOTAL IDIOT?

Piece 20
AIMS. HOPES.

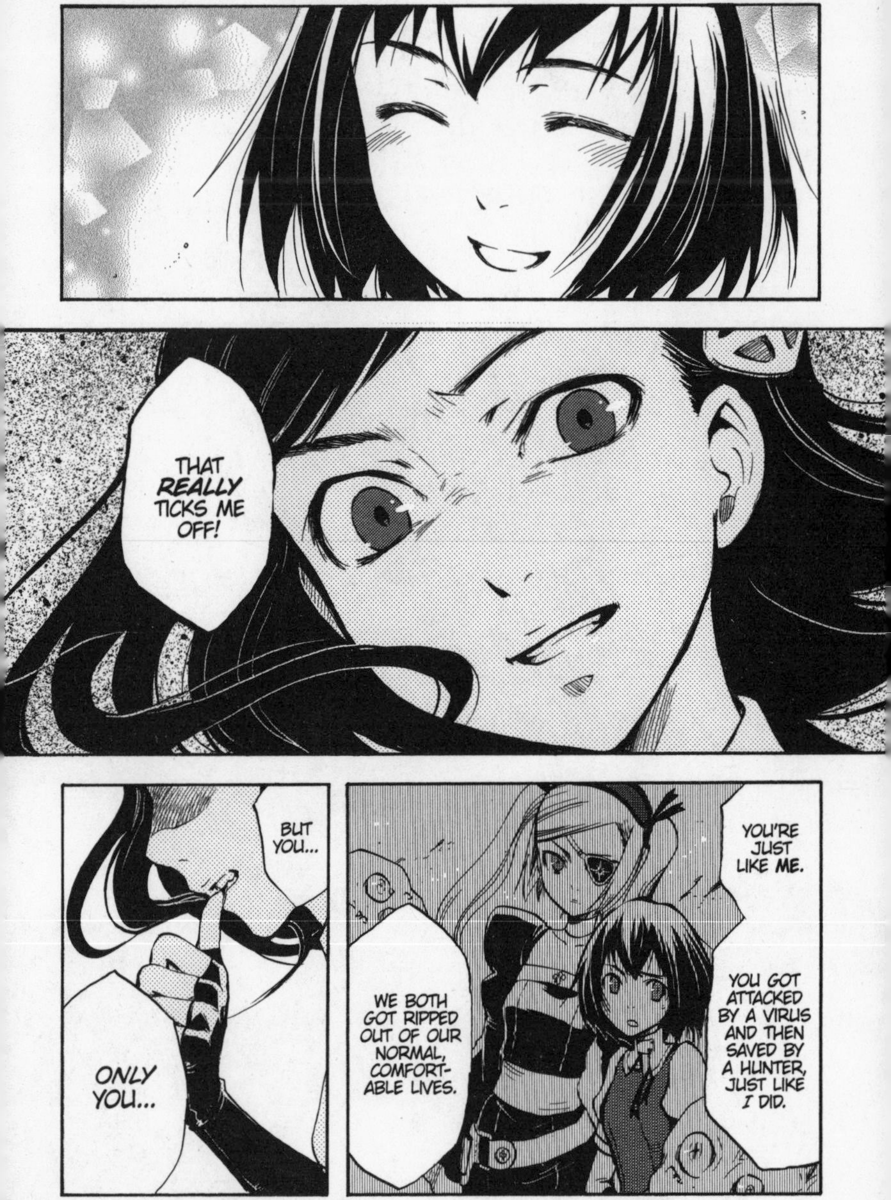
THAT *REALLY* TICKS ME OFF!
YOU'RE JUST LIKE ME.
YOU GOT ATTACKED BY A VIRUS AND THEN SAVED BY A HUNTER, JUST LIKE *I* DID.
WE BOTH GOT RIPPED OUT OF OUR NORMAL, COMFORT-ABLE LIVES.
BUT YOU...
ONLY YOU...

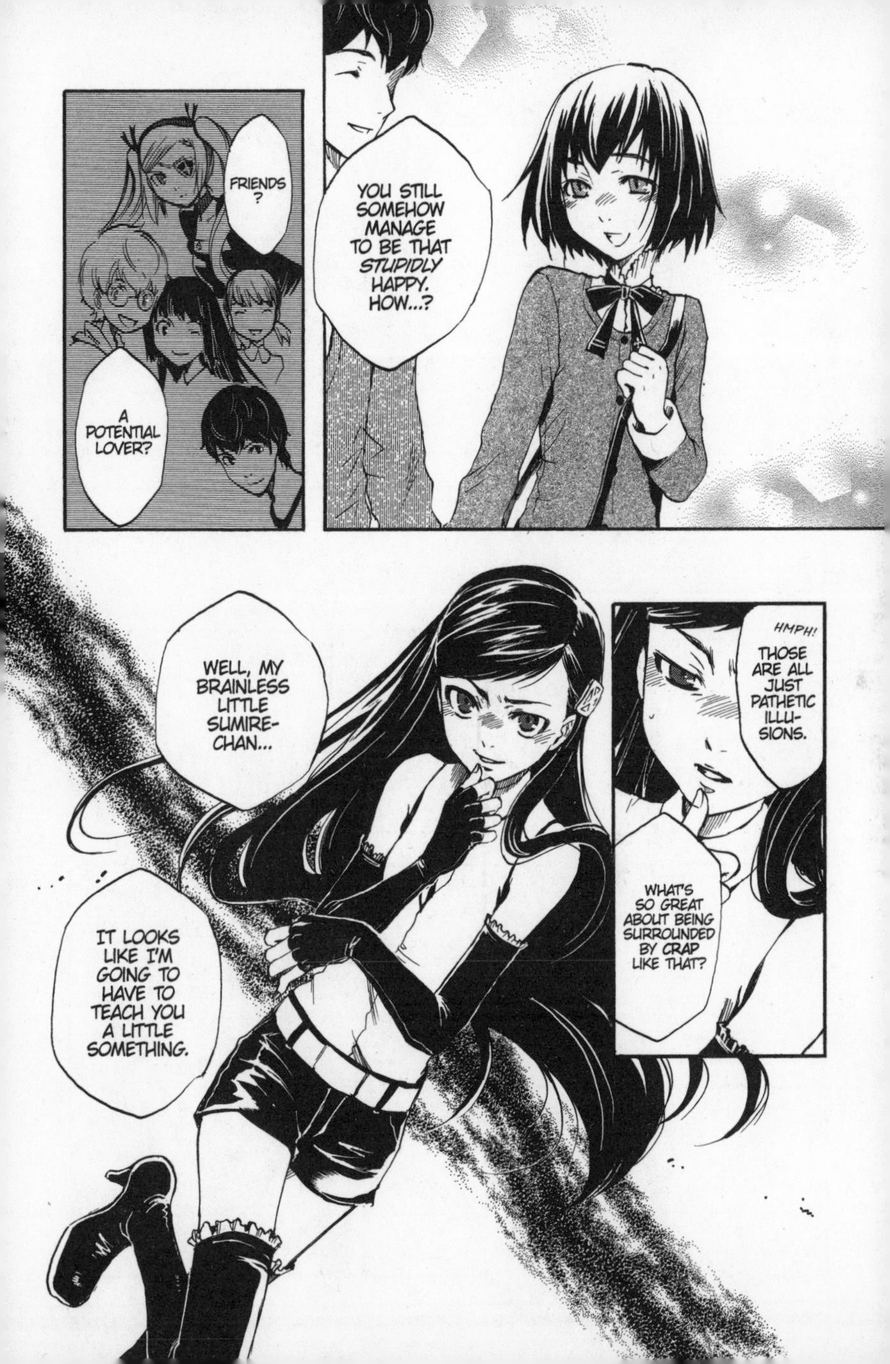
YOU STILL SOMEHOW MANAGE TO BE THAT *STUPIDLY* HAPPY. HOW...?
FRIENDS?
A POTENTIAL LOVER?
HMPH!
THOSE ARE ALL JUST PATHETIC ILLUSIONS.
WHAT'S SO GREAT ABOUT BEING SURROUNDED BY CRAP LIKE THAT?
WELL, MY BRAINLESS LITTLE SUMIRE-CHAN...
IT LOOKS LIKE I'M GOING TO HAVE TO TEACH YOU A LITTLE SOMETHING.

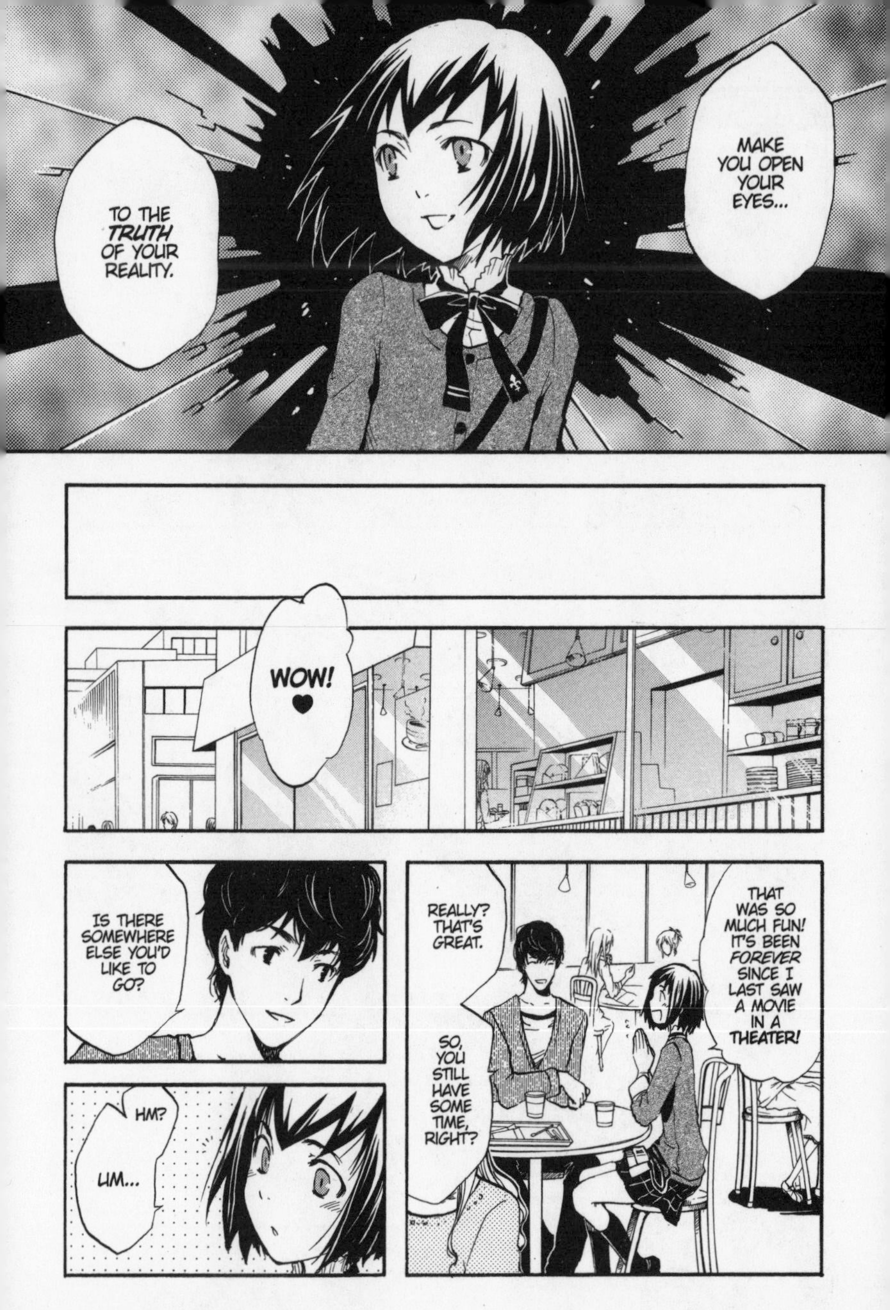
MAKE YOU OPEN YOUR EYES...
TO THE *TRUTH* OF YOUR REALITY.
WOW! ♥
THAT WAS SO MUCH FUN! IT'S BEEN *FOREVER* SINCE I LAST SAW A MOVIE IN A THEATER!
REALLY? THAT'S GREAT.
SO, YOU STILL HAVE SOME TIME, RIGHT?
IS THERE SOMEWHERE ELSE YOU'D LIKE TO GO?
HM?
UM...

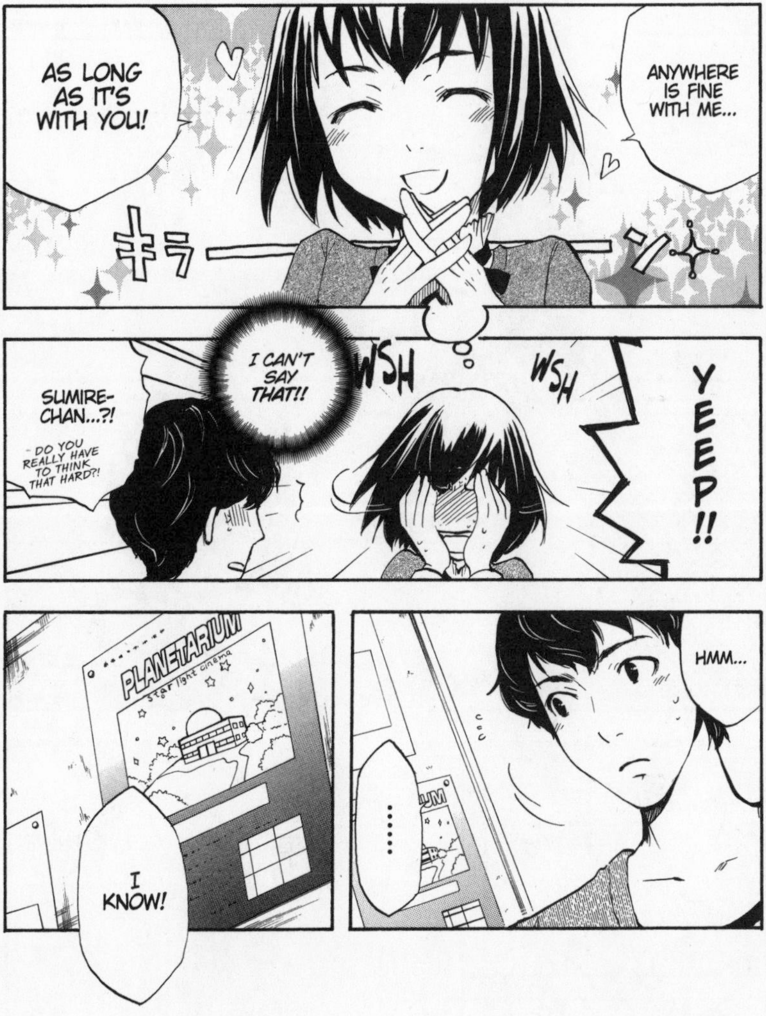
ANYWHERE IS FINE WITH ME...
AS LONG AS IT'S WITH YOU!
キラーン
YEEP!!
WSH
WSH
I CAN'T SAY THAT!!
SUMIRE-CHAN...?!
DO YOU REALLY HAVE TO THINK THAT HARD?!
HMM...
......
PLANETARIUM
starlight cinema
I KNOW!

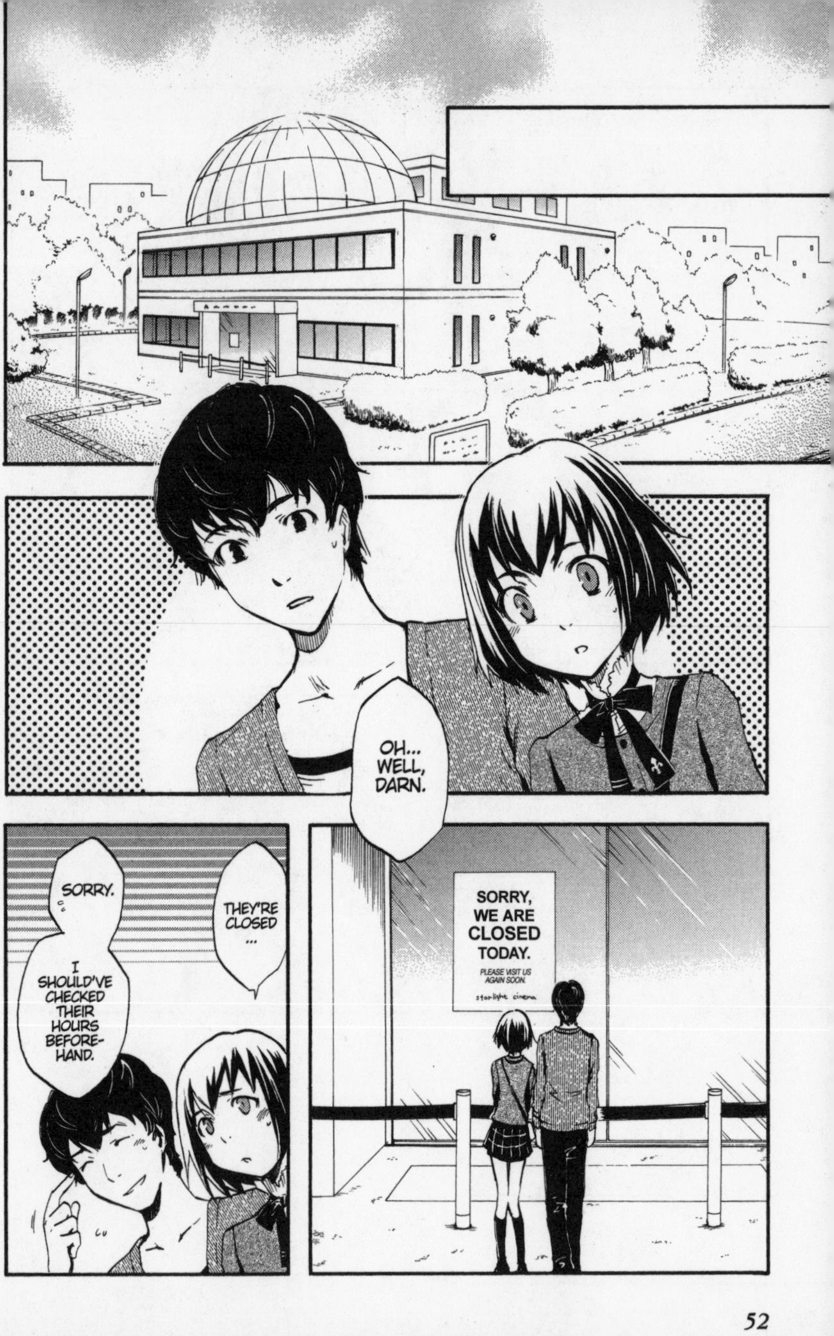
OH... WELL, DARN.
SORRY, WE ARE CLOSED TODAY.
PLEASE VISIT US AGAIN SOON.
starlight cinema
THEY'RE CLOSED ...
SORRY.
I SHOULD'VE CHECKED THEIR HOURS BEFORE-HAND.

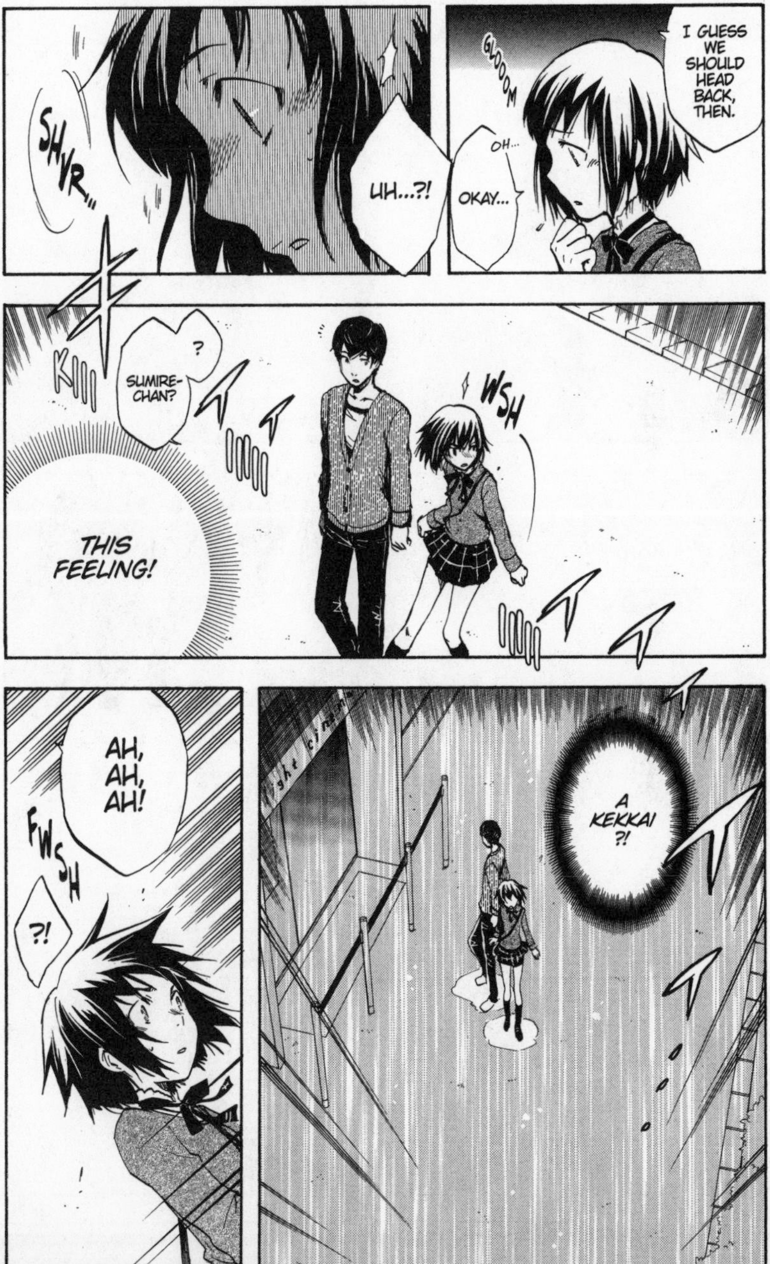
I GUESS WE SHOULD HEAD BACK, THEN.
GLOOOM
OH... OKAY...
UH...?!
SHVR...
WSH
? SUMIRE-CHAN?
KIII
THIS FEELING!
A KEKKAI ?!
AH, AH, AH!
FWSH
?!

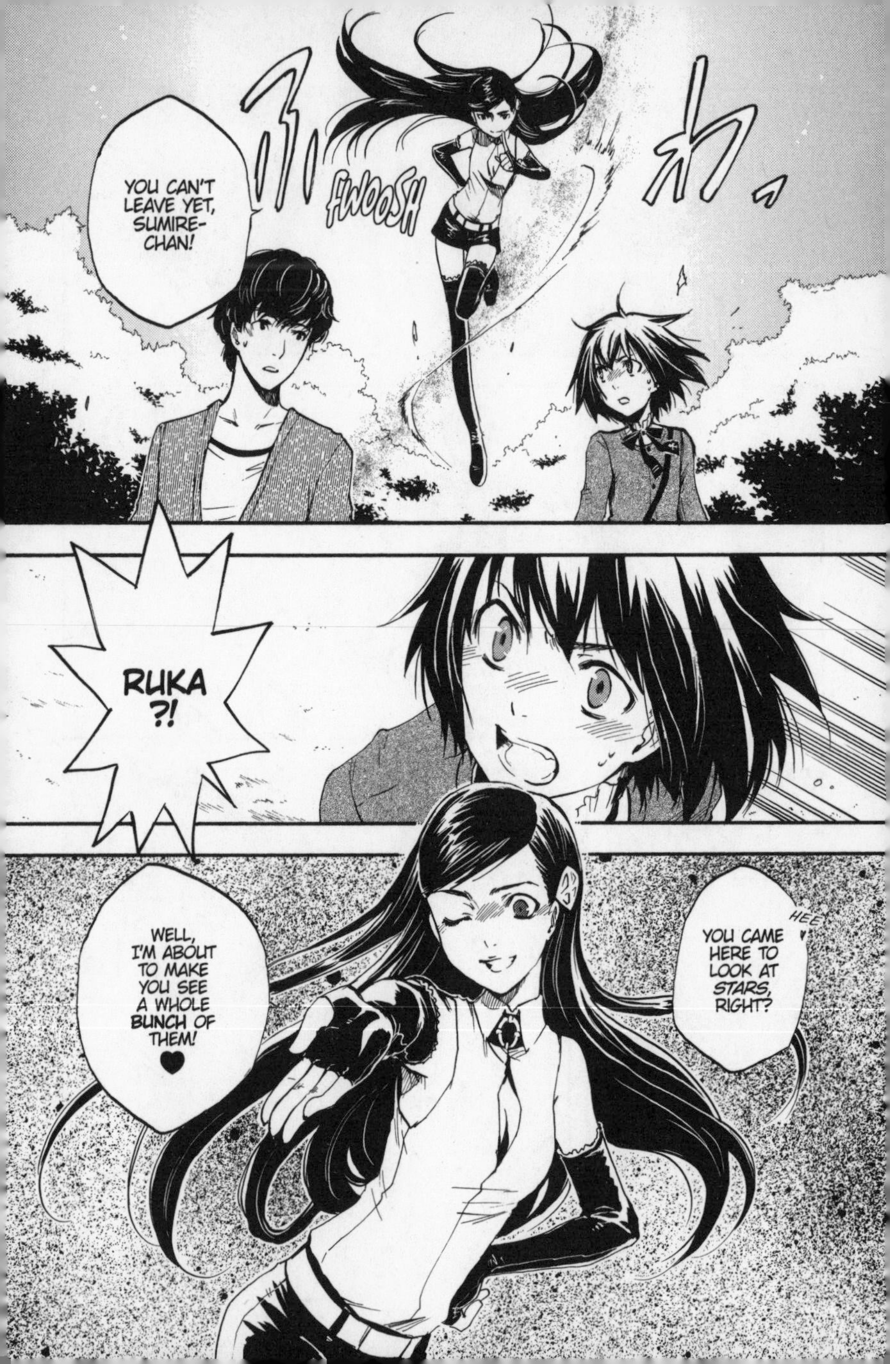
ふわっ
FWOOSH
YOU CAN'T LEAVE YET, SUMIRE-CHAN!
RUKA ?!
YOU CAME HERE TO LOOK AT STARS, RIGHT?
HEE
WELL, I'M ABOUT TO MAKE YOU SEE A WHOLE BUNCH OF THEM! ♥

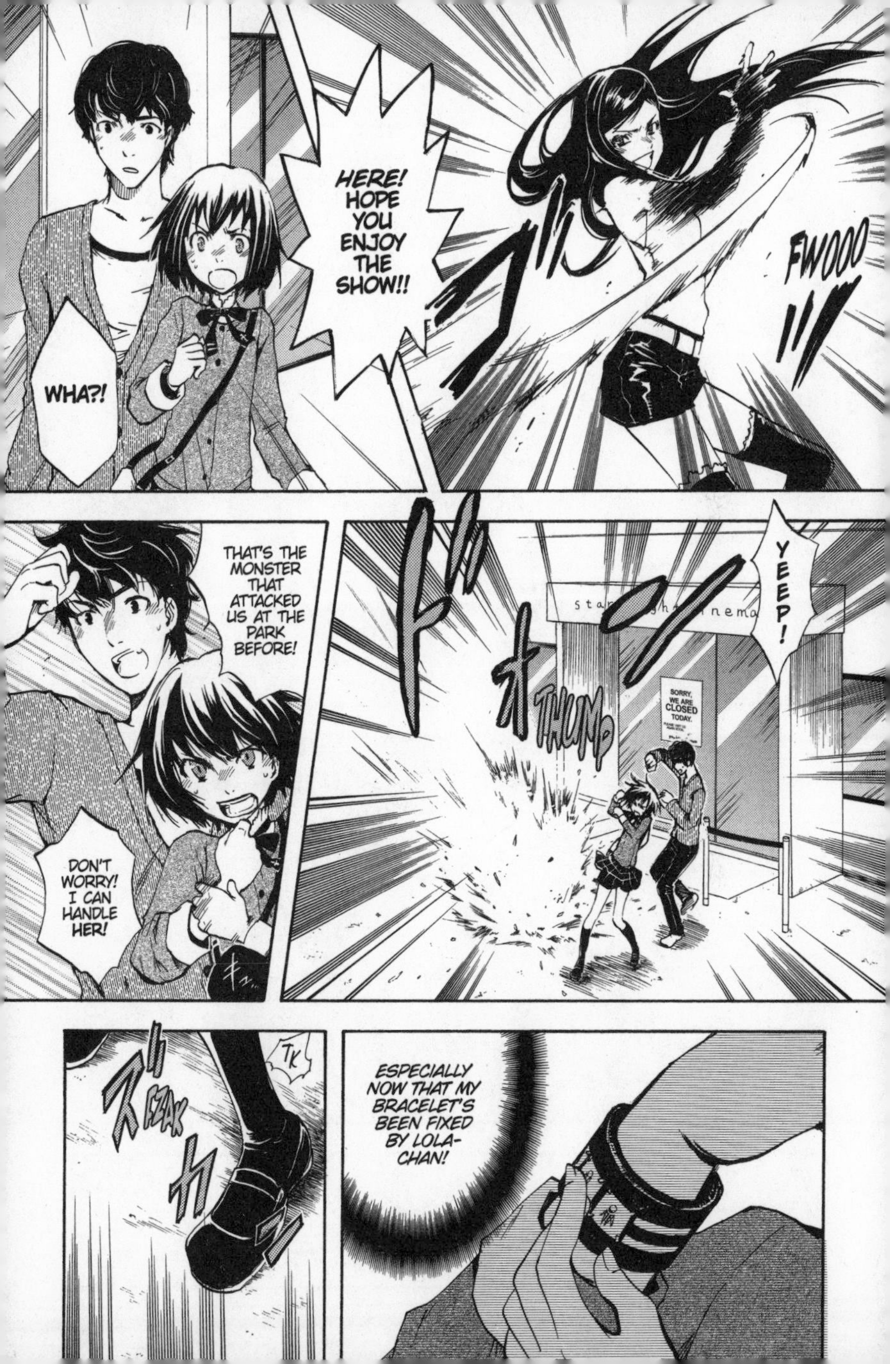
HERE! HOPE YOU ENJOY THE SHOW!!
FWOOO
WHA?!
YEEP!
THUMP
SORRY, WE ARE CLOSED TODAY.
THAT'S THE MONSTER THAT ATTACKED US AT THE PARK BEFORE!
DON'T WORRY! I CAN HANDLE HER!
ESPECIALLY NOW THAT MY BRACELET'S BEEN FIXED BY LOLA-CHAN!
TK
FZAK

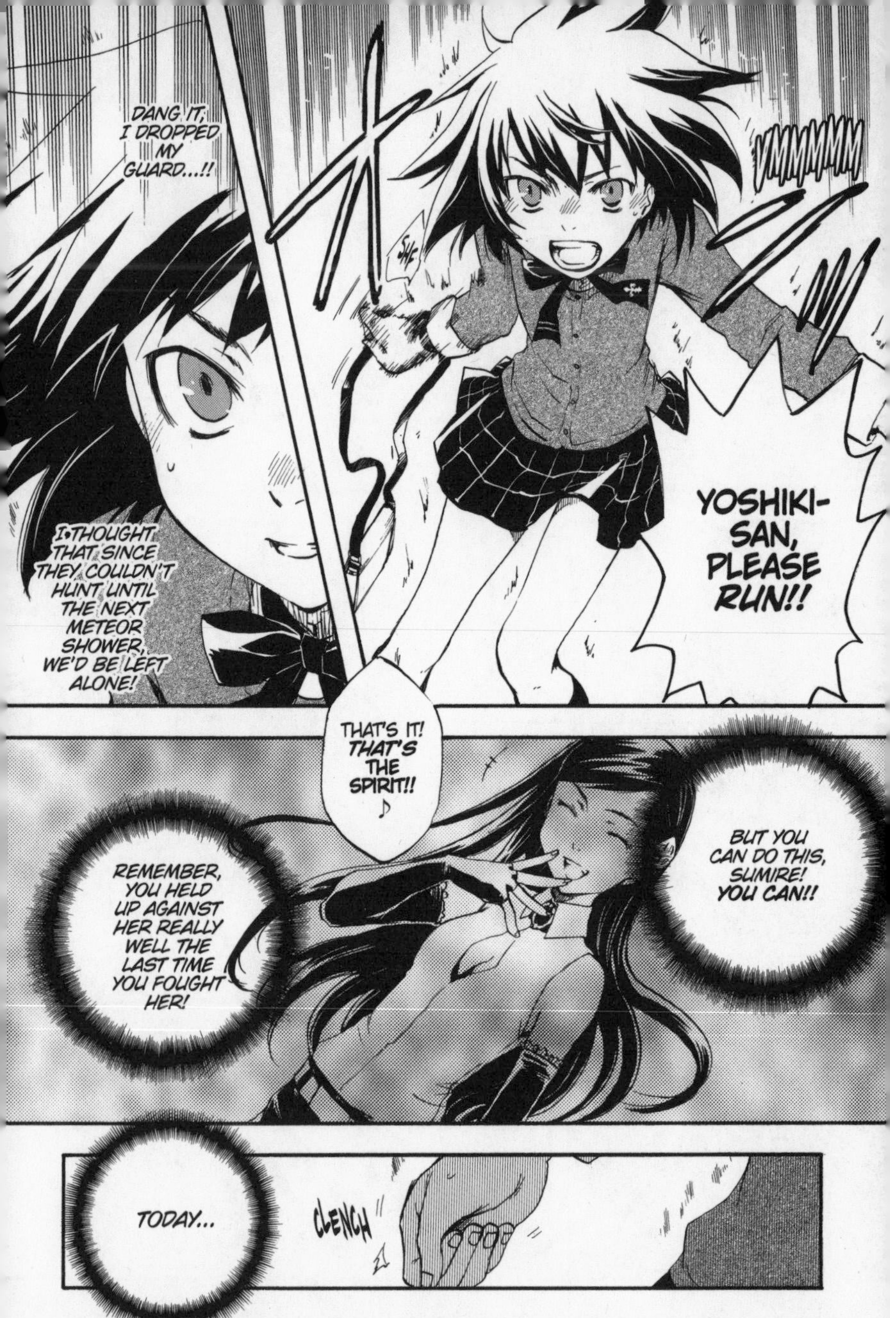
VMMMMM
YOSHIKI-SAN, PLEASE RUN!!
DANG IT, I DROPPED MY GUARD...!!
I THOUGHT THAT SINCE THEY COULDN'T HUNT UNTIL THE NEXT METEOR SHOWER, WE'D BE LEFT ALONE!
THAT'S IT! THAT'S THE SPIRIT!! ♪
BUT YOU CAN DO THIS, SUMIRE! YOU CAN!!
REMEMBER, YOU HELD UP AGAINST HER REALLY WELL THE LAST TIME YOU FOUGHT HER!
CLENCH
TODAY...

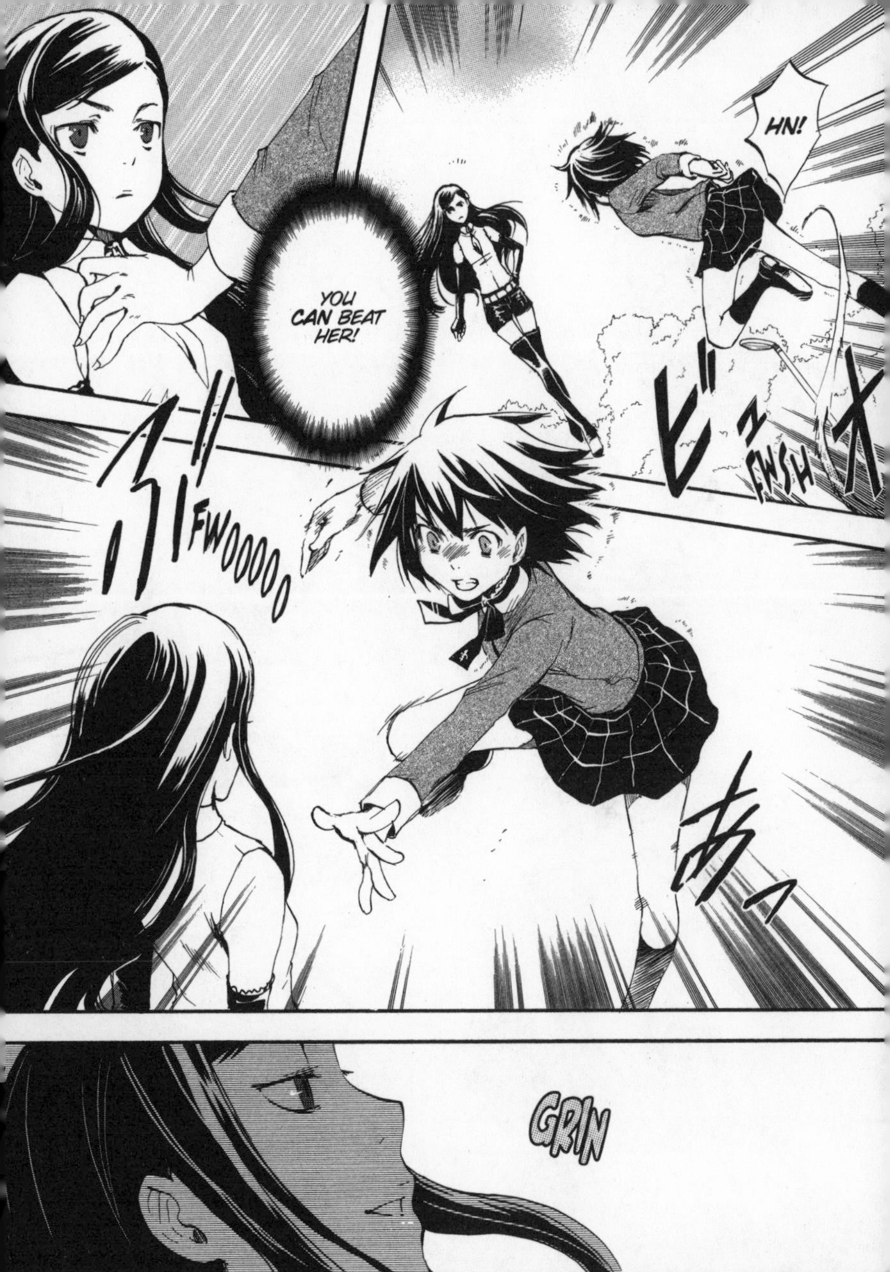
HN!
FWSH
YOU CAN BEAT HER!
FWOOOOO
GRIN

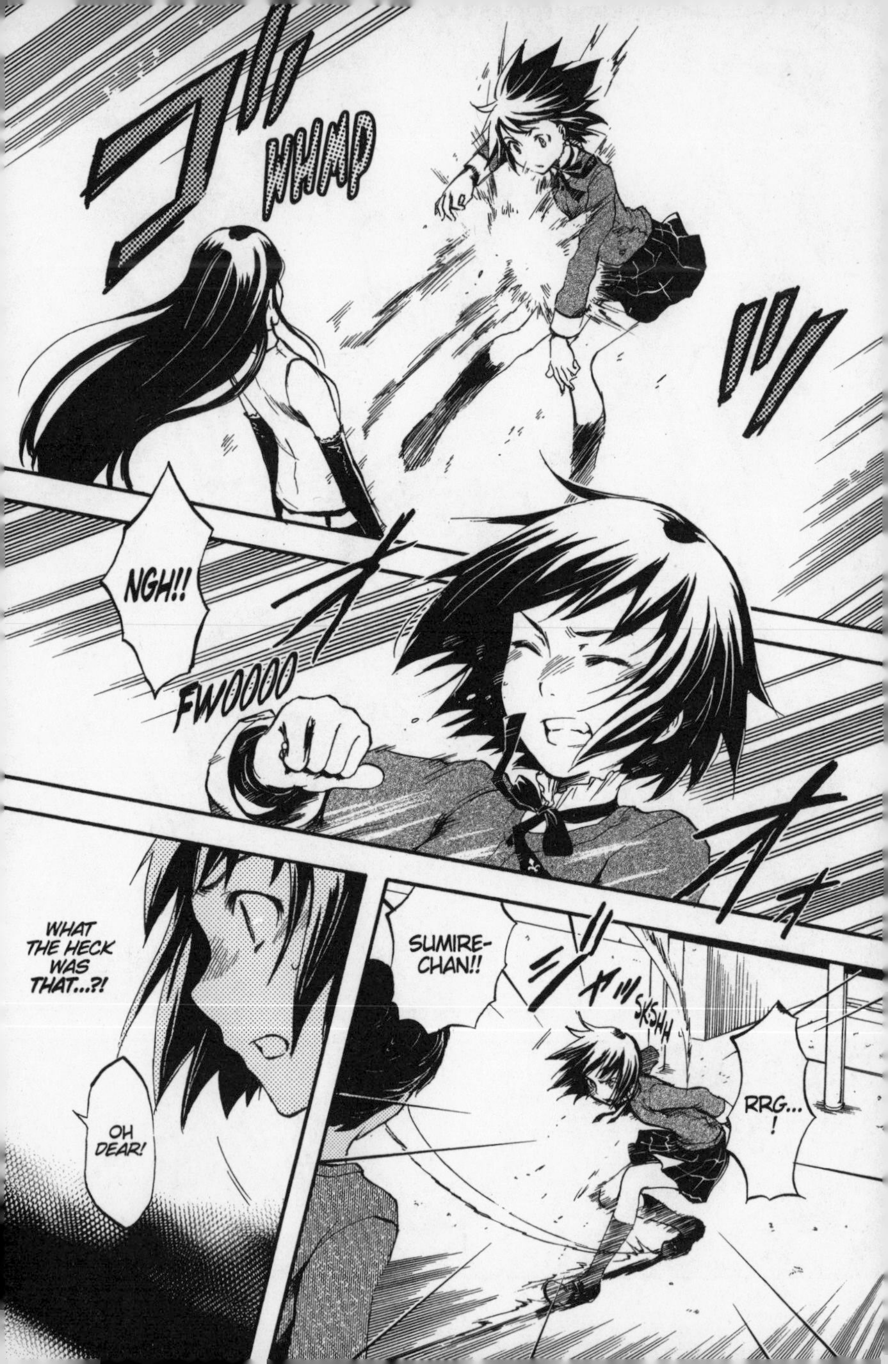
WHMP
NGH!!
FWOOOO
SUMIRE-CHAN!!
SKSHH
RRG... !
WHAT THE HECK WAS THAT...?!
OH DEAR!

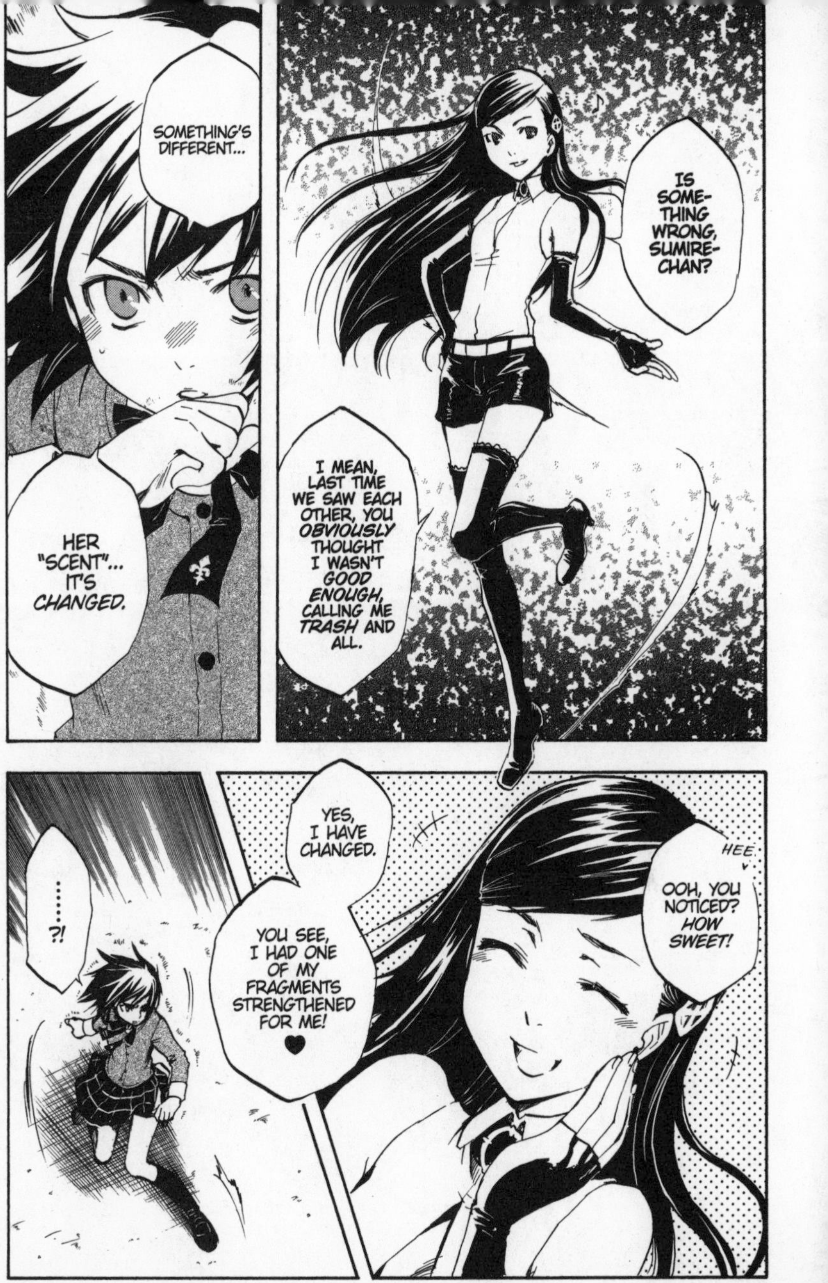
IS SOMETHING WRONG, SUMIRE-CHAN?
I MEAN, LAST TIME WE SAW EACH OTHER, YOU OBVIOUSLY THOUGHT I WASN'T GOOD ENOUGH, CALLING ME TRASH AND ALL.
SOMETHING'S DIFFERENT...
HER "SCENT"... IT'S CHANGED.
HEE
OOH, YOU NOTICED? HOW SWEET!
YES, I HAVE CHANGED.
YOU SEE, I HAD ONE OF MY FRAGMENTS STRENGTHENED FOR ME!
......?!

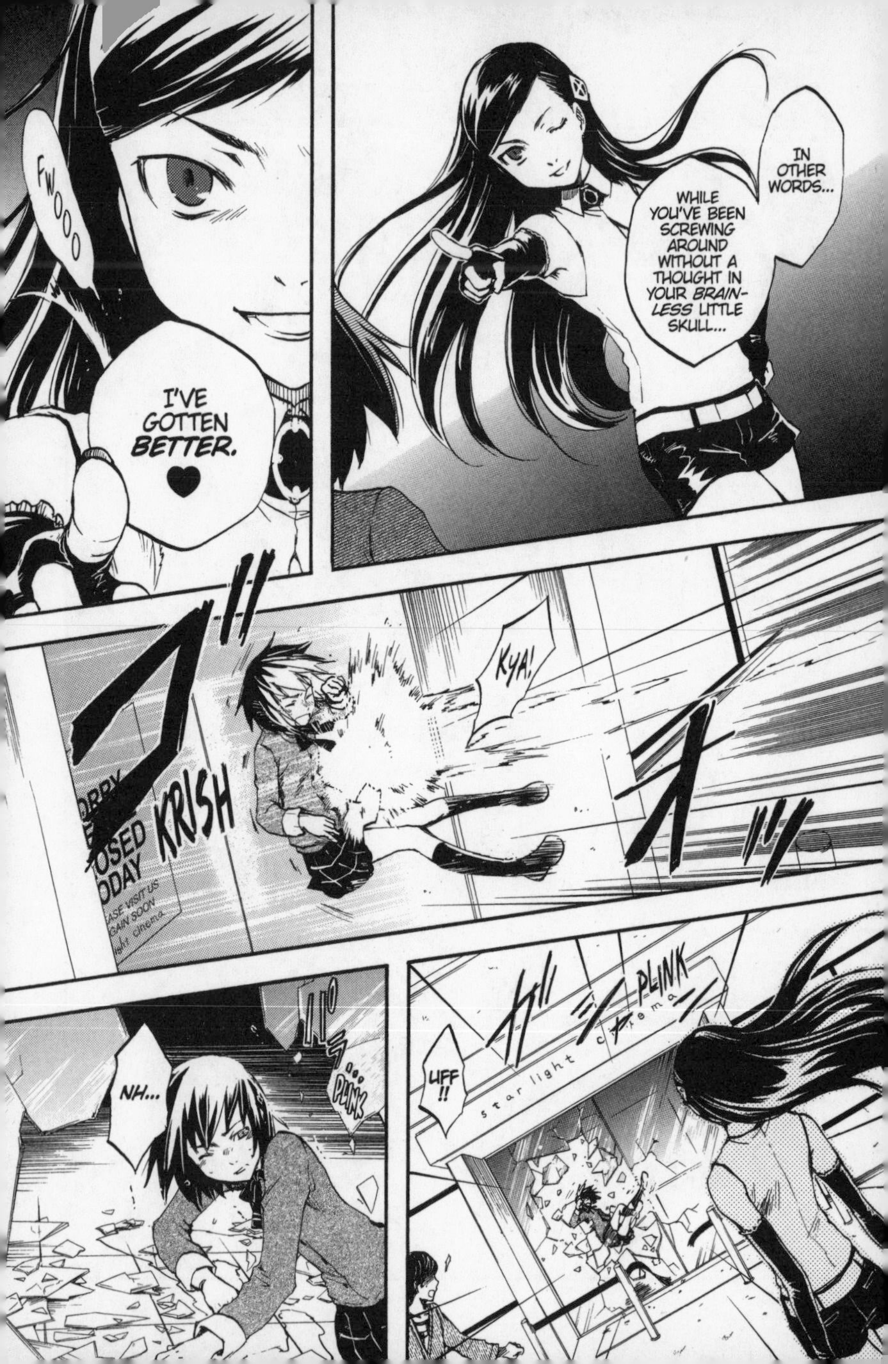
IN OTHER WORDS...
WHILE YOU'VE BEEN SCREWING AROUND WITHOUT A THOUGHT IN YOUR *BRAIN-LESS* LITTLE SKULL...
FWOOOO
I'VE GOTTEN *BETTER.* ♥
KYA!
KRISH
PLINK
UFF!!
star light
NH...
PLINK

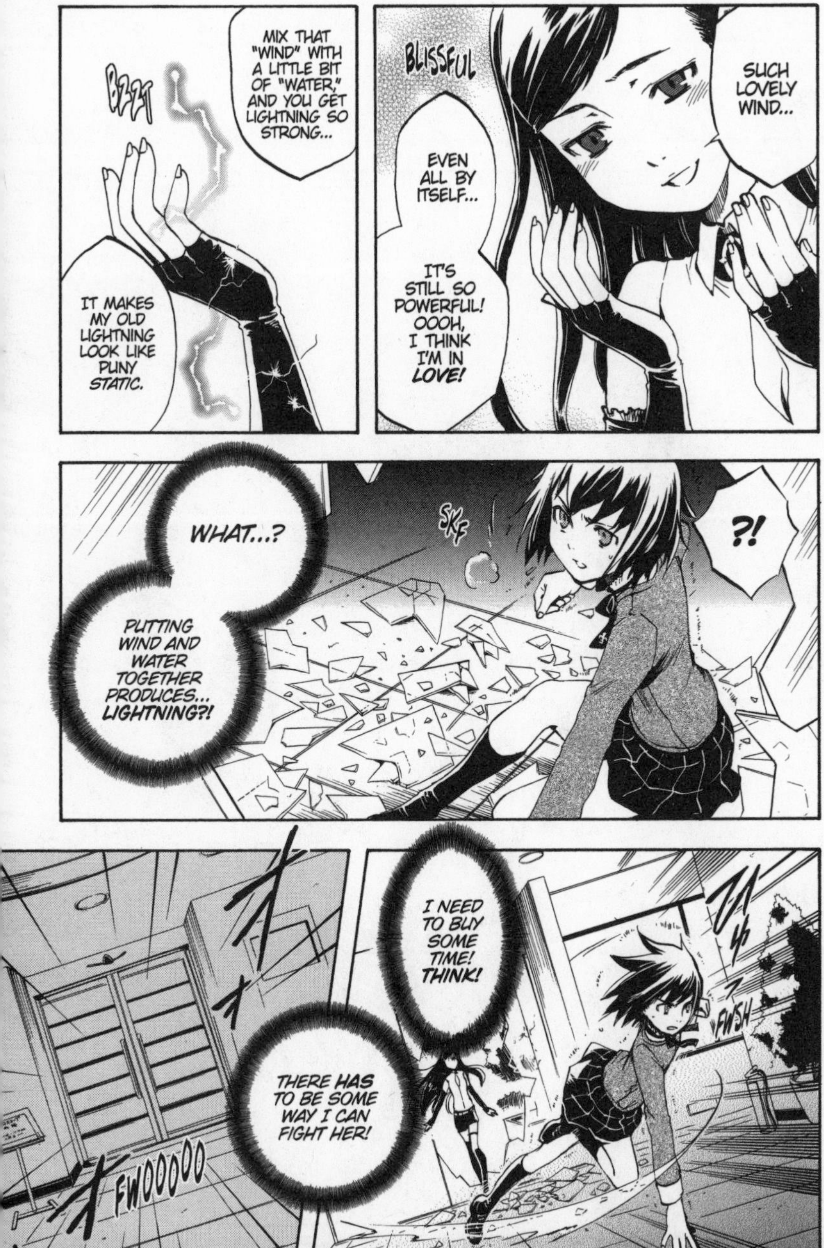
SUCH LOVELY WIND...
BLISSFUL
EVEN ALL BY ITSELF...
IT'S STILL SO POWERFUL! OOOH, I THINK I'M IN **LOVE!**
MIX THAT "WIND" WITH A LITTLE BIT OF "WATER," AND YOU GET LIGHTNING SO STRONG...
BZZZT
IT MAKES MY OLD LIGHTNING LOOK LIKE PUNY STATIC.
?!
SKF
WHAT...?
PUTTING WIND AND WATER TOGETHER PRODUCES... **LIGHTNING?!**
FWSH
I NEED TO BUY SOME TIME! **THINK!**
THERE **HAS** TO BE SOME WAY I CAN FIGHT HER!
FWOOOOO

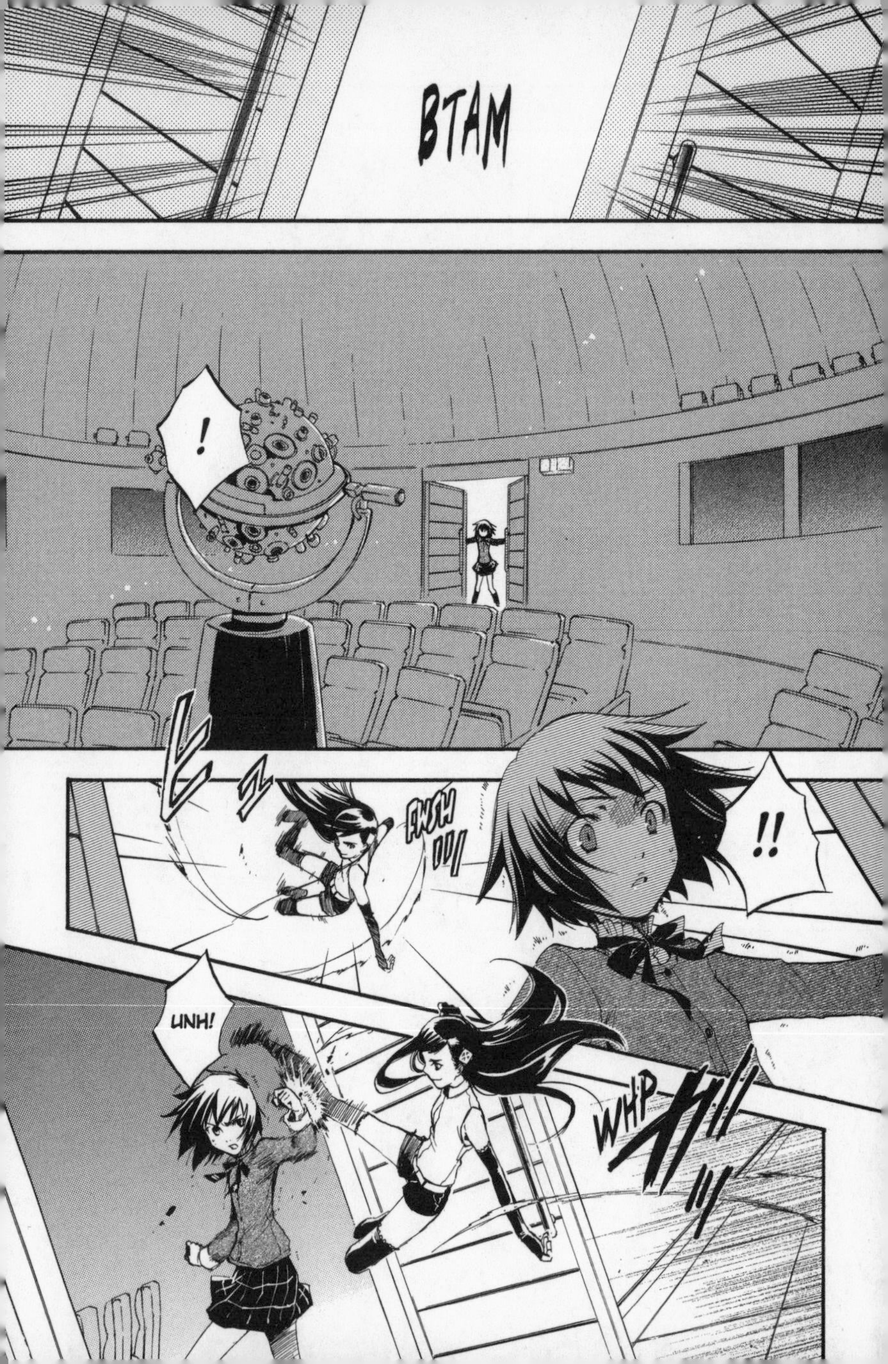

BTAM
!
!!
FWSH
WHP
UNH!

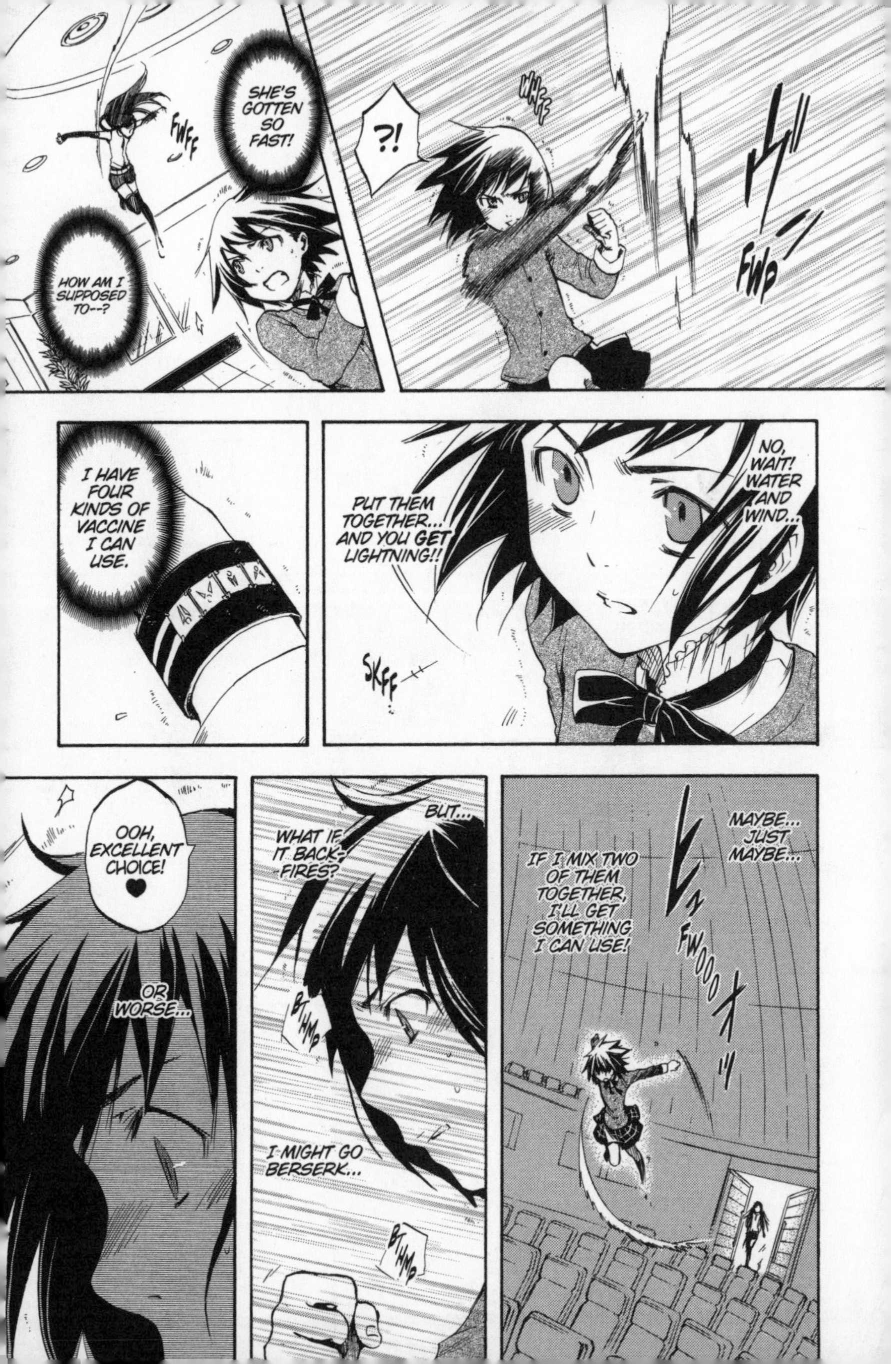
WHFF
?!
FWP
SHE'S GOTTEN SO FAST!
FWFF
HOW AM I SUPPOSED TO--?
NO, WAIT! WATER AND WIND...
PUT THEM TOGETHER... AND YOU GET LIGHTNING!!
SKFF
I HAVE FOUR KINDS OF VACCINE I CAN USE.
MAYBE... JUST MAYBE...
IF I MIX TWO OF THEM TOGETHER, I'LL GET SOMETHING I CAN USE!
FWOOO
BUT...
WHAT IF IT BACK-FIRES?
BTHMP
I MIGHT GO BERSERK...
BTHMP
OOH, EXCELLENT CHOICE!
OR WORSE...

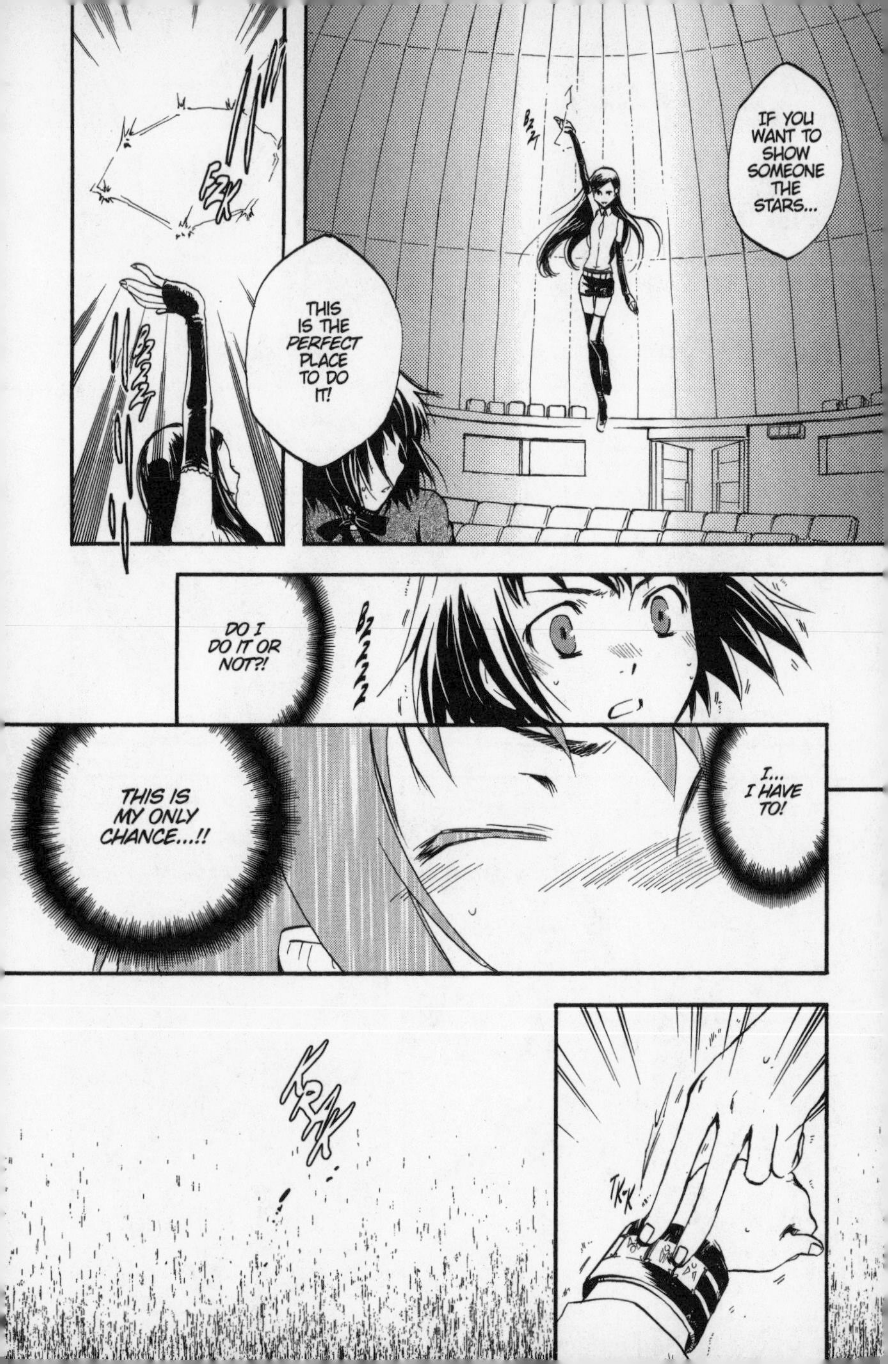
IF YOU WANT TO SHOW SOMEONE THE STARS...
THIS IS THE PERFECT PLACE TO DO IT!
BZK
DO I DO IT OR NOT?!
I... I HAVE TO!
THIS IS MY ONLY CHANCE...!!
TK-K
KRAK

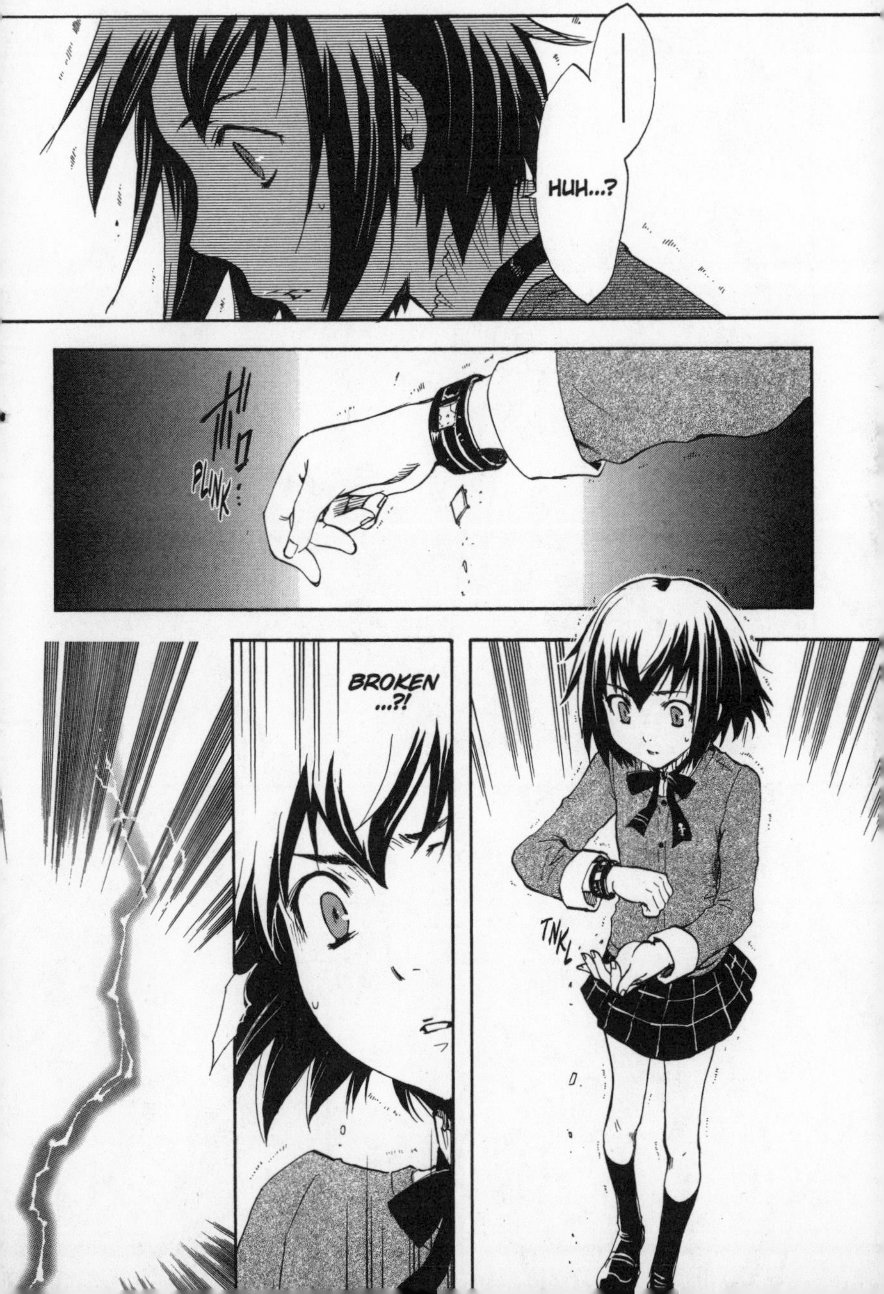
HUH...?
ポロ
PLINK
TNKL
BROKEN ...?!

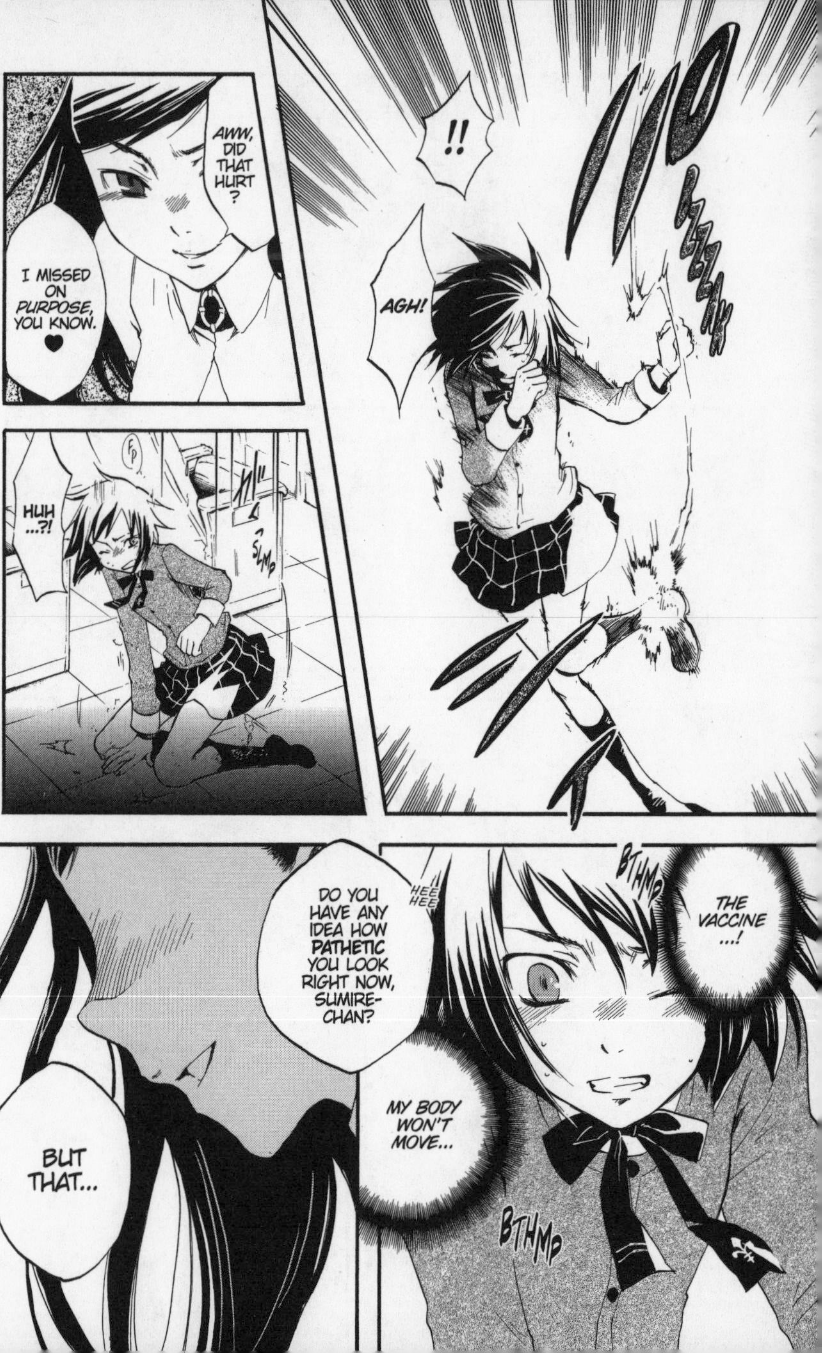
!!
AGH!
AWW, DID THAT HURT?
I MISSED ON PURPOSE, YOU KNOW. ♥
HUH ...?!
SLMP
BTHMP
THE VACCINE ...!
HEE HEE
DO YOU HAVE ANY IDEA HOW PATHETIC YOU LOOK RIGHT NOW, SUMIRE-CHAN?
MY BODY WON'T MOVE...
BTHMP
BUT THAT...

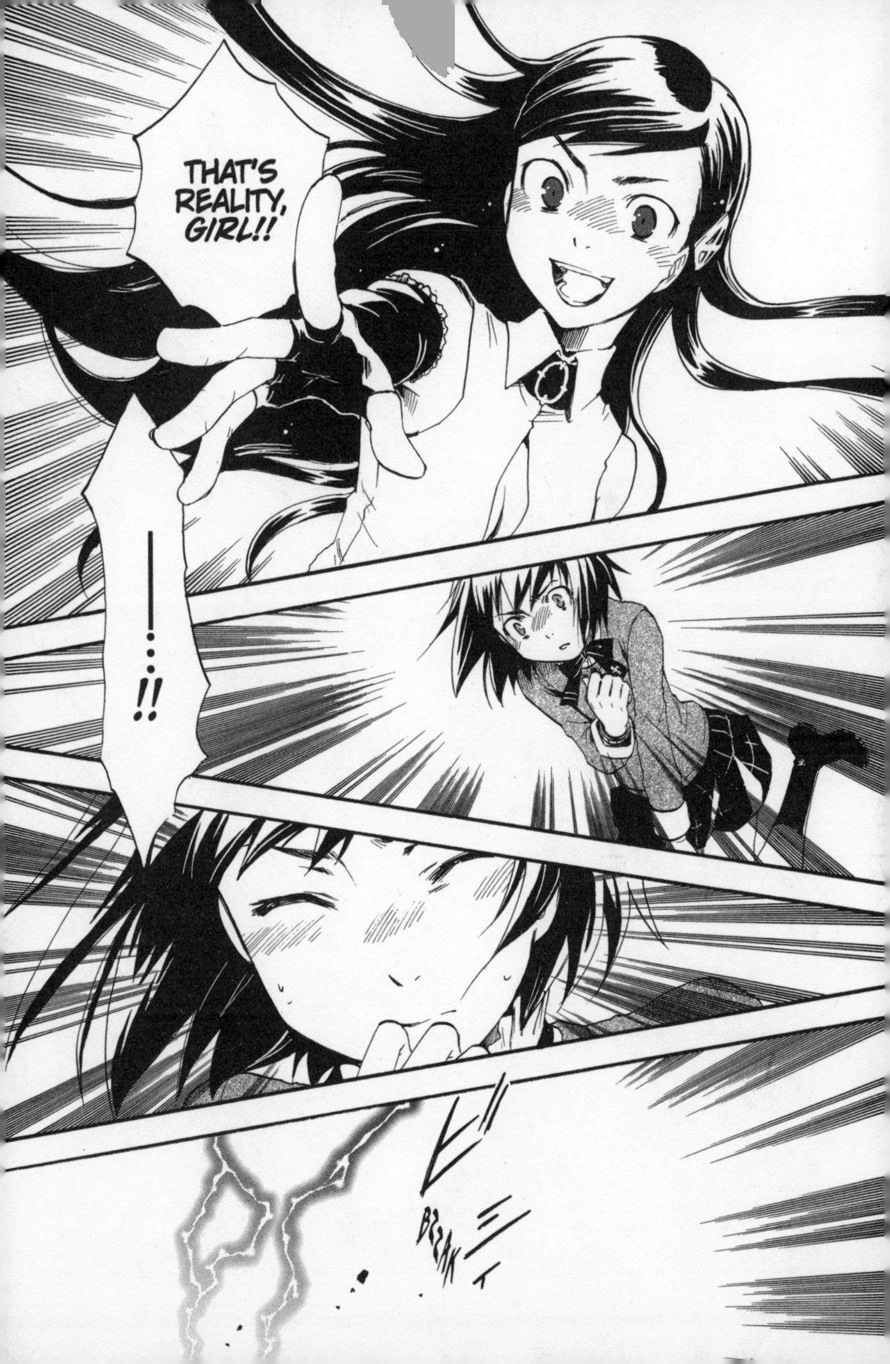
THAT'S REALITY, GIRL!!
——...!!
BZZAK

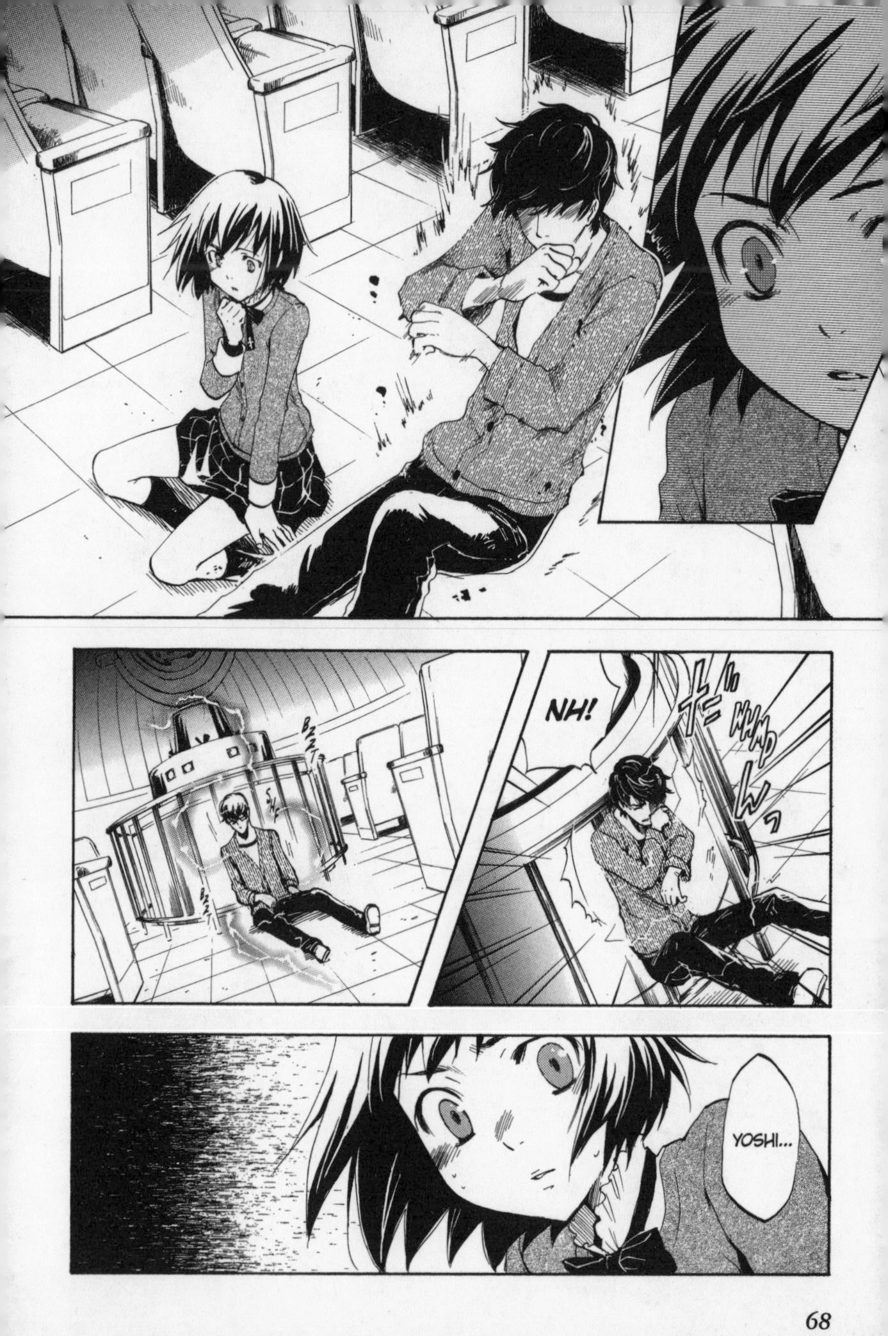
NH!
WHMP
BZZT
BZZT
YOSHI...

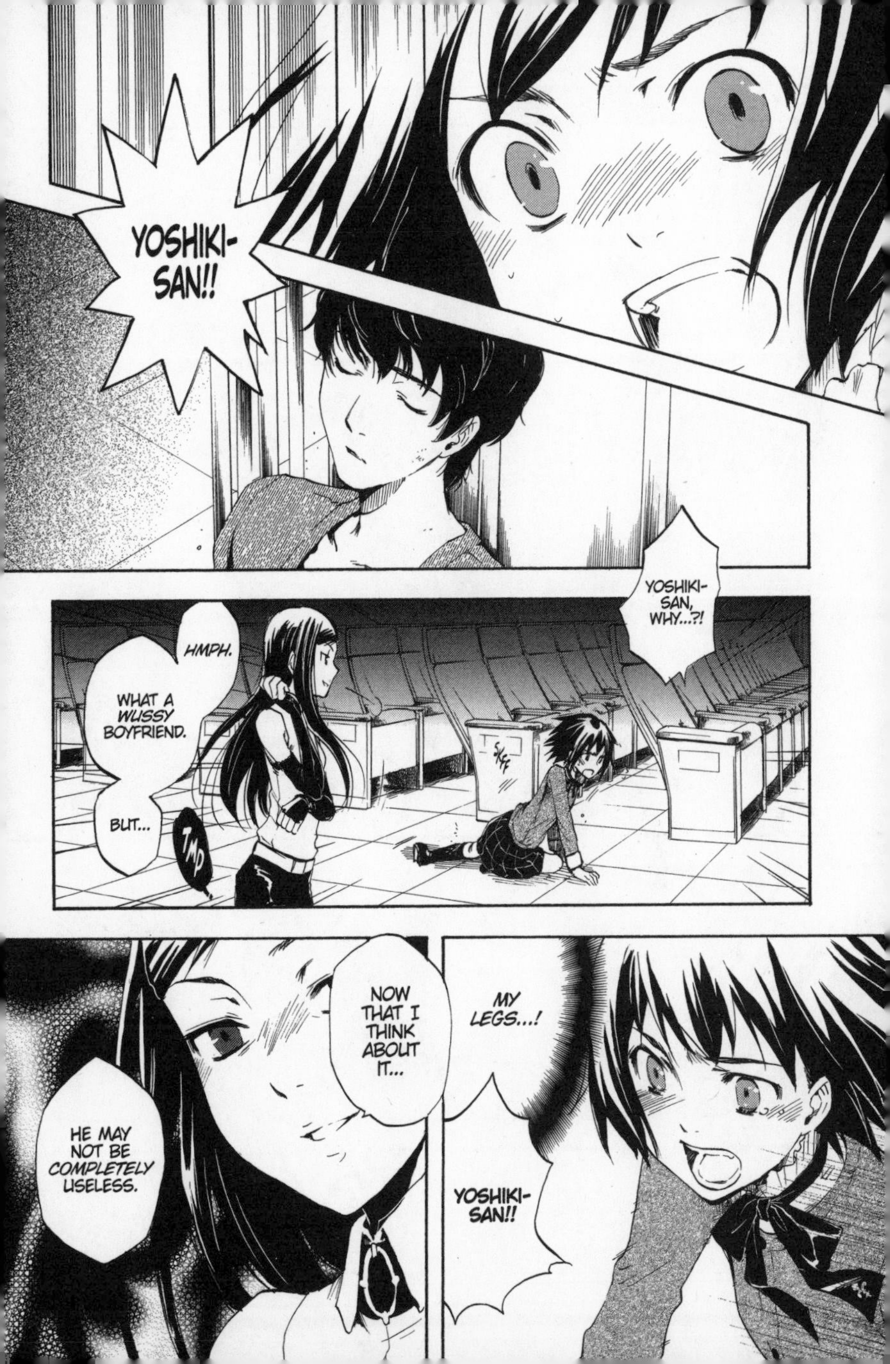
YOSHIKI-SAN!!
YOSHIKI-SAN, WHY...?!
SKFF
HMPH.
WHAT A *WUSSY* BOYFRIEND.
BUT...
TMP
MY LEGS...!
YOSHIKI-SAN!!
NOW THAT I THINK ABOUT IT...
HE MAY NOT BE *COMPLETELY* USELESS.

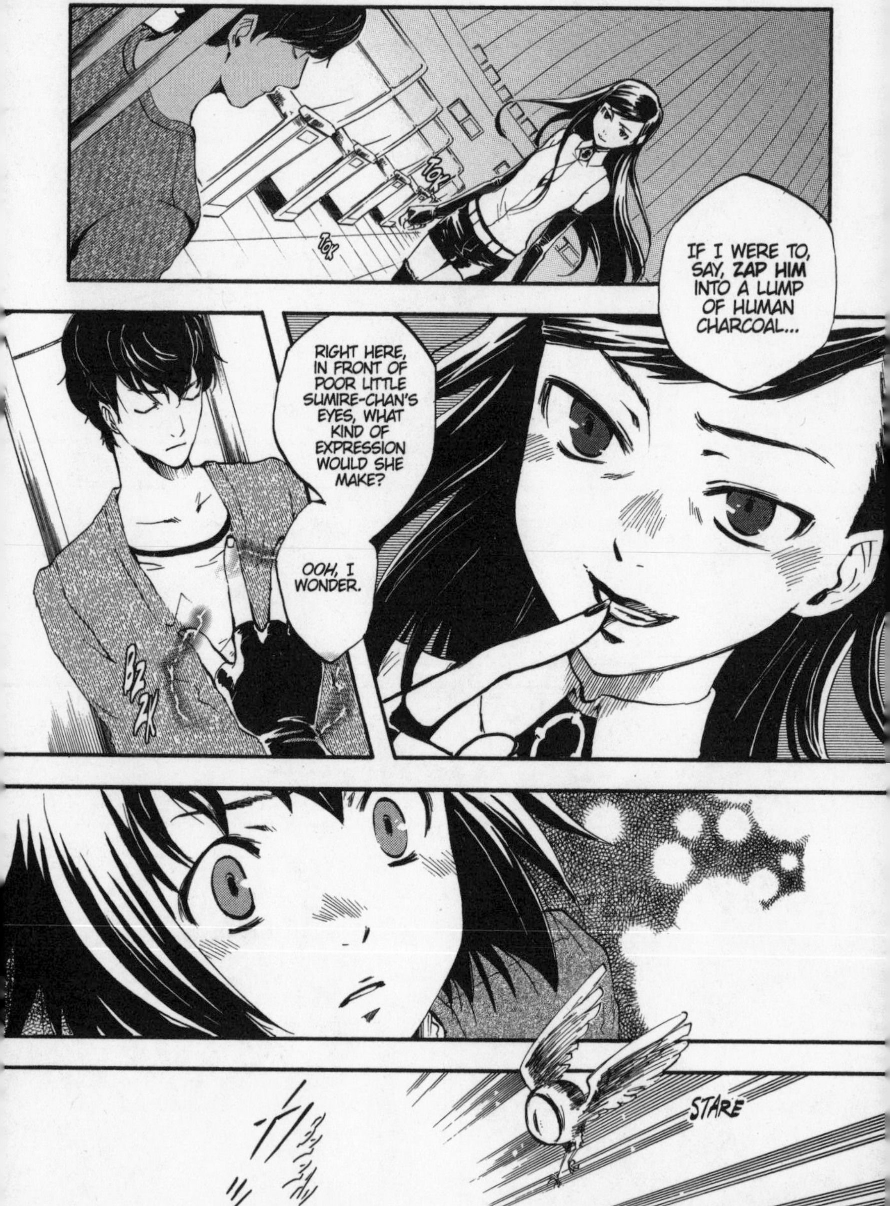

TOK
TOK
IF I WERE TO, SAY, ZAP HIM INTO A LUMP OF HUMAN CHARCOAL...
RIGHT HERE, IN FRONT OF POOR LITTLE SUMIRE-CHAN'S EYES, WHAT KIND OF EXPRESSION WOULD SHE MAKE?
OOH, I WONDER.
BZZK
STARE

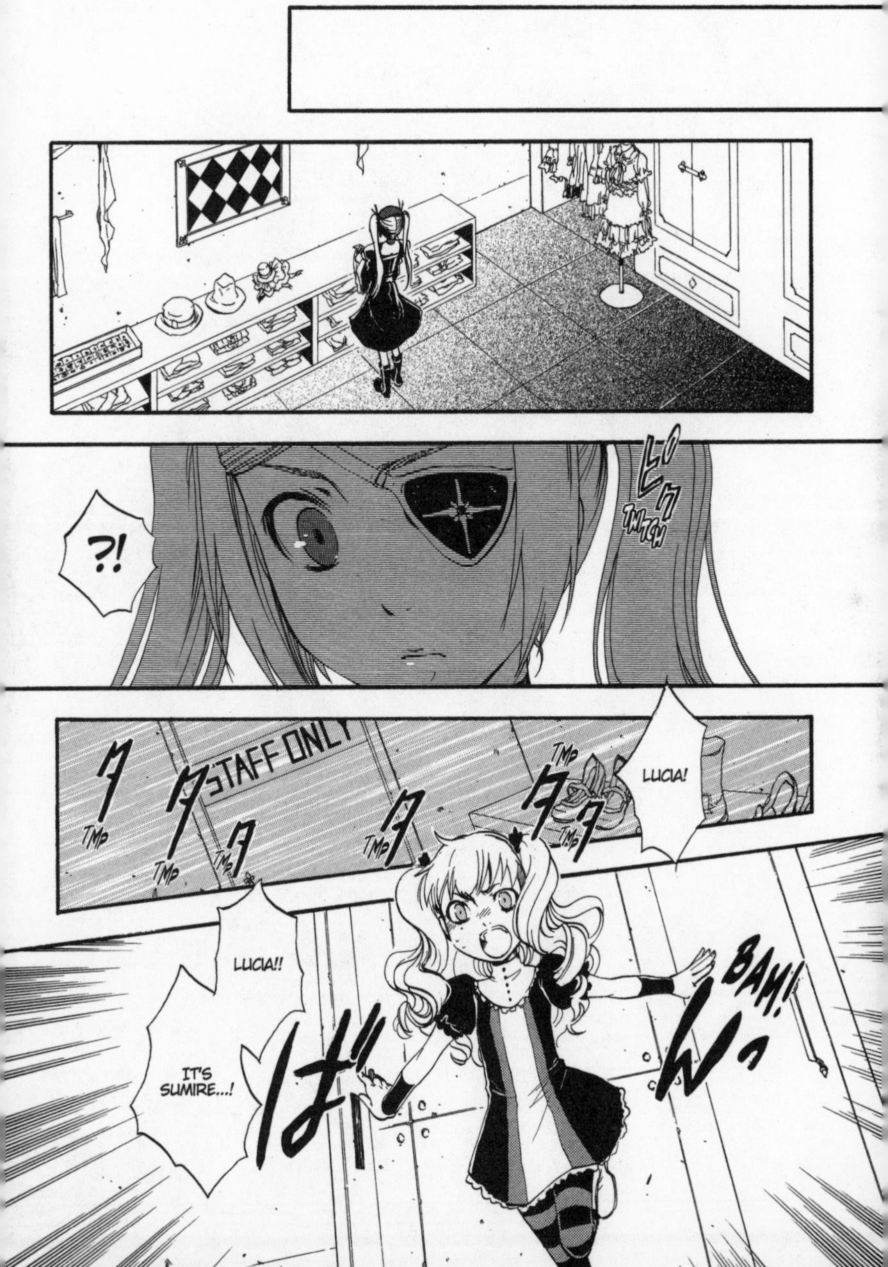

ピク
TWITCH
?!
LUCIA!
STAFF ONLY
TMP
TMP
TMP
TMP
TMP
TMP
BAM!
LUCIA!!
IT'S SUMIRE...!

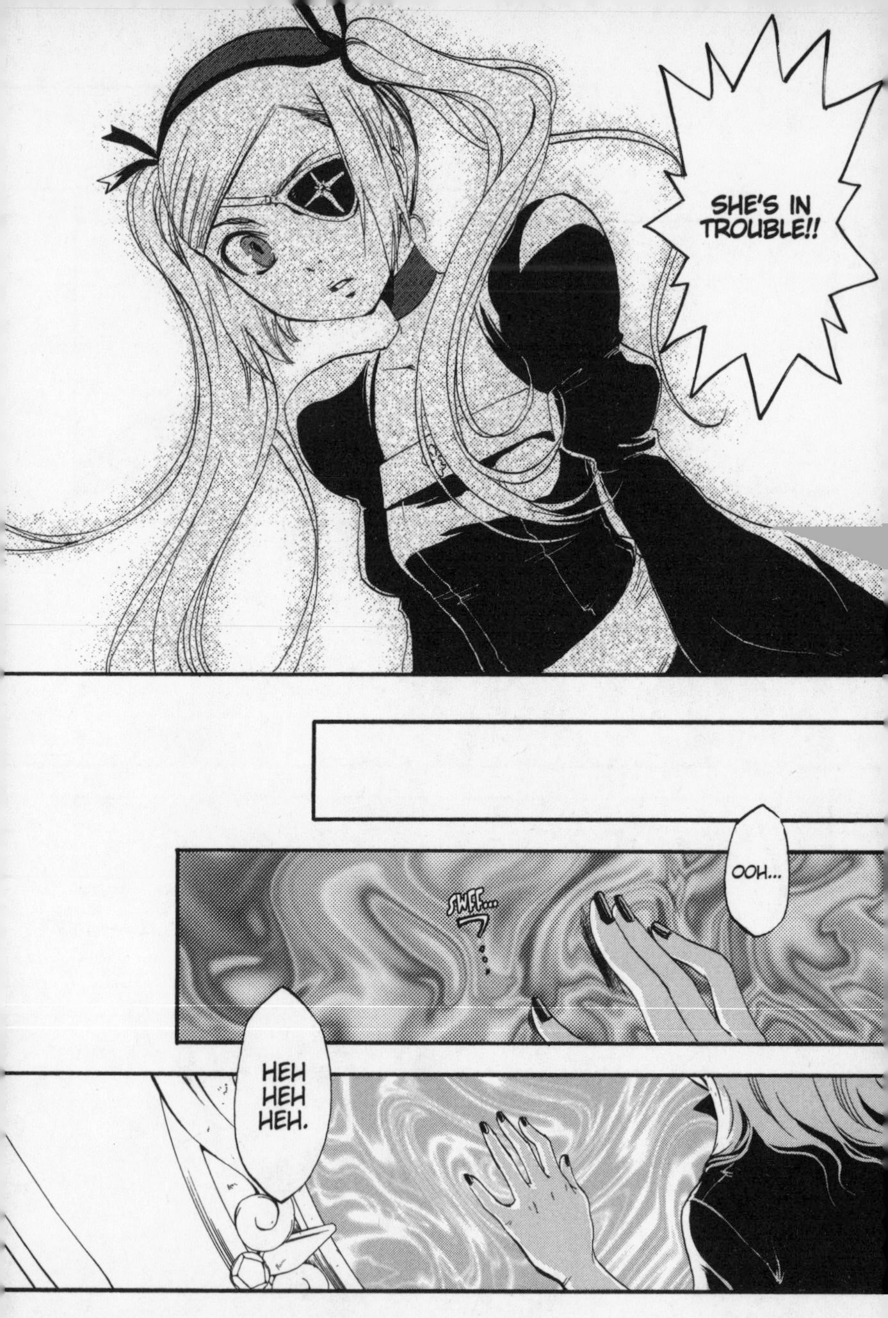
SHE'S IN TROUBLE!!
OOH...
SWFF...
HEH HEH HEH.

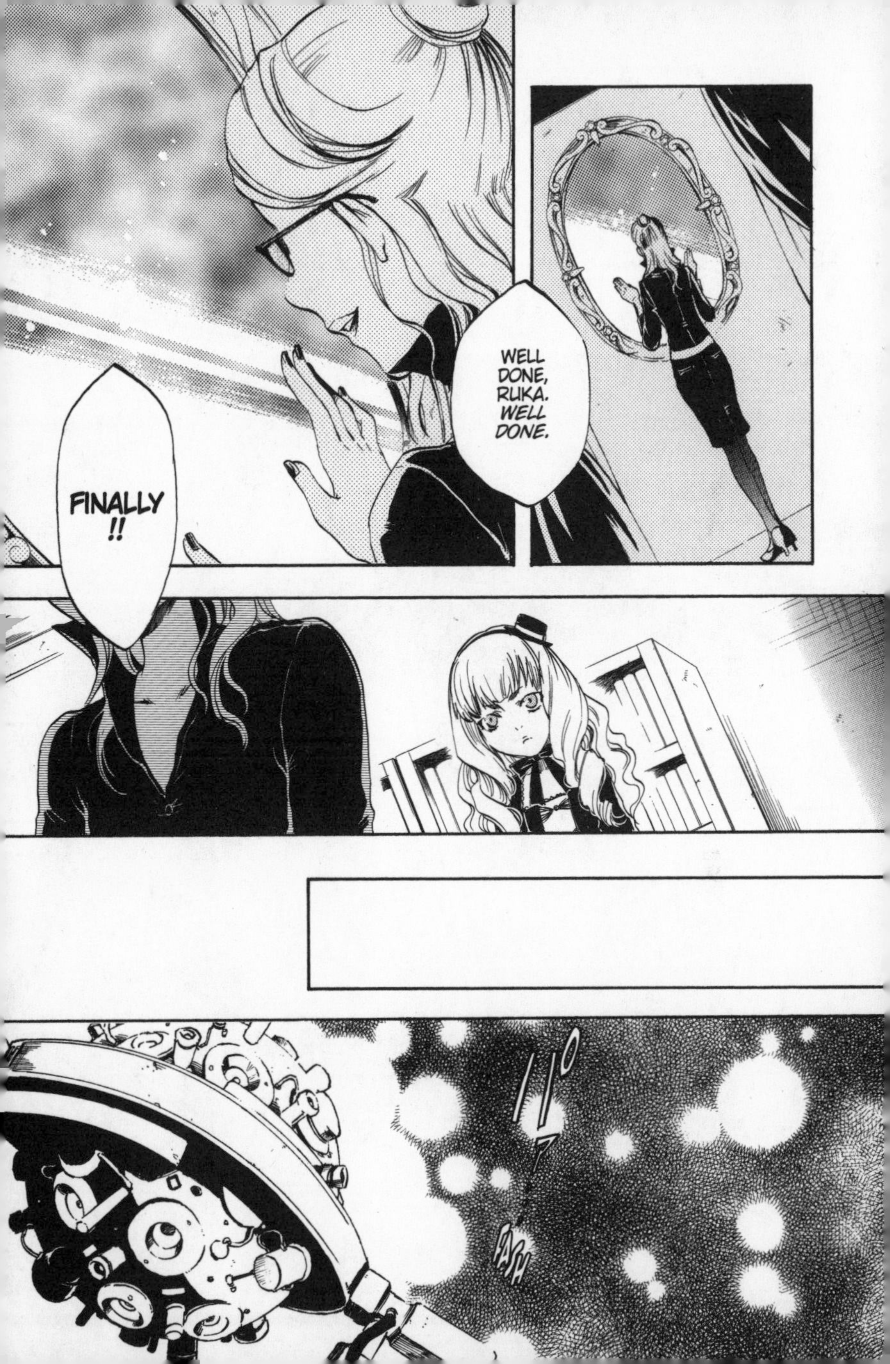
WELL DONE, RUKA. WELL DONE.
FINALLY!!
FASH

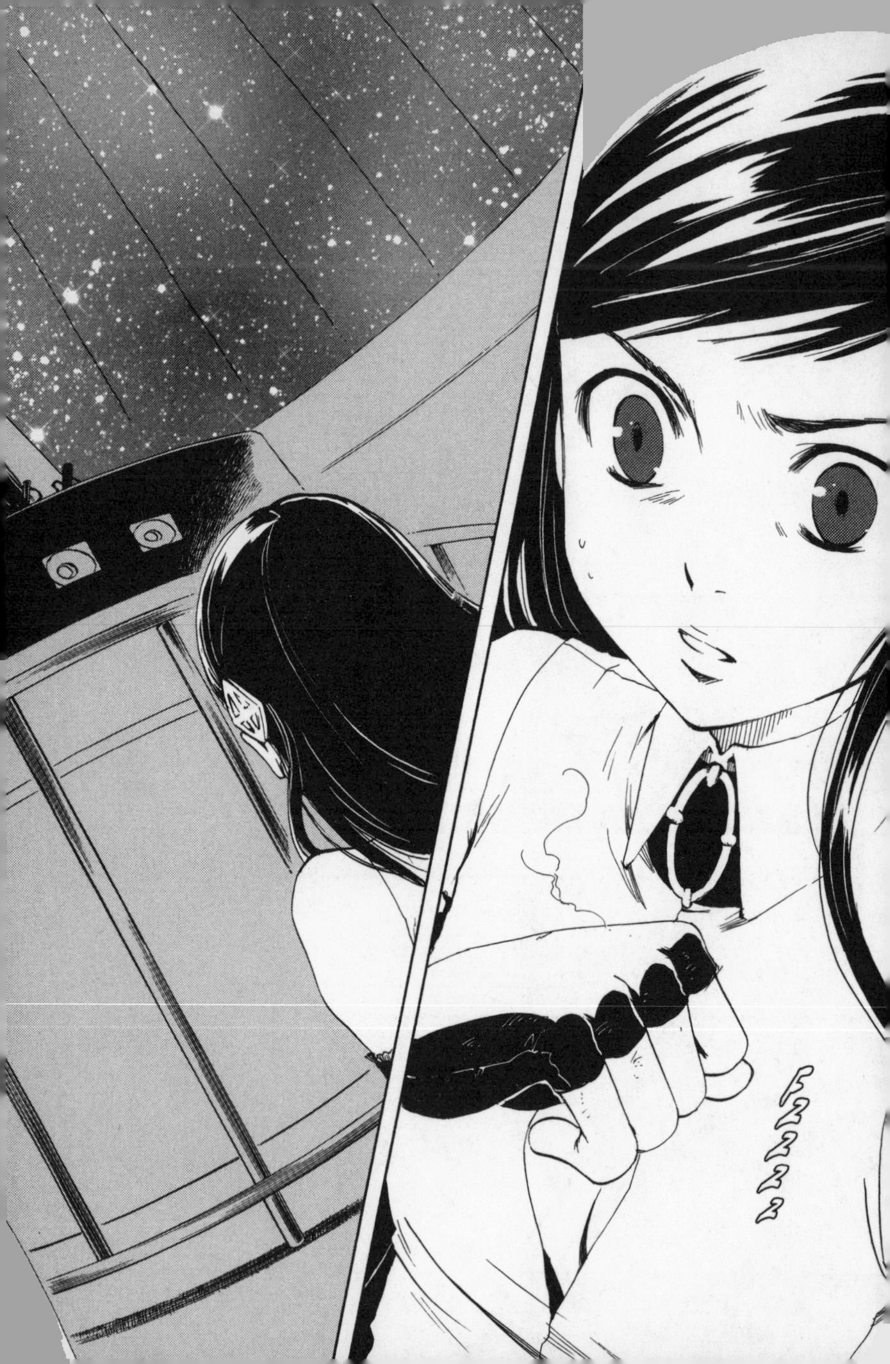
FZZZZ

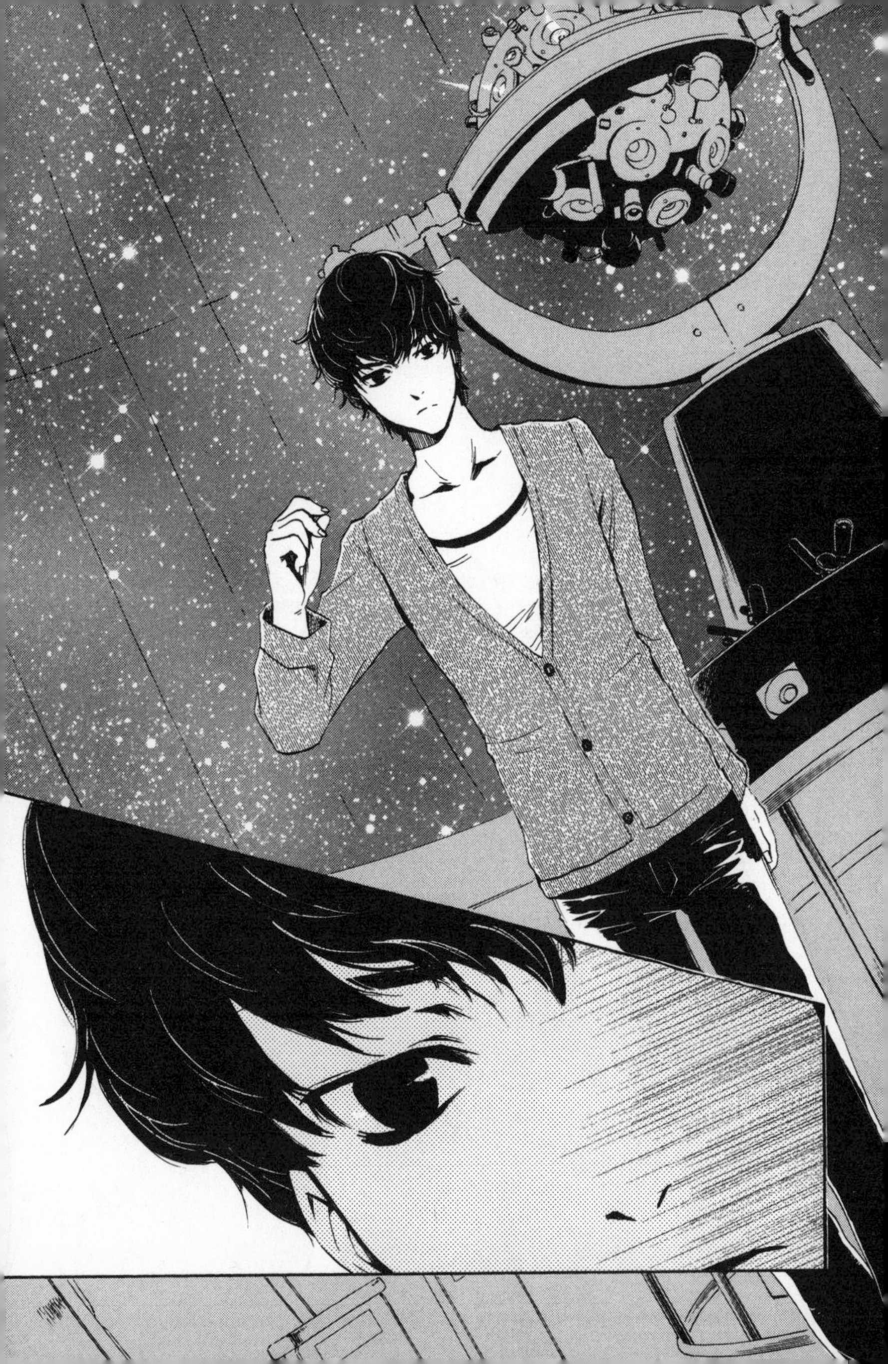

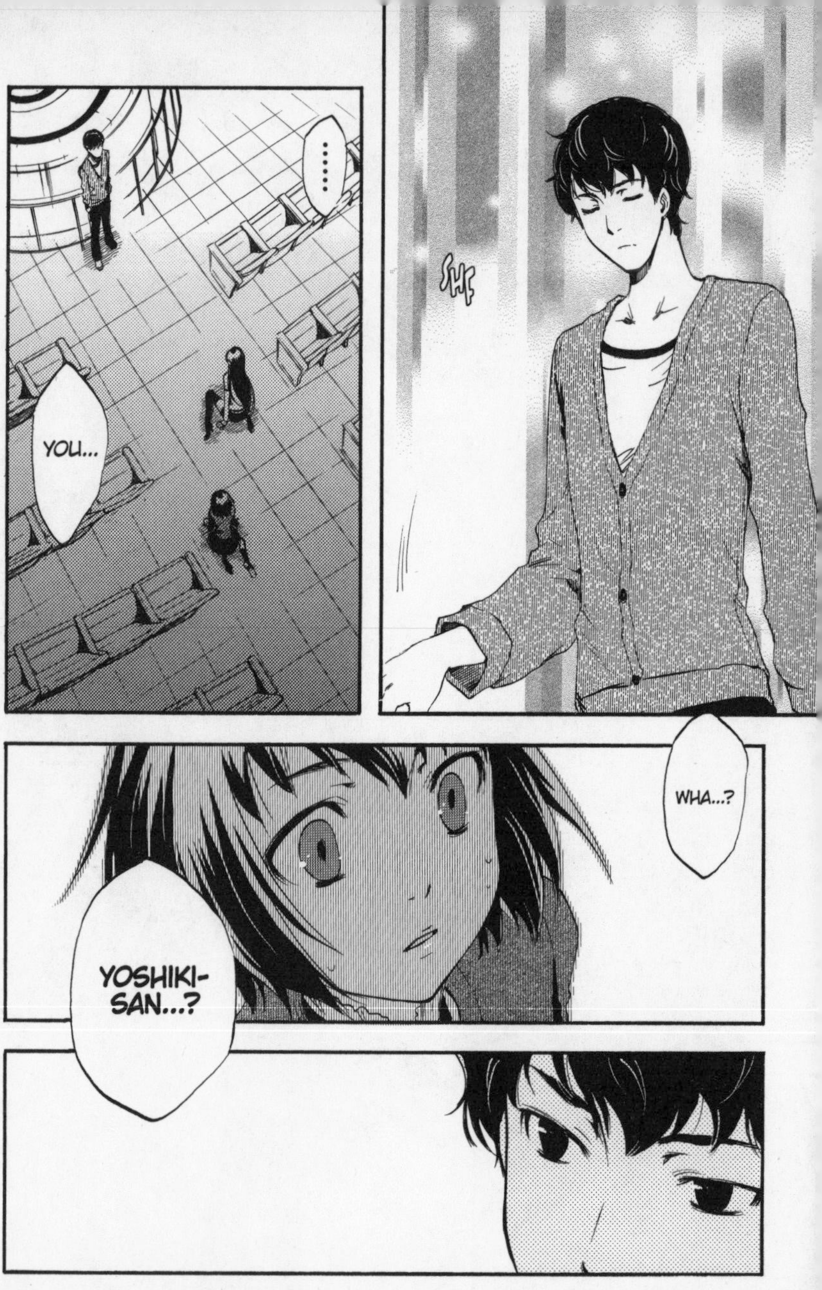
SHF
......
YOU...
WHA...?
YOSHIKI-SAN...?

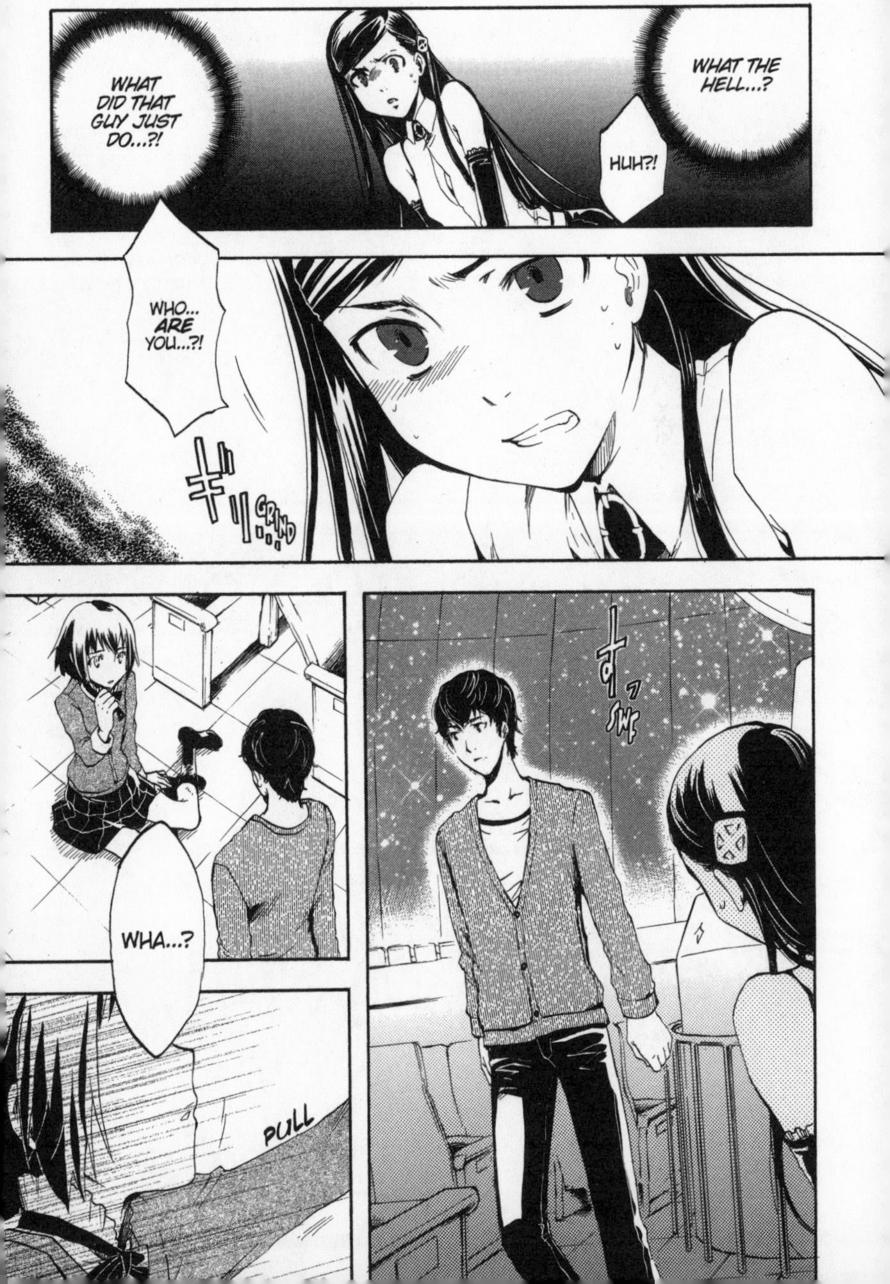
WHAT THE HELL...?
HUH?!
WHAT DID THAT GUY JUST DO...?!
WHO... ARE YOU...?!
GRIND
SWF
WHA...?
PULL

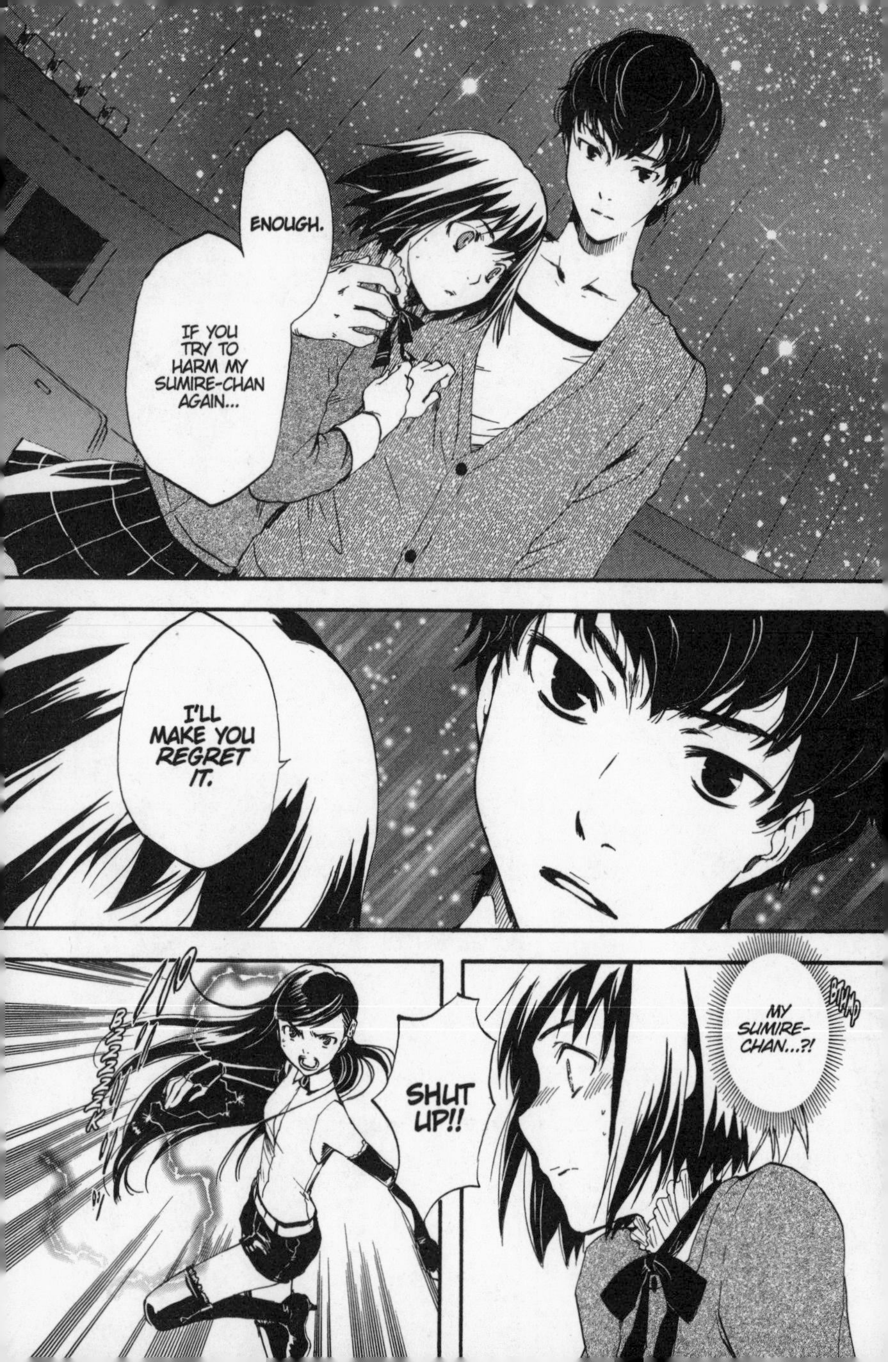
ENOUGH.
IF YOU TRY TO HARM MY SUMIRE-CHAN AGAIN...
I'LL MAKE YOU REGRET IT.
MY SUMIRE-CHAN...?!
SHUT UP!!

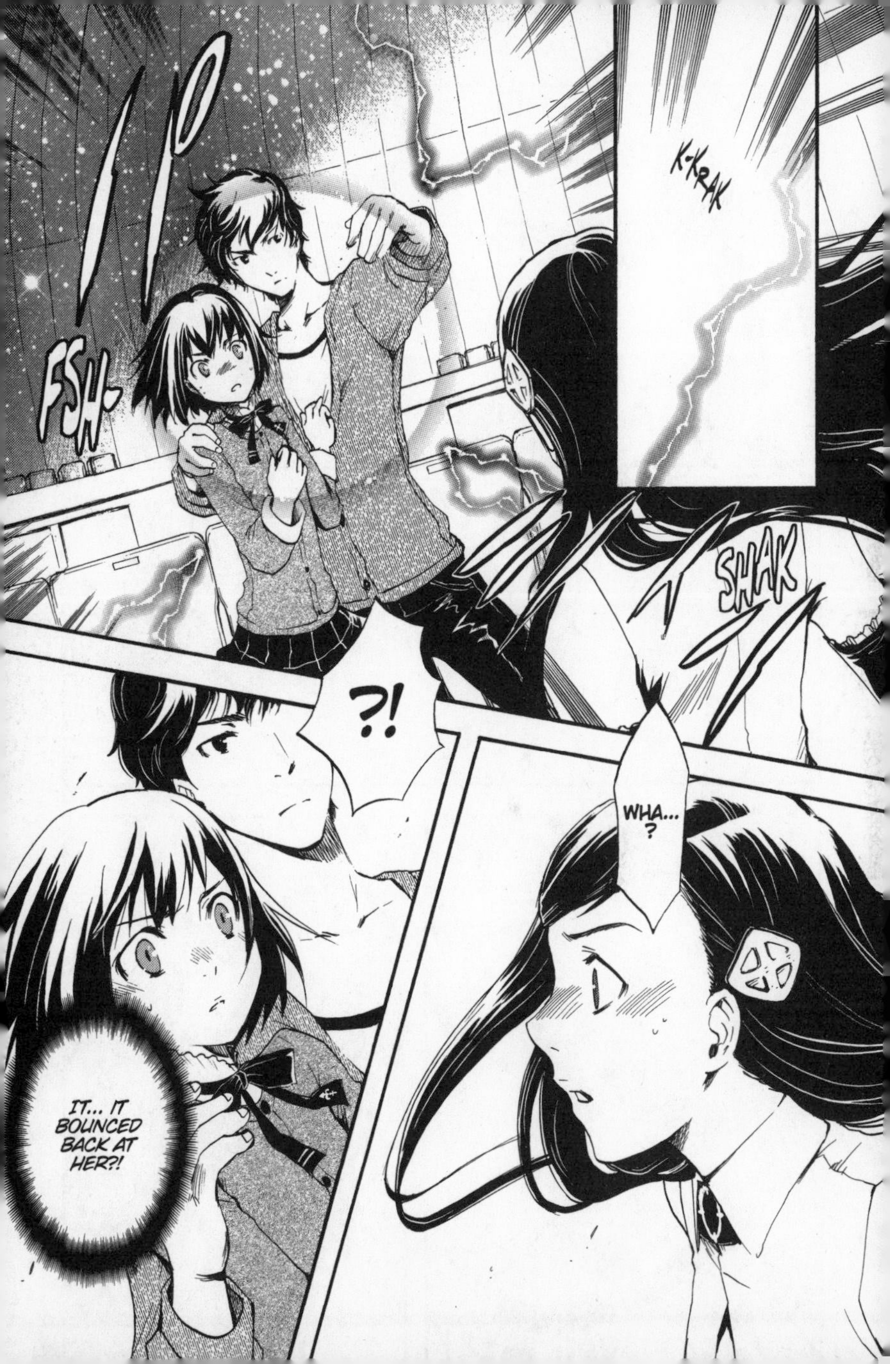
K-KRAK
SHAK
FSH-
WHA...?
?!
IT... IT BOUNCED BACK AT HER?!

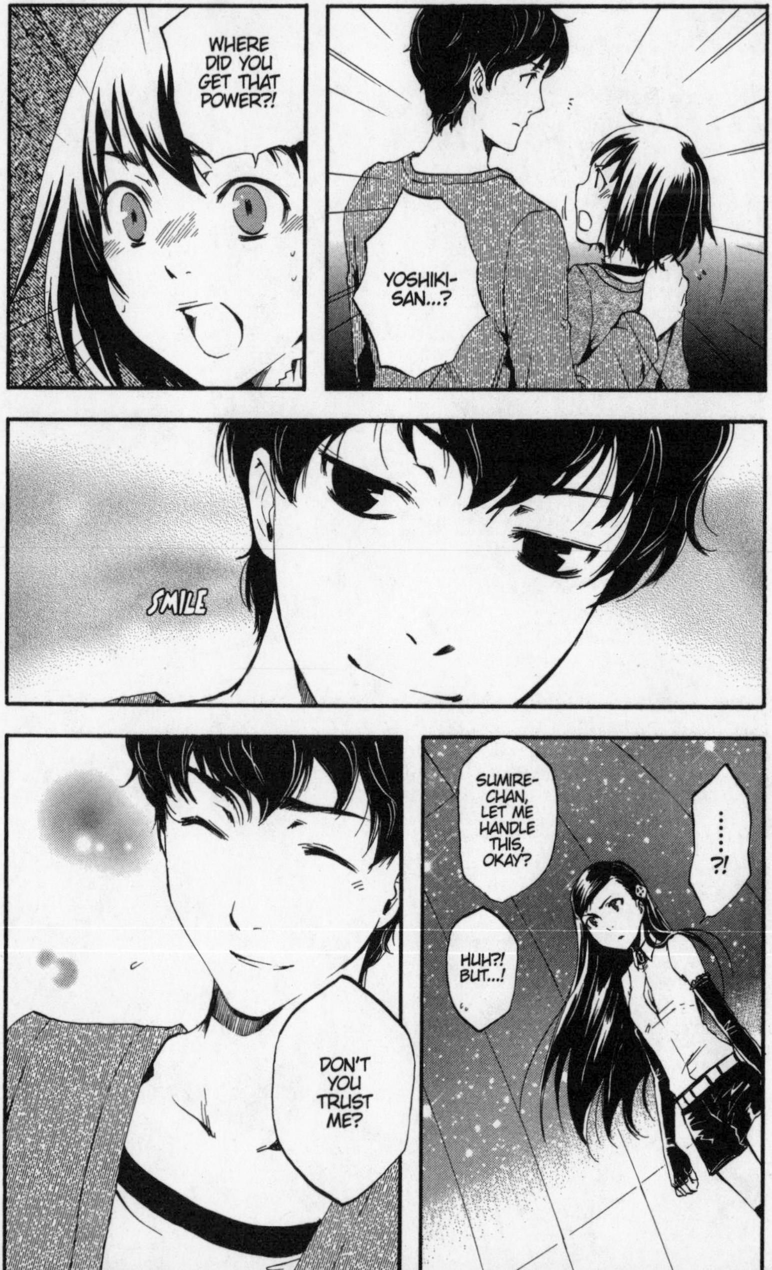
YOSHIKI-SAN...?
WHERE DID YOU GET THAT POWER?!
SMILE
......?!
SUMIRE-CHAN, LET ME HANDLE THIS, OKAY?
HUH?! BUT...!
DON'T YOU TRUST ME?

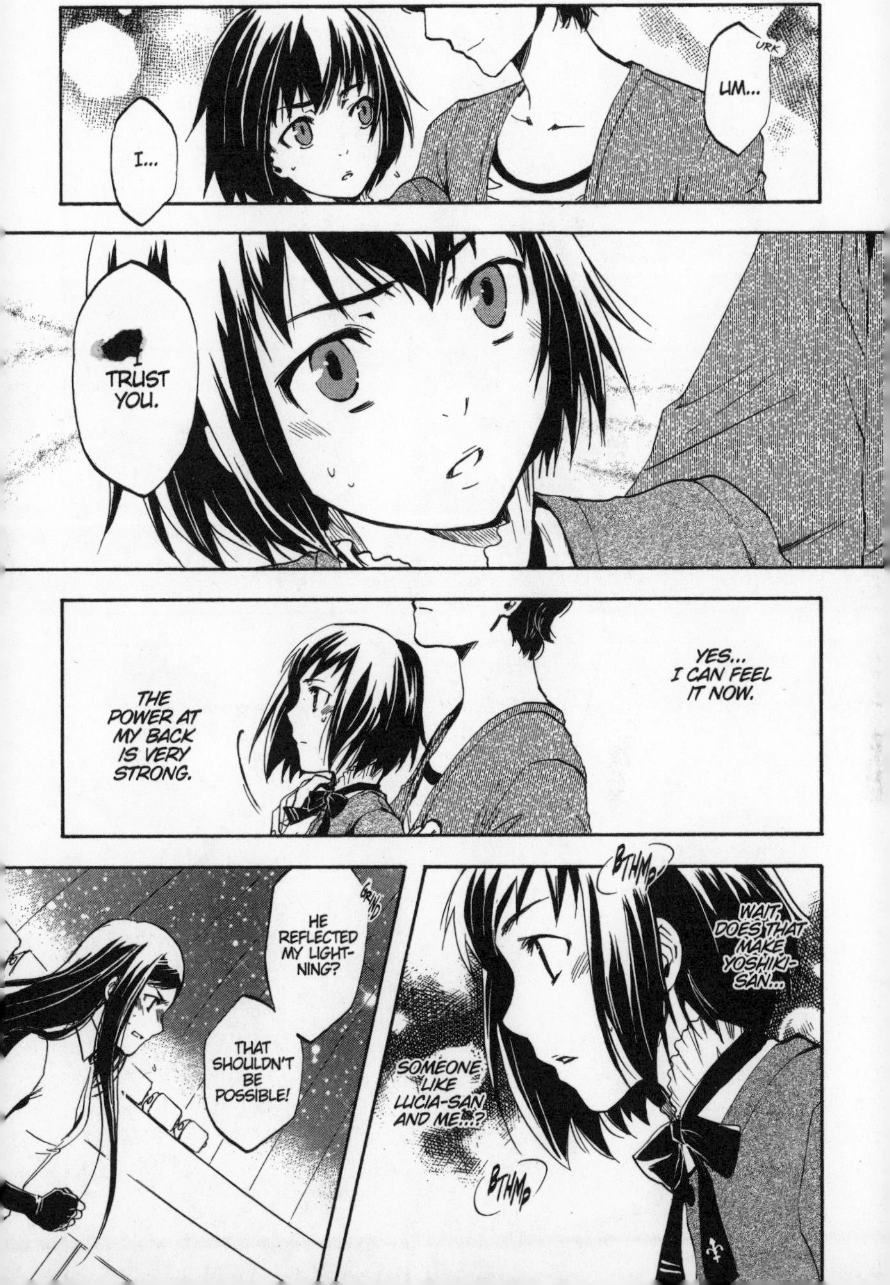
URK
UM...
I...
I TRUST YOU.
YES... I CAN FEEL IT NOW.
THE POWER AT MY BACK IS VERY STRONG.
BTHMP
WAIT, DOES THAT MAKE YOSHIKI-SAN...
SOMEONE LIKE LUCIA-SAN AND ME...?
BTHMP
GRIND
HE REFLECTED MY LIGHTNING?
THAT SHOULDN'T BE POSSIBLE!

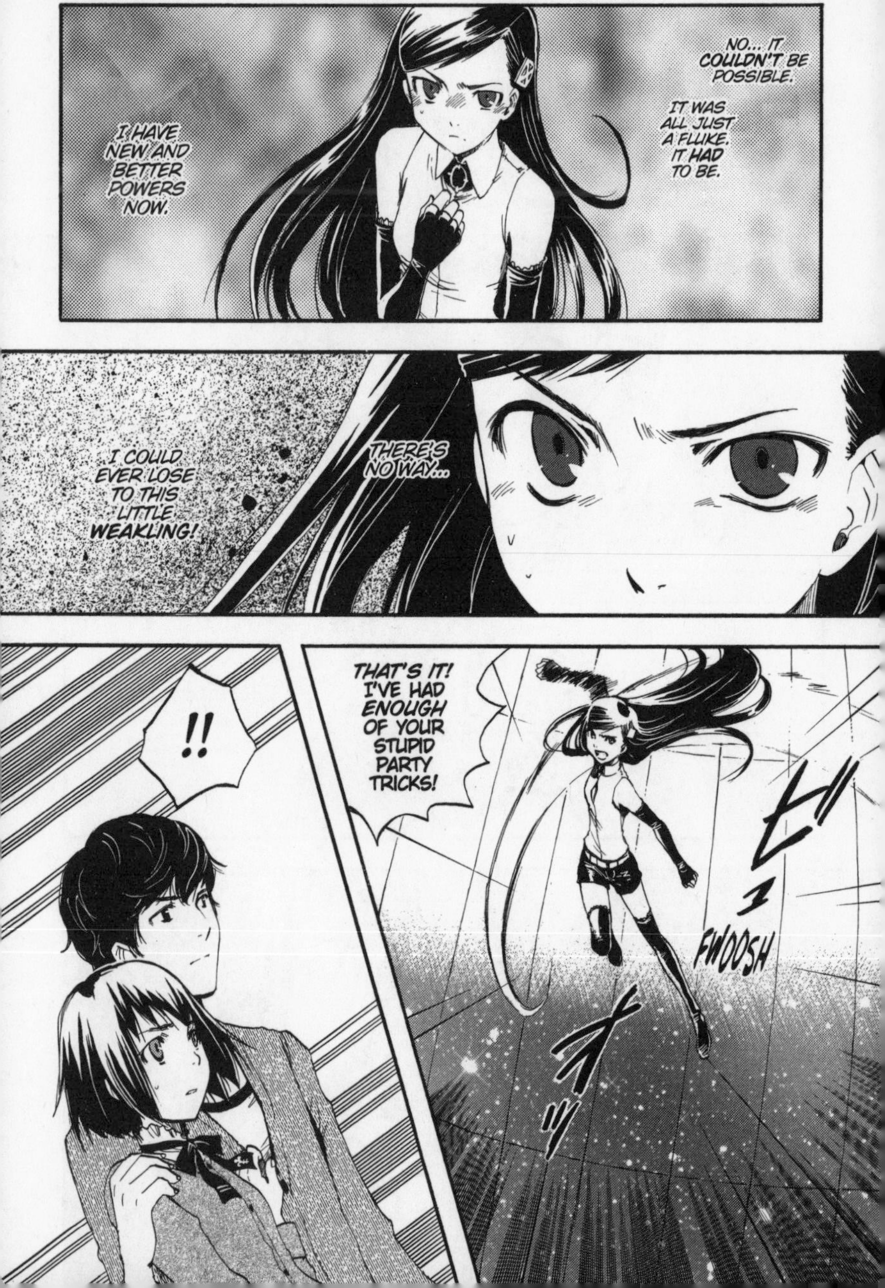
NO... IT COULDN'T BE POSSIBLE.
IT WAS ALL JUST A FLUKE. IT HAD TO BE.
I HAVE NEW AND BETTER POWERS NOW.
THERE'S NO WAY...
I COULD EVER LOSE TO THIS LITTLE WEAKLING!
THAT'S IT! I'VE HAD ENOUGH OF YOUR STUPID PARTY TRICKS!
FWOOSH
!!

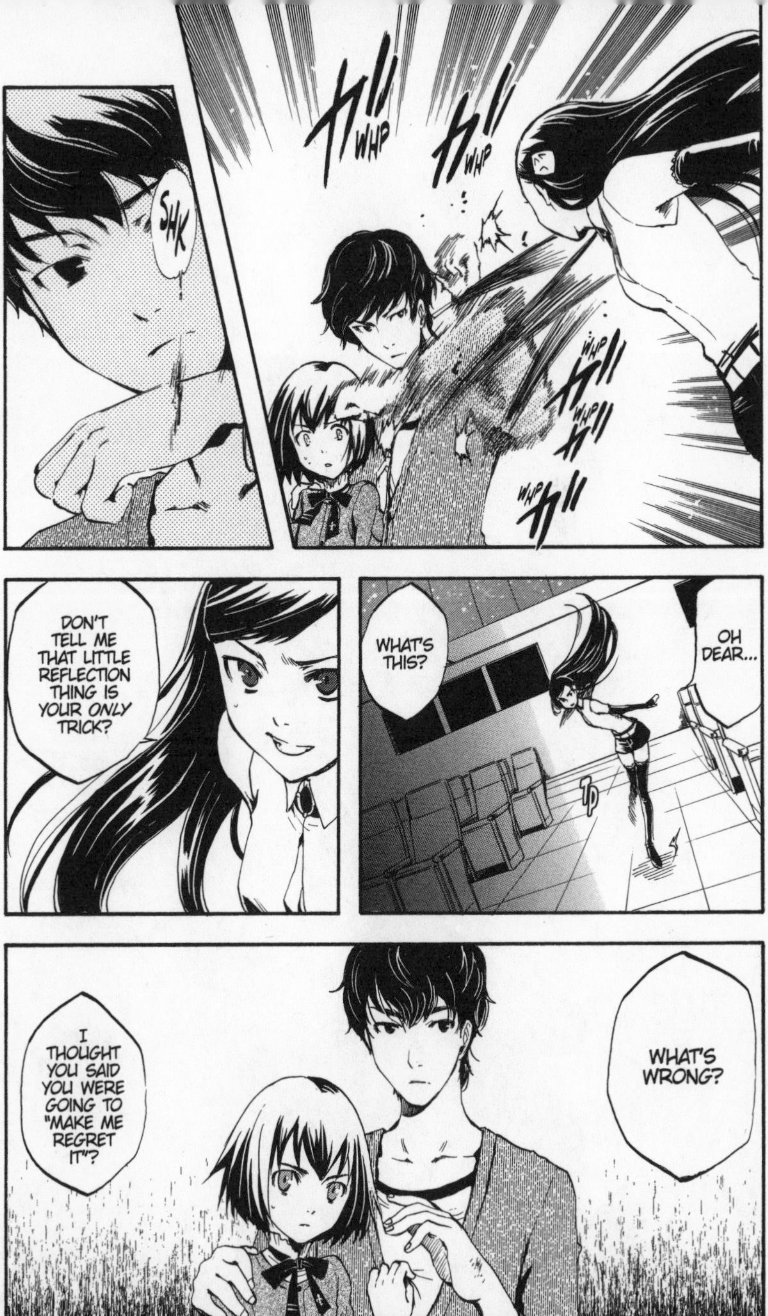
WHP
WHP
WHP
WHP
WHP
SHK
OH DEAR...
WHAT'S THIS?
TP
DON'T TELL ME THAT LITTLE REFLECTION THING IS YOUR *ONLY* TRICK?
WHAT'S WRONG?
I THOUGHT YOU SAID YOU WERE GOING TO "MAKE ME REGRET IT"?

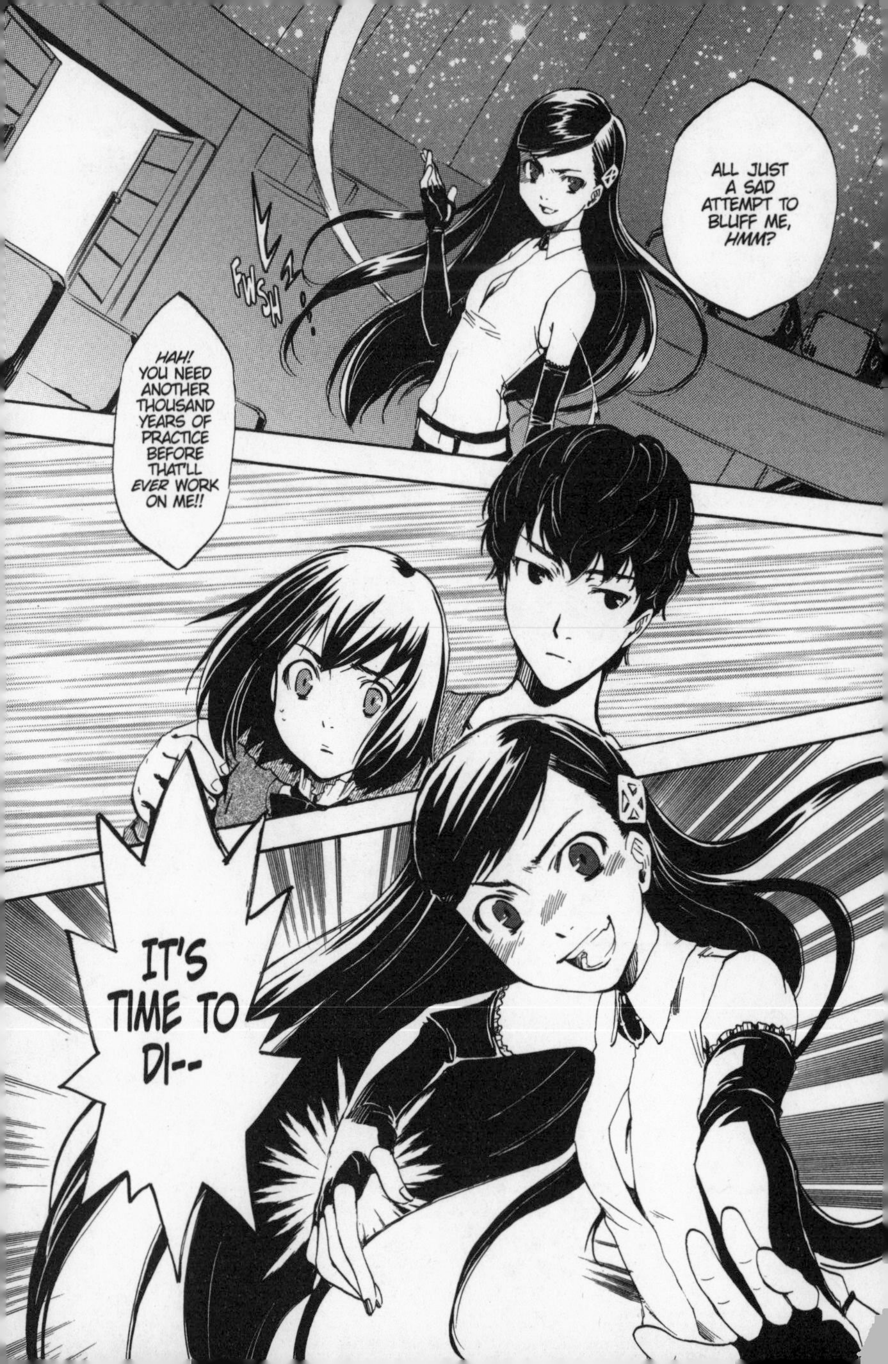
ALL JUST A SAD ATTEMPT TO BLUFF ME, HMM?
FWSH
HAH! YOU NEED ANOTHER THOUSAND YEARS OF PRACTICE BEFORE THAT'LL EVER WORK ON ME!!
IT'S TIME TO DI--

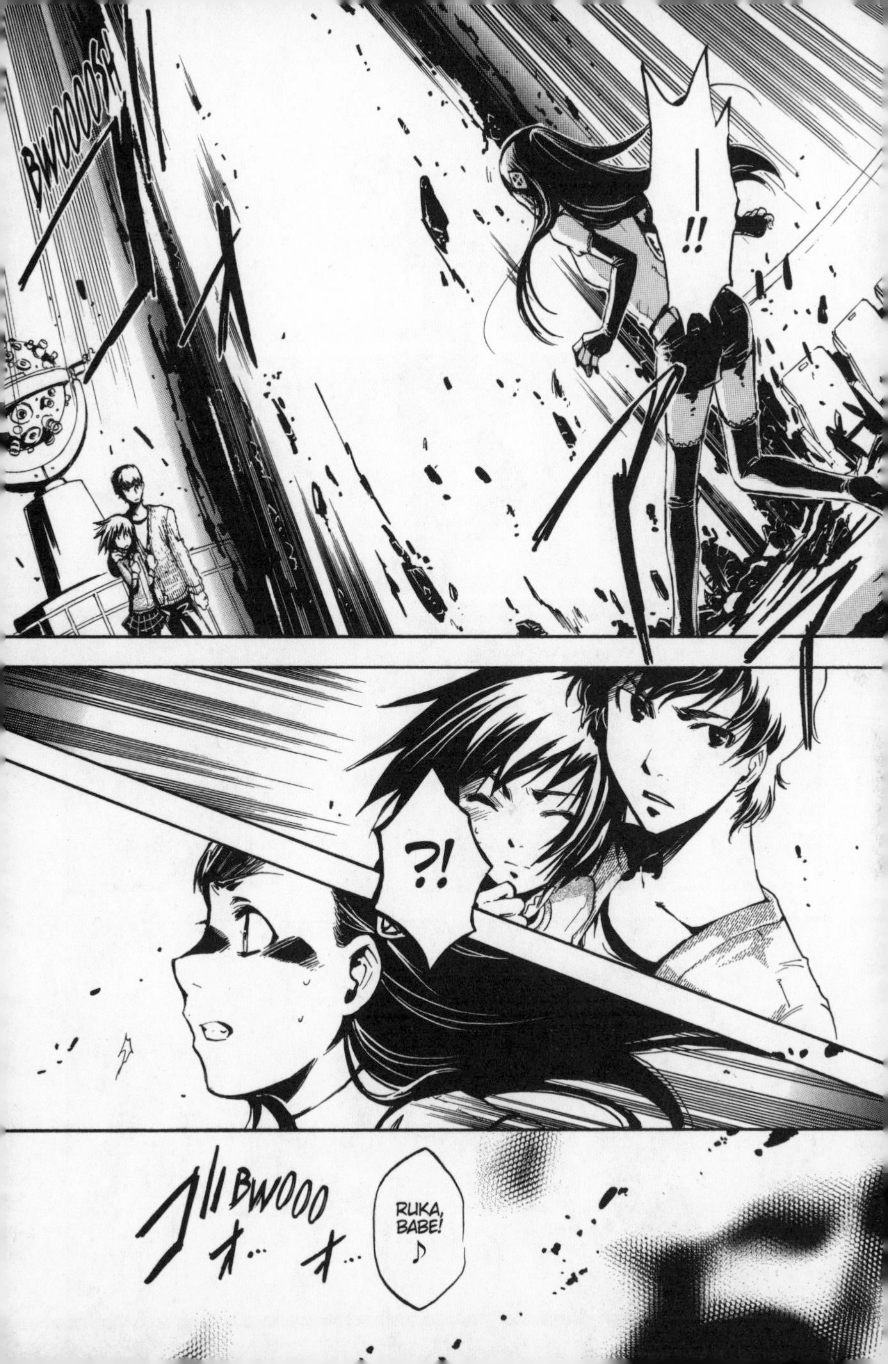
!!
BWOOOOSH
?!
RUKA, BABE! ♪
BWOOO

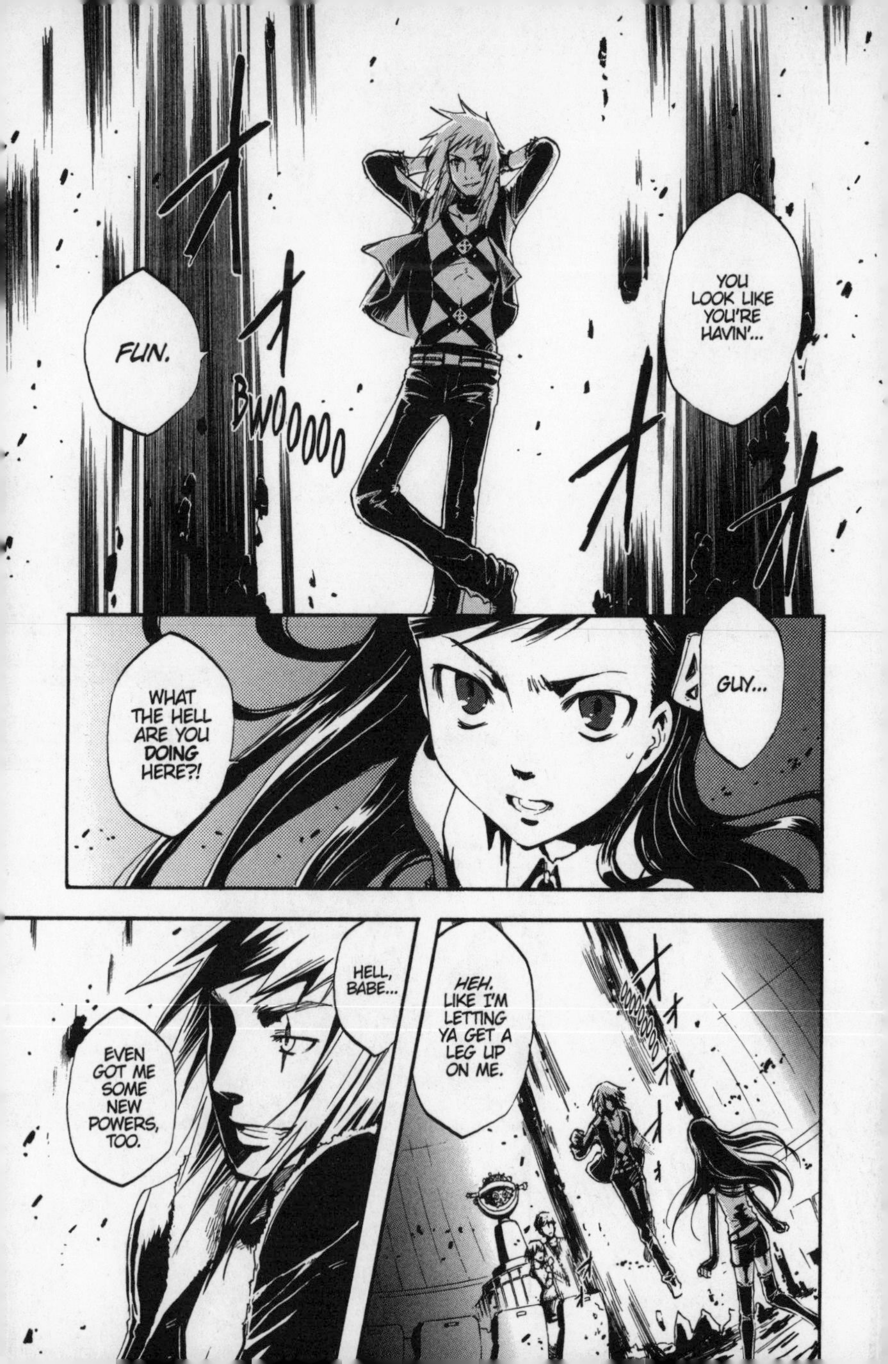
YOU LOOK LIKE YOU'RE HAVIN'...
FUN.
BWOOOOO
GUY...
WHAT THE HELL ARE YOU DOING HERE?!
HEH. LIKE I'M LETTING YA GET A LEG UP ON ME.
HELL, BABE...
EVEN GOT ME SOME NEW POWERS, TOO.

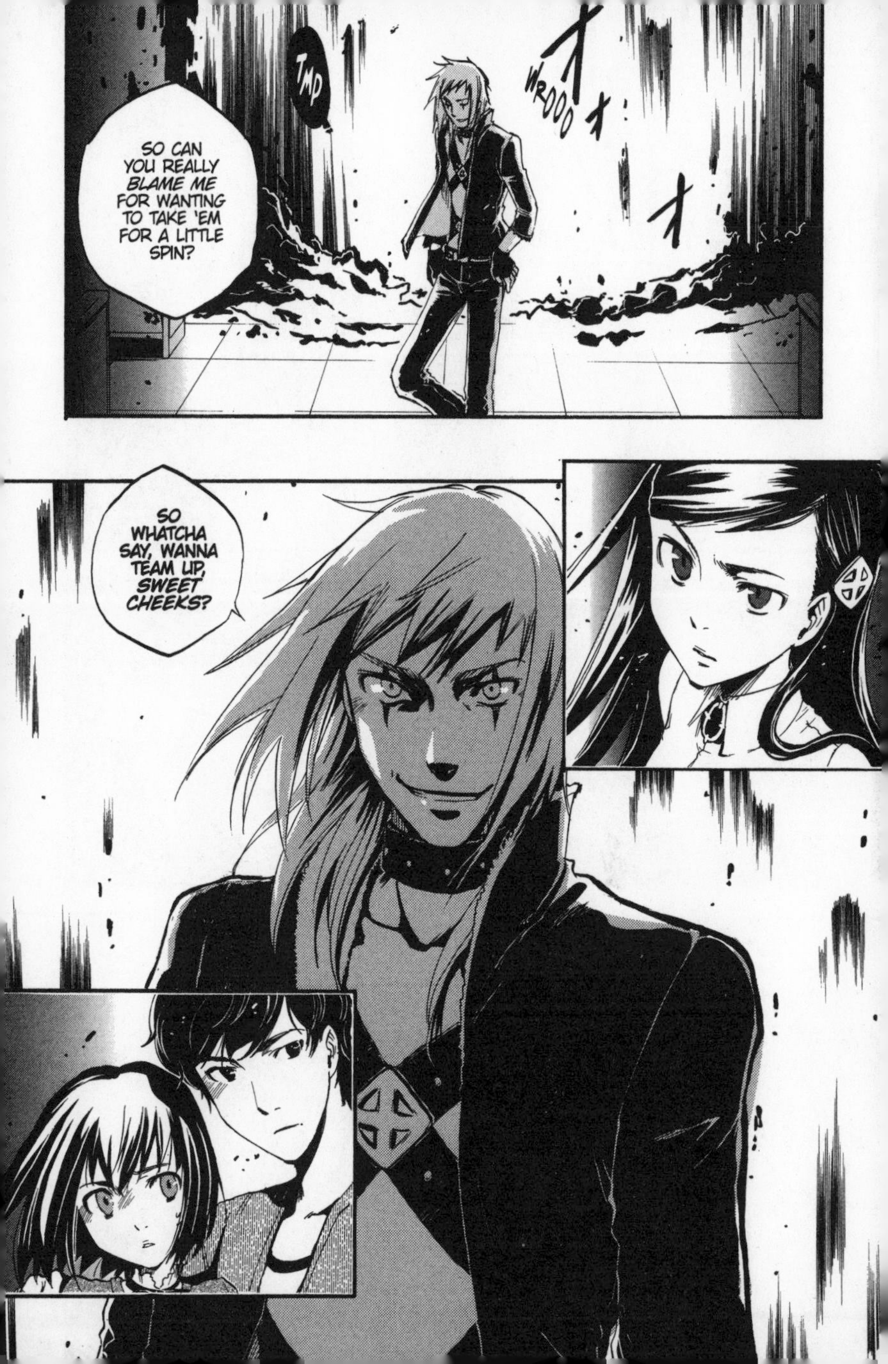
TMP
WROOO
SO CAN YOU REALLY *BLAME ME* FOR WANTING TO TAKE 'EM FOR A LITTLE SPIN?
SO WHATCHA SAY, WANNA TEAM UP, *SWEET CHEEKS?*

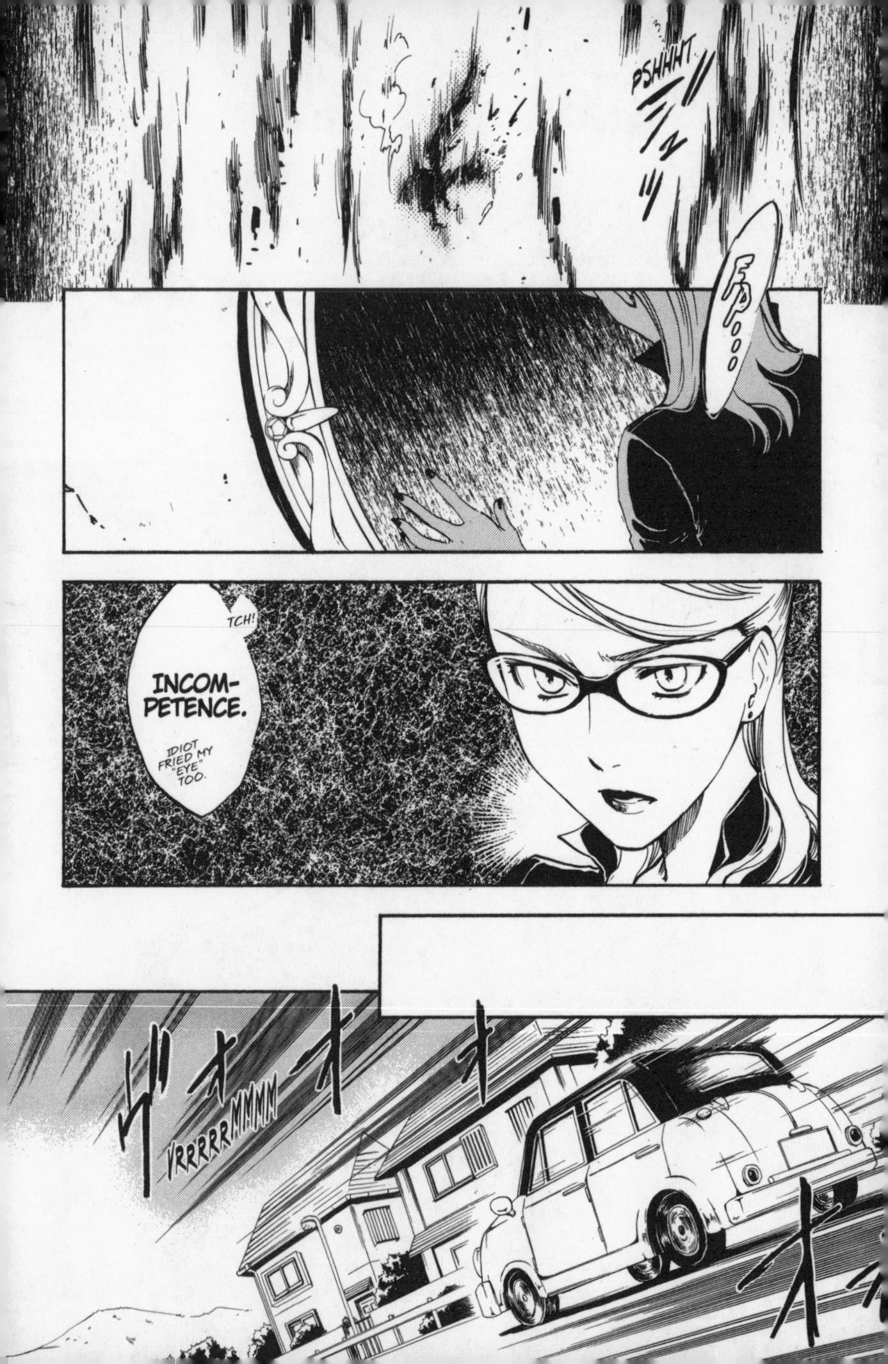

PSHHHT
FP...
TCH!
INCOM-PETENCE.
IDIOT FRIED MY "EYE" TOO.
VRRRRRMMMM

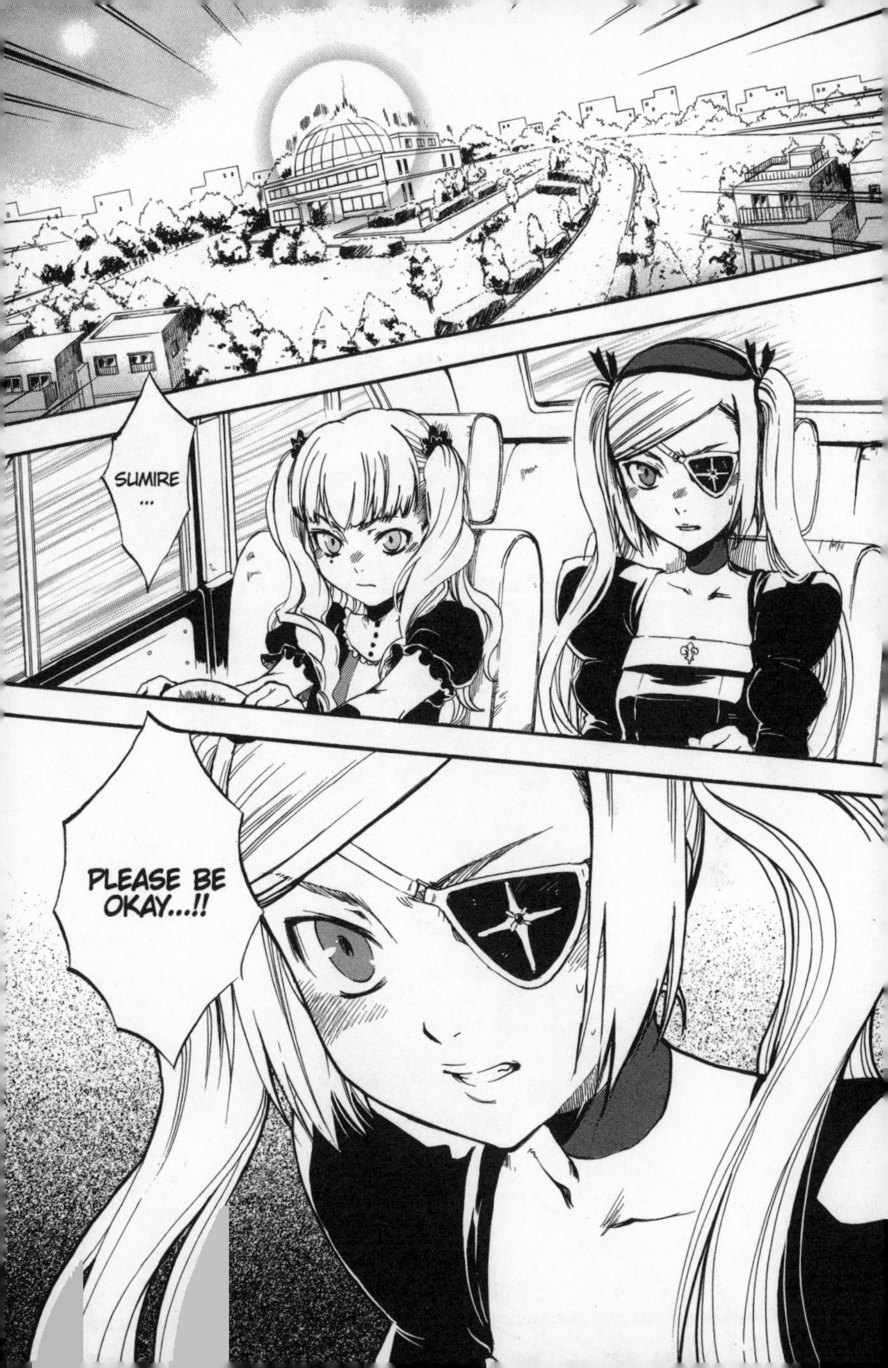
SUMIRE ...
PLEASE BE OKAY...!!

Jewelry
and
Clothes

Venus Vangard

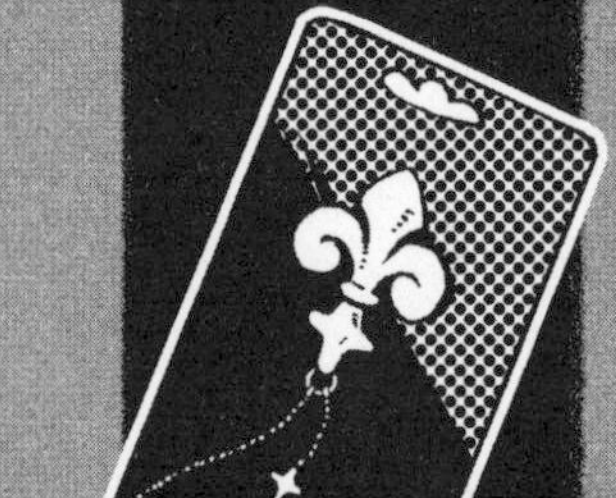
Venus Vangard

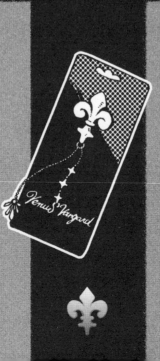

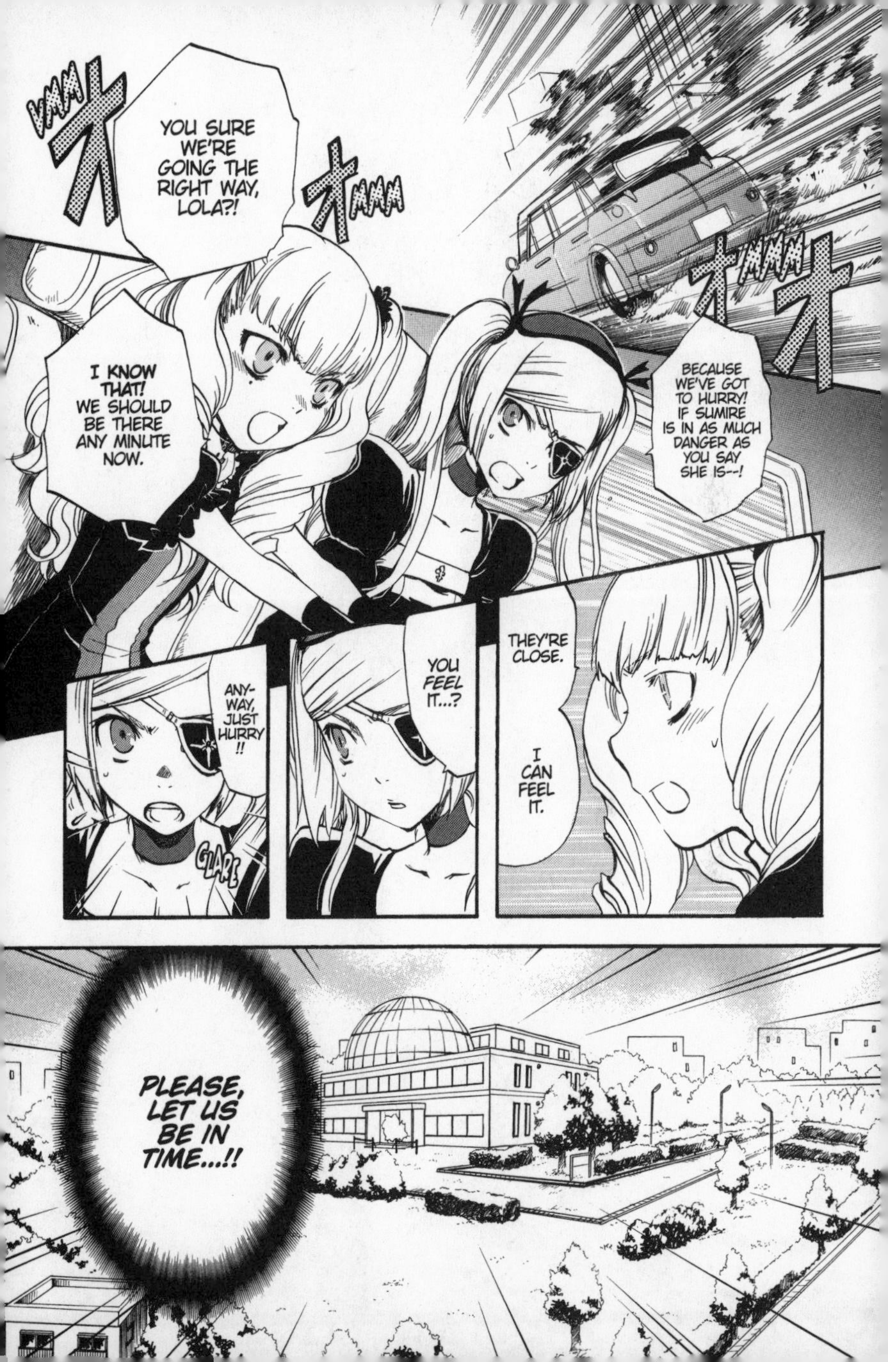
MMMM
VMMM
MMMM
YOU SURE WE'RE GOING THE RIGHT WAY, LOLA?!
BECAUSE WE'VE GOT TO HURRY! IF SUMIRE IS IN AS MUCH DANGER AS YOU SAY SHE IS--!
I KNOW THAT! WE SHOULD BE THERE ANY MINUTE NOW.
THEY'RE CLOSE.
I CAN FEEL IT.
YOU FEEL IT...?
ANY-WAY, JUST HURRY!!
GLARE
PLEASE, LET US BE IN TIME...!!

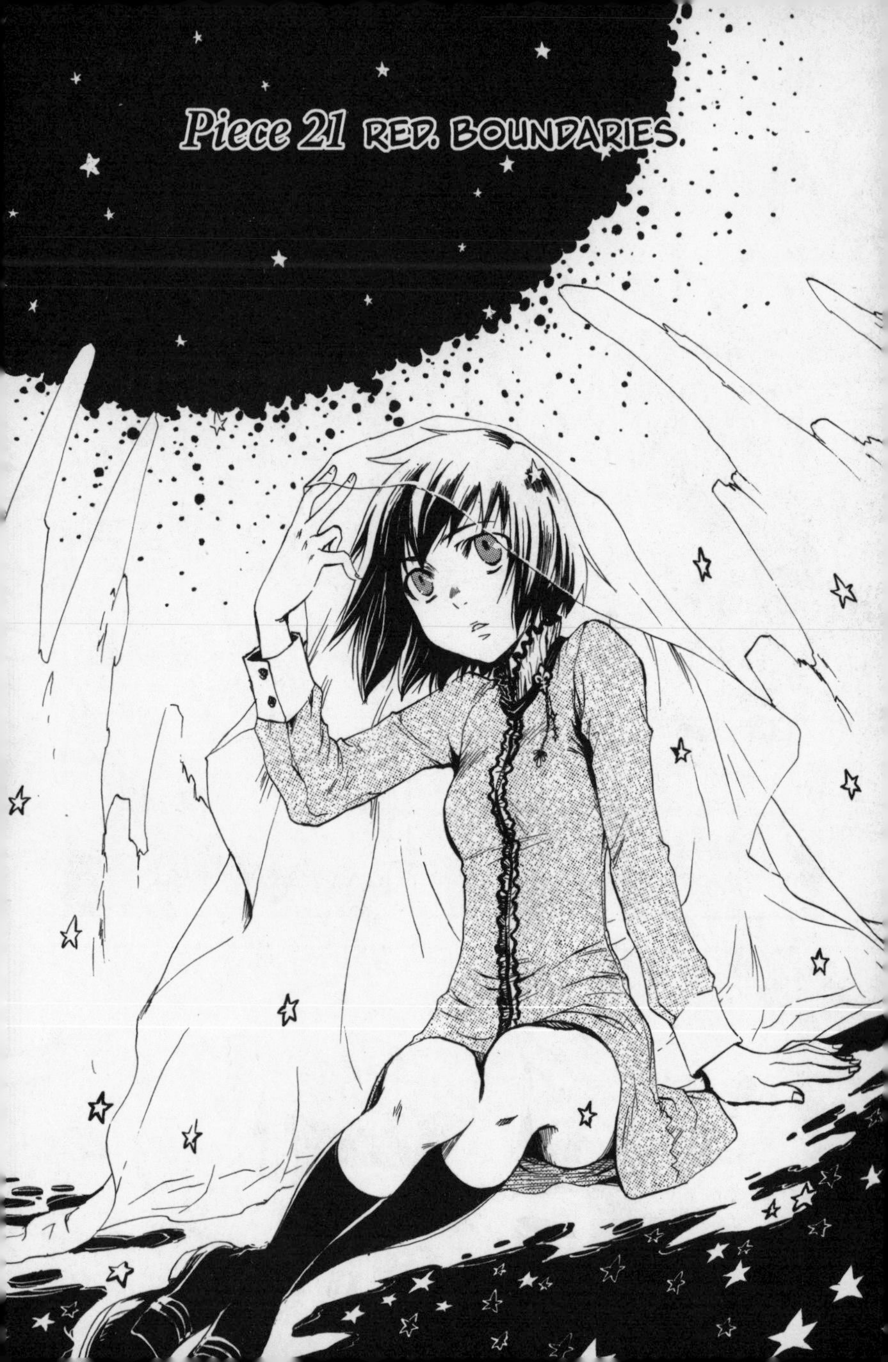
Piece 21 RED. BOUNDARIES.

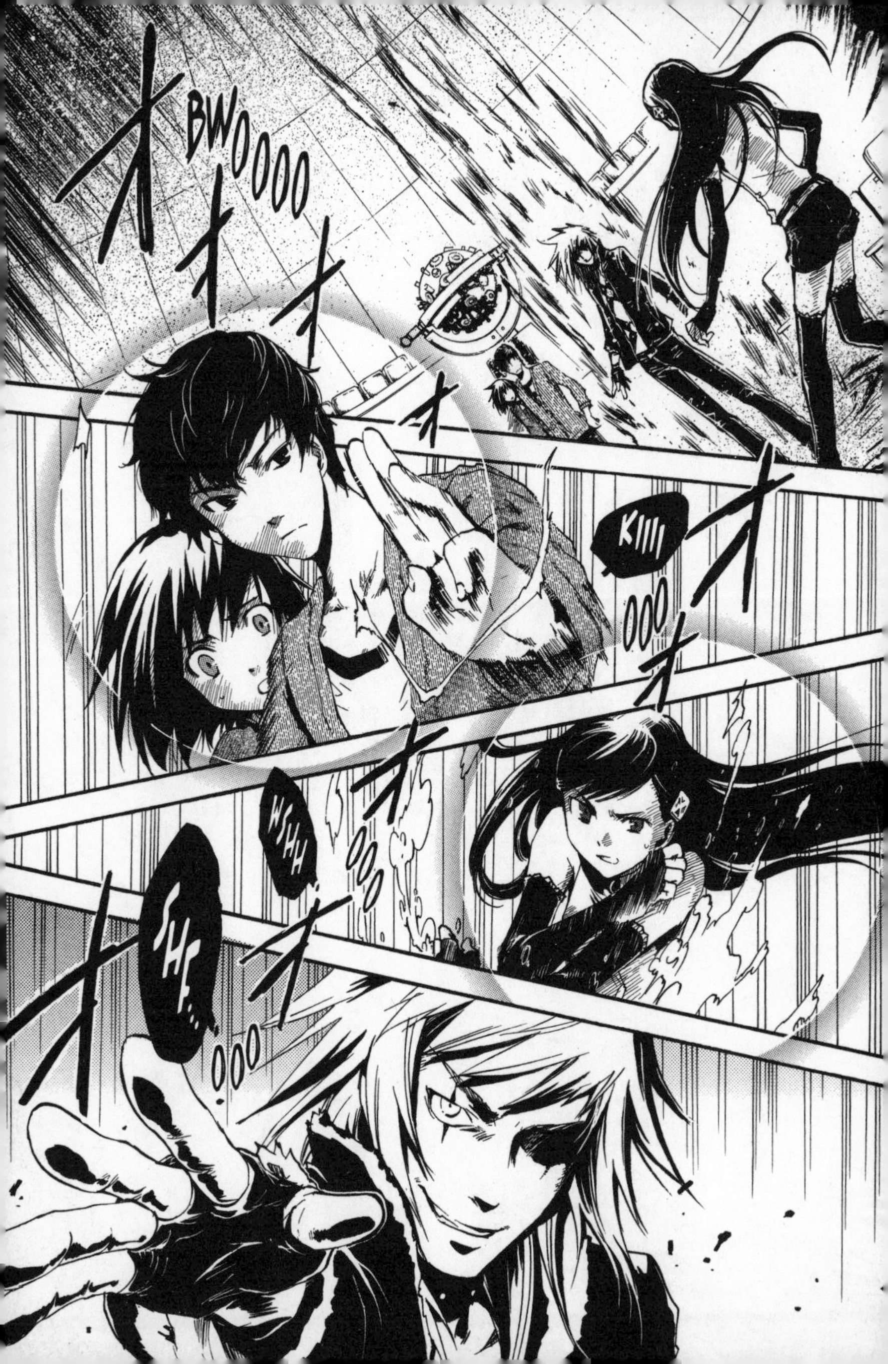
BWOOOO
KIIII
OOO
WSHH
OOOO
SHF...
OOO

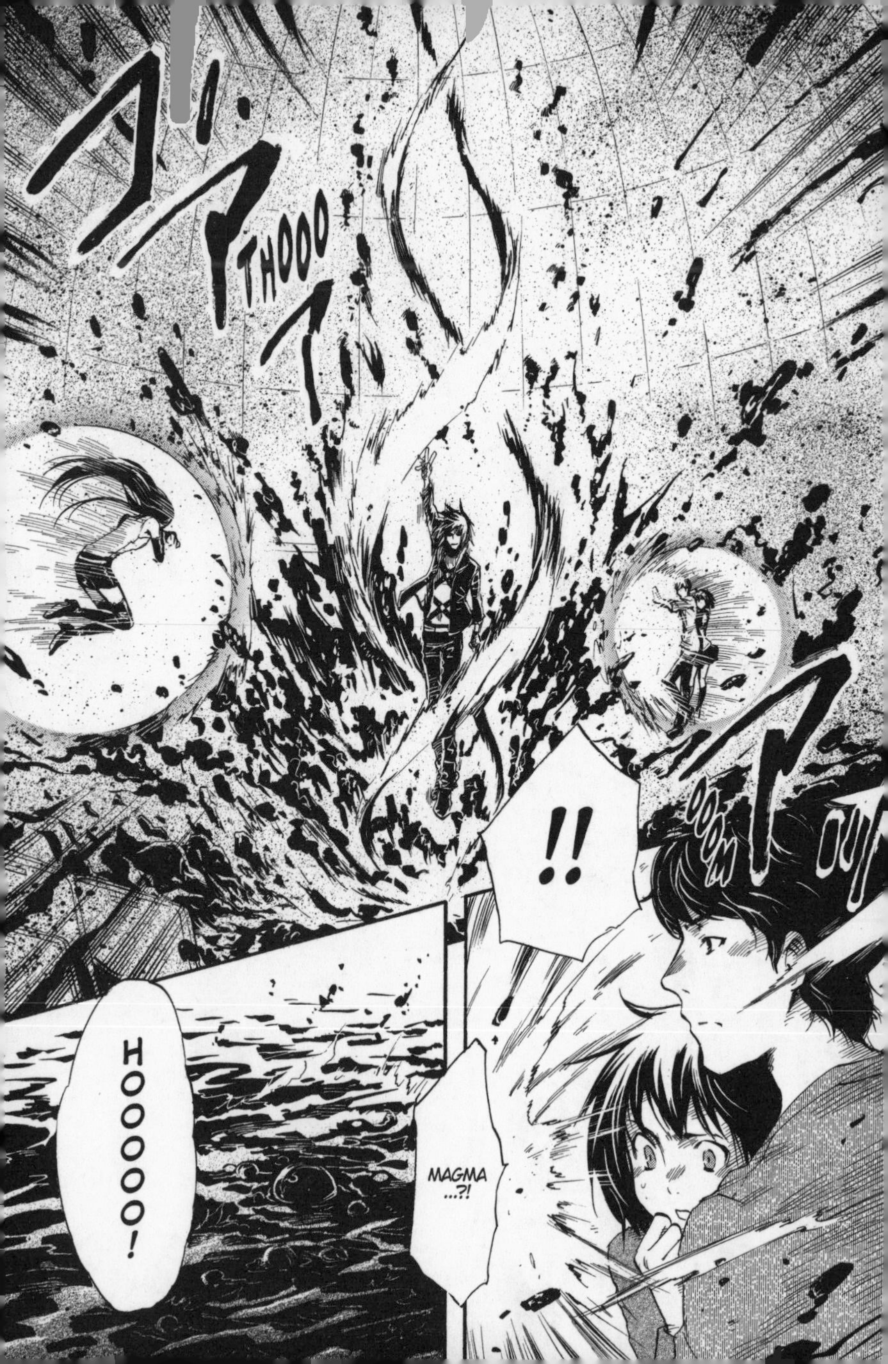
THOOO
OOOM
!!
MAGMA ...?!
HOOOOOO!

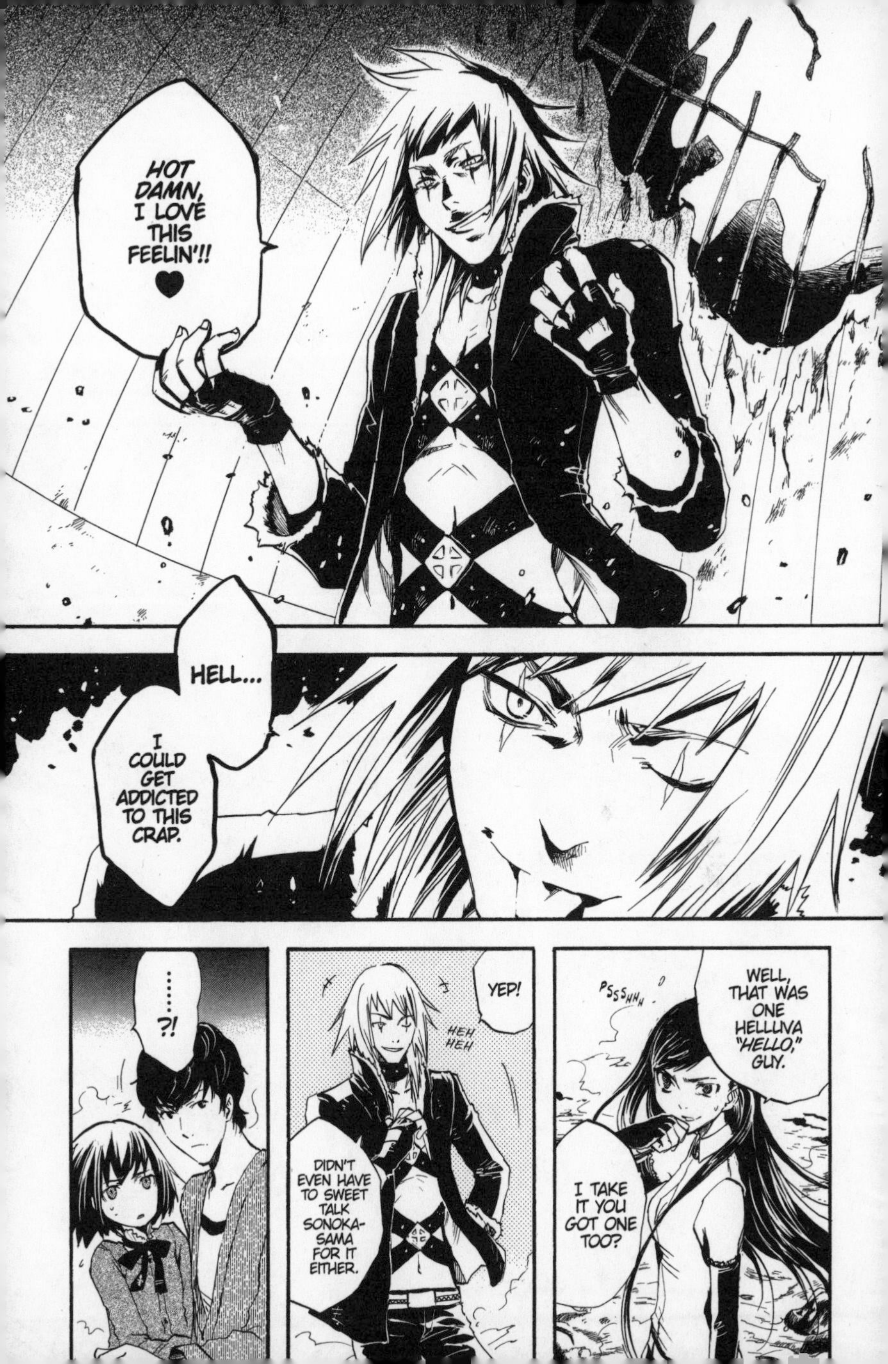
HOT DAMN, I LOVE THIS FEELIN'!! ♥
HELL...
I COULD GET ADDICTED TO THIS CRAP.
WELL, THAT WAS ONE HELLUVA "HELLO," GUY.
PSSSHHH
I TAKE IT YOU GOT ONE TOO?
YEP!
HEH HEH
DIDN'T EVEN HAVE TO SWEET TALK SONOKA-SAMA FOR IT EITHER.
......?!

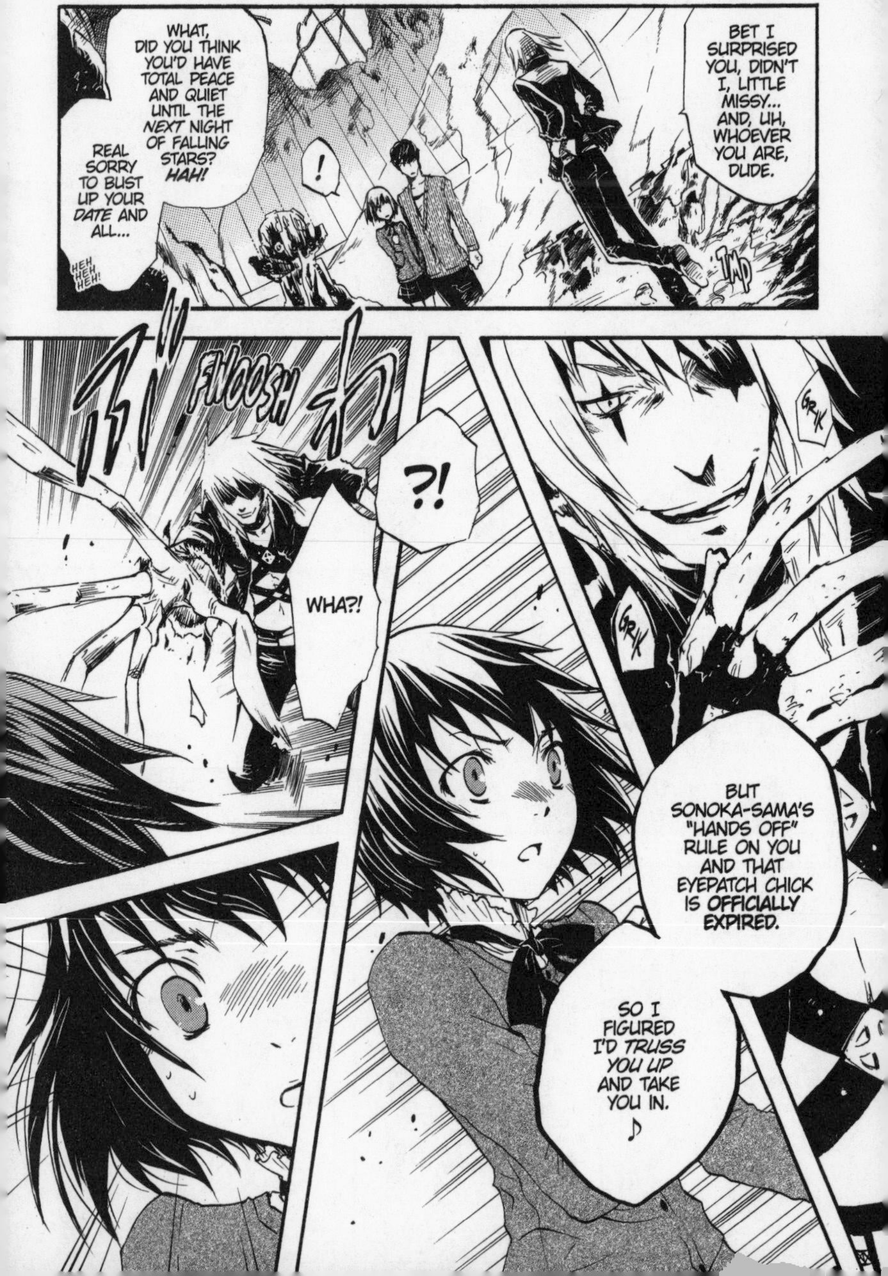
BET I SURPRISED YOU, DIDN'T I, LITTLE MISSY... AND, UH, WHOEVER YOU ARE, DUDE.
TMP
!
WHAT, DID YOU THINK YOU'D HAVE TOTAL PEACE AND QUIET UNTIL THE *NEXT* NIGHT OF FALLING STARS? *HAH!*
REAL SORRY TO BUST UP YOUR *DATE* AND ALL...
HEH HEH HEH!
GRIK
GRIK
BUT SONOKA-SAMA'S "HANDS OFF" RULE ON YOU AND THAT EYEPATCH CHICK IS **OFFICIALLY** EXPIRED.
SO I FIGURED I'D *TRUSS YOU UP* AND TAKE YOU IN. ♪
?!
FWOOSH
WHA?!

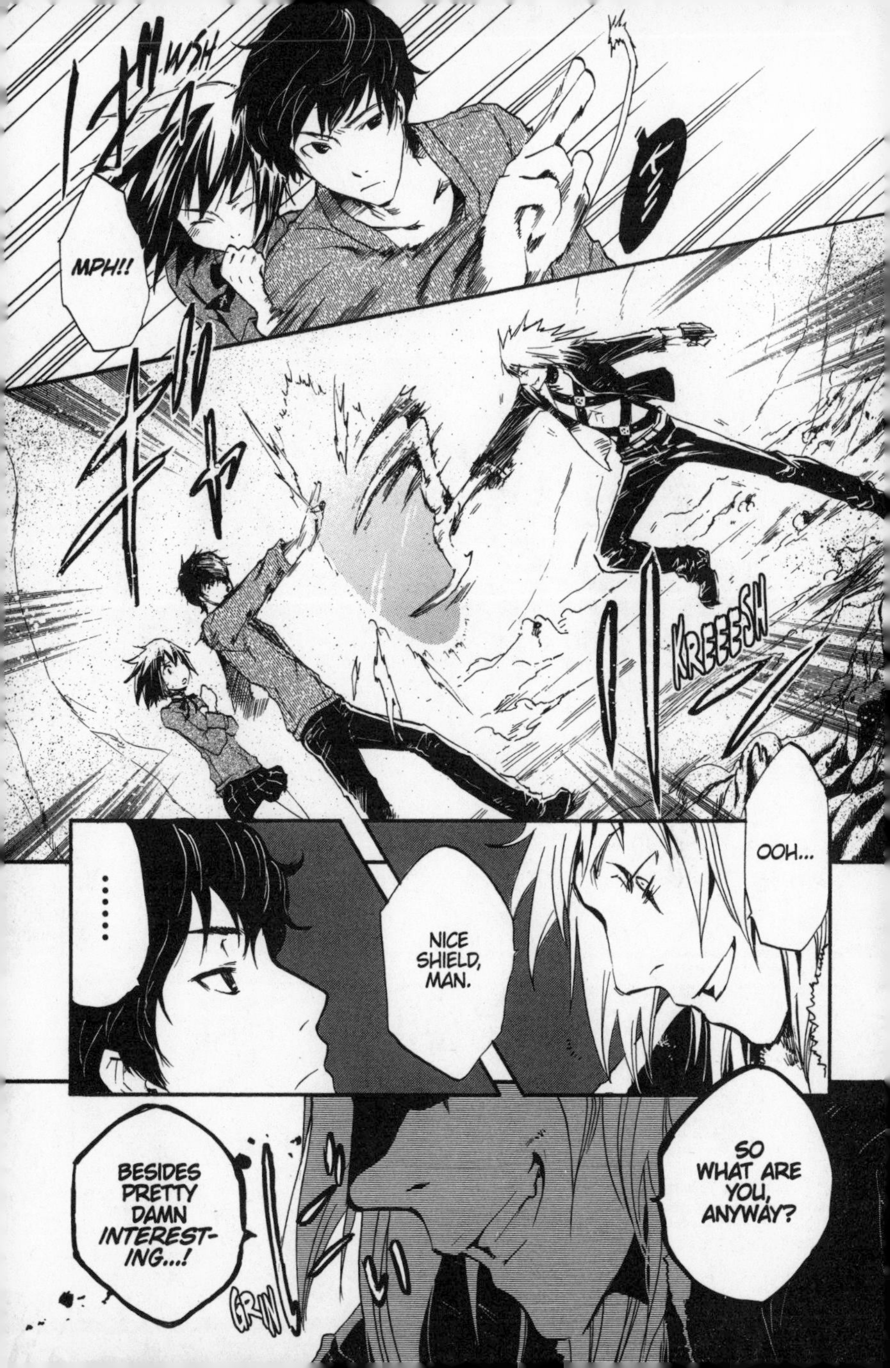

WSH
MPH!!
KREEESH
OOH...
NICE SHIELD, MAN.
......
SO WHAT ARE YOU, ANYWAY?
BESIDES PRETTY DAMN INTERESTING...!
GRIN

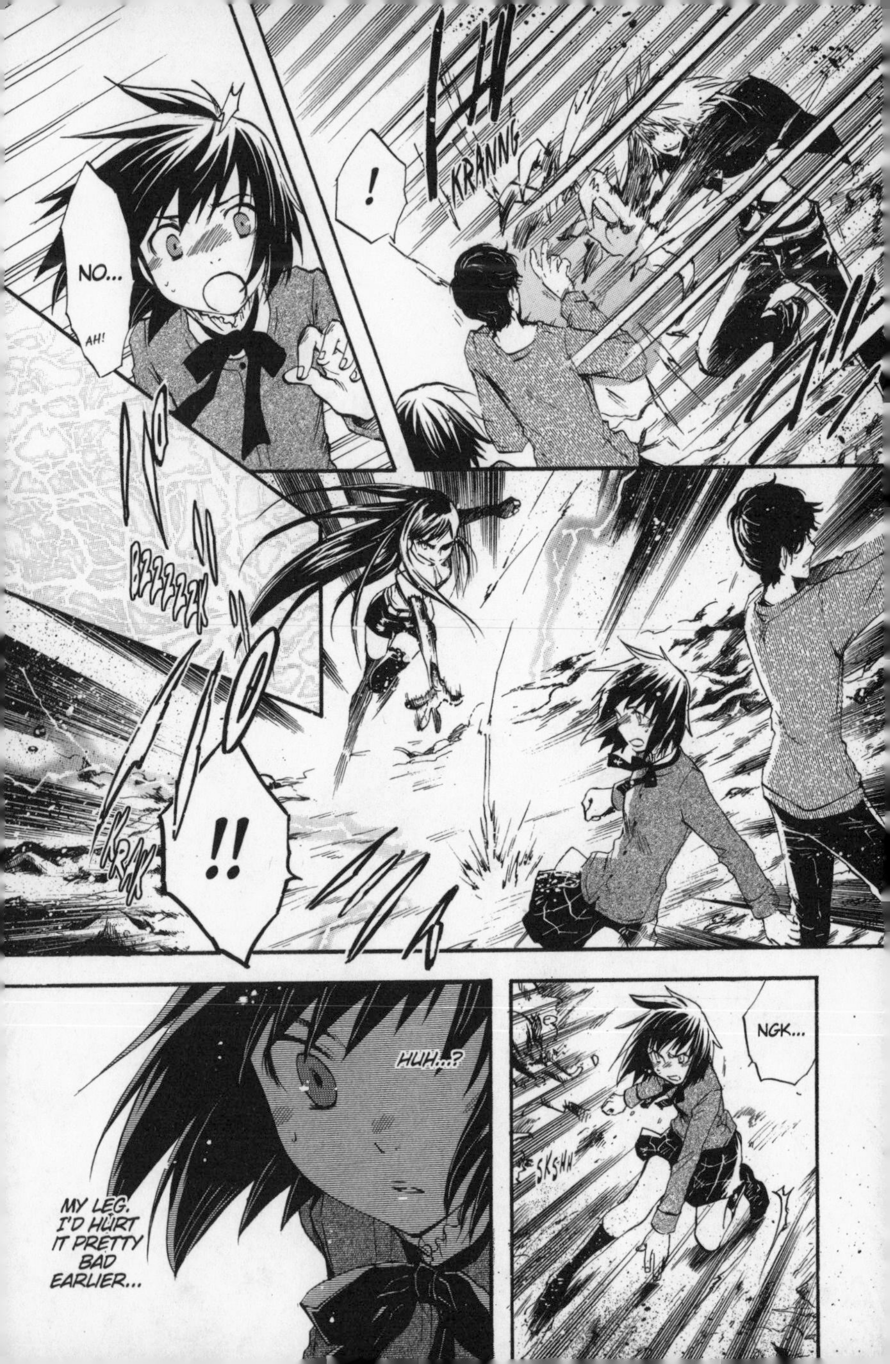
!
KRANNG
NO...
AH!
BZZZZZZK
!!
KRAK
NGK...
SKSHH
HUH...?
MY LEG. I'D HURT IT PRETTY BAD EARLIER...

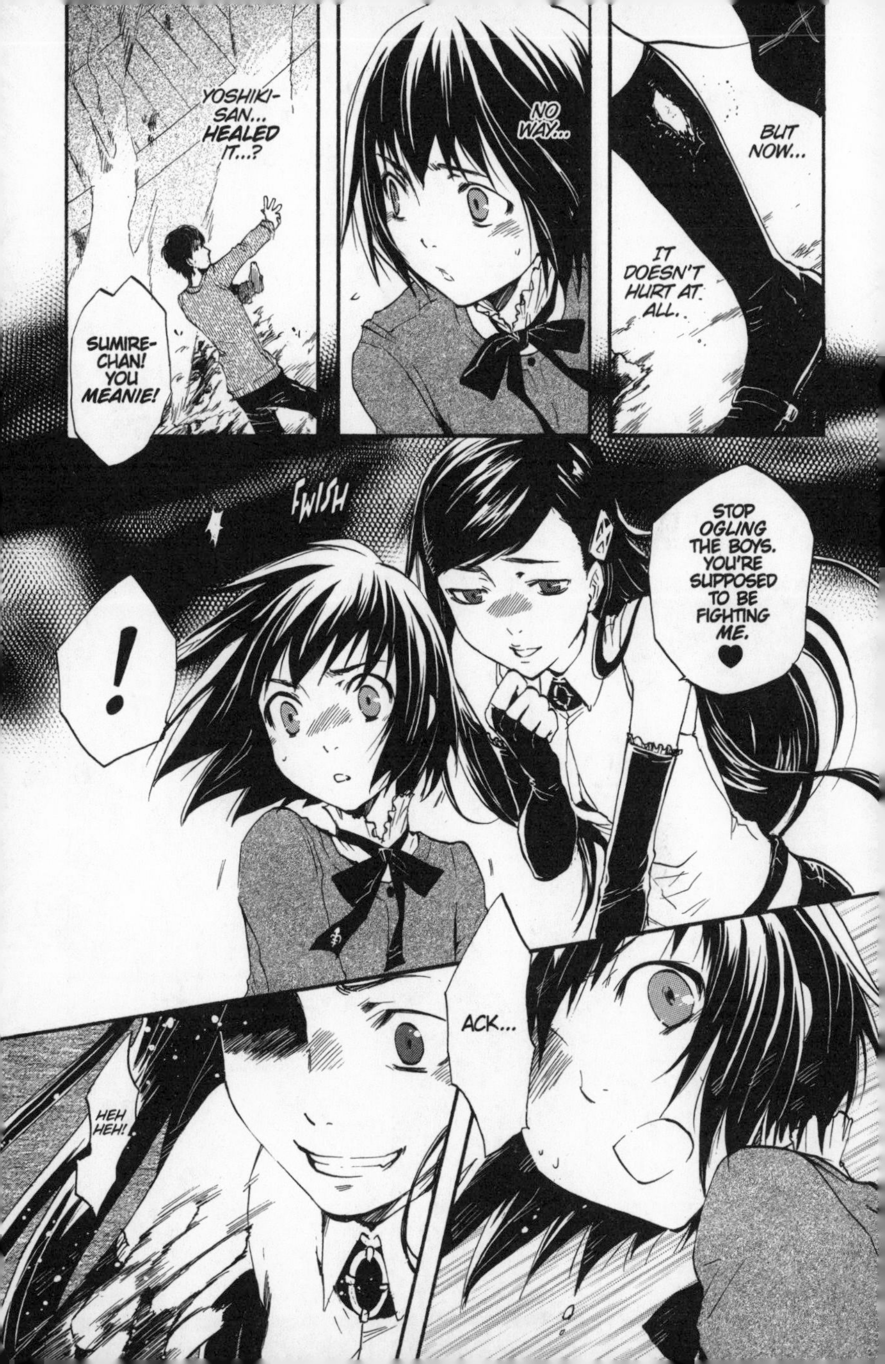
BUT NOW...
IT DOESN'T HURT AT ALL.
NO WAY...
YOSHIKI-SAN... HEALED IT...?
SUMIRE-CHAN! YOU MEANIE!
STOP OGLING THE BOYS. YOU'RE SUPPOSED TO BE FIGHTING ME. ♥
FWISH
!
ACK...
HEH HEH!

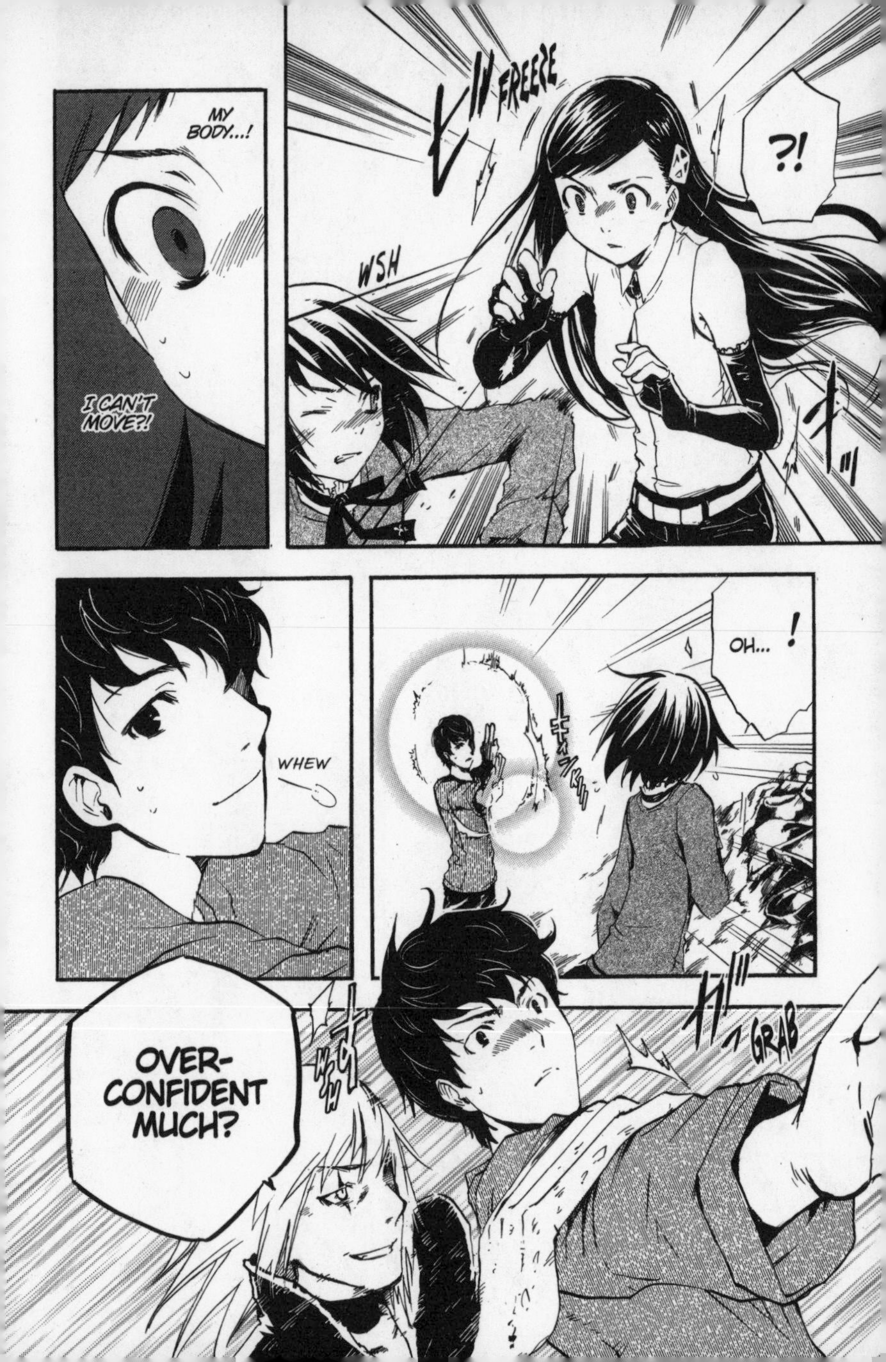
FREEZE
?!
WSH
MY BODY...!
I CAN'T MOVE?!
OH... !
WHEW
GRAB
OVER-CONFIDENT MUCH?

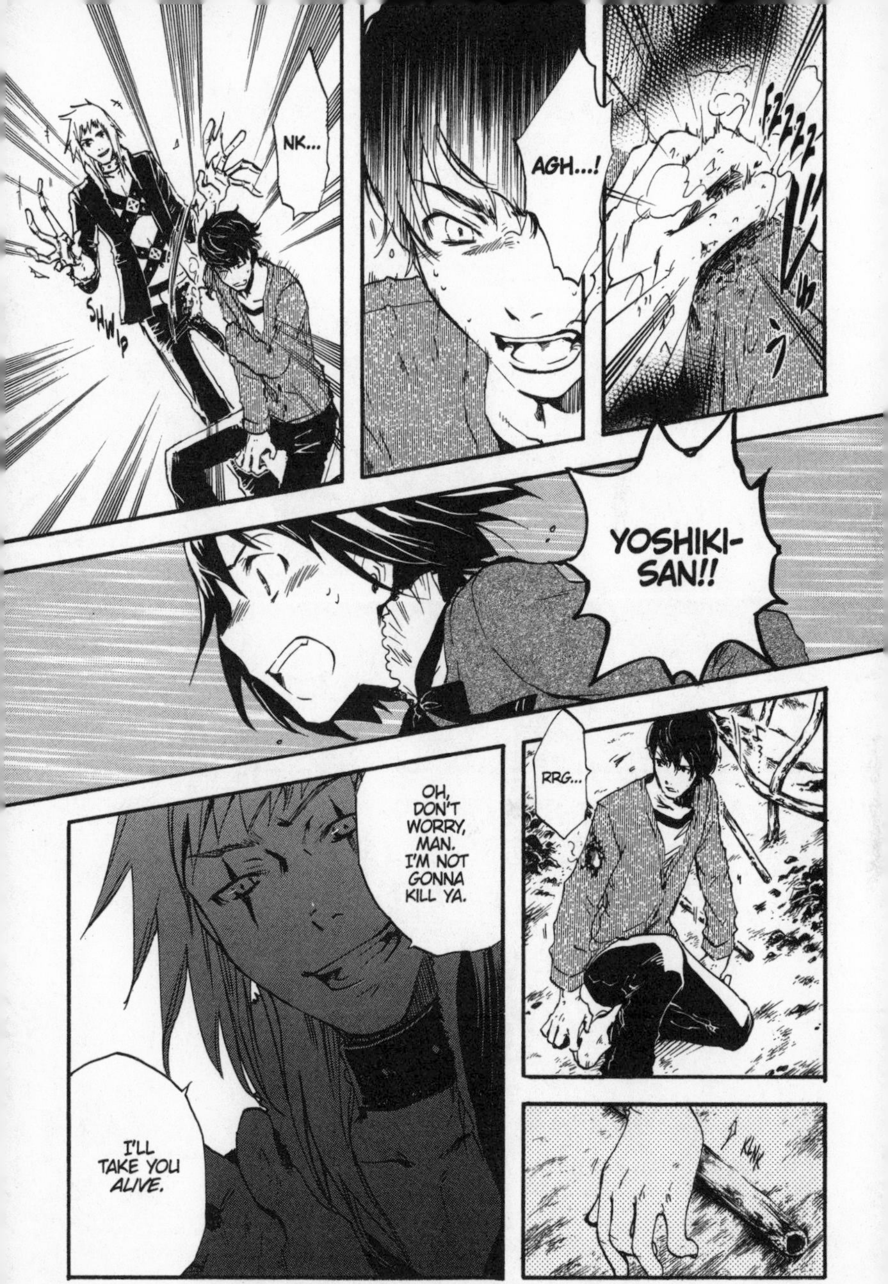
AGH...!
NK...
SHWIP
YOSHIKI-SAN!!
RRG...
OH, DON'T WORRY, MAN. I'M NOT GONNA KILL YA.
I'LL TAKE YOU *ALIVE.*

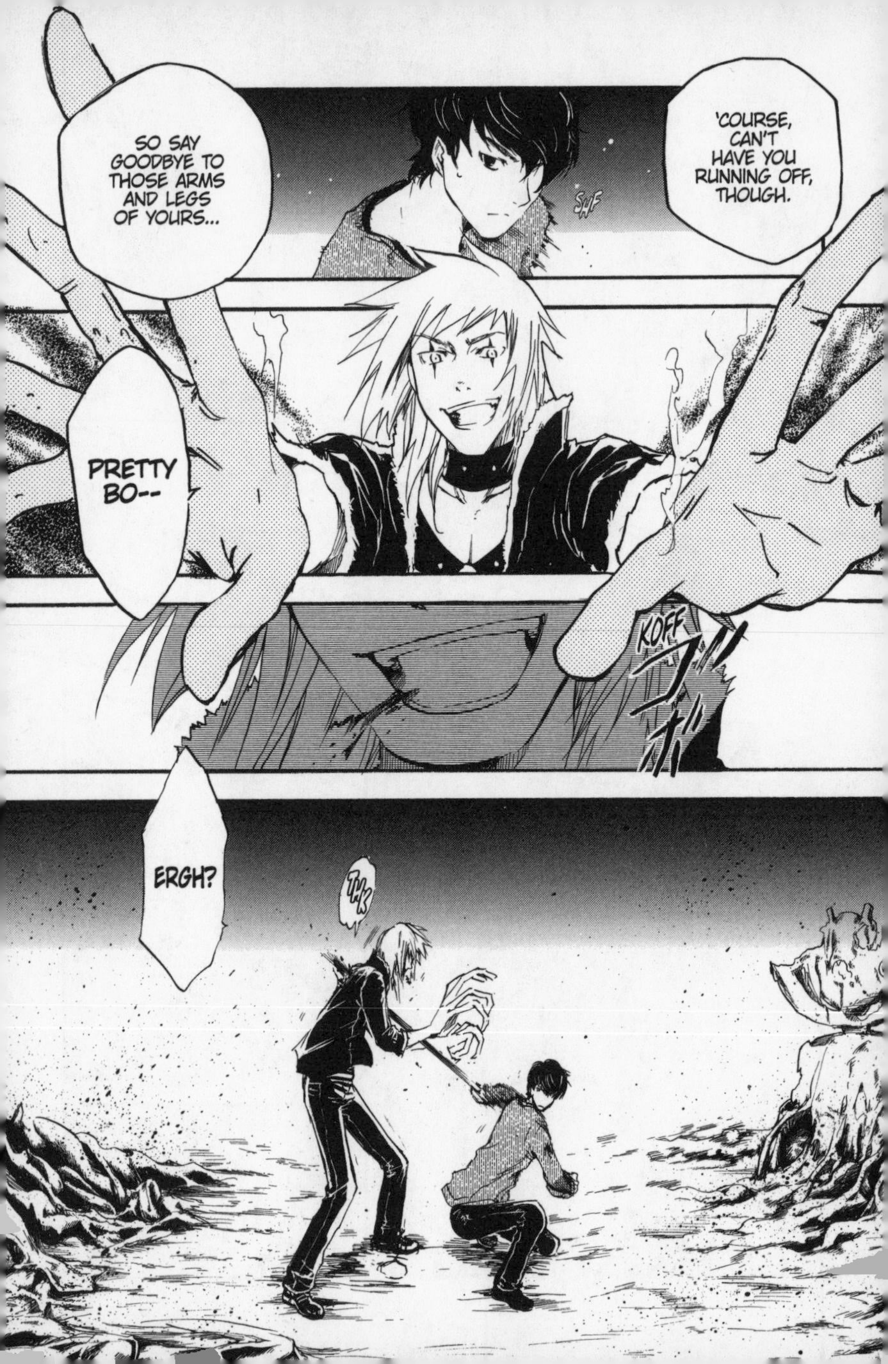
'COURSE, CAN'T HAVE YOU RUNNING OFF, THOUGH.
SHF
SO SAY GOODBYE TO THOSE ARMS AND LEGS OF YOURS...
PRETTY BO--
KOFF
ERGH?
THK

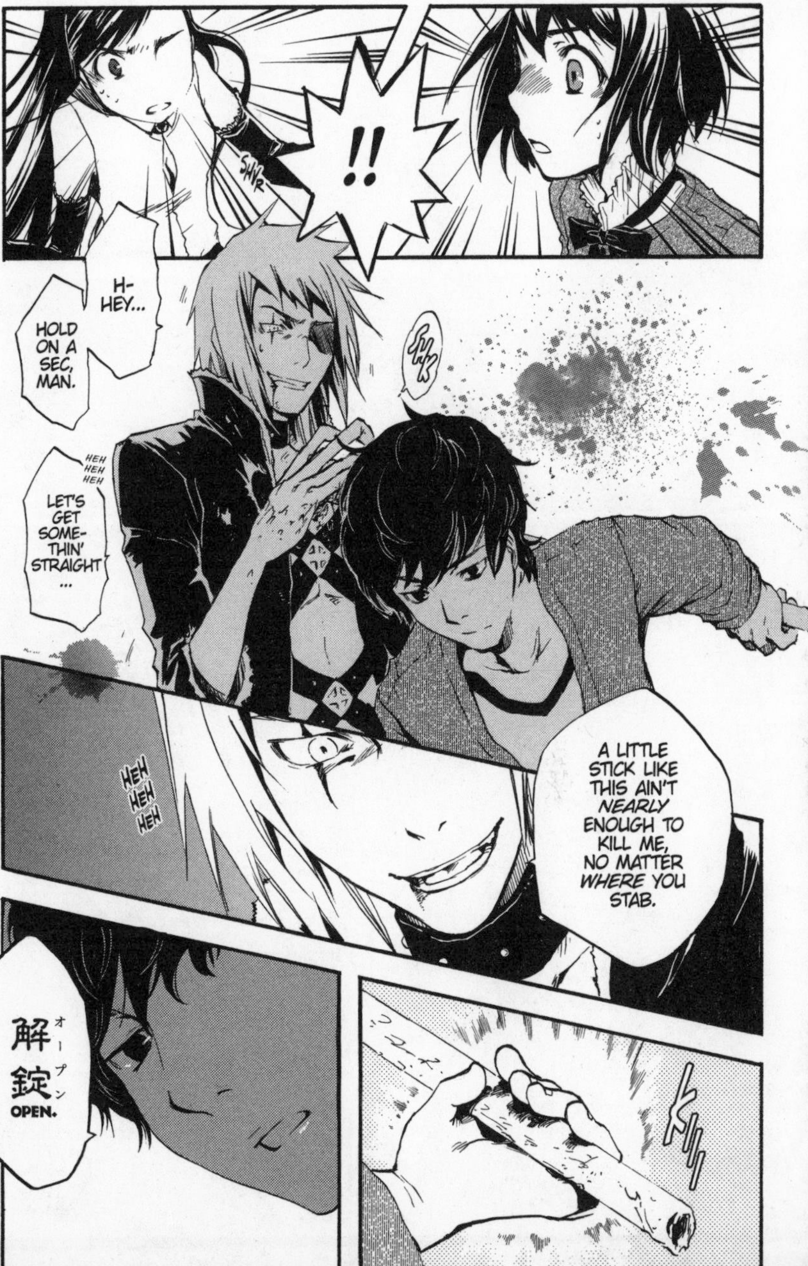
!!
SHVR
H- HEY...
HOLD ON A SEC, MAN.
SHK
HEH HEH HEH
LET'S GET SOME-THIN' STRAIGHT...
A LITTLE STICK LIKE THIS AIN'T *NEARLY* ENOUGH TO KILL ME, NO MATTER *WHERE* YOU STAB.
HEH HEH HEH
KIII
解錠 オープン
OPEN.

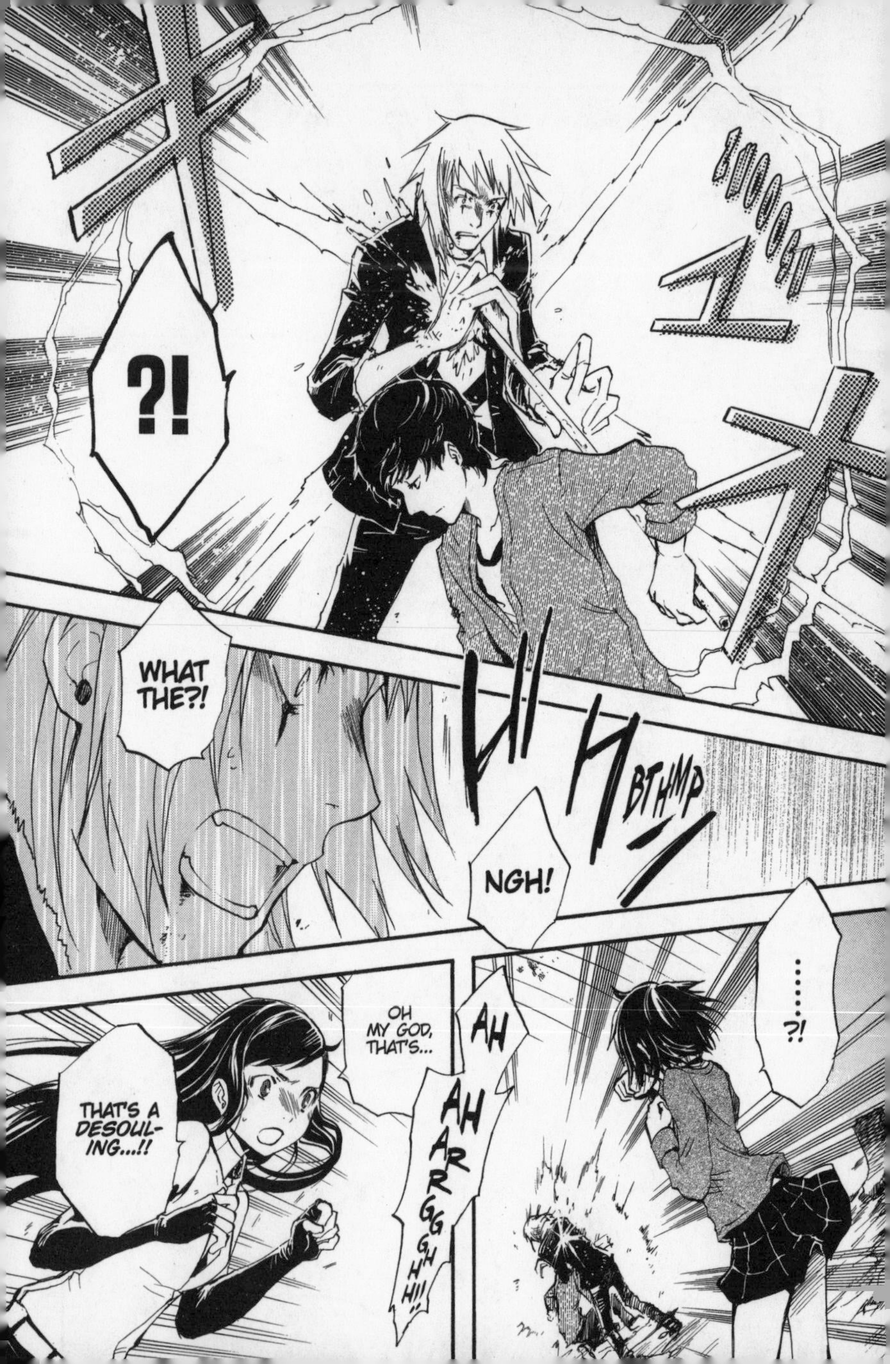
?!
BTHMP
NGH!
WHAT THE?!
……?!
AH AH ARRGGGHH!!
OH MY GOD, THAT'S...
THAT'S A DESOUL-ING...!!

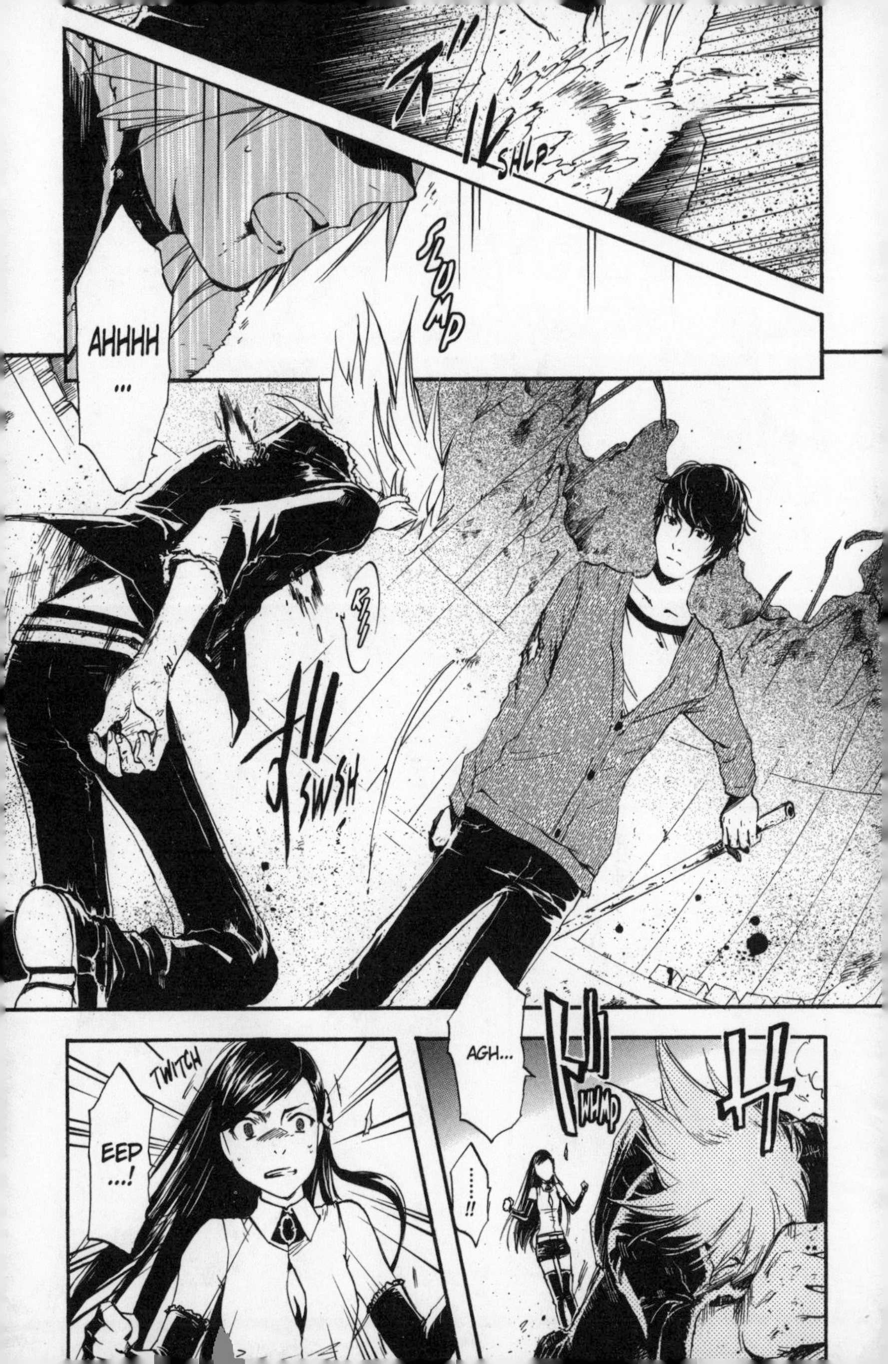
SHLP
SLUMP
AHHHH ...
SWISH
AGH...
WHMP
......!!
TWITCH
EEP ...!

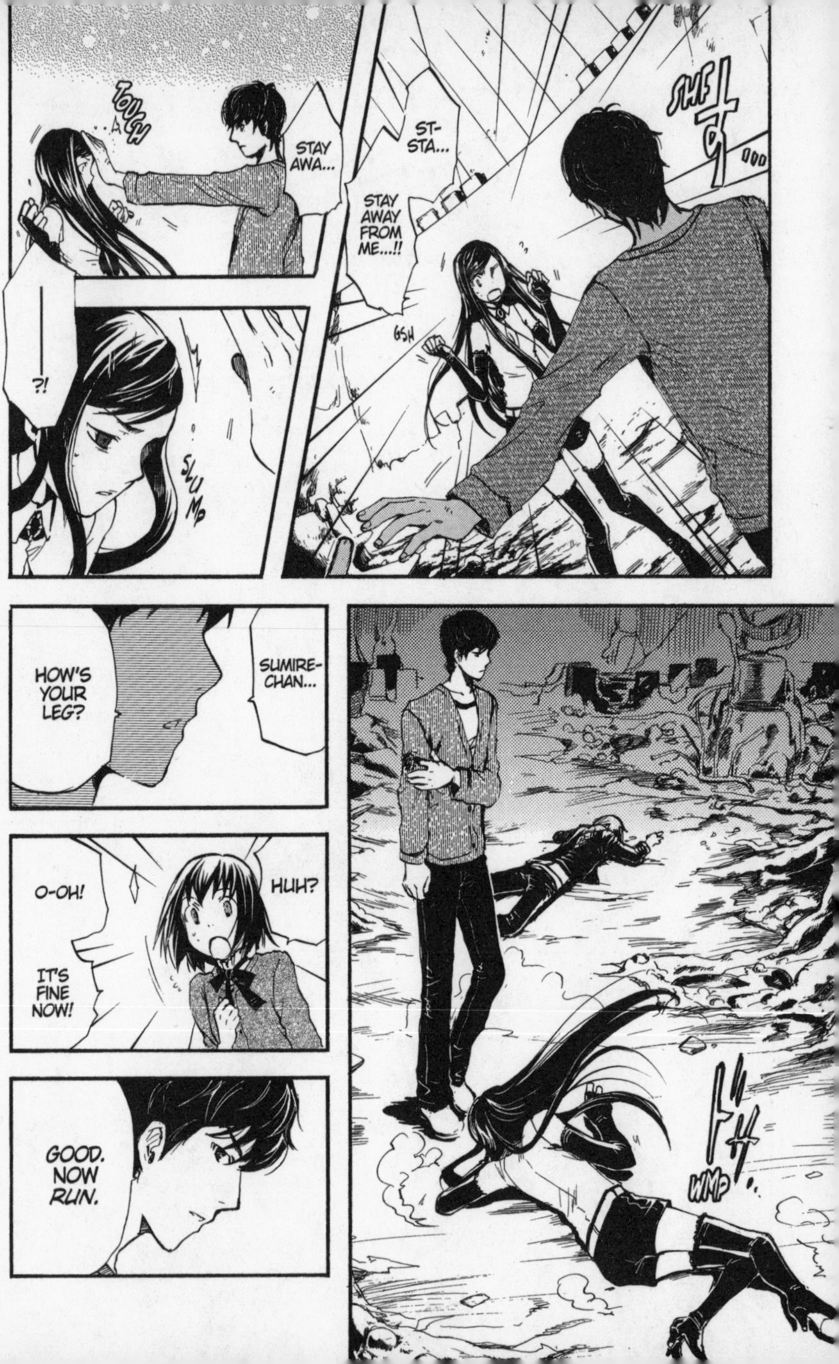
SHF
ST-STA...
STAY AWAY FROM ME...!!
GSH
TOUCH
STAY AWA...
?!
SLUMP
WMP
SUMIRE-CHAN...
HOW'S YOUR LEG?
HUH?
O-OH!
IT'S FINE NOW!
GOOD. NOW RUN.

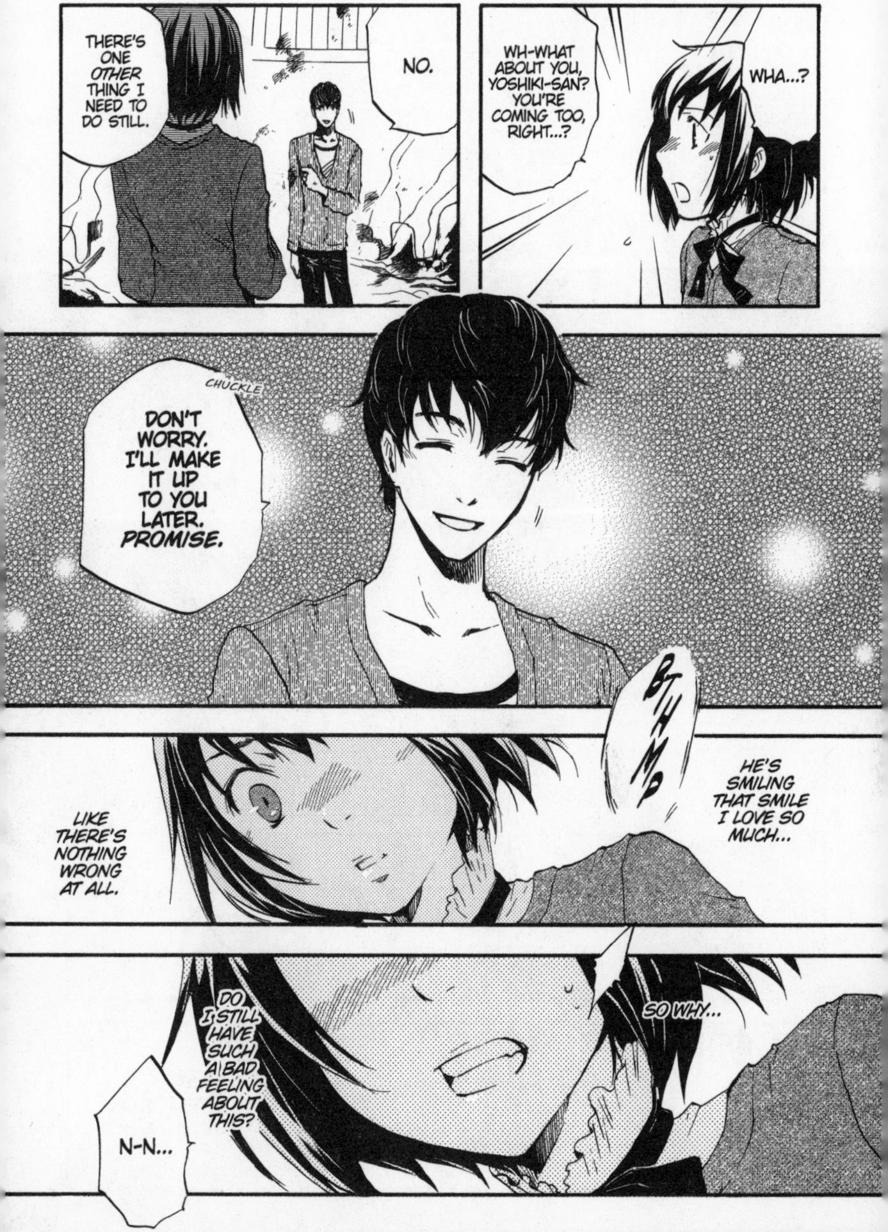
WHA...?
WH-WHAT ABOUT YOU, YOSHIKI-SAN? YOU'RE COMING TOO, RIGHT...?
NO.
THERE'S ONE OTHER THING I NEED TO DO STILL.
CHUCKLE
DON'T WORRY. I'LL MAKE IT UP TO YOU LATER. PROMISE.
BTHMP
HE'S SMILING THAT SMILE I LOVE SO MUCH...
LIKE THERE'S NOTHING WRONG AT ALL.
SO WHY...
DO I STILL HAVE SUCH A BAD FEELING ABOUT THIS?
N-N...

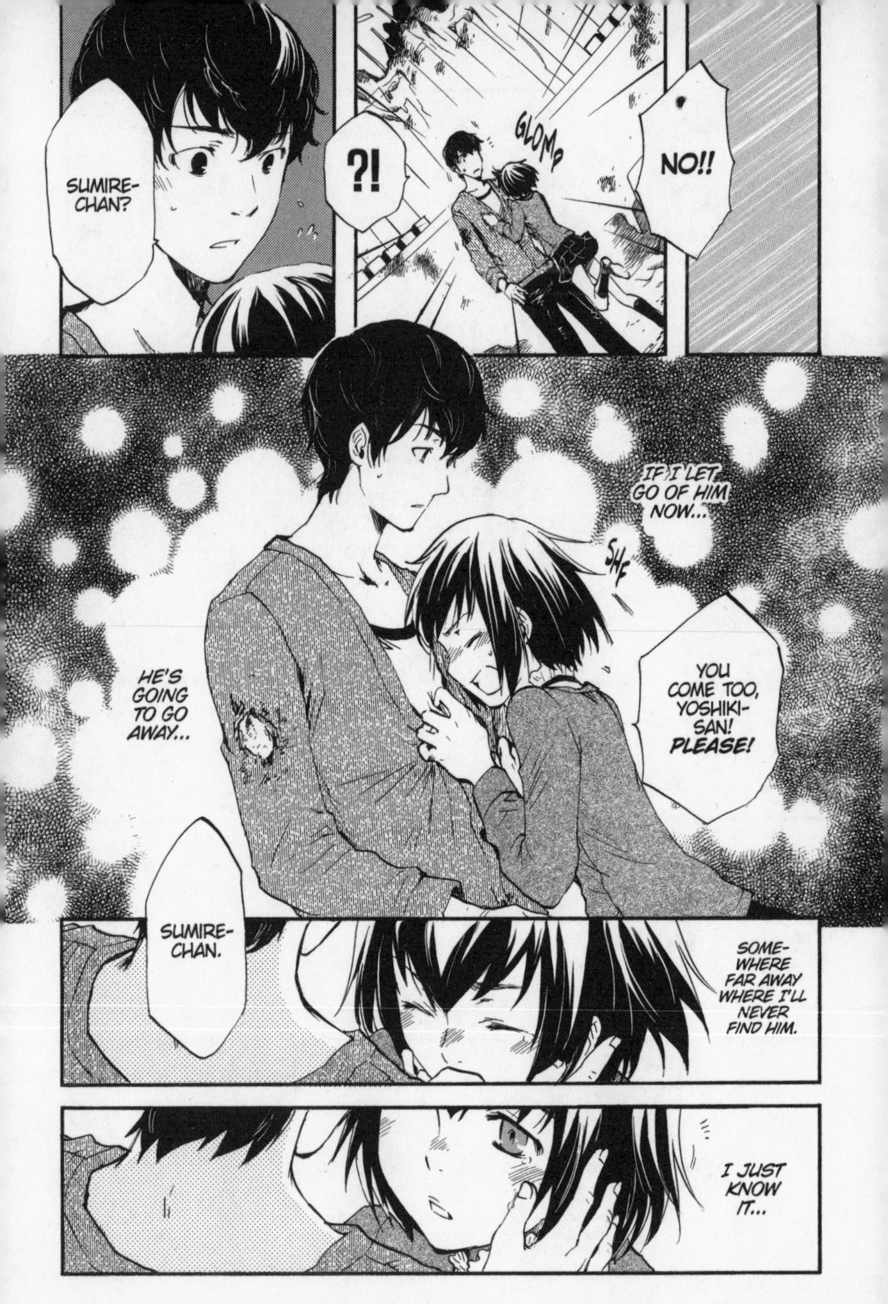
NO!!
GLOMP
?!
SUMIRE-CHAN?
IF I LET GO OF HIM NOW...
SHF
YOU COME TOO, YOSHIKI-SAN! PLEASE!
HE'S GOING TO GO AWAY...
SOME-WHERE FAR AWAY WHERE I'LL NEVER FIND HIM.
SUMIRE-CHAN.
I JUST KNOW IT...

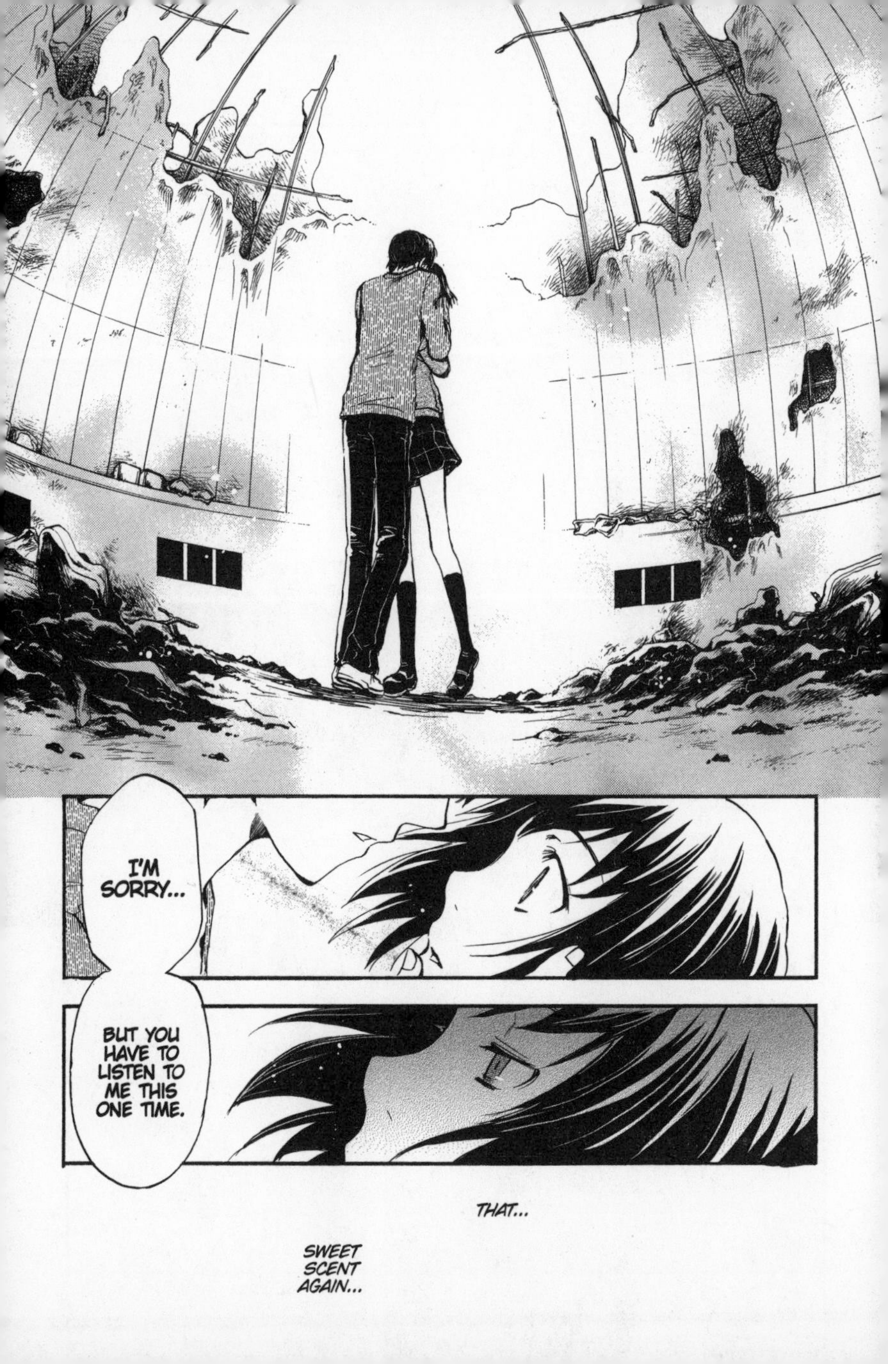
I'M SORRY...
BUT YOU HAVE TO LISTEN TO ME THIS ONE TIME.
THAT...
SWEET SCENT AGAIN...

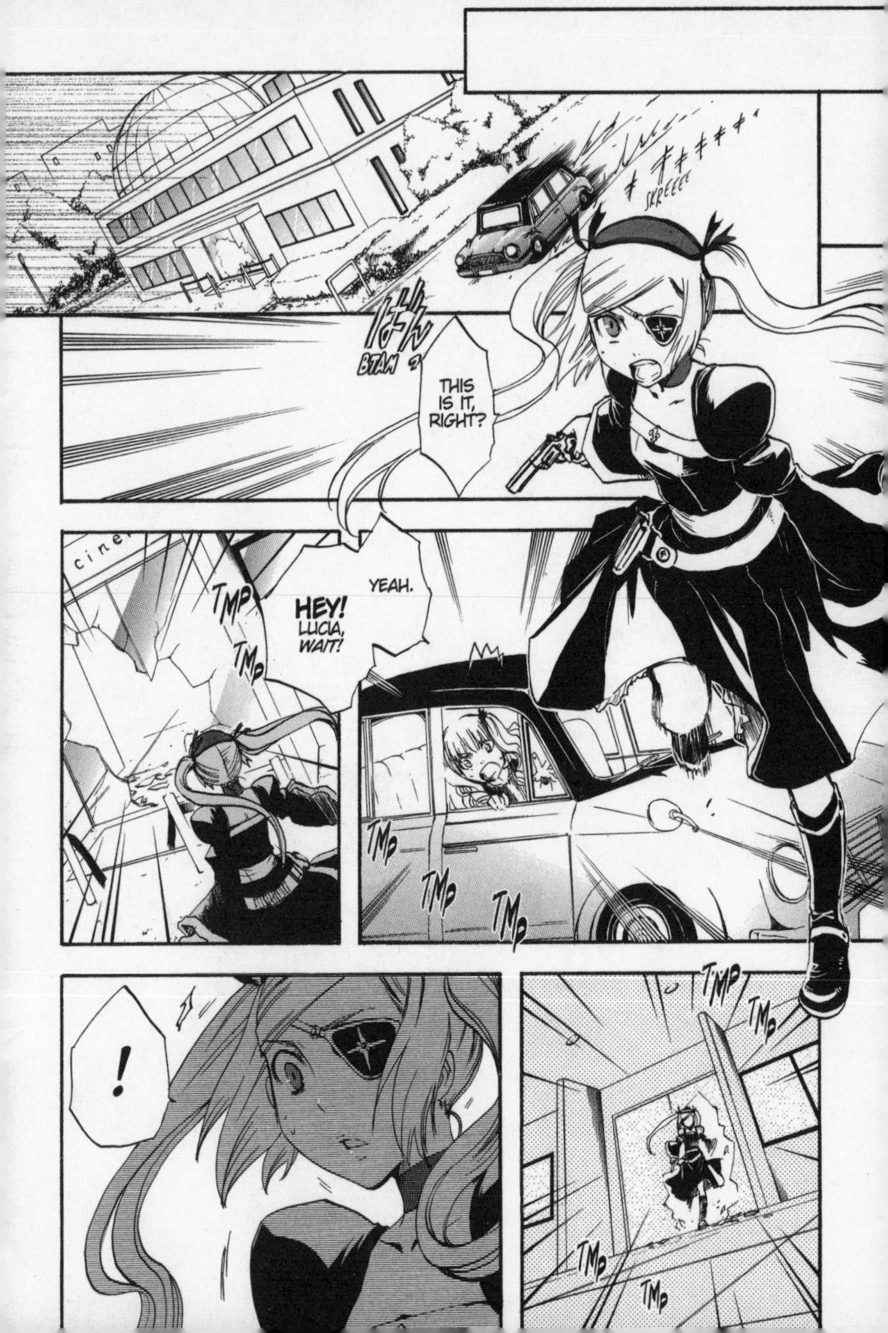
SKREEEE
BTAM
THIS IS IT, RIGHT?
YEAH.
HEY! LUCIA, WAIT!
TMP
TMP
TMP
TMP
TMP
TMP
TMP
TMP
TMP
!

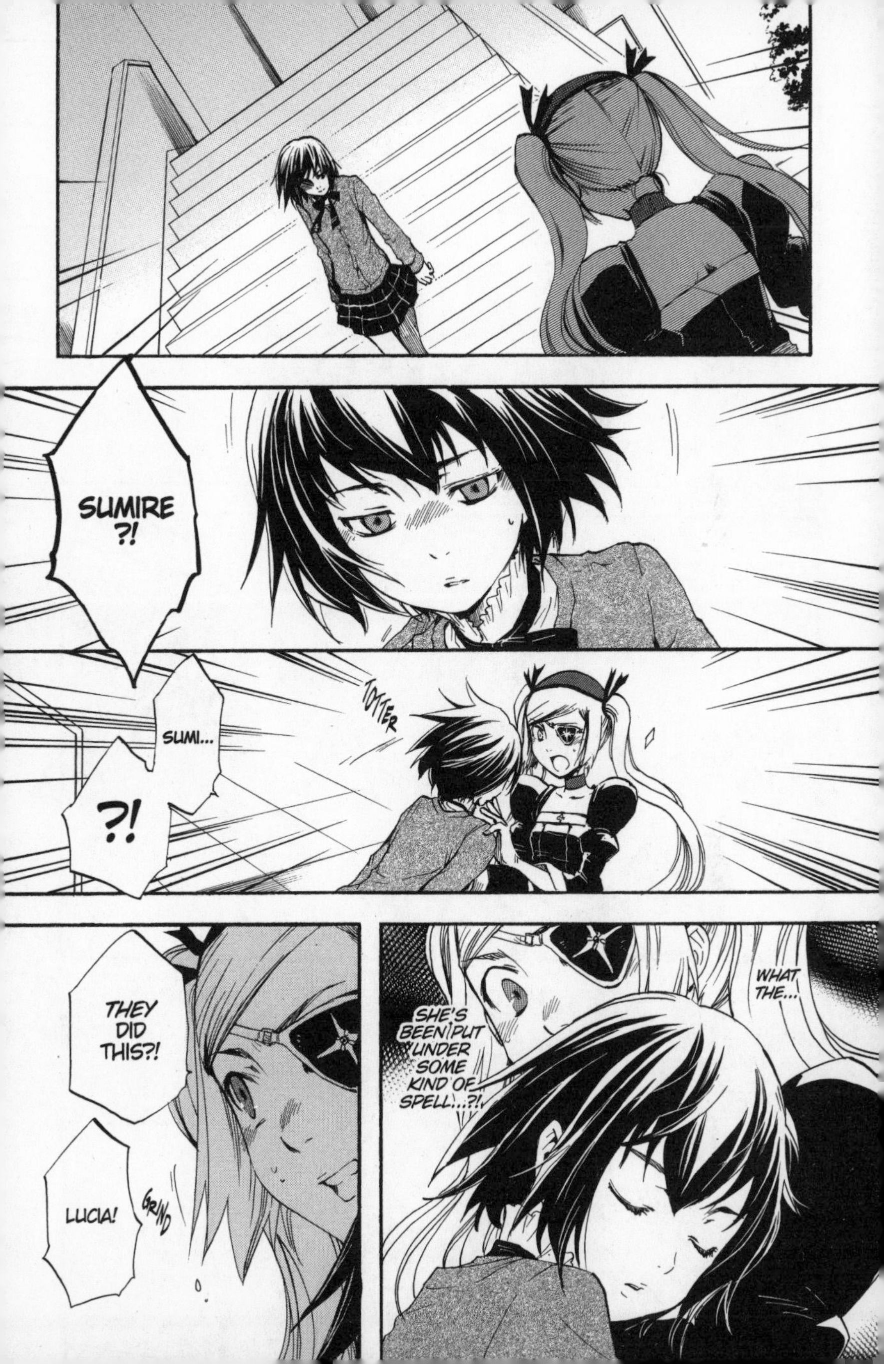
SUMIRE ?!
TOTTER
SUMI...
?!
WHAT THE...
SHE'S BEEN PUT UNDER SOME KIND OF SPELL...?!
THEY DID THIS?!
GRIND
LUCIA!

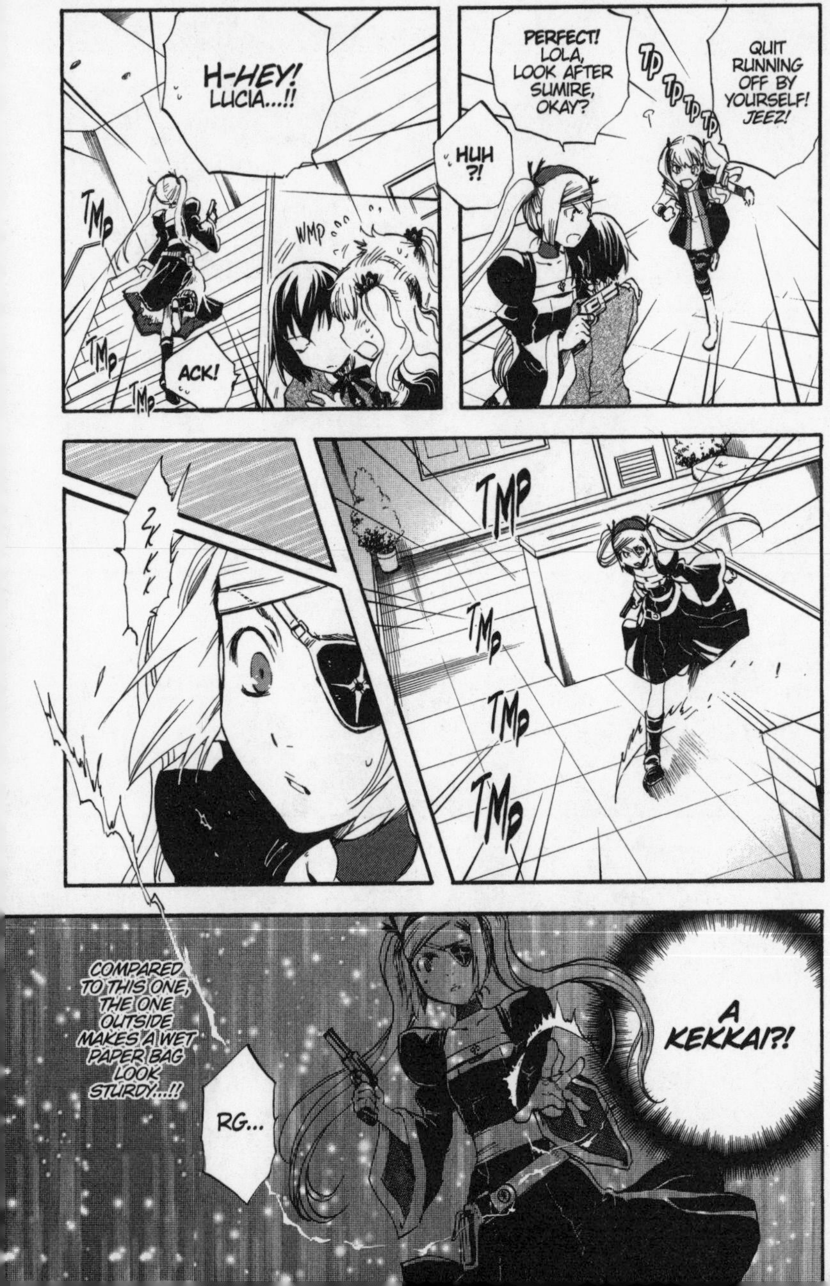
QUIT RUNNING OFF BY YOURSELF! JEEZ!
TP TP TP TP TP
PERFECT! LOLA, LOOK AFTER SUMIRE, OKAY?
HUH ?!
H-HEY! LUCIA...!!
TMP
WMP
ACK!
TMP
TMP
TMP
TMP
TMP
TMP
ZKKK
A KEKKAI?!
RG...
COMPARED TO THIS ONE, THE ONE OUTSIDE MAKES A WET PAPER BAG LOOK STURDY...!!

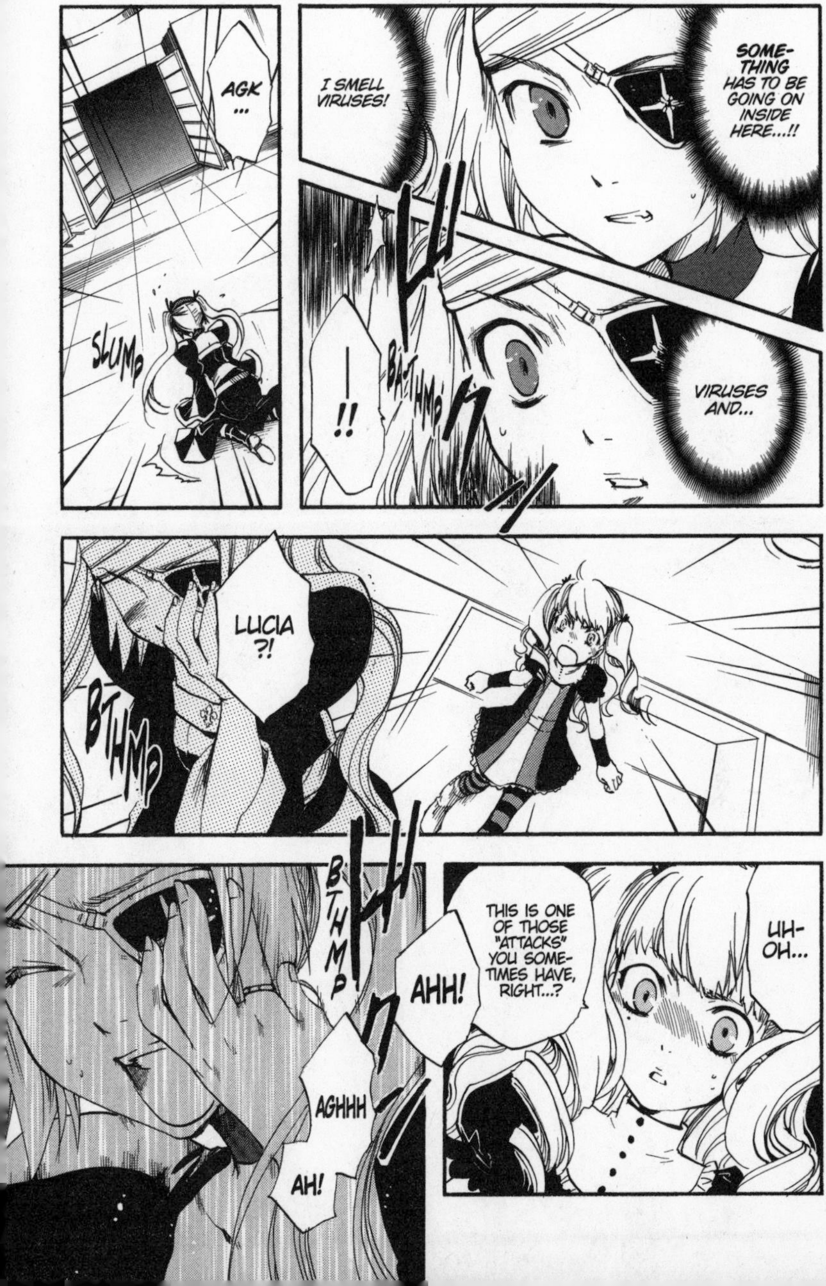
SOME-THING HAS TO BE GOING ON INSIDE HERE...!!
I SMELL VIRUSES!
VIRUSES AND...
BA-THMP
!!
AGK ...
SLUMP
LUCIA ?!
BTHMP
UH-OH...
THIS IS ONE OF THOSE "ATTACKS" YOU SOME-TIMES HAVE, RIGHT...?
BTHMP
AHH!
AGHHH
AH!

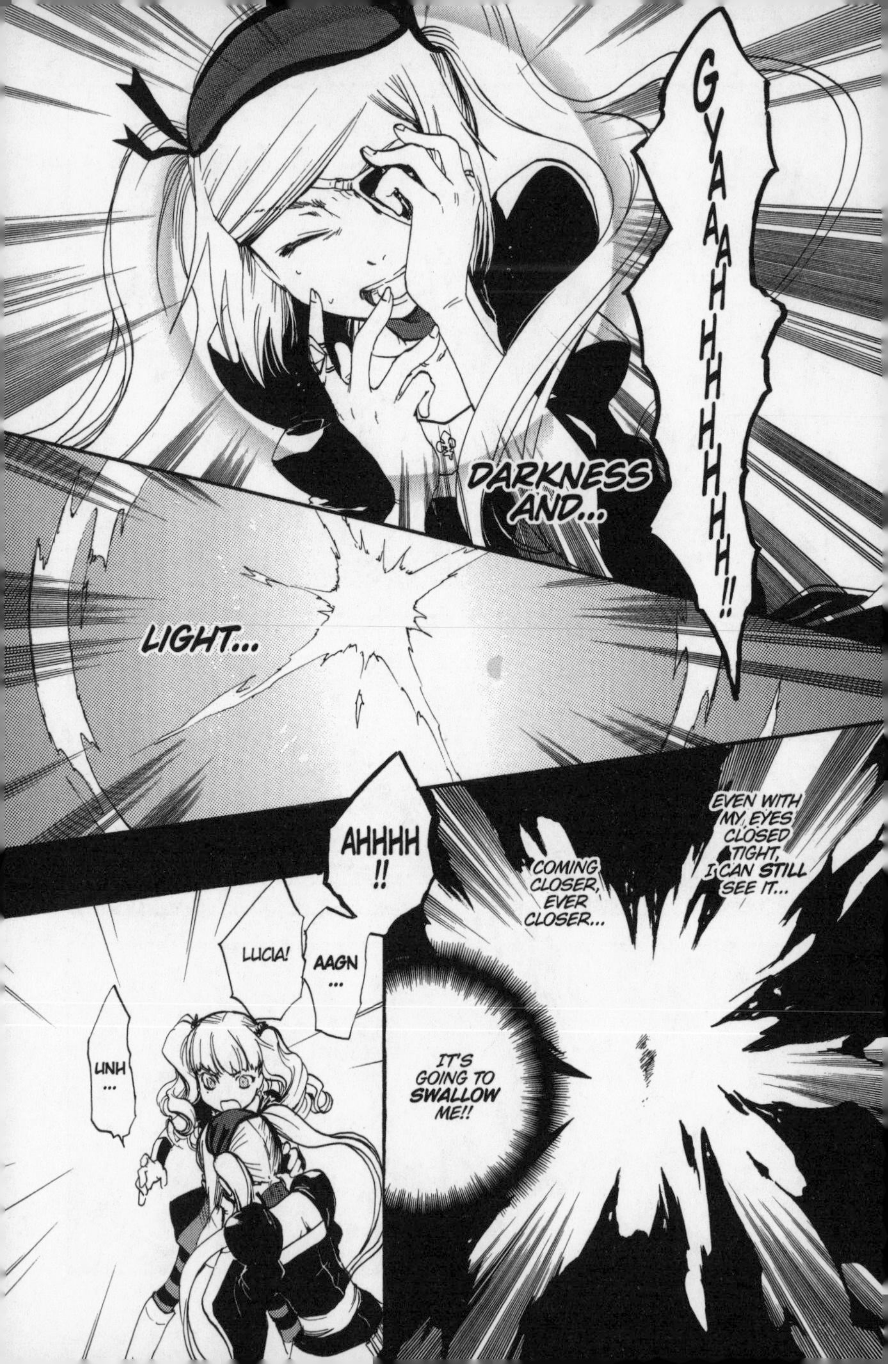
GYAAAHHHHHHH!!
DARKNESS AND...
LIGHT...
EVEN WITH MY EYES CLOSED TIGHT, I CAN STILL SEE IT...
COMING CLOSER, EVER CLOSER...
IT'S GOING TO SWALLOW ME!!
AHHHH!!
AAGN...
LUCIA!
UNH...

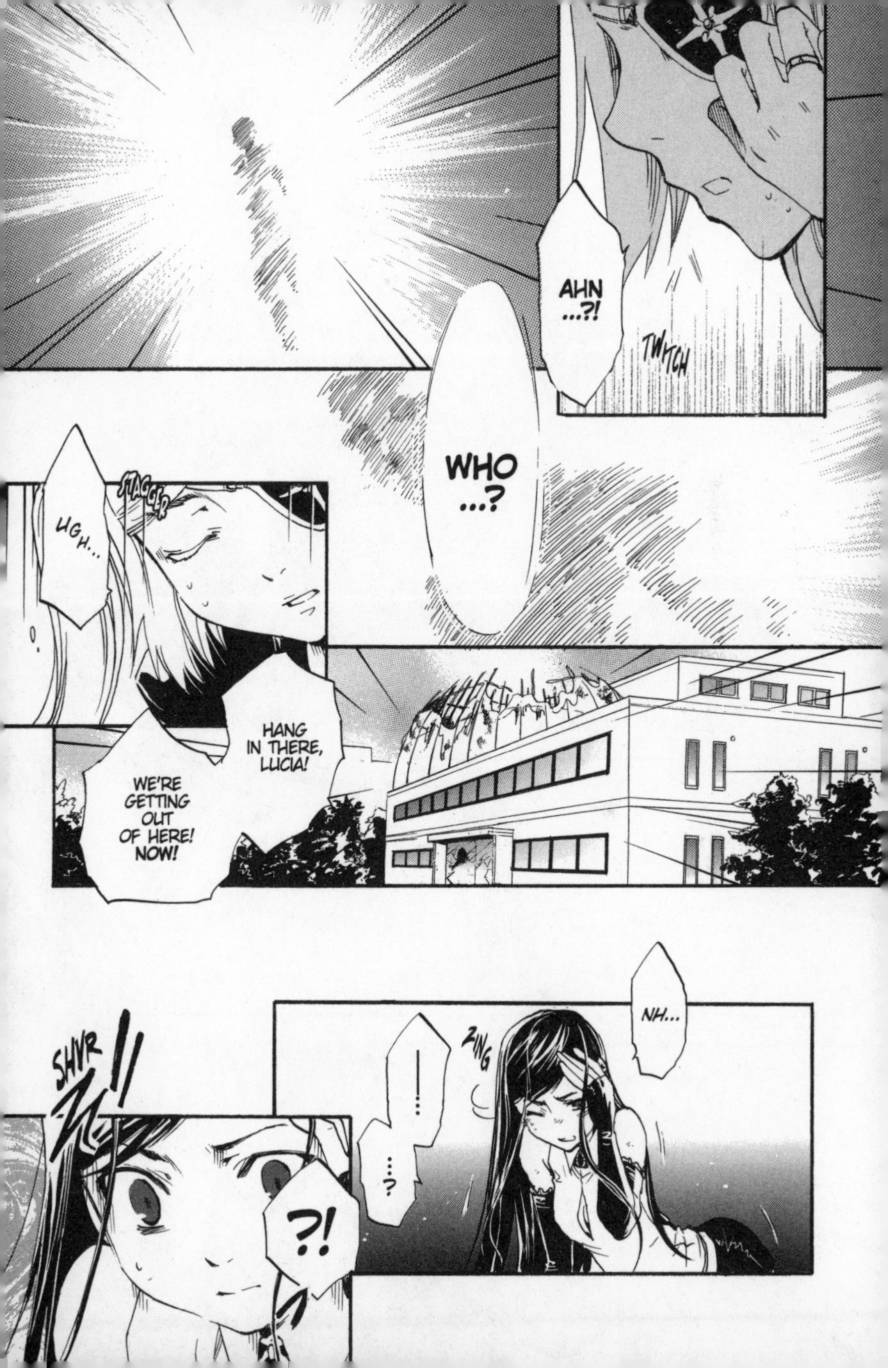

AHN ...?!
TWITCH
WHO ...?
STAGGER
UGH...
HANG IN THERE, LUCIA!
WE'RE GETTING OUT OF HERE! NOW!
NH...
ZING
......?
SHVR
?!

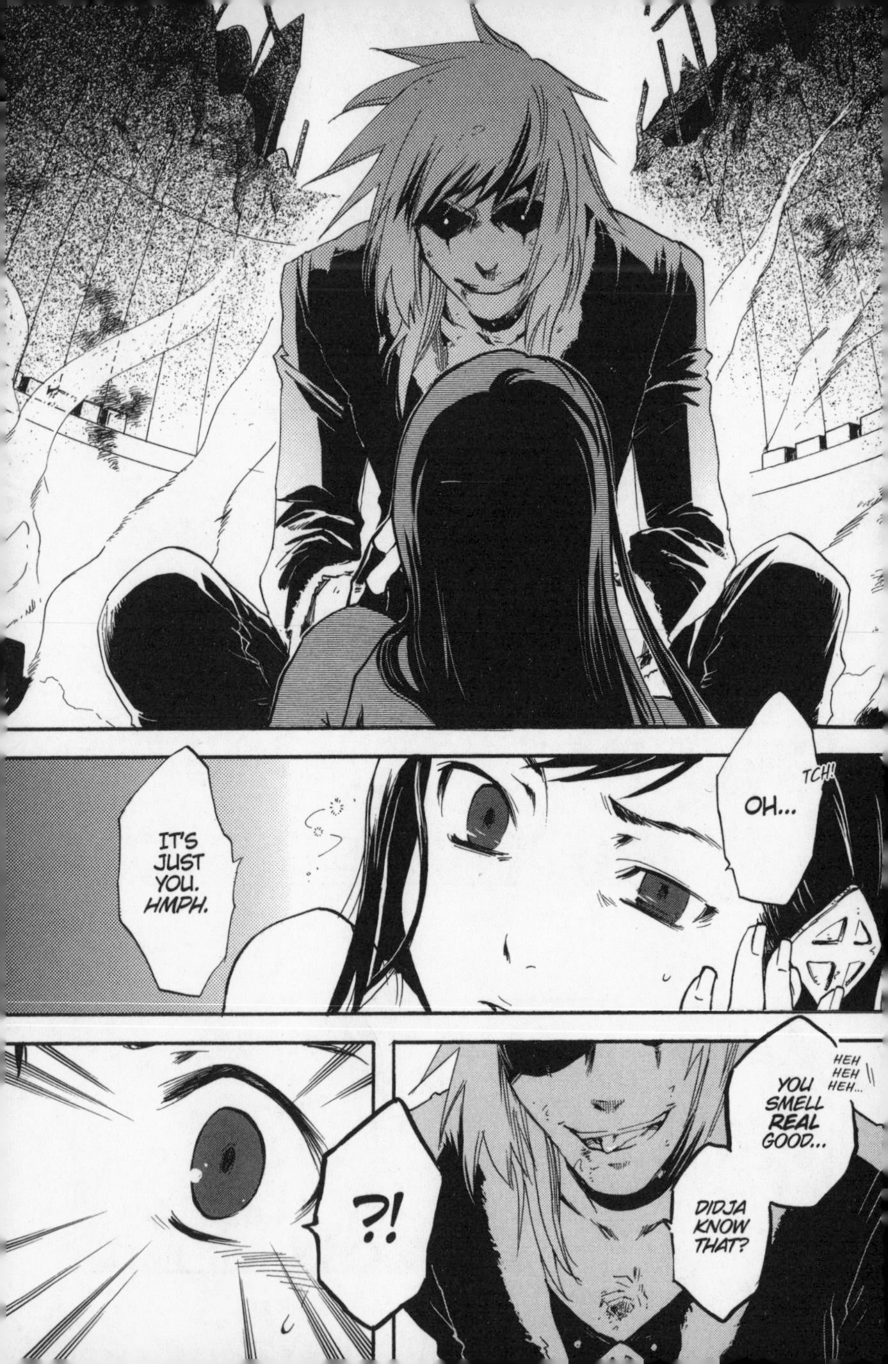
TCH!
OH...
IT'S JUST YOU. HMPH.
HEH HEH HEH...
YOU SMELL REAL GOOD...
DIDJA KNOW THAT?
?!

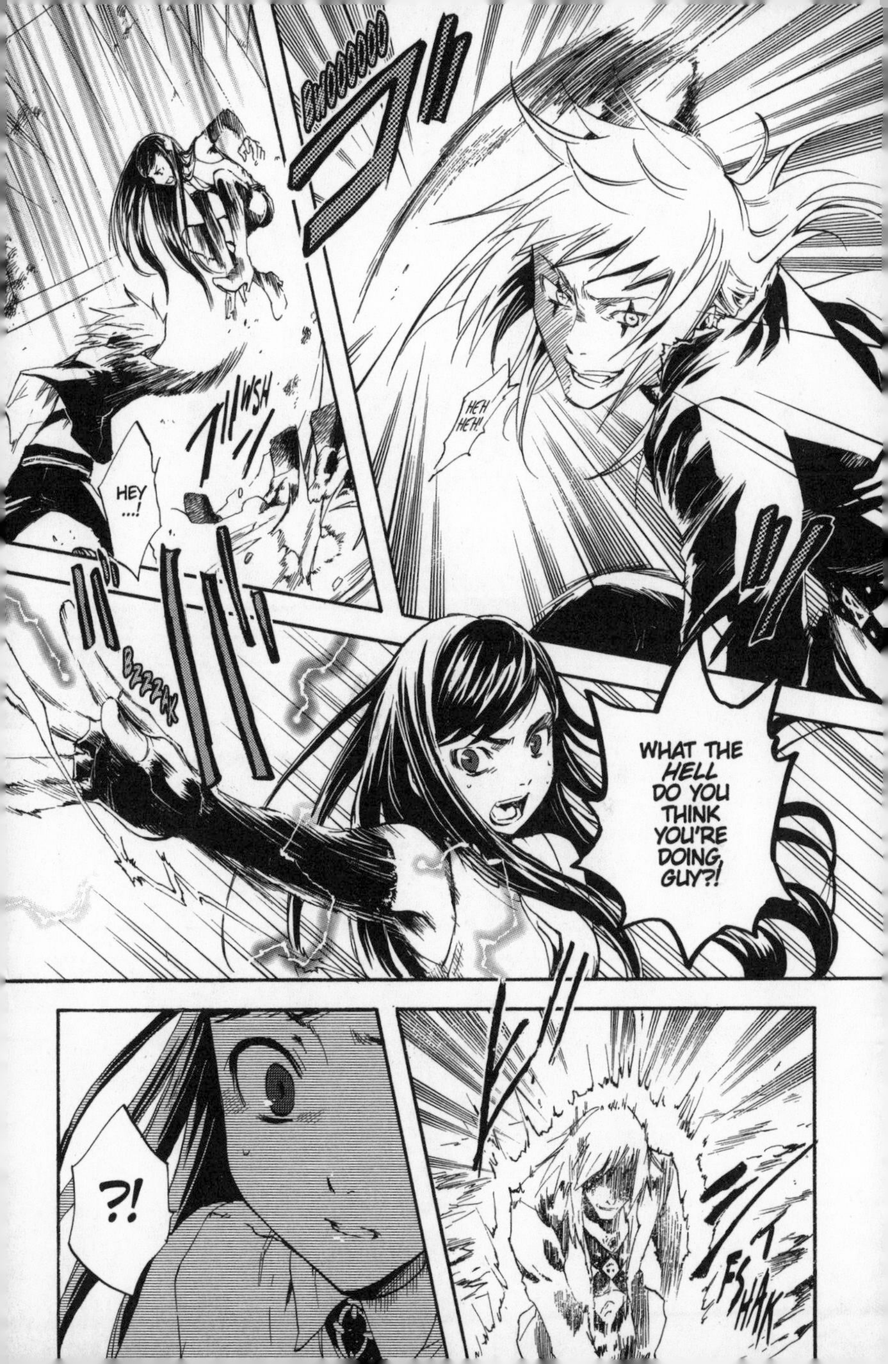
BWOOOOOOO
HEH HEH!
WSH
HEY ...!
BZZZAK
WHAT THE *HELL* DO YOU THINK YOU'RE DOING, GUY?!
FSHAK
?!

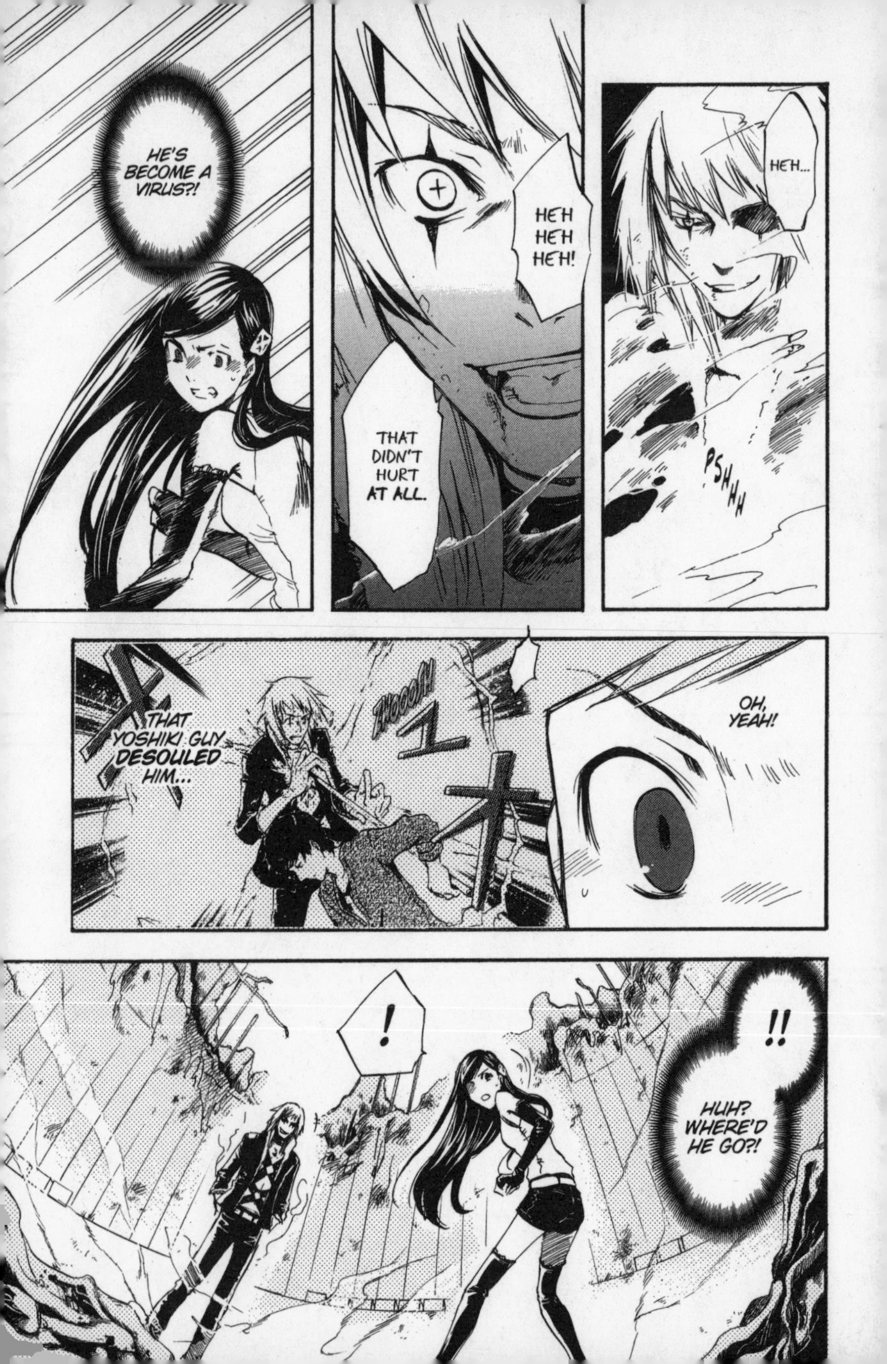
HEH...
PSHHH
HEH HEH HEH!
THAT DIDN'T HURT AT ALL.
HE'S BECOME A VIRUS?!
OH, YEAH!
THAT YOSHIKI GUY DESOULED HIM...
!!
HUH? WHERE'D HE GO?!
!

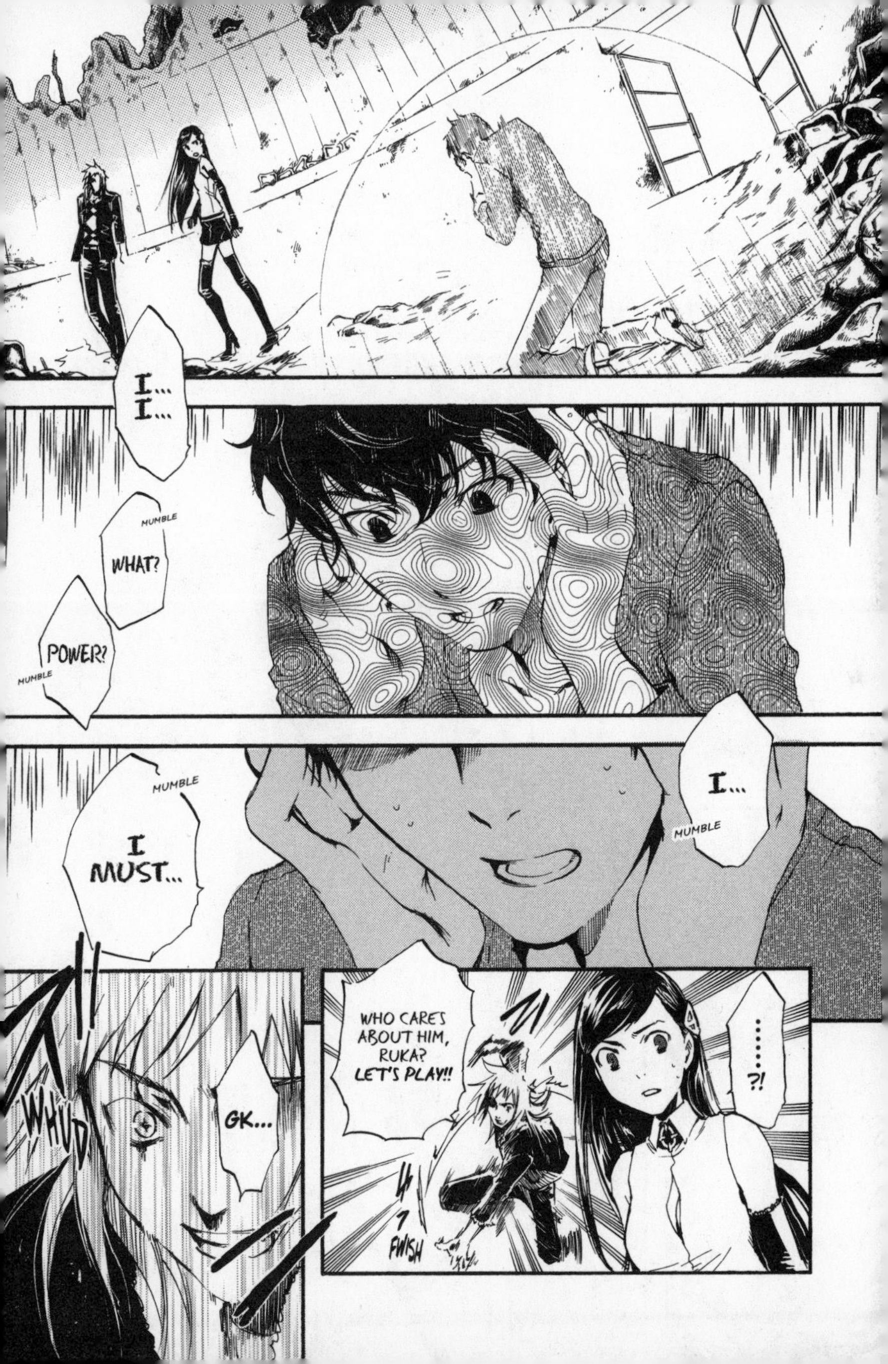
I... I...
MUMBLE
WHAT?
POWER?
MUMBLE
I...
MUMBLE
MUMBLE
I MUST...
......?!
WHO CARES ABOUT HIM, RUKA? LET'S PLAY!!
FWISH
WHUD
GK...

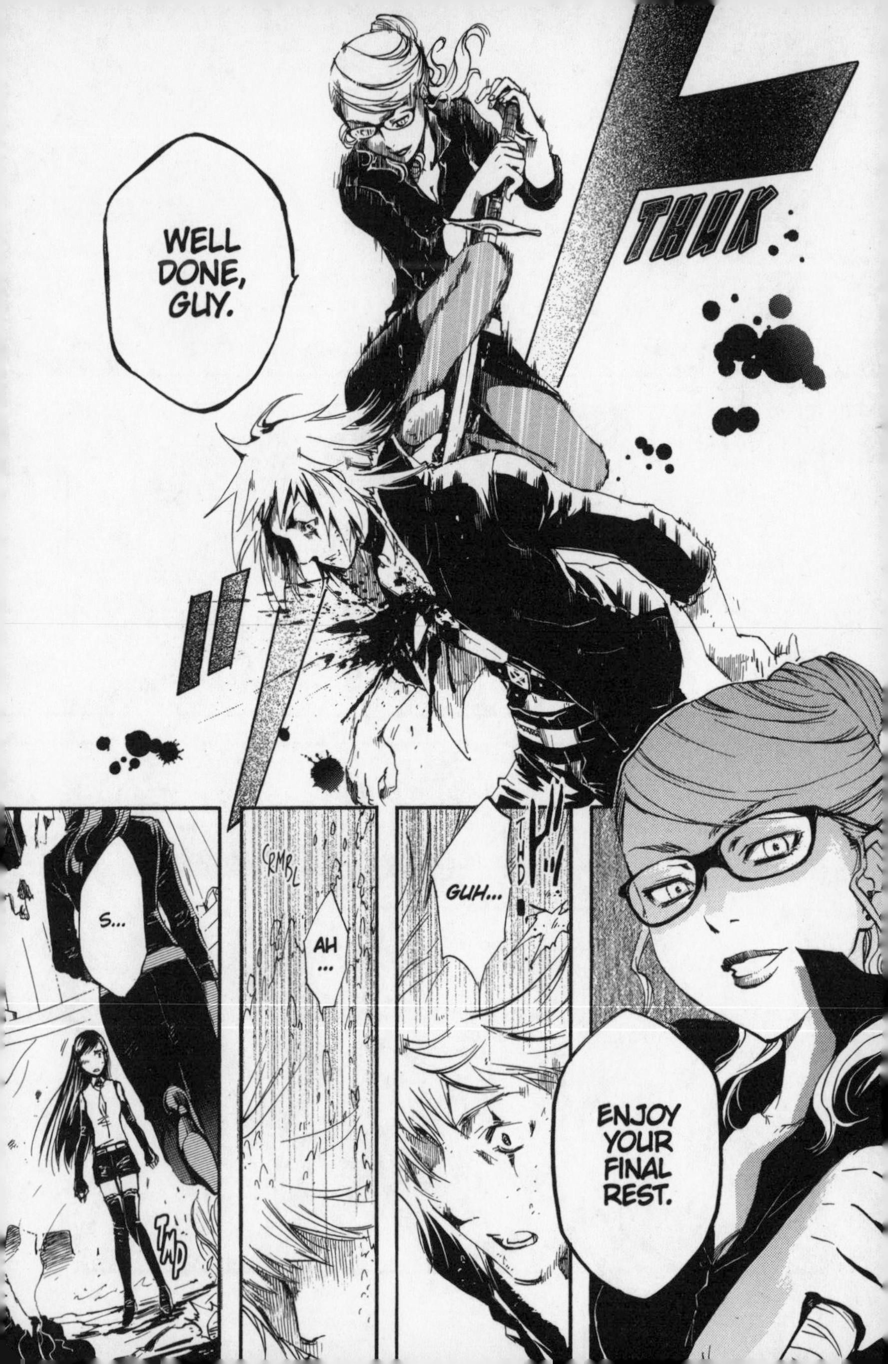
THUK
WELL DONE, GUY.
ENJOY YOUR FINAL REST.
THD
GUH...
CRMBL
AH ...
S...
TMP

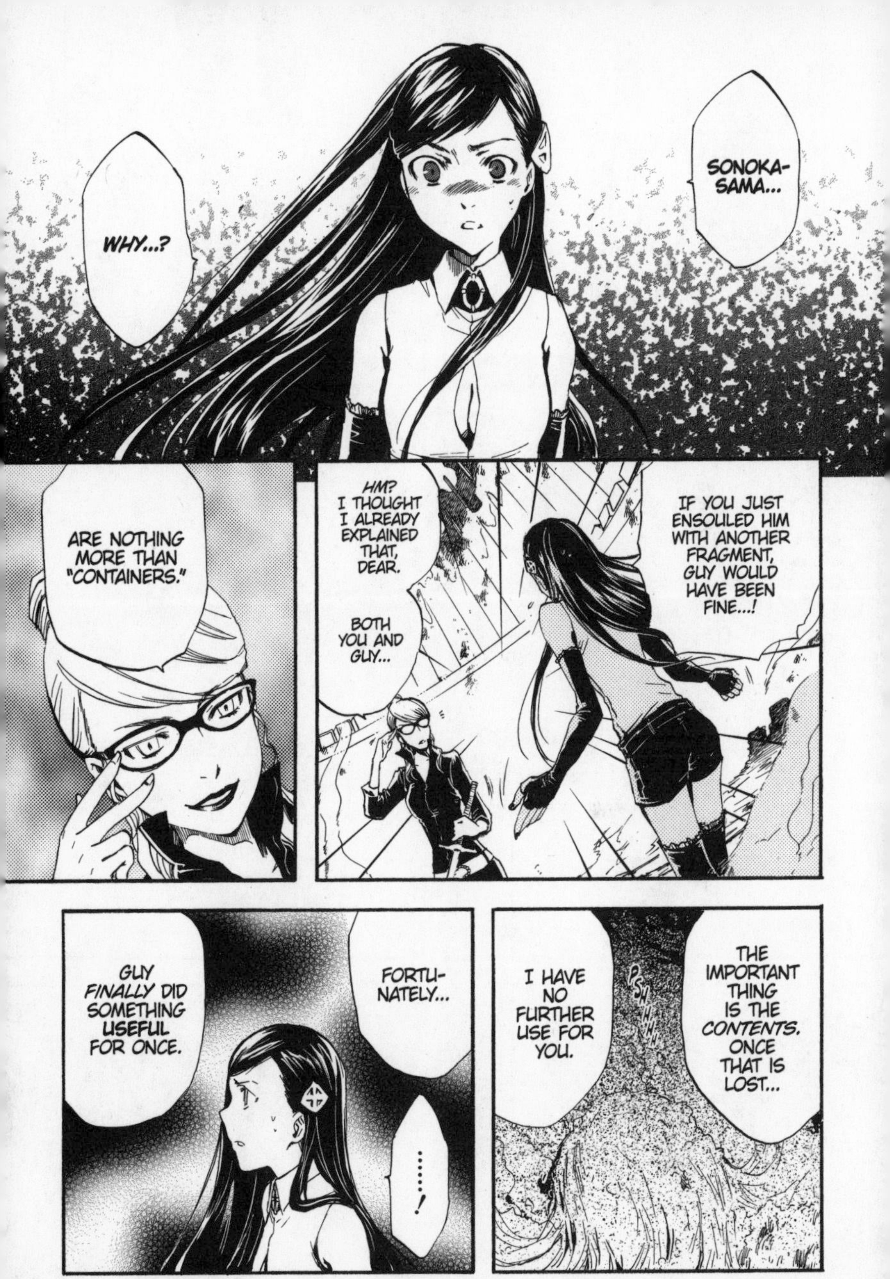
SONOKA-SAMA...
WHY...?
IF YOU JUST ENSOULED HIM WITH ANOTHER FRAGMENT, GUY WOULD HAVE BEEN FINE...!
HM? I THOUGHT I ALREADY EXPLAINED THAT, DEAR.
BOTH YOU AND GUY...
ARE NOTHING MORE THAN "CONTAINERS."
THE IMPORTANT THING IS THE CONTENTS. ONCE THAT IS LOST...
PSHHHH
I HAVE NO FURTHER USE FOR YOU.
FORTU-NATELY...
GUY FINALLY DID SOMETHING USEFUL FOR ONCE.
......!

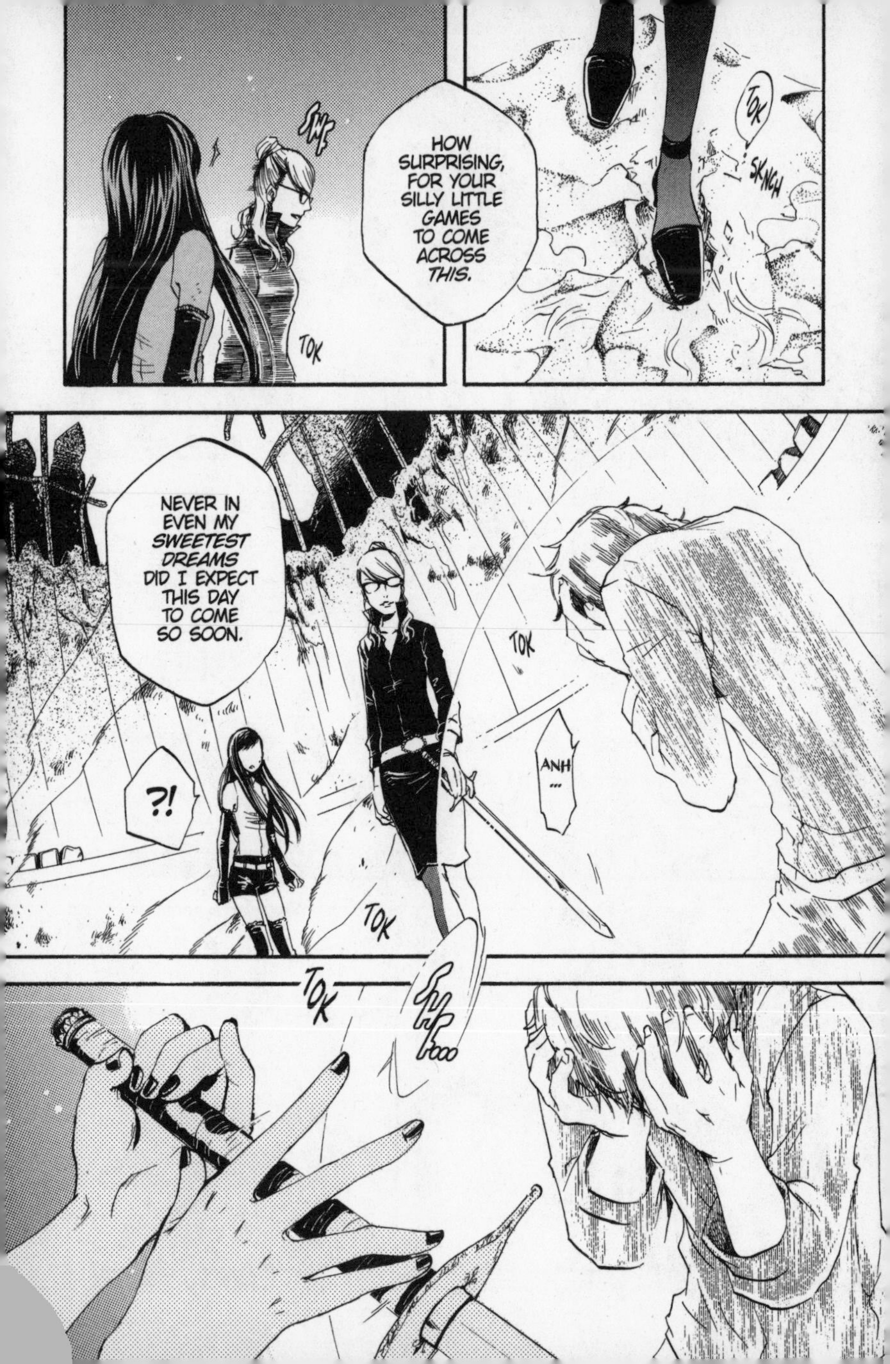

TOK
SKNCH
HOW SURPRISING, FOR YOUR SILLY LITTLE GAMES TO COME ACROSS THIS.
TOK
TOK
ANH ...
NEVER IN EVEN MY SWEETEST DREAMS DID I EXPECT THIS DAY TO COME SO SOON.
?!
TOK
TOK

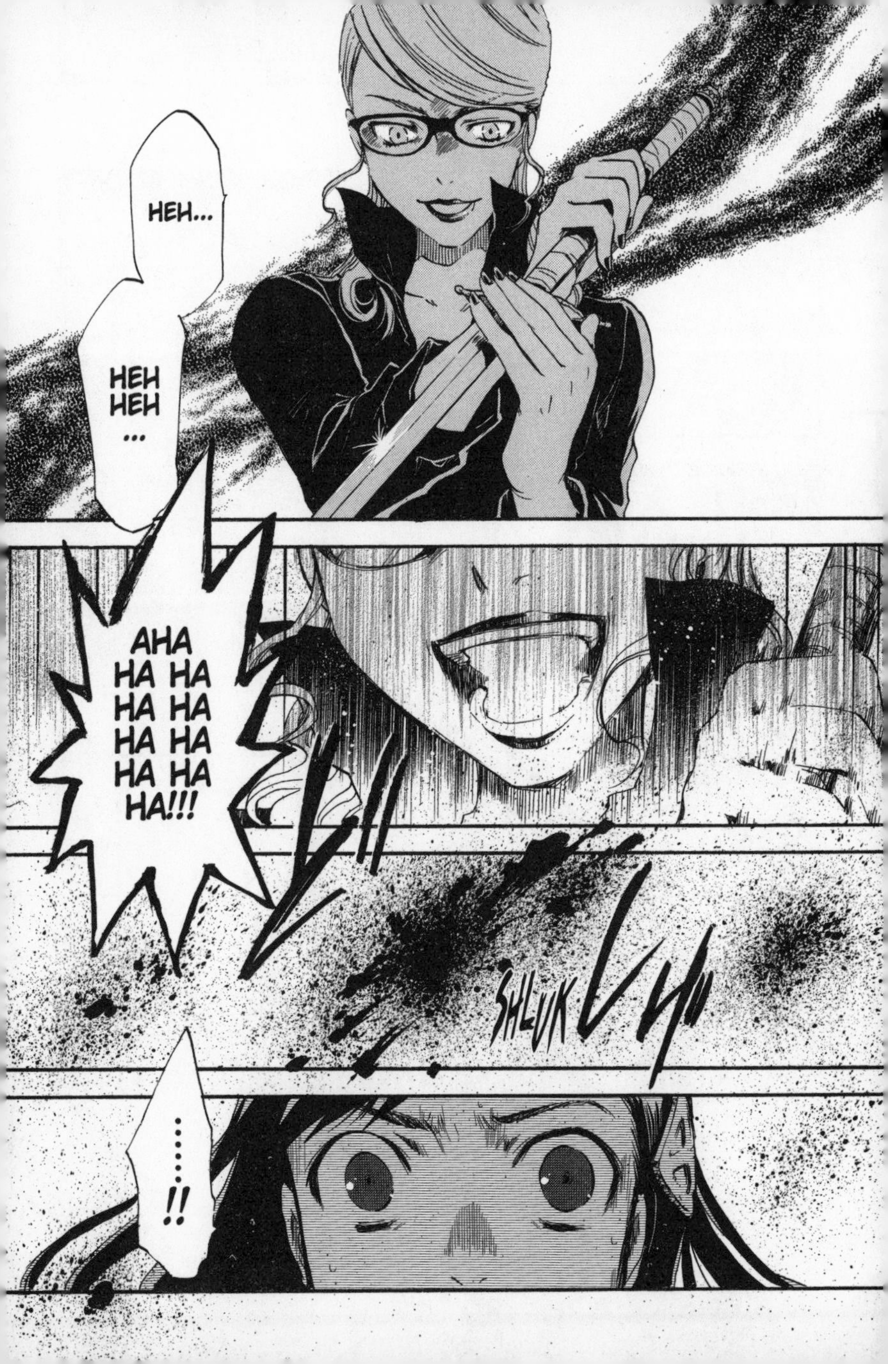
HEH...
HEH HEH ...
AHA HA HA HA HA HA HA HA HA HA!!!
SHLUK
......!!

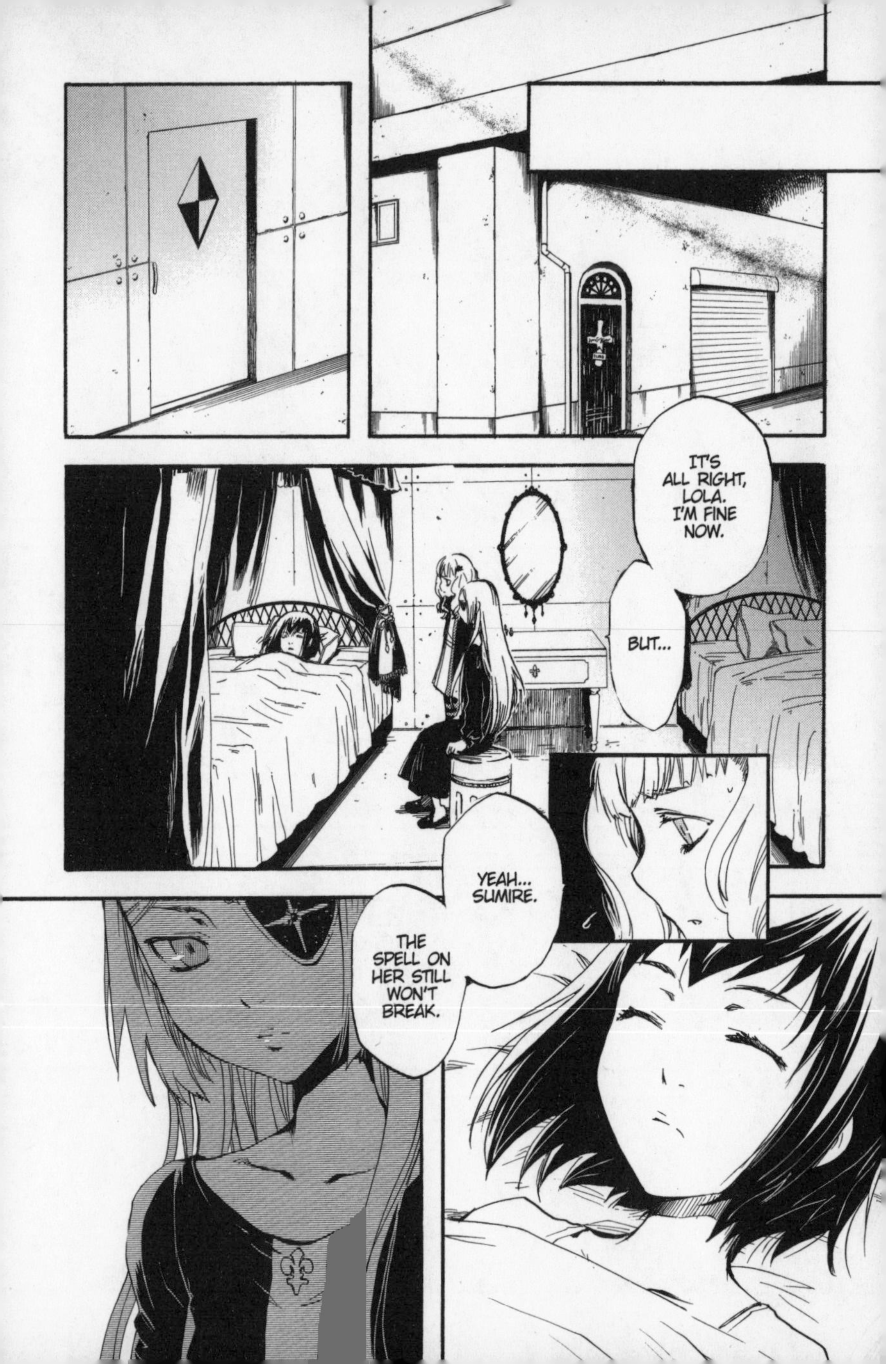
IT'S ALL RIGHT, LOLA. I'M FINE NOW.
BUT...
YEAH... SUMIRE.
THE SPELL ON HER STILL WON'T BREAK.

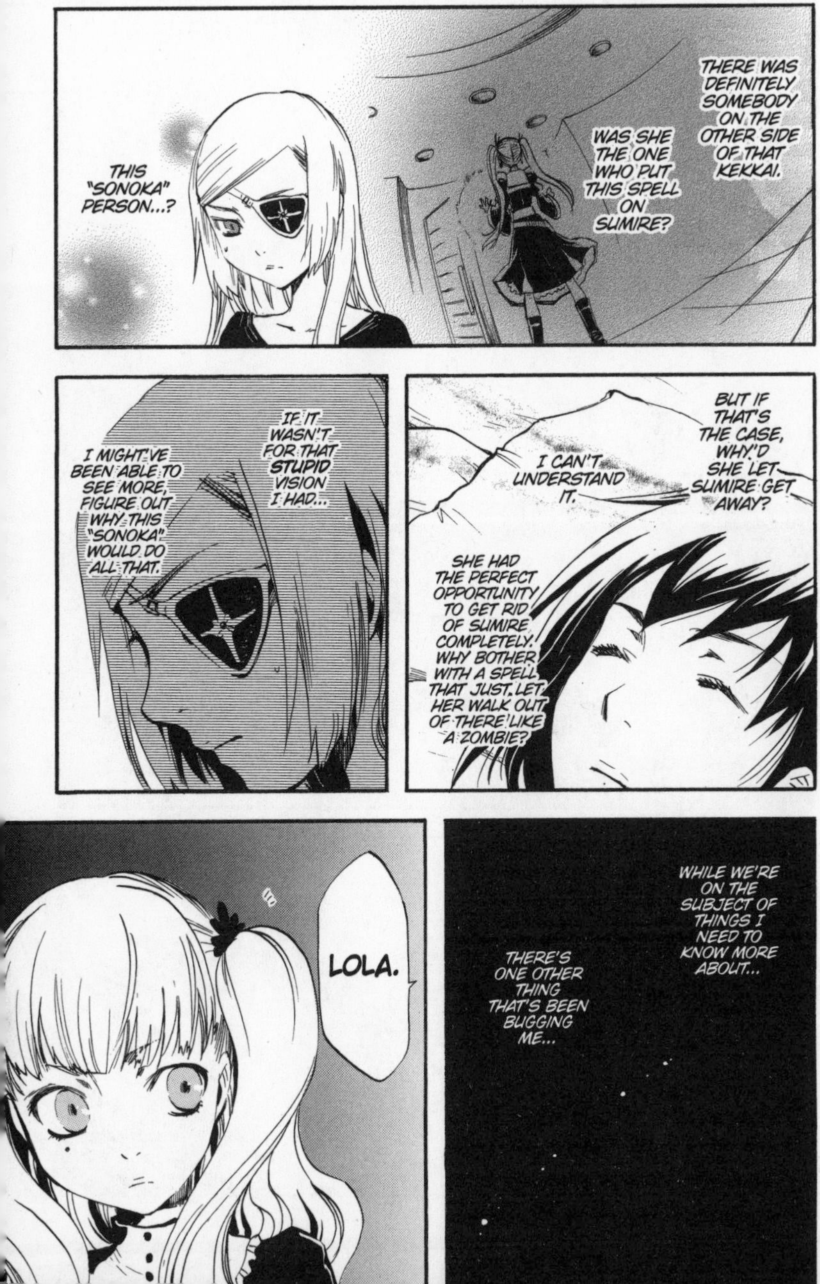
THERE WAS DEFINITELY SOMEBODY ON THE OTHER SIDE OF THAT KEKKAI.
WAS SHE THE ONE WHO PUT THIS SPELL ON SUMIRE?
THIS "SONOKA" PERSON...?
BUT IF THAT'S THE CASE, WHY'D SHE LET SUMIRE GET AWAY?
I CAN'T UNDERSTAND IT.
SHE HAD THE PERFECT OPPORTUNITY TO GET RID OF SUMIRE COMPLETELY. WHY BOTHER WITH A SPELL THAT JUST LET HER WALK OUT OF THERE LIKE A ZOMBIE?
IF IT WASN'T FOR THAT **STUPID** VISION I HAD...
I MIGHT'VE BEEN ABLE TO SEE MORE, FIGURE OUT WHY THIS "SONOKA" WOULD DO ALL THAT.
WHILE WE'RE ON THE SUBJECT OF THINGS I NEED TO KNOW MORE ABOUT...
THERE'S ONE OTHER THING THAT'S BEEN BUGGING ME...
LOLA.

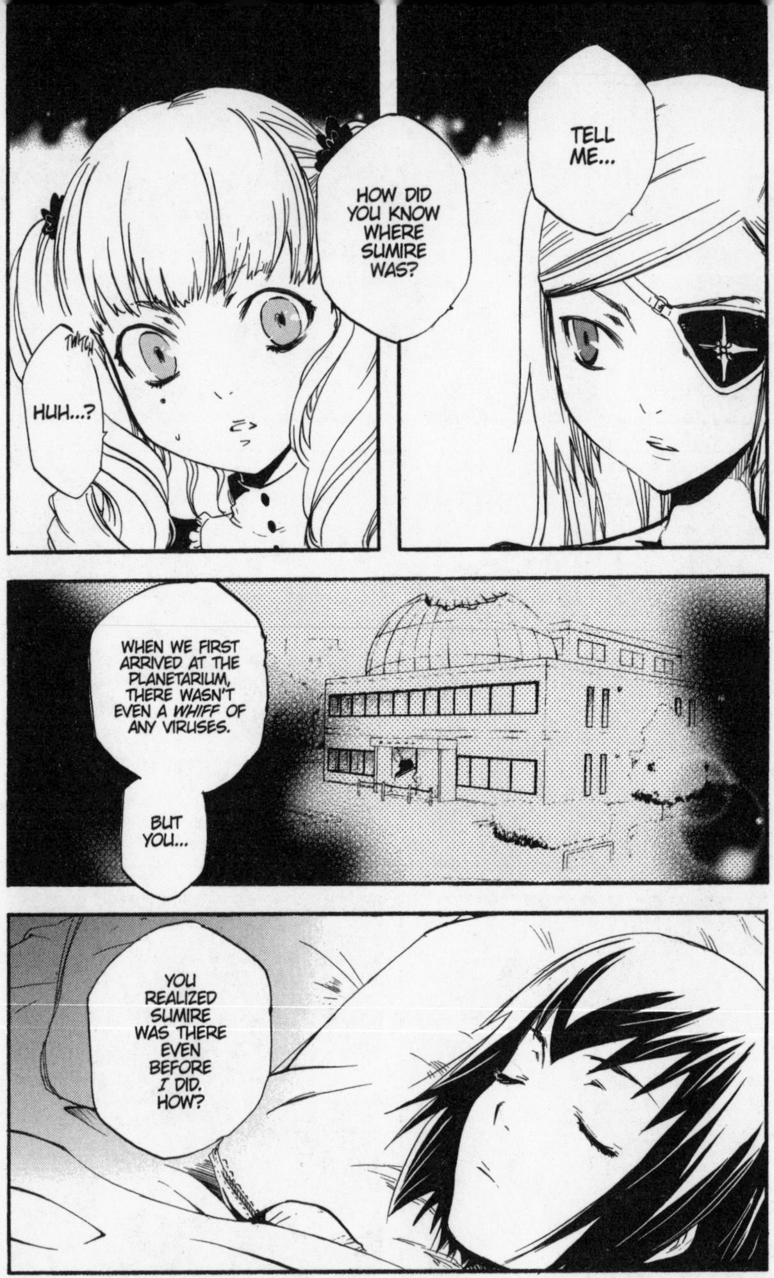
TELL ME...
HOW DID YOU KNOW WHERE SUMIRE WAS?
TWITCH
HUH...?
WHEN WE FIRST ARRIVED AT THE PLANETARIUM, THERE WASN'T EVEN A *WHIFF* OF ANY VIRUSES.
BUT YOU...
YOU REALIZED SUMIRE WAS THERE EVEN BEFORE *I* DID. HOW?

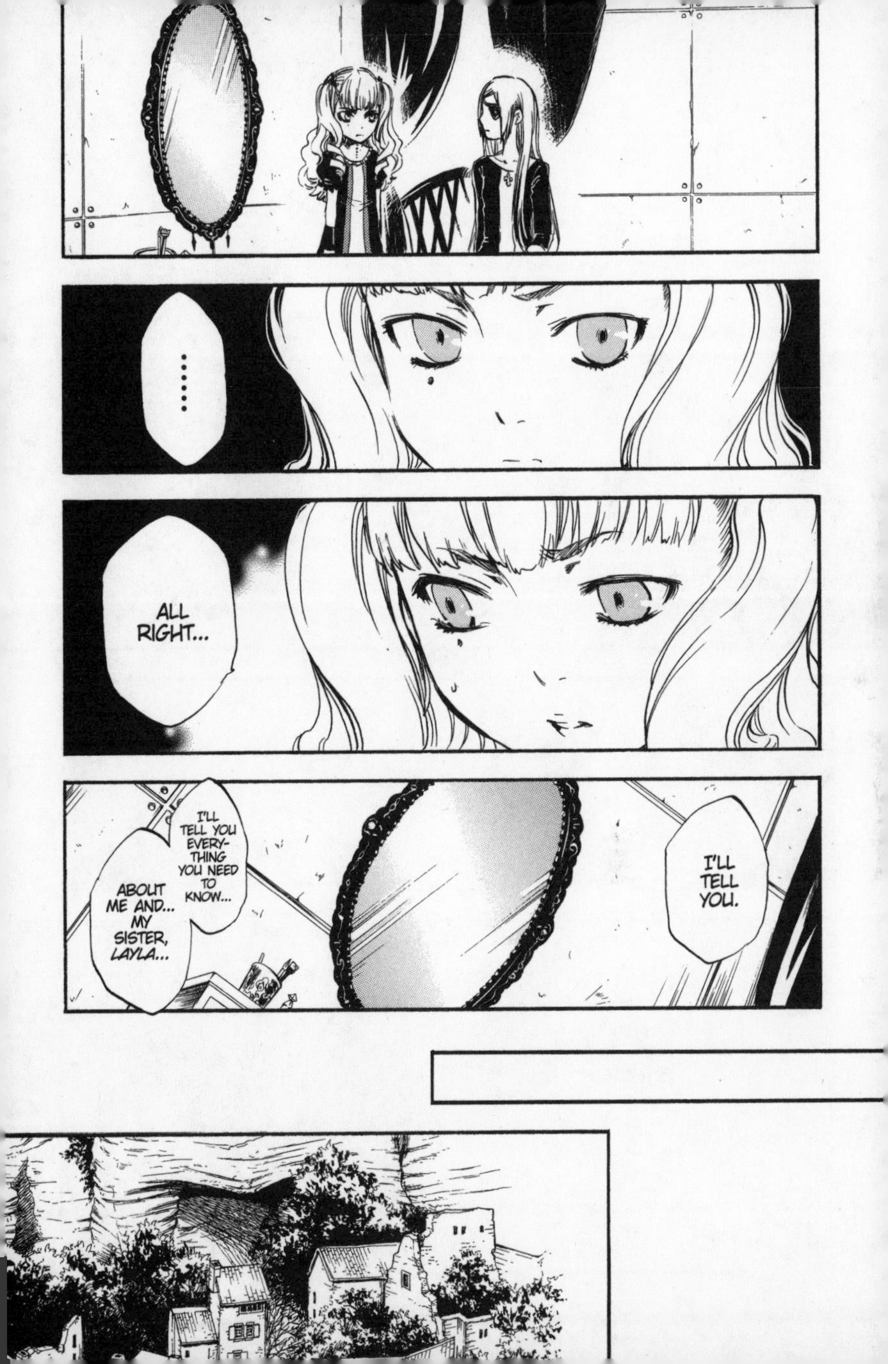
......
ALL RIGHT...
I'LL TELL YOU.
I'LL TELL YOU EVERYTHING YOU NEED TO KNOW...
ABOUT ME AND... MY SISTER, *LAYLA*...

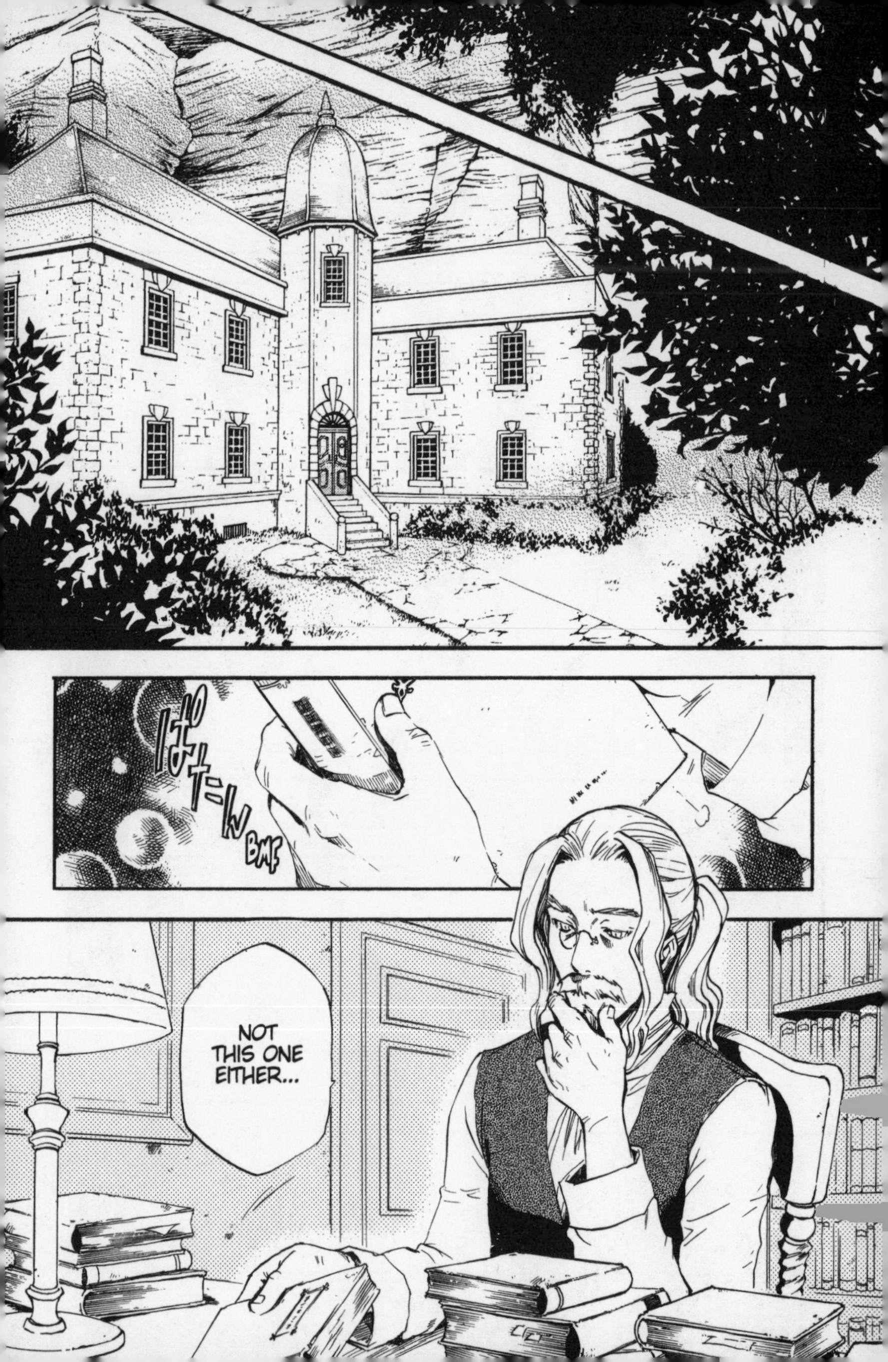
ぱたーん
BMF
NOT THIS ONE EITHER...

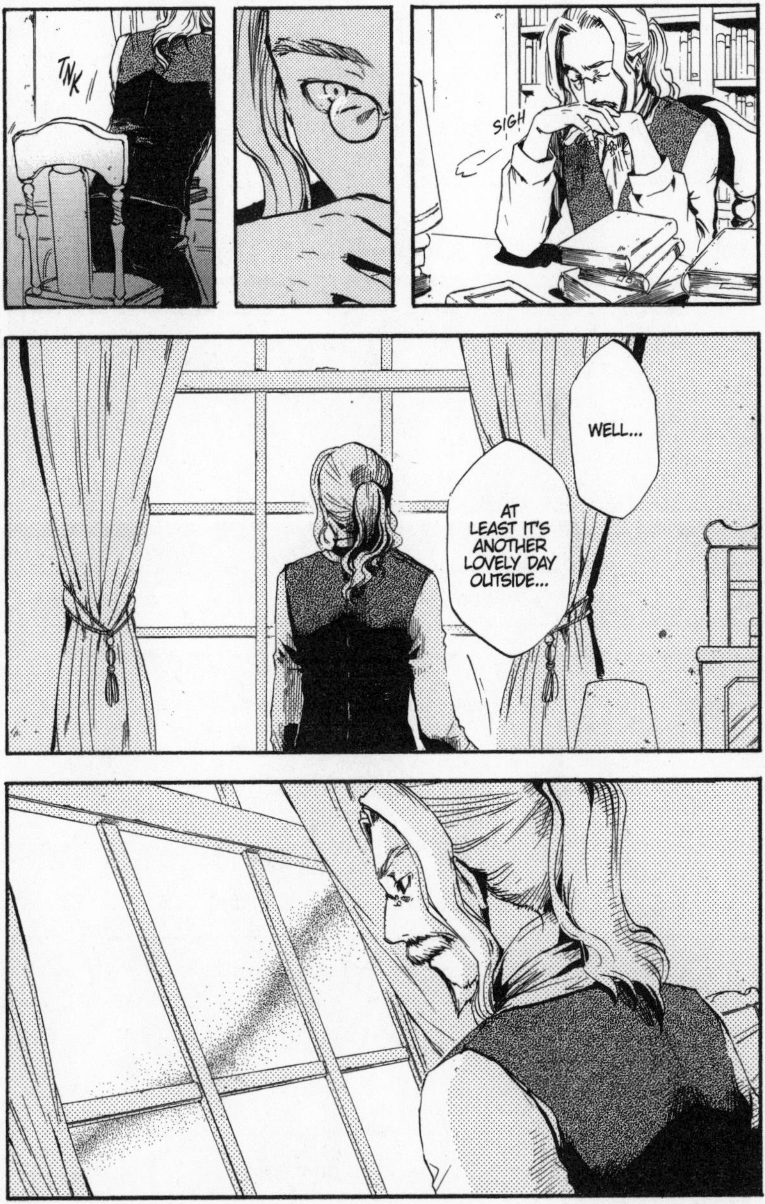
SIGH
TNK
WELL...
AT LEAST IT'S ANOTHER LOVELY DAY OUTSIDE...

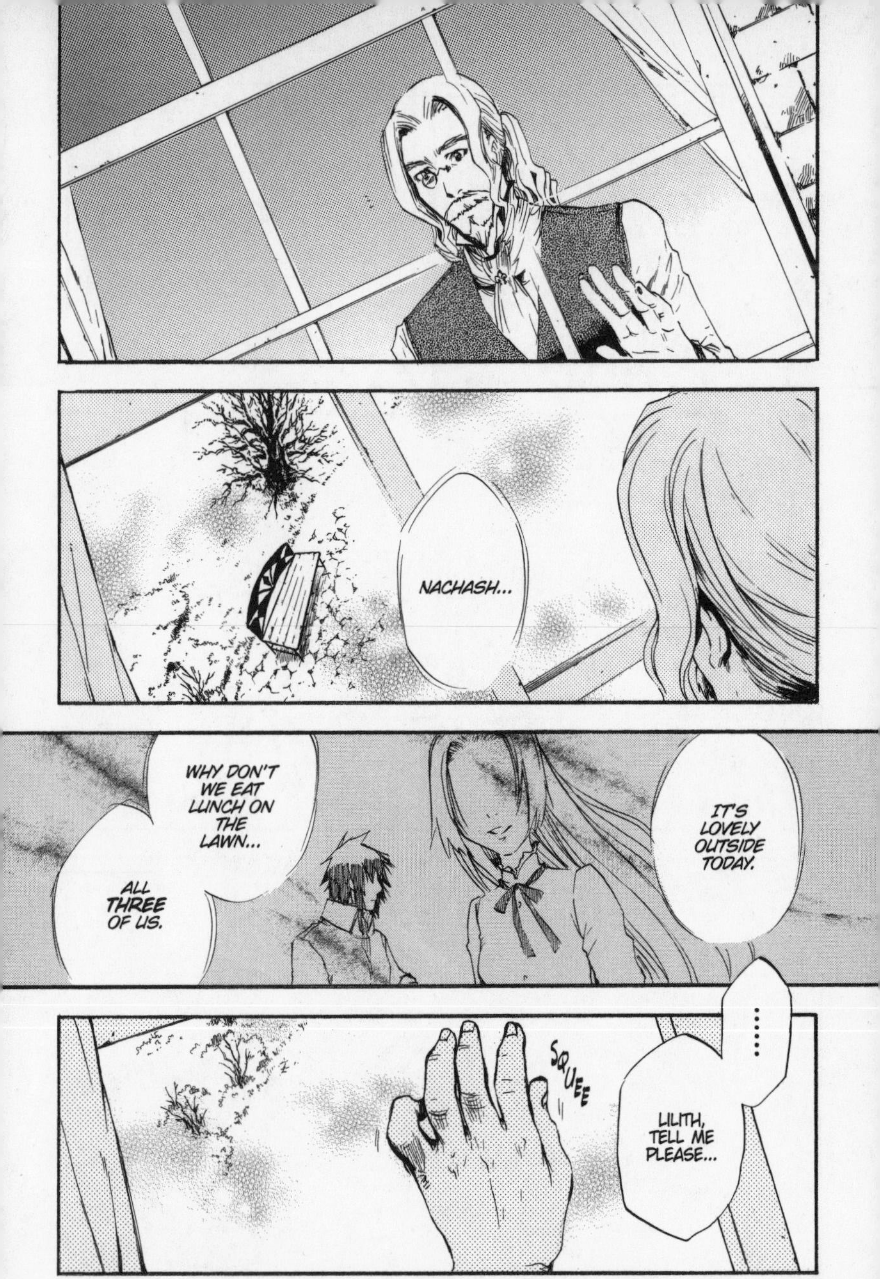
NACHASH...
IT'S LOVELY OUTSIDE TODAY.
WHY DON'T WE EAT LUNCH ON THE LAWN...
ALL THREE OF US.
......
SQUEE
LILITH, TELL ME PLEASE...

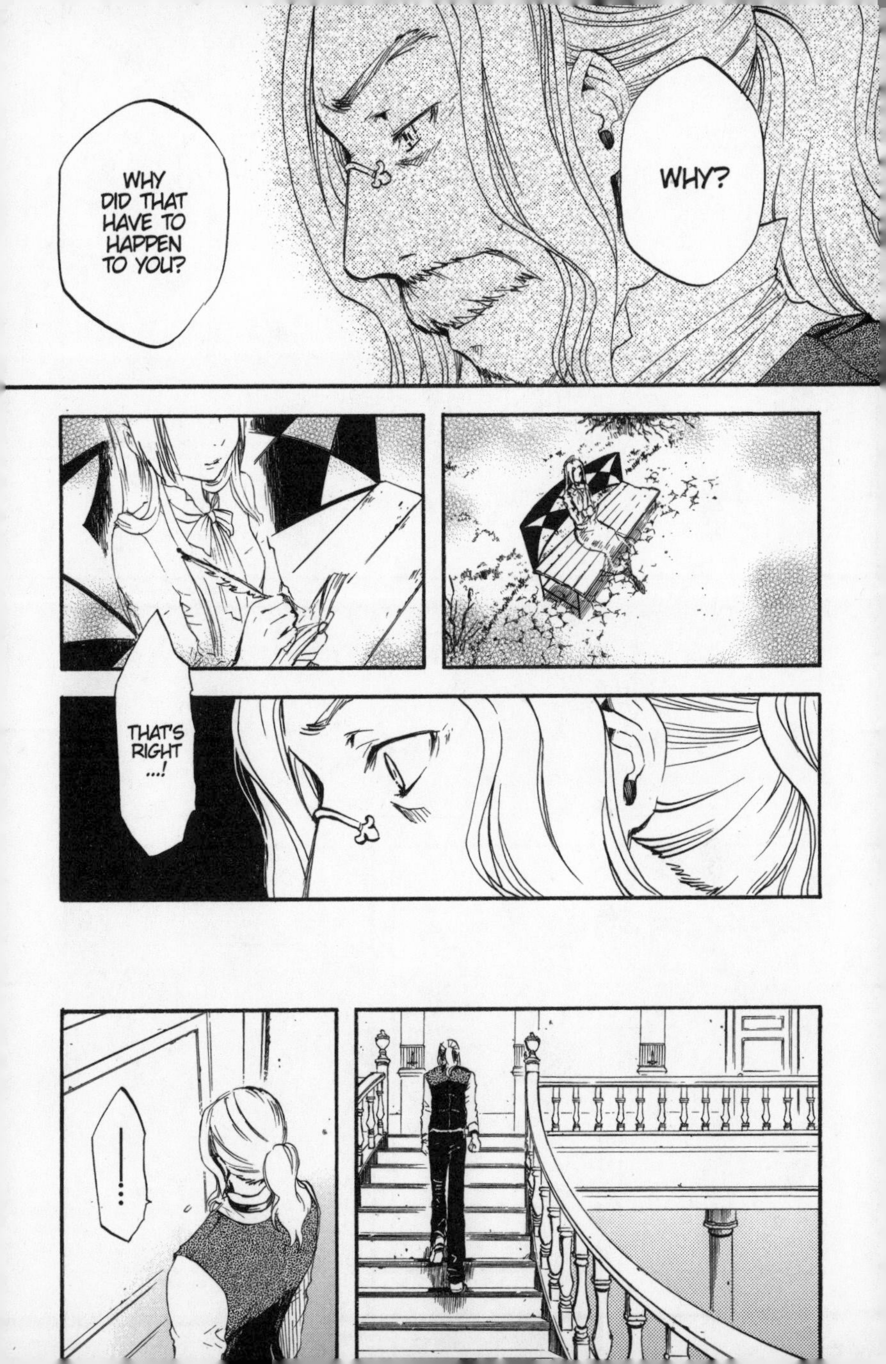
WHY?
WHY DID THAT HAVE TO HAPPEN TO YOU?
THAT'S RIGHT ...!
...!

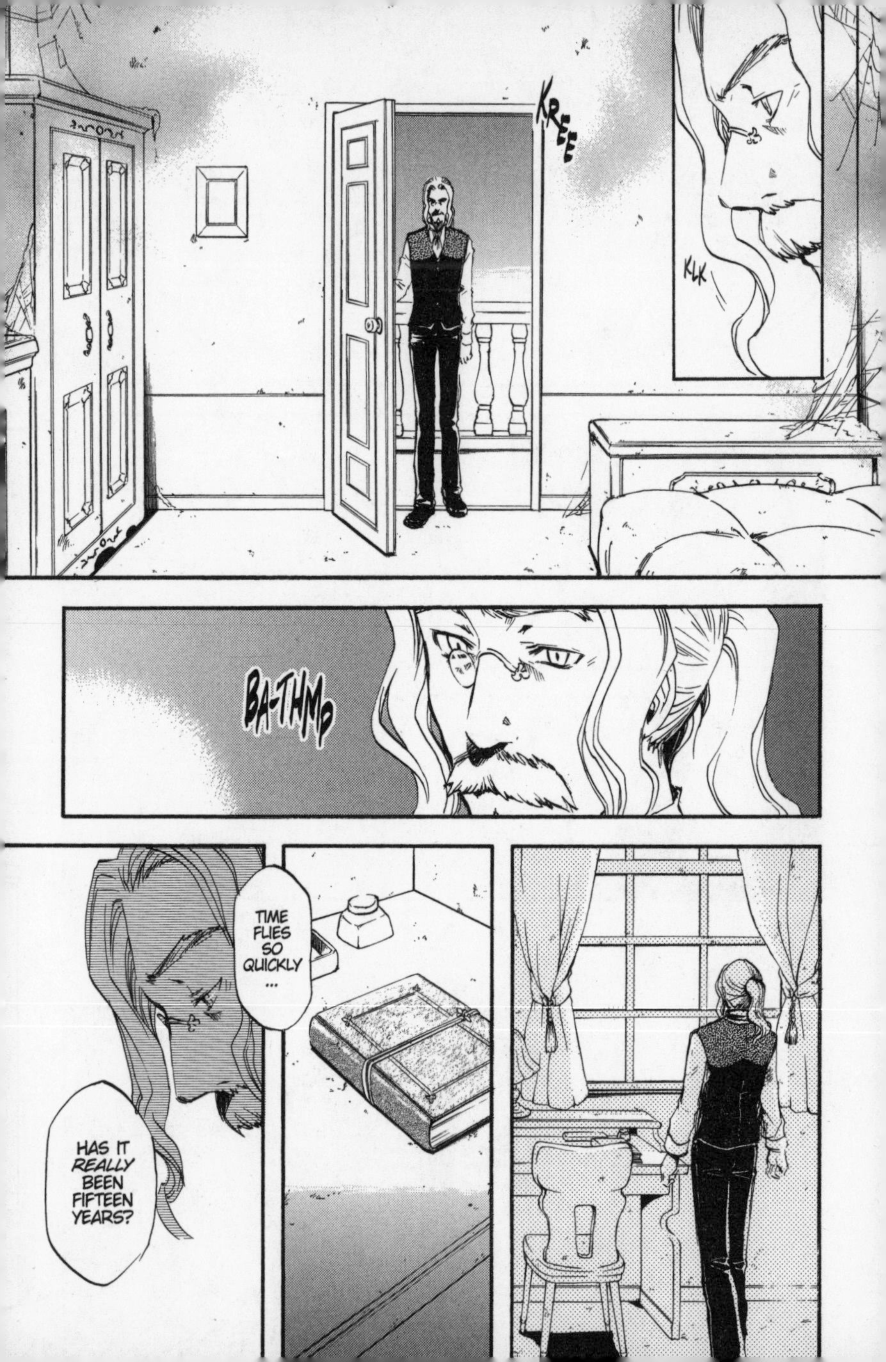
KREE
KLK
BA-THMP
TIME FLIES SO QUICKLY ...
HAS IT *REALLY* BEEN FIFTEEN YEARS?

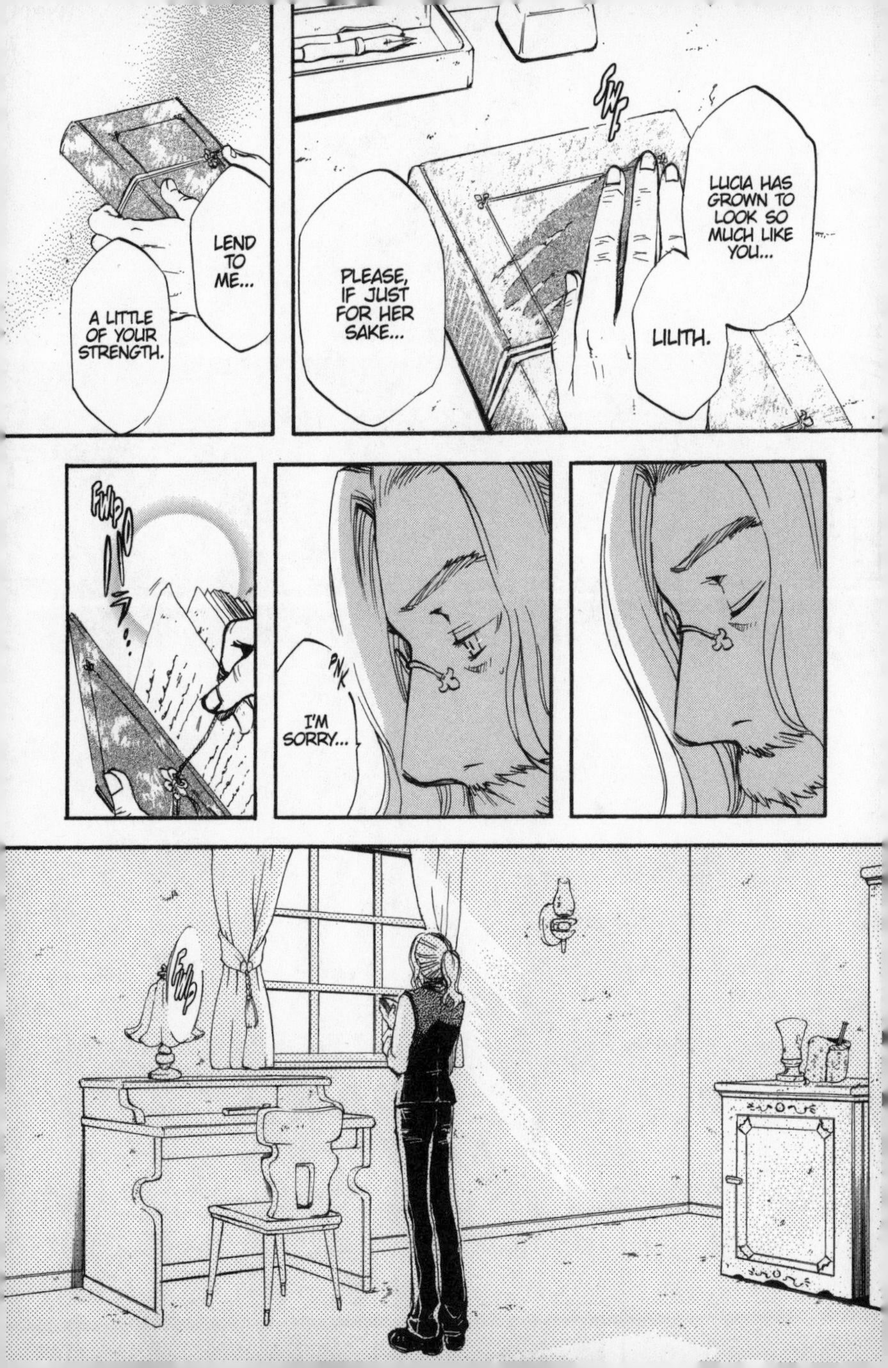
LUCIA HAS GROWN TO LOOK SO MUCH LIKE YOU...
LILITH.
PLEASE, IF JUST FOR HER SAKE...
LEND TO ME...
A LITTLE OF YOUR STRENGTH.
PNK
I'M SORRY...

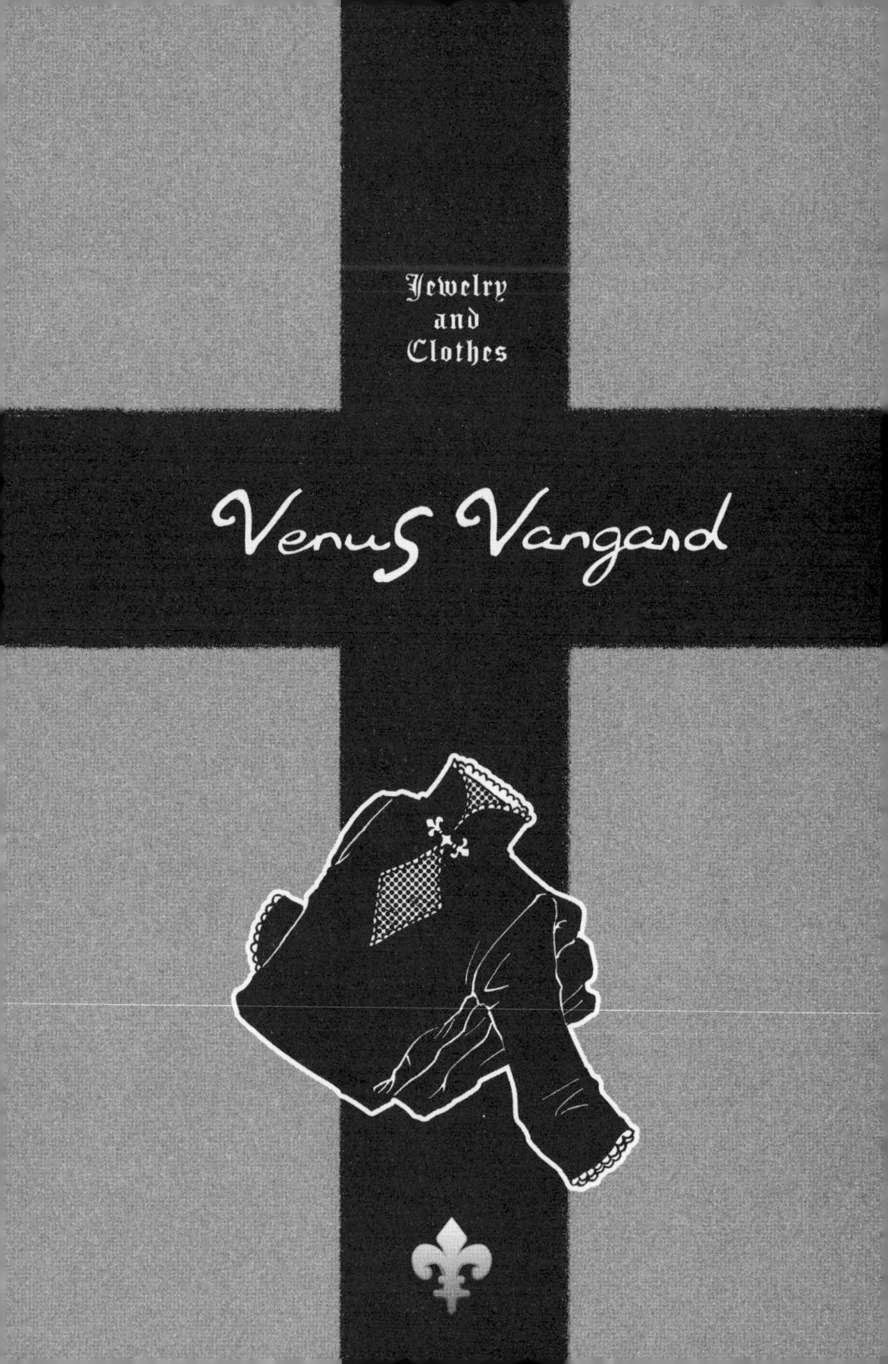
Jewelry
and
Clothes
Venus Vangard

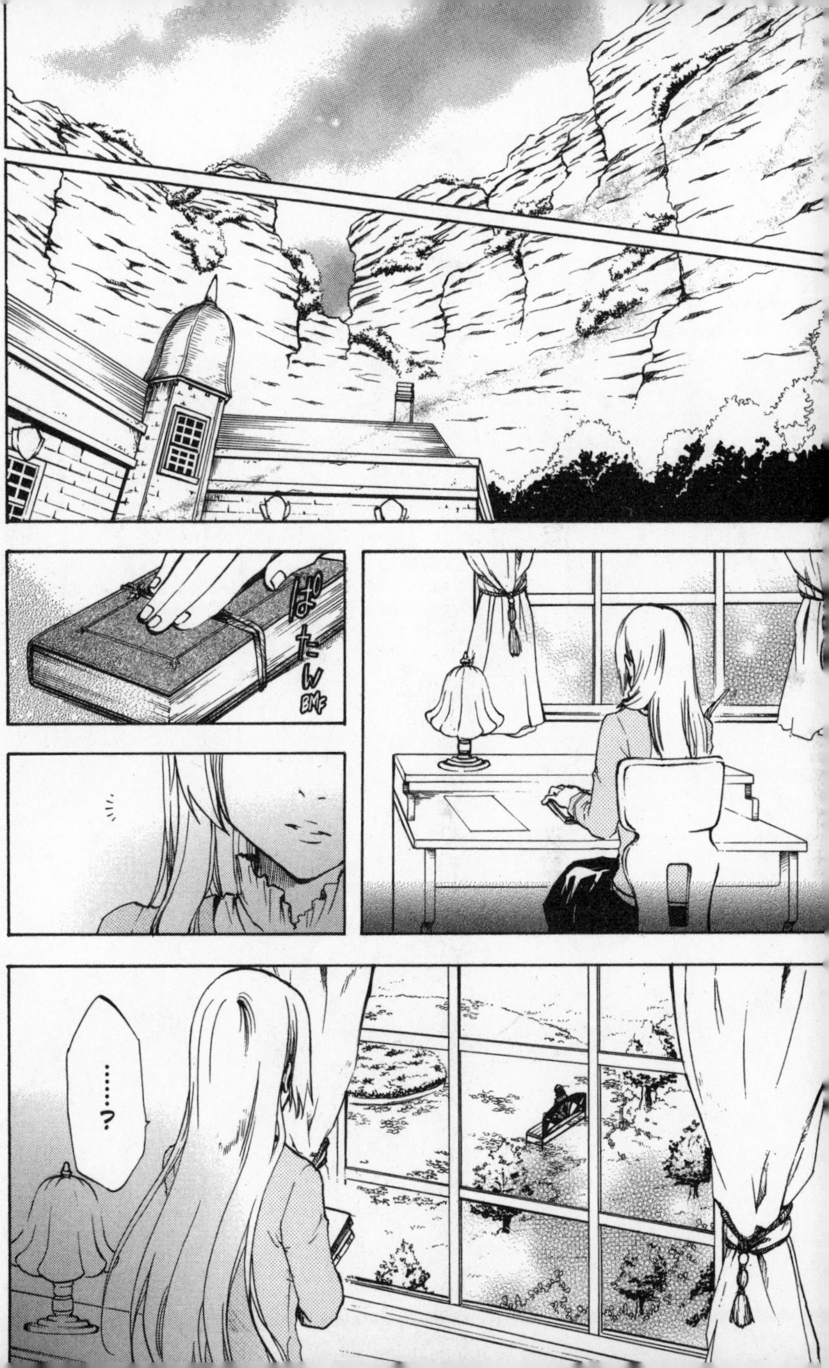
ぱたん
BMF
……っ

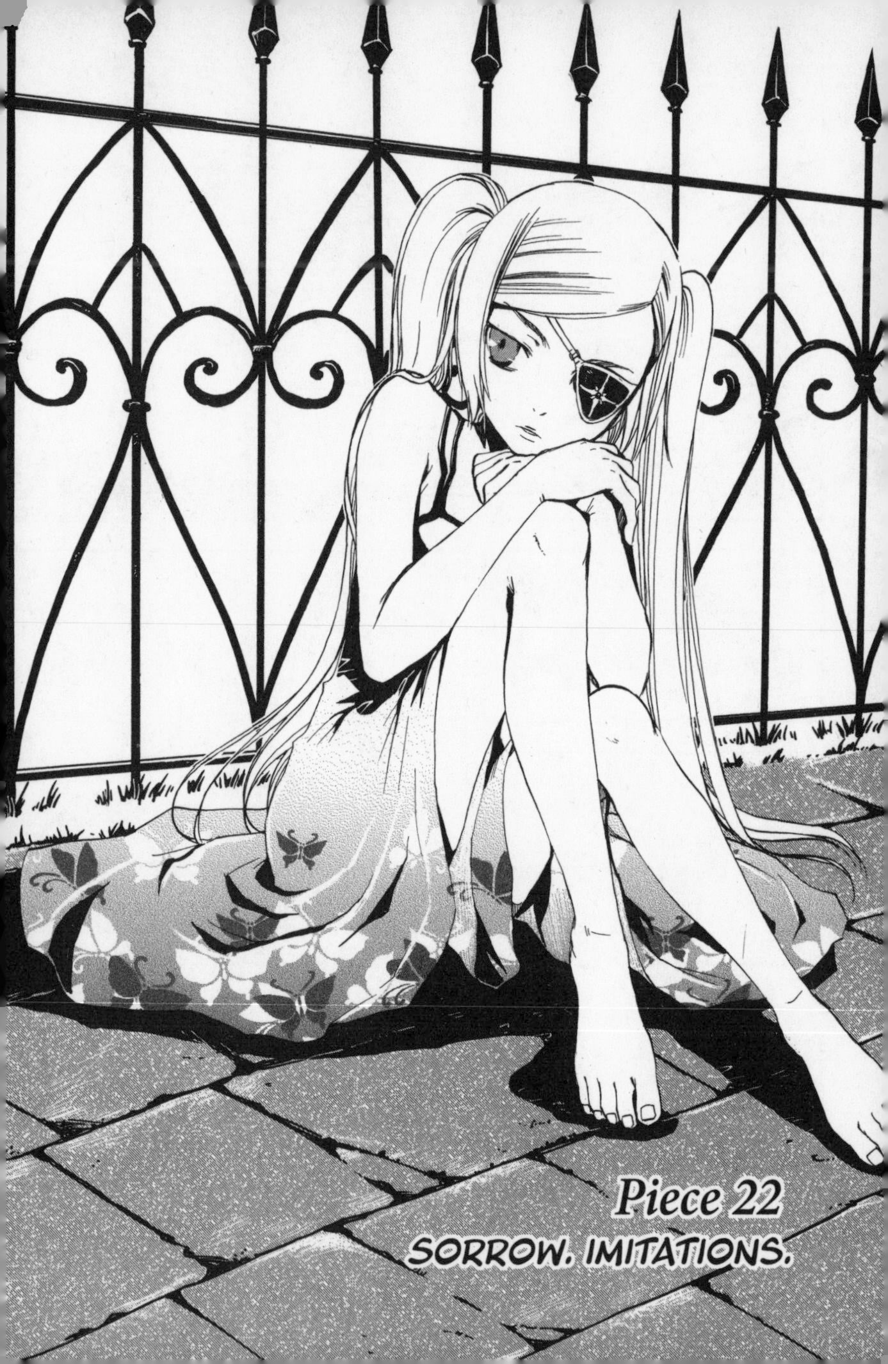
Piece 22
SORROW. IMITATIONS.

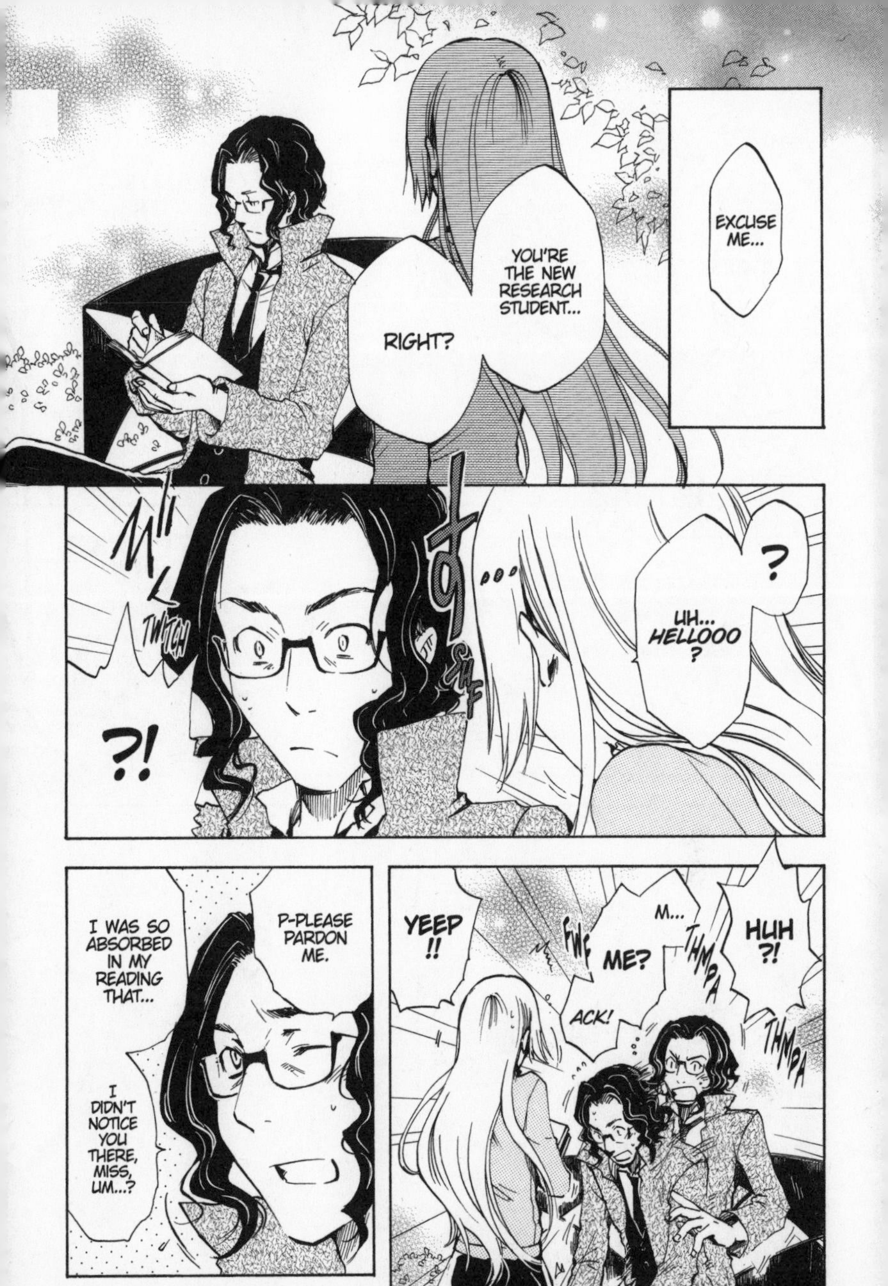
EXCUSE ME...
YOU'RE THE NEW RESEARCH STUDENT...
RIGHT?
?
UH... HELLOOO ?
...
SHF
TWITCH
?!
HUH ?!
THMPA
M...
ME?
FWG
YEEP !!
ACK!
THMPA
P-PLEASE PARDON ME.
I WAS SO ABSORBED IN MY READING THAT...
I DIDN'T NOTICE YOU THERE, MISS, UM...?

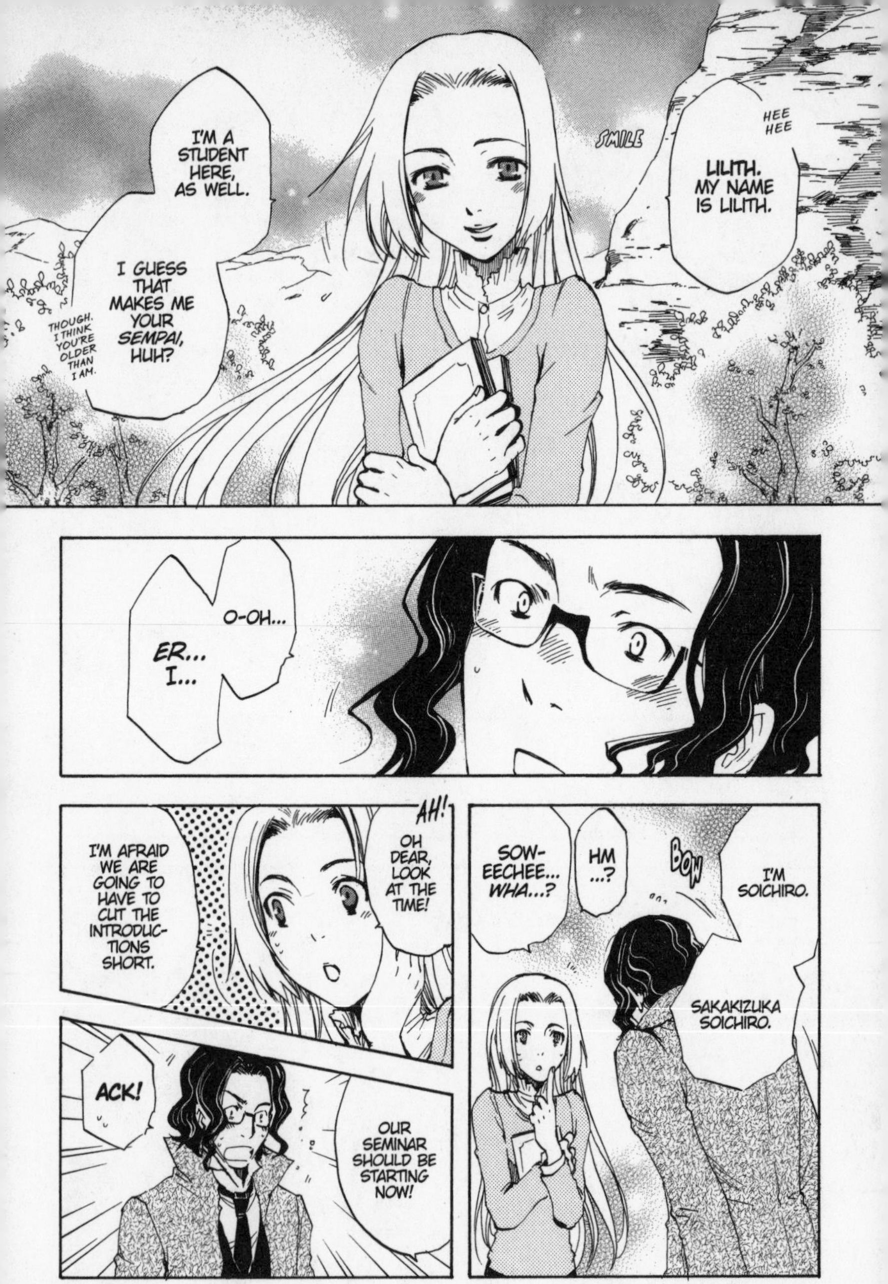
HEE HEE
LILITH. MY NAME IS LILITH.
SMILE
I'M A STUDENT HERE, AS WELL.
I GUESS THAT MAKES ME YOUR *SEMPAI*, HUH?
THOUGH. I THINK YOU'RE OLDER THAN I AM.
O-OH...
ER... I...
I'M SOICHIRO.
BOW
SAKAKIZUKA SOICHIRO.
HM ...?
SOW-EECHEE... *WHA...?*
AH!
OH DEAR, LOOK AT THE TIME!
I'M AFRAID WE ARE GOING TO HAVE TO CUT THE INTRODUCTIONS SHORT.
OUR SEMINAR SHOULD BE STARTING NOW!
ACK!

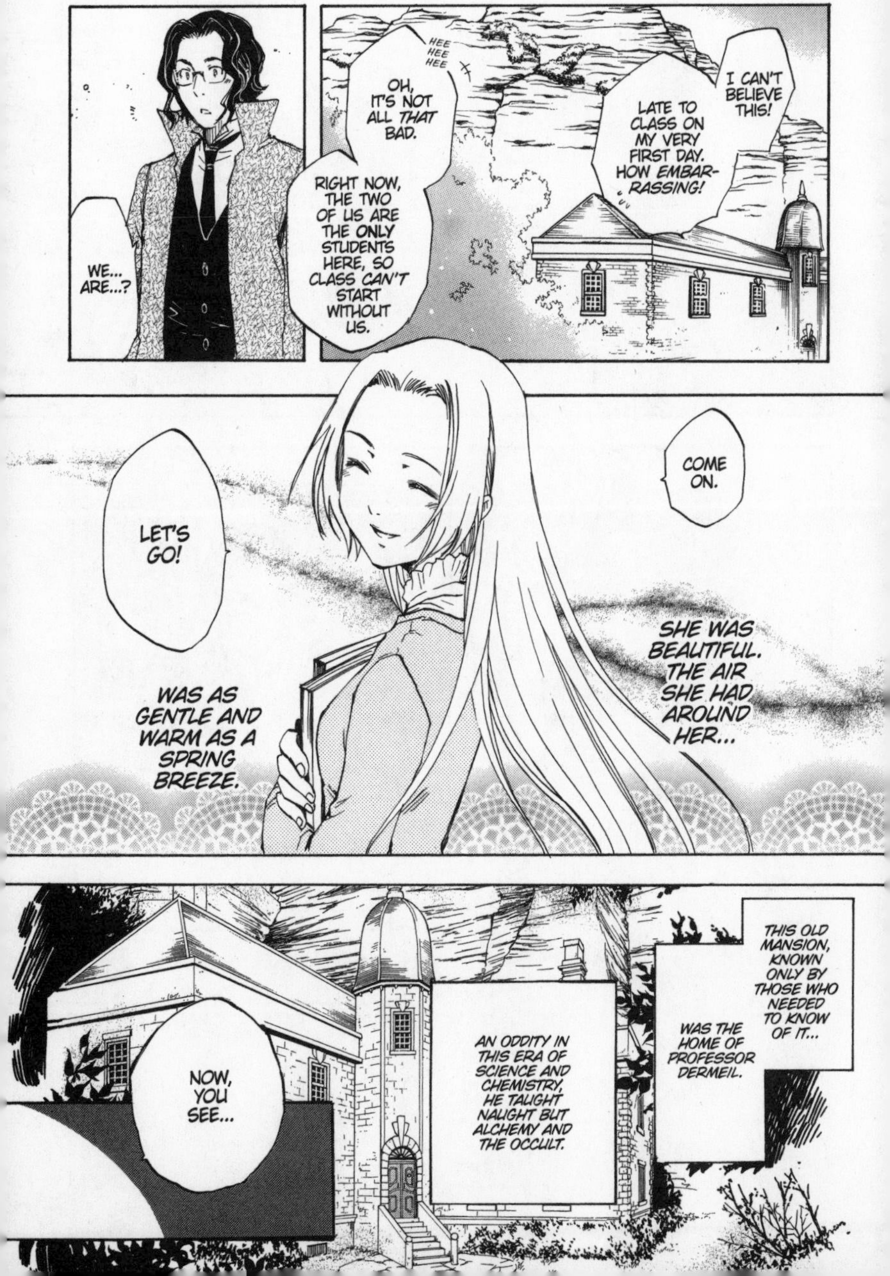
I CAN'T BELIEVE THIS!
LATE TO CLASS ON MY VERY FIRST DAY. HOW EMBARRASSING!
HEE HEE HEE
OH, IT'S NOT ALL *THAT* BAD.
RIGHT NOW, THE TWO OF US ARE THE ONLY STUDENTS HERE, SO CLASS *CAN'T* START WITHOUT US.
WE... ARE...?
COME ON.
LET'S GO!
SHE WAS BEAUTIFUL. THE AIR SHE HAD AROUND HER...
WAS AS GENTLE AND WARM AS A SPRING BREEZE.
THIS OLD MANSION, KNOWN ONLY BY THOSE WHO NEEDED TO KNOW OF IT...
WAS THE HOME OF PROFESSOR DERMEIL.
AN ODDITY IN THIS ERA OF SCIENCE AND CHEMISTRY, HE TAUGHT NAUGHT BUT ALCHEMY AND THE OCCULT.
NOW, YOU SEE...

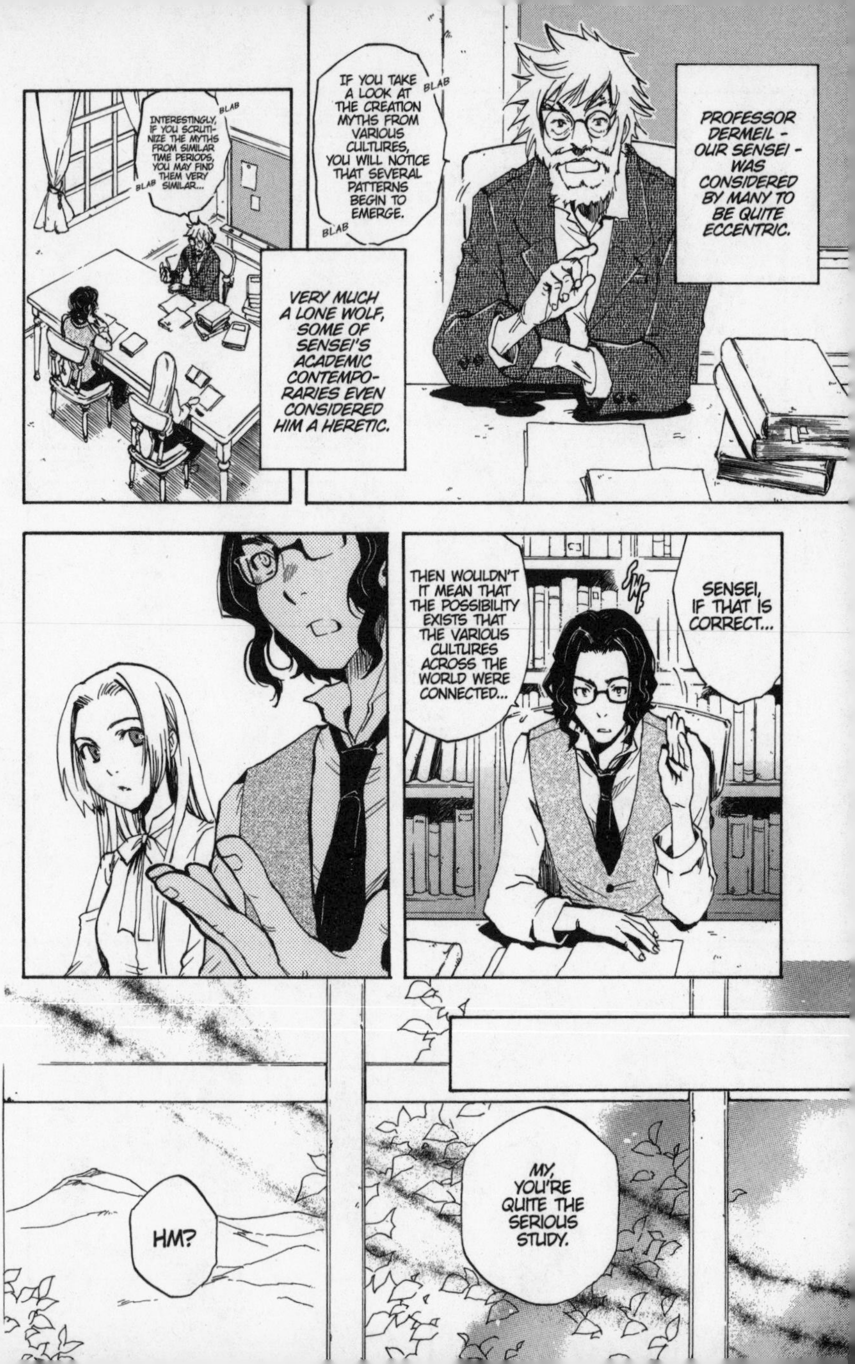
PROFESSOR DERMEIL - OUR SENSEI - WAS CONSIDERED BY MANY TO BE QUITE ECCENTRIC.
IF YOU TAKE A LOOK AT THE CREATION MYTHS FROM VARIOUS CULTURES, YOU WILL NOTICE THAT SEVERAL PATTERNS BEGIN TO EMERGE.
BLAB
BLAB
VERY MUCH A LONE WOLF, SOME OF SENSEI'S ACADEMIC CONTEMPORARIES EVEN CONSIDERED HIM A HERETIC.
INTERESTINGLY, IF YOU SCRUTINIZE THE MYTHS FROM SIMILAR TIME PERIODS, YOU MAY FIND THEM VERY SIMILAR...
BLAB
BLAB
SENSEI, IF THAT IS CORRECT...
THEN WOULDN'T IT MEAN THAT THE POSSIBILITY EXISTS THAT THE VARIOUS CULTURES ACROSS THE WORLD WERE CONNECTED...
MY, YOU'RE QUITE THE SERIOUS STUDY.
HM?

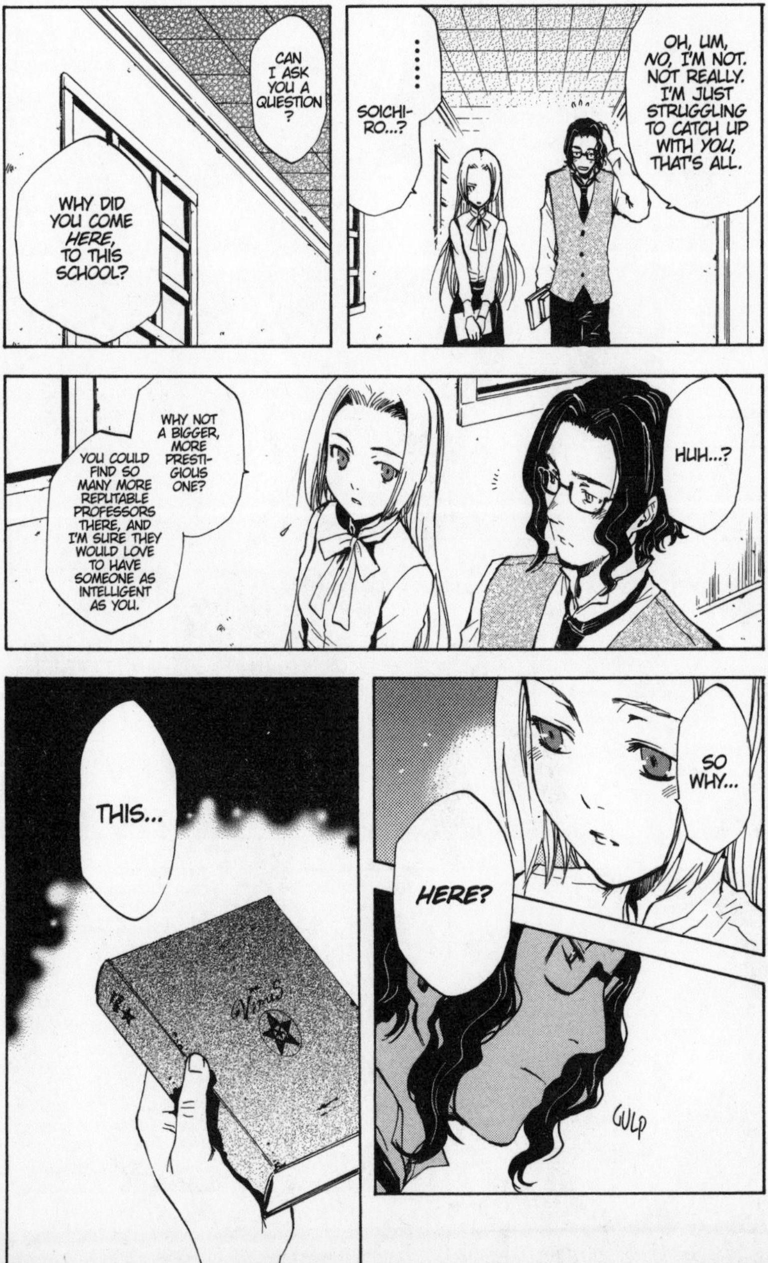
OH, UM, NO, I'M NOT. NOT REALLY. I'M JUST STRUGGLING TO CATCH UP WITH YOU, THAT'S ALL.
......
SOICHI-RO...?
CAN I ASK YOU A QUESTION?
WHY DID YOU COME HERE, TO THIS SCHOOL?
HUH...?
WHY NOT A BIGGER, MORE PRESTI-GIOUS ONE?
YOU COULD FIND SO MANY MORE REPUTABLE PROFESSORS THERE, AND I'M SURE THEY WOULD LOVE TO HAVE SOMEONE AS INTELLIGENT AS YOU.
SO WHY...
HERE?
GULP
THIS...

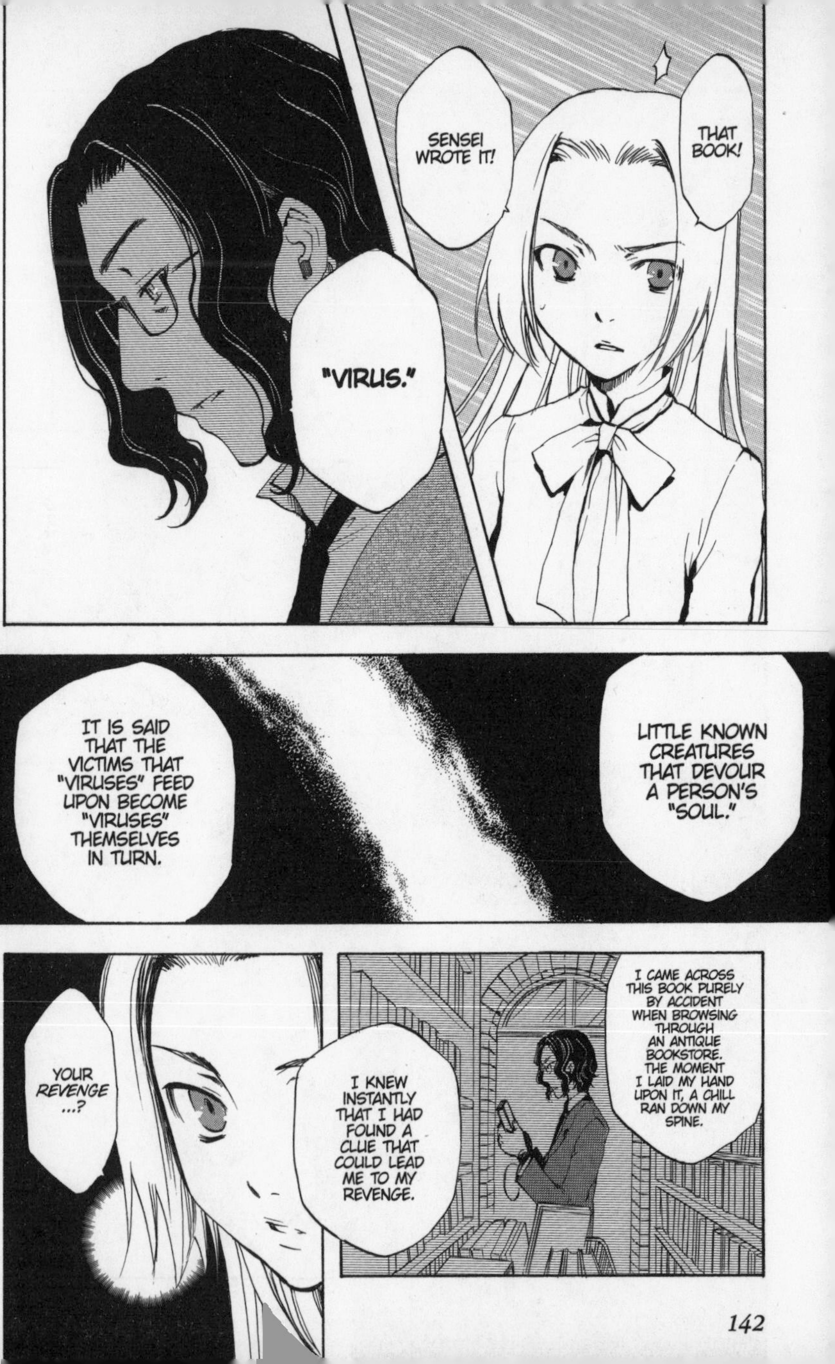
THAT BOOK!
SENSEI WROTE IT!
"VIRUS."
LITTLE KNOWN CREATURES THAT DEVOUR A PERSON'S "SOUL."
IT IS SAID THAT THE VICTIMS THAT "VIRUSES" FEED UPON BECOME "VIRUSES" THEMSELVES IN TURN.
I CAME ACROSS THIS BOOK PURELY BY ACCIDENT WHEN BROWSING THROUGH AN ANTIQUE BOOKSTORE. THE MOMENT I LAID MY HAND UPON IT, A CHILL RAN DOWN MY SPINE.
I KNEW INSTANTLY THAT I HAD FOUND A CLUE THAT COULD LEAD ME TO MY REVENGE.
YOUR REVENGE ...?

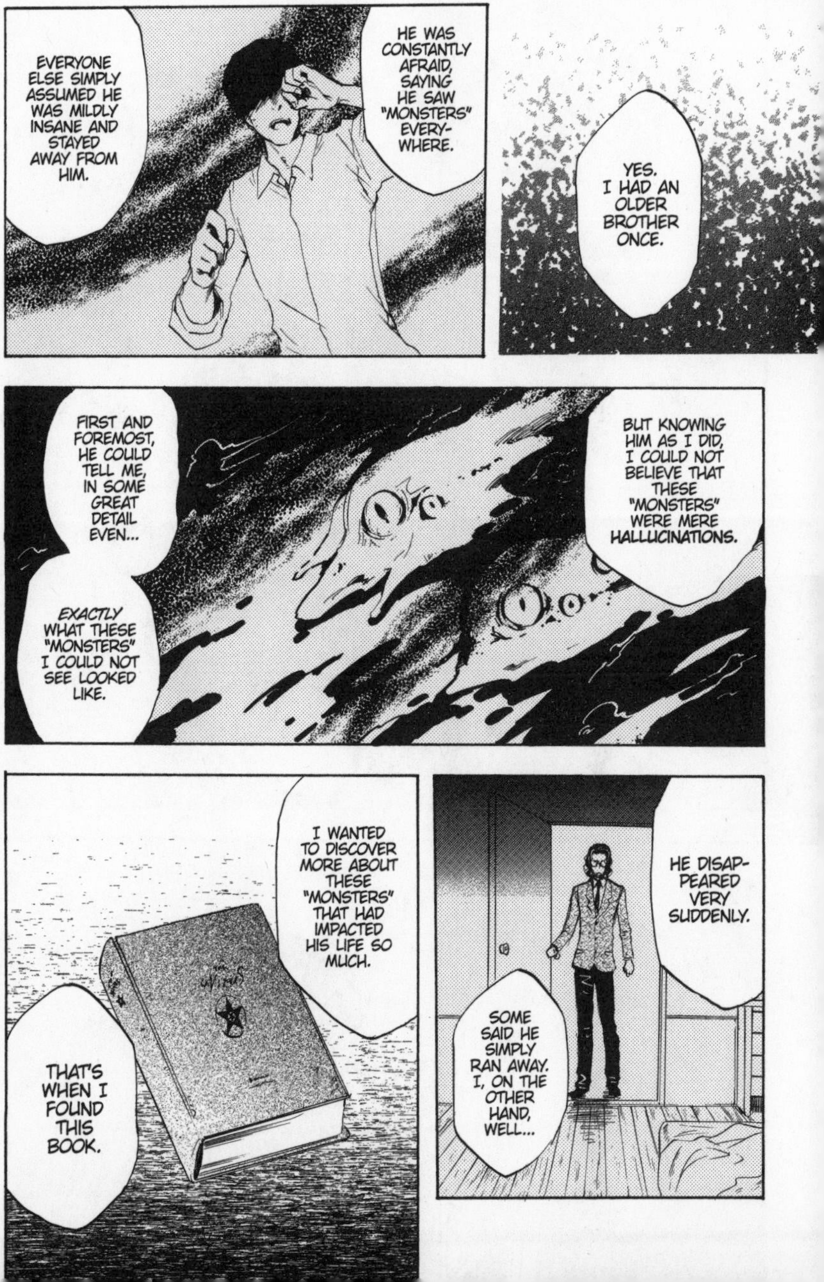
YES. I HAD AN OLDER BROTHER ONCE.
HE WAS CONSTANTLY AFRAID, SAYING HE SAW "MONSTERS" EVERY-WHERE.
EVERYONE ELSE SIMPLY ASSUMED HE WAS MILDLY INSANE AND STAYED AWAY FROM HIM.
BUT KNOWING HIM AS I DID, I COULD NOT BELIEVE THAT THESE "MONSTERS" WERE MERE HALLUCINATIONS.
FIRST AND FOREMOST, HE COULD TELL ME, IN SOME GREAT DETAIL EVEN...
EXACTLY WHAT THESE "MONSTERS" I COULD NOT SEE LOOKED LIKE.
HE DISAP-PEARED VERY SUDDENLY.
SOME SAID HE SIMPLY RAN AWAY. I, ON THE OTHER HAND, WELL...
I WANTED TO DISCOVER MORE ABOUT THESE "MONSTERS" THAT HAD IMPACTED HIS LIFE SO MUCH.
THAT'S WHEN I FOUND THIS BOOK.

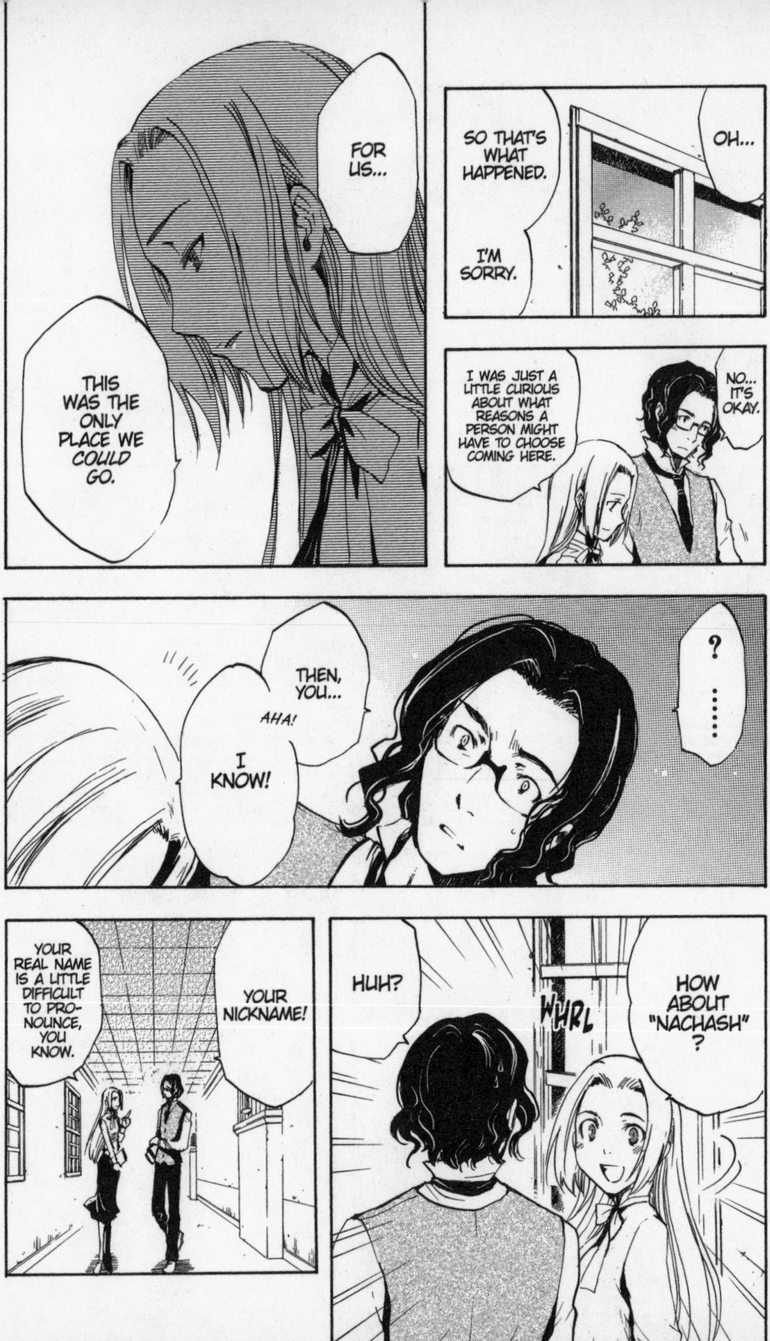
OH...
SO THAT'S WHAT HAPPENED.
I'M SORRY.
NO... IT'S OKAY.
I WAS JUST A LITTLE CURIOUS ABOUT WHAT REASONS A PERSON MIGHT HAVE TO CHOOSE COMING HERE.
FOR US...
THIS WAS THE ONLY PLACE WE COULD GO.
?
......
THEN, YOU...
AHA!
I KNOW!
HOW ABOUT "NACHASH"?
WHRL
HUH?
YOUR NICKNAME!
YOUR REAL NAME IS A LITTLE DIFFICULT TO PRONOUNCE, YOU KNOW.

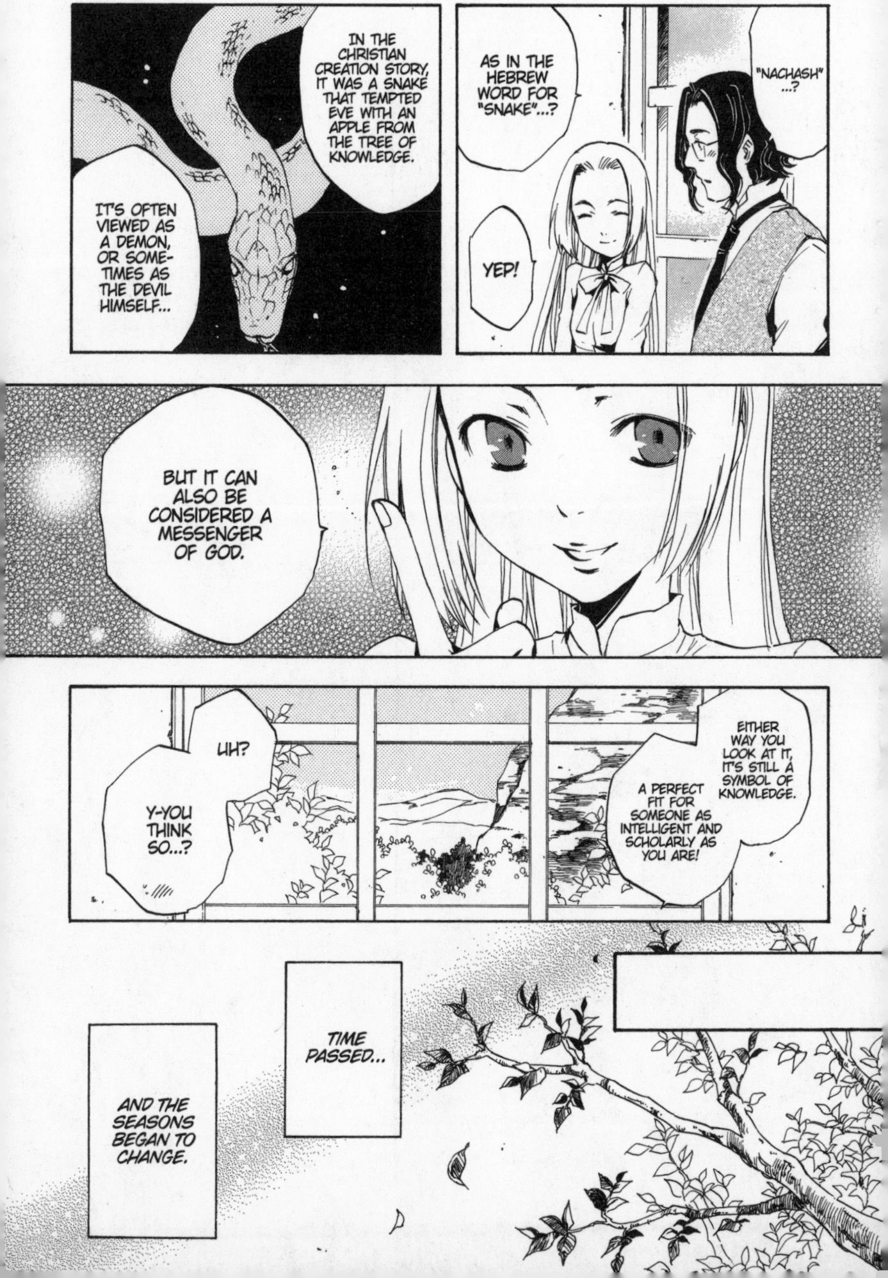
"NACHASH"...?
AS IN THE HEBREW WORD FOR "SNAKE"...?
YEP!
IN THE CHRISTIAN CREATION STORY, IT WAS A SNAKE THAT TEMPTED EVE WITH AN APPLE FROM THE TREE OF KNOWLEDGE.
IT'S OFTEN VIEWED AS A DEMON, OR SOME-TIMES AS THE DEVIL HIMSELF...
BUT IT CAN ALSO BE CONSIDERED A MESSENGER OF GOD.
EITHER WAY YOU LOOK AT IT, IT'S STILL A SYMBOL OF KNOWLEDGE.
A PERFECT FIT FOR SOMEONE AS INTELLIGENT AND SCHOLARLY AS YOU ARE!
UH?
Y-YOU THINK SO...?
TIME PASSED...
AND THE SEASONS BEGAN TO CHANGE.

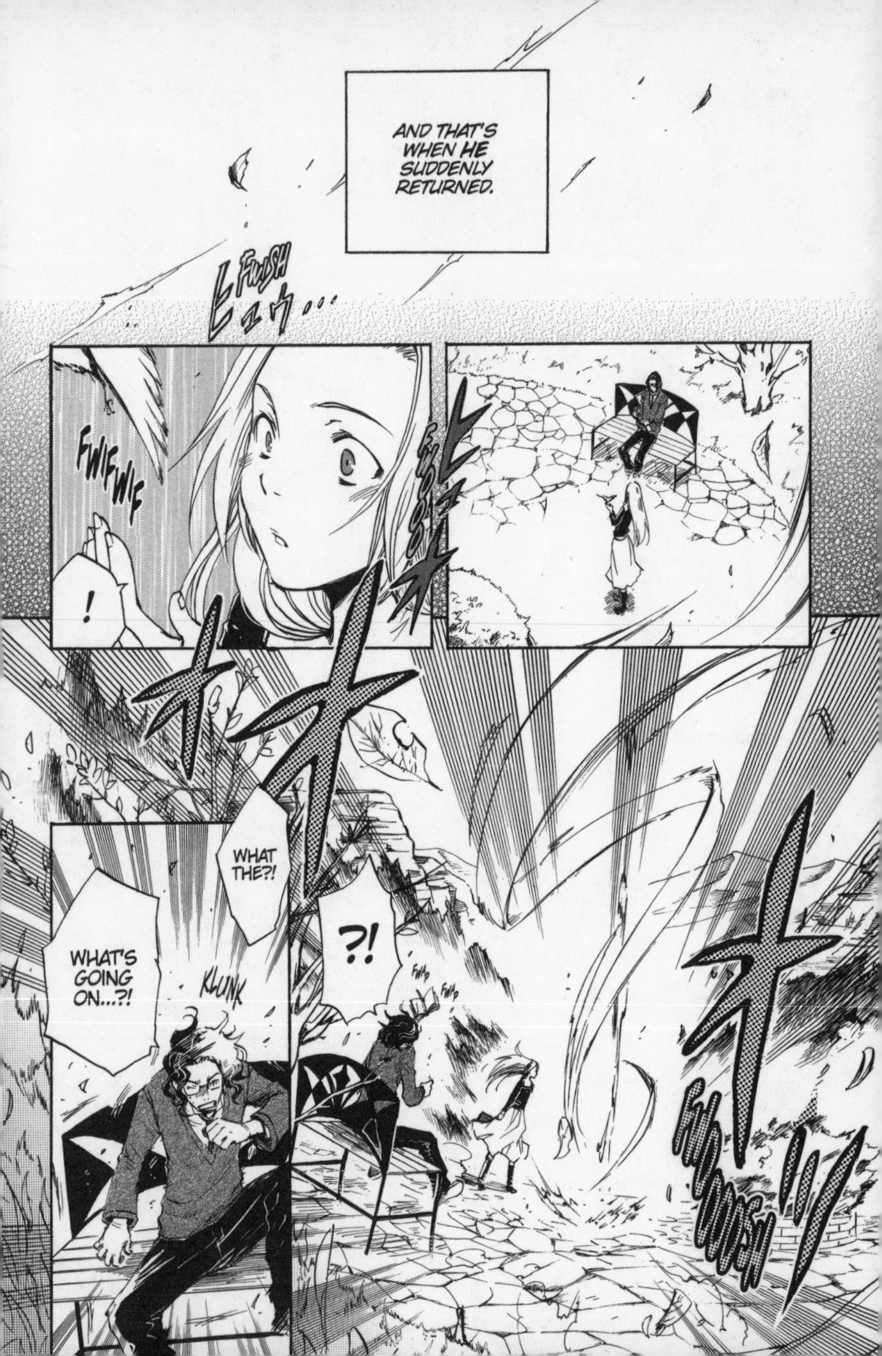
AND THAT'S WHEN HE SUDDENLY RETURNED.
FWISH
ヒュウ...
FWIFWIF
!
?!
FWAP
FWAP
WHAT THE?!
WHAT'S GOING ON...?!
KLUNK

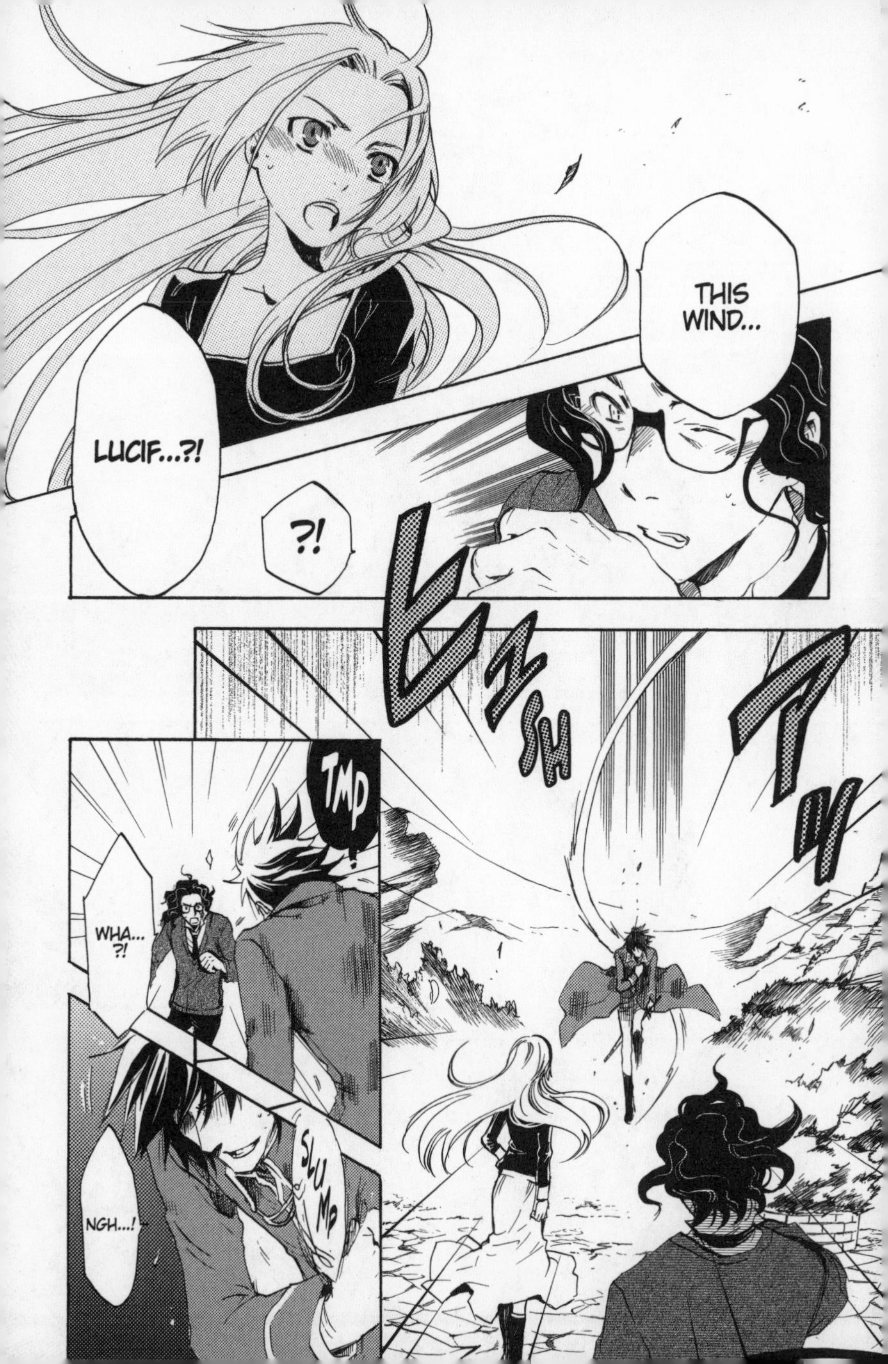
LUCIF...?!
THIS WIND...
?!
TMP
WHA... ?!
SLUMP
NGH...!

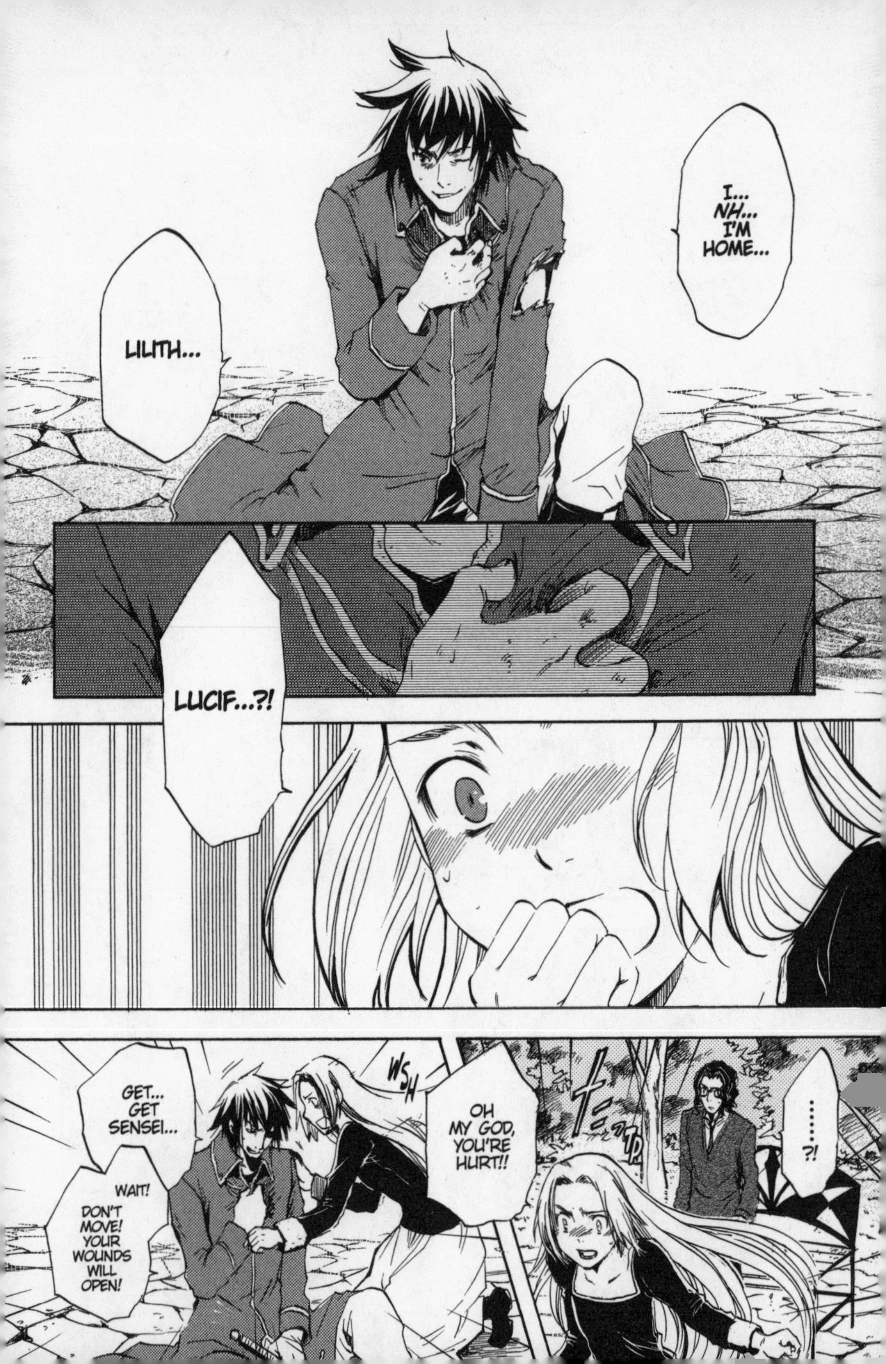
I... NH... I'M HOME...
LILITH...
LUCIF...?!
......?!
OH MY GOD, YOU'RE HURT!!
WSH
GET... GET SENSEI...
WAIT! DON'T MOVE! YOUR WOUNDS WILL OPEN!

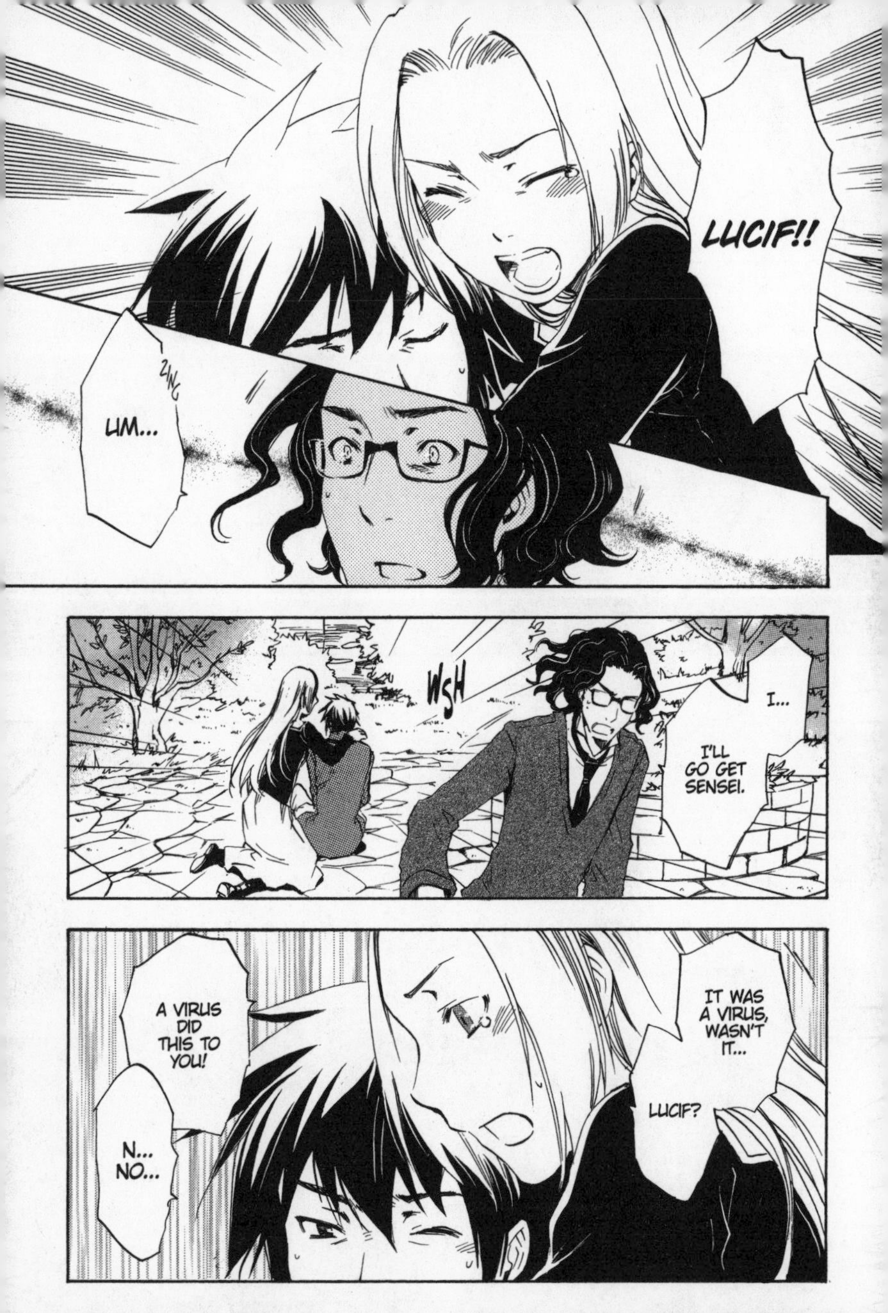
LUCIF!!
ZING
UM...
I...
I'LL GO GET SENSEI.
WSH
IT WAS A VIRUS, WASN'T IT...
LUCIF?
A VIRUS DID THIS TO YOU!
N... NO...

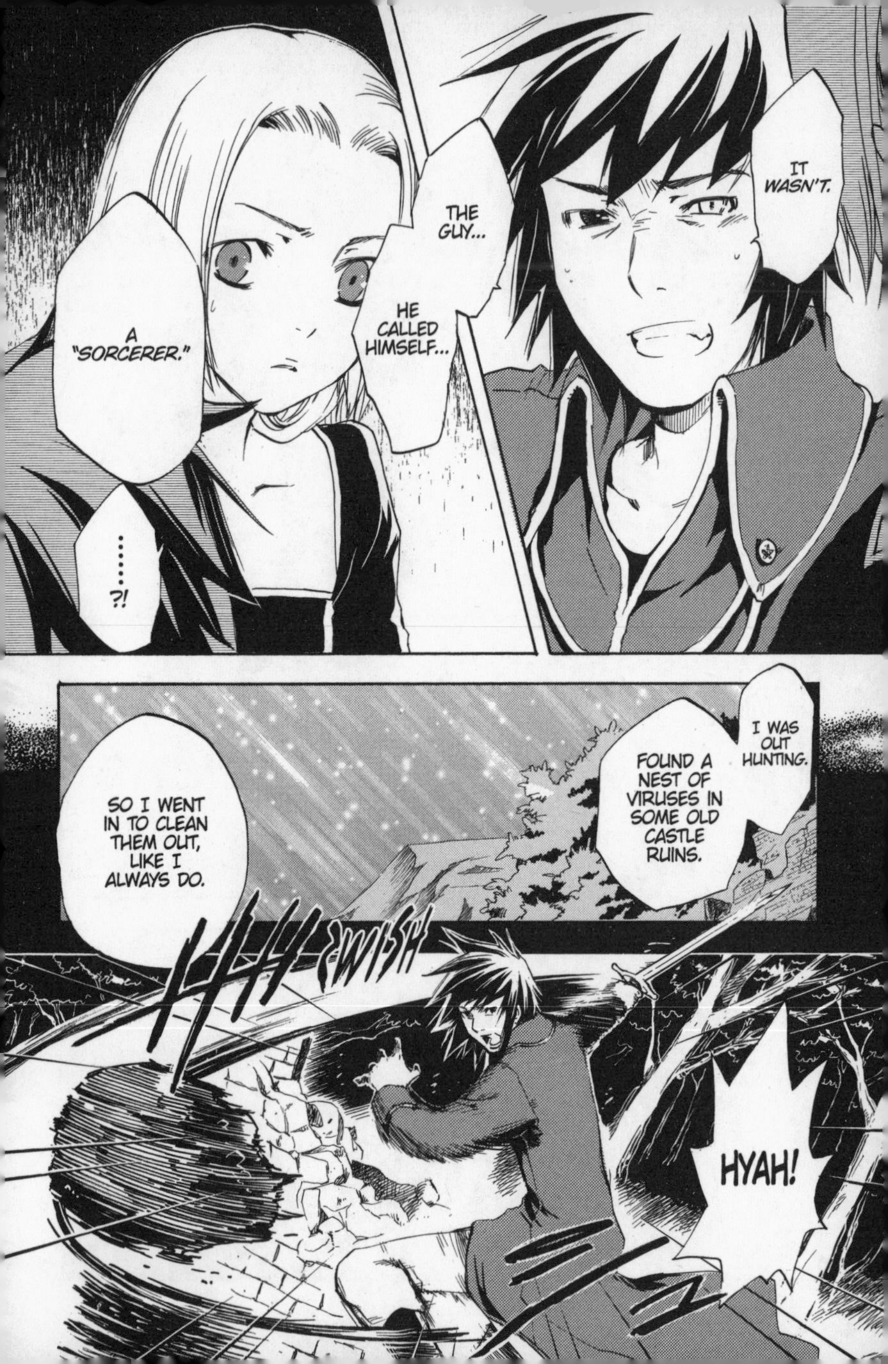
IT WASN'T.
THE GUY...
HE CALLED HIMSELF...
A "SORCERER."
......?!
I WAS OUT HUNTING.
FOUND A NEST OF VIRUSES IN SOME OLD CASTLE RUINS.
SO I WENT IN TO CLEAN THEM OUT, LIKE I ALWAYS DO.
HYAH!

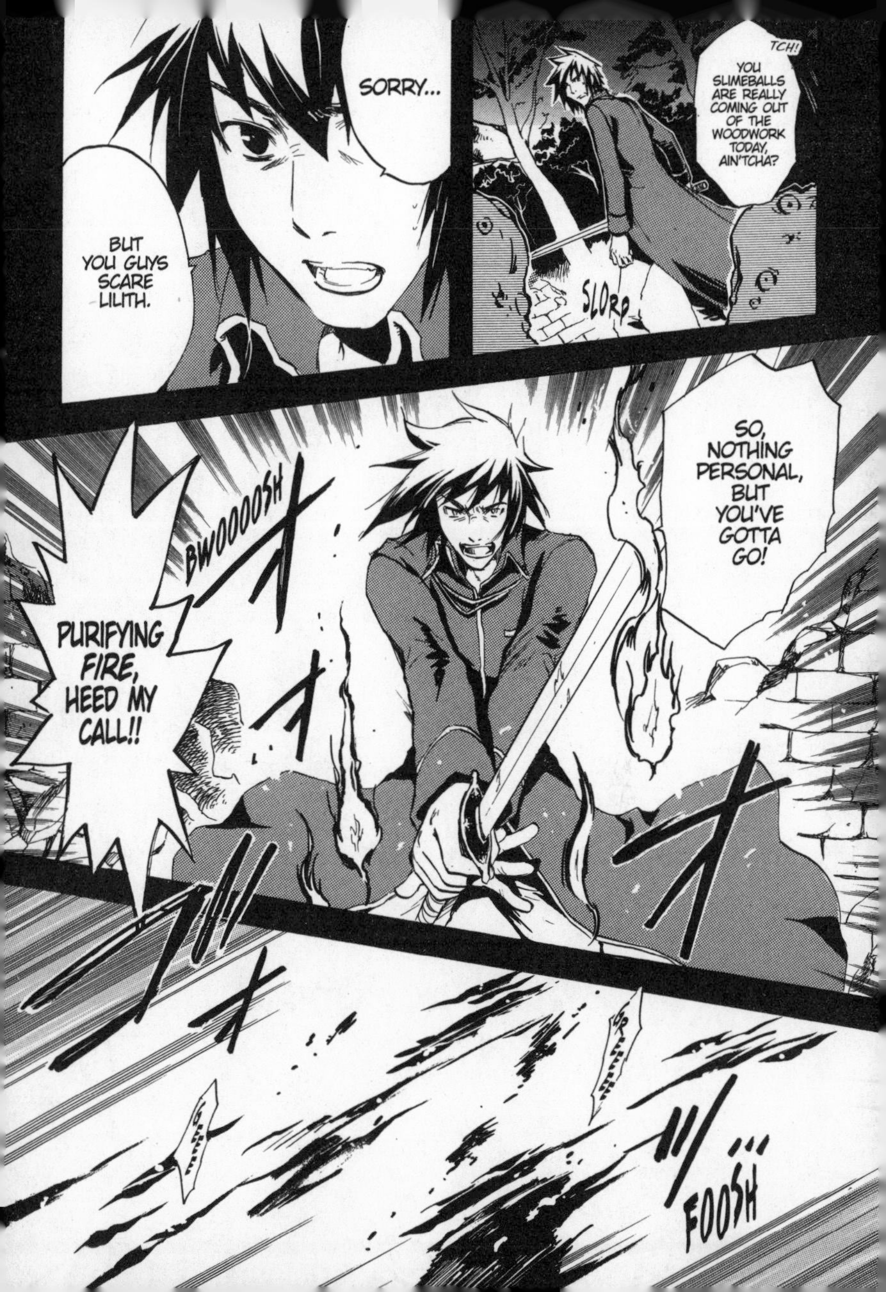
TCH!
YOU SLIMEBALLS ARE REALLY COMING OUT OF THE WOODWORK TODAY, AIN'TCHA?
SLORP
SORRY...
BUT YOU GUYS SCARE LILITH.
SO, NOTHING PERSONAL, BUT YOU'VE GOTTA GO!
BWOOOOOSH
PURIFYING FIRE, HEED MY CALL!!
FOOSH

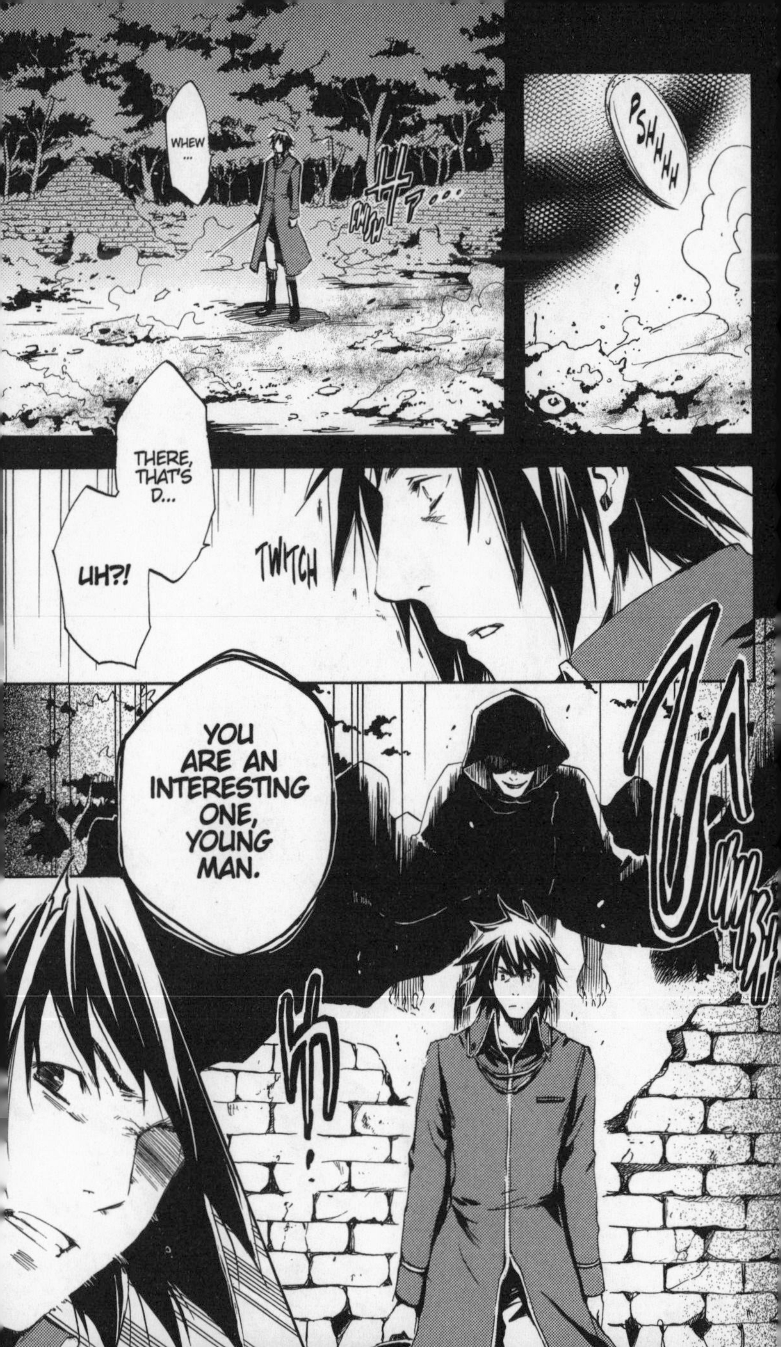
PSHHHH
WHEW ...
FWSH
THERE, THAT'S D...
UH?!
TWITCH
YOU ARE AN INTERESTING ONE, YOUNG MAN.

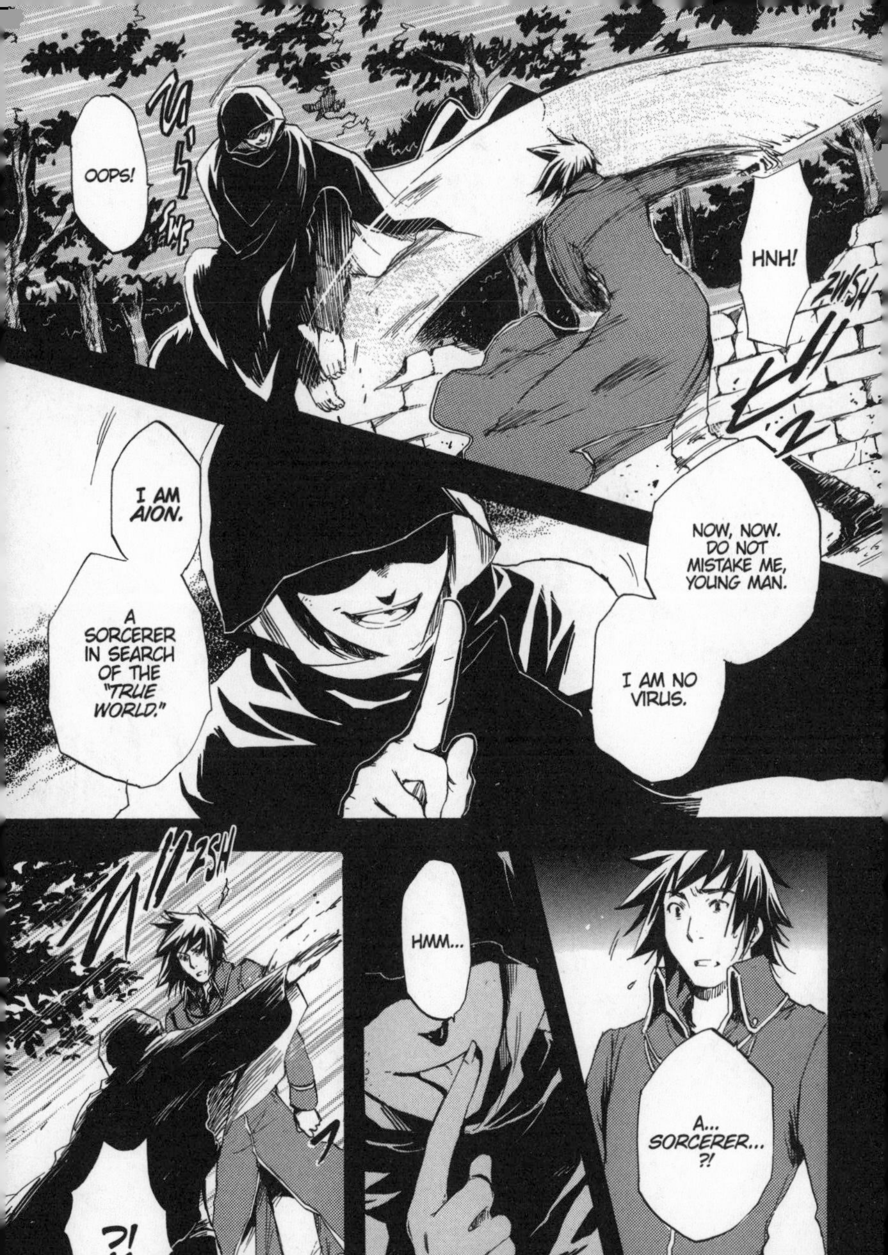
HNH!
ZWSH
OOPS!
NOW, NOW. DO NOT MISTAKE ME, YOUNG MAN.
I AM NO VIRUS.
I AM AION.
A SORCERER IN SEARCH OF THE "TRUE WORLD."
A... SORCERER... ?!
HMM...
?!

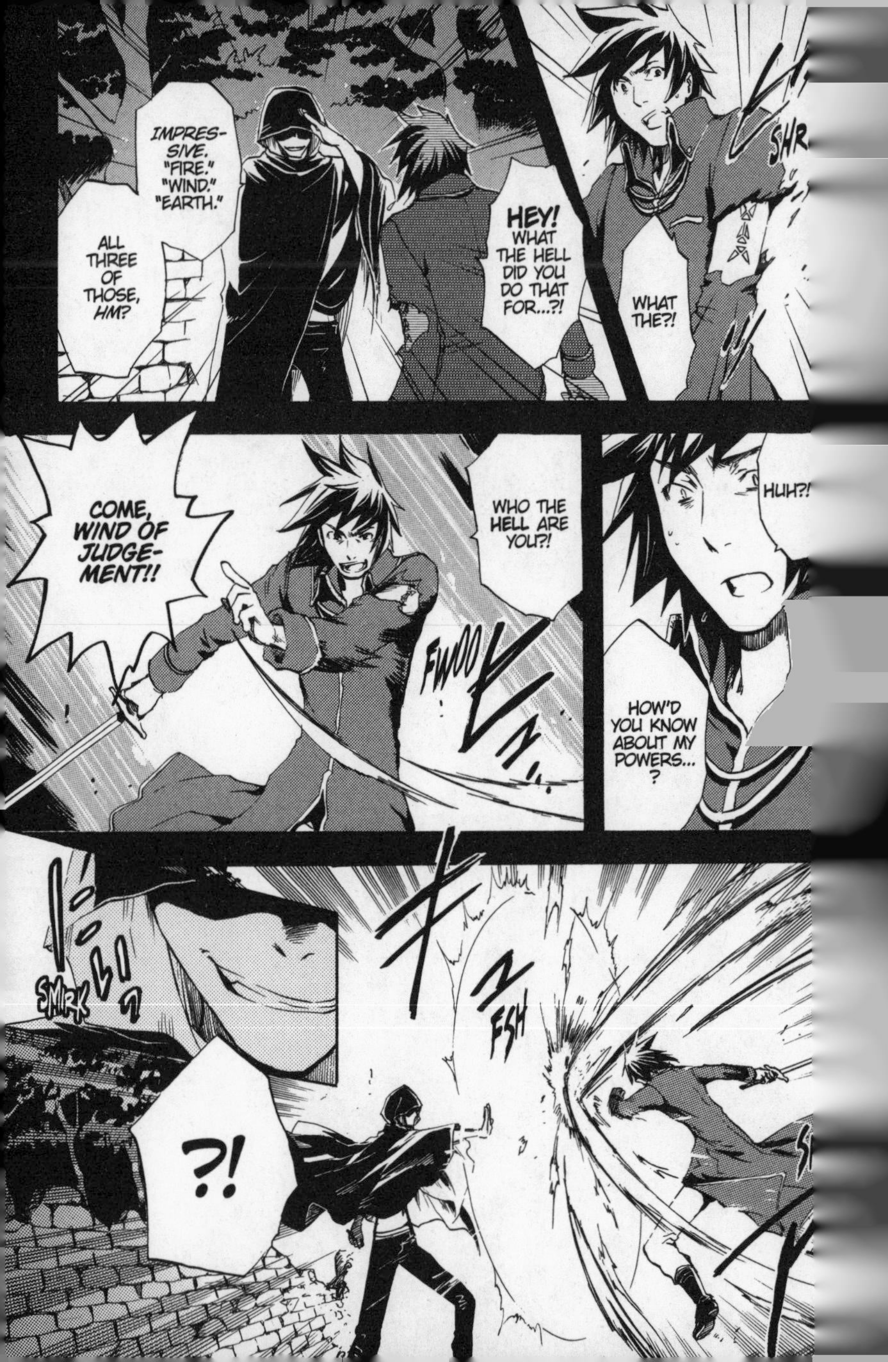
SHR
WHAT THE?!
HEY! WHAT THE HELL DID YOU DO THAT FOR...?!
IMPRESSIVE. "FIRE." "WIND." "EARTH."
ALL THREE OF THOSE, HM?
HUH?!
HOW'D YOU KNOW ABOUT MY POWERS...?
WHO THE HELL ARE YOU?!
FWOO
COME, WIND OF JUDGEMENT!!
FSH
SMIRK
?!

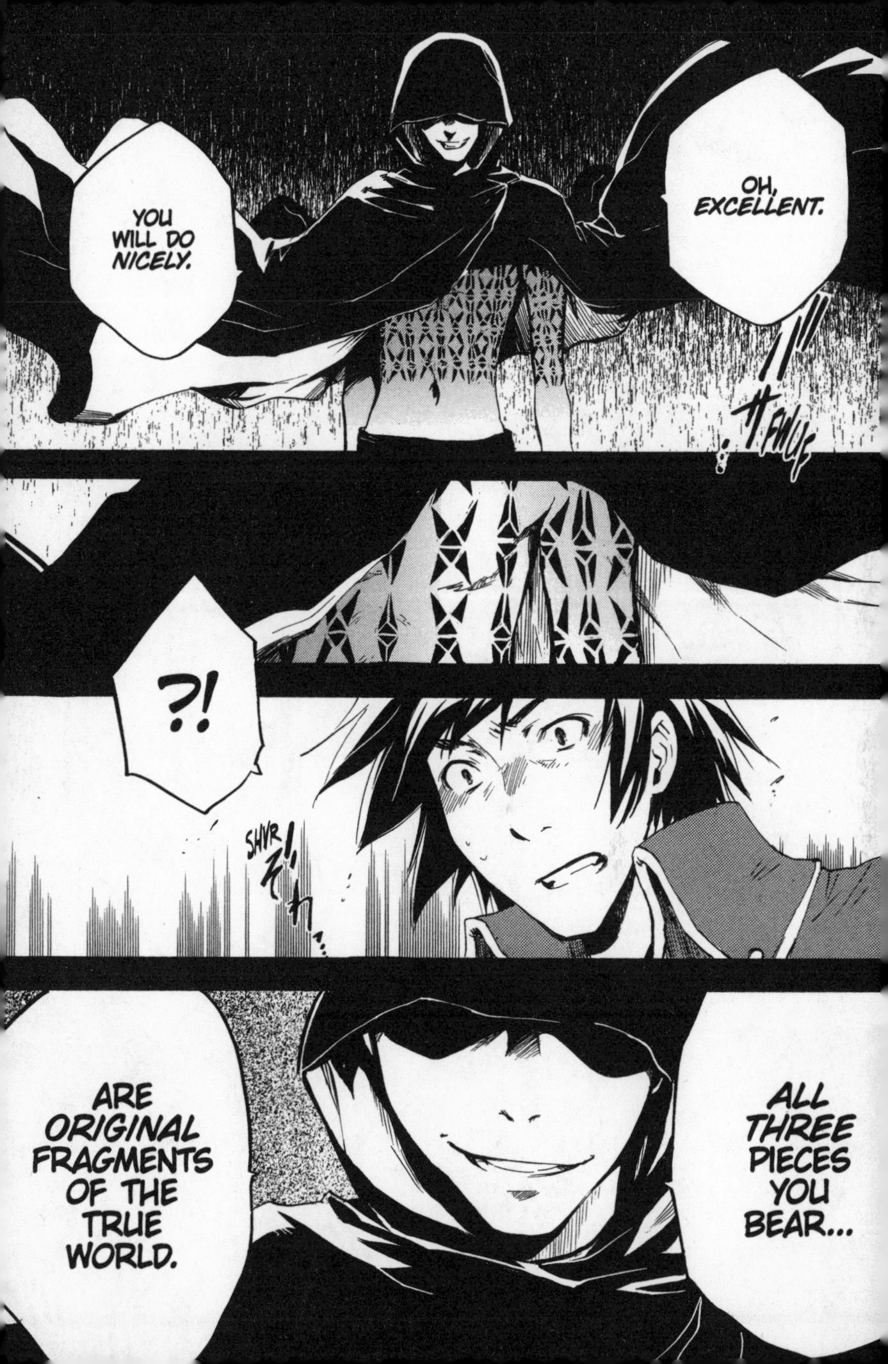
OH, EXCELLENT.
YOU WILL DO NICELY.
?!
SHVR
ALL THREE PIECES YOU BEAR...
ARE ORIGINAL FRAGMENTS OF THE TRUE WORLD.

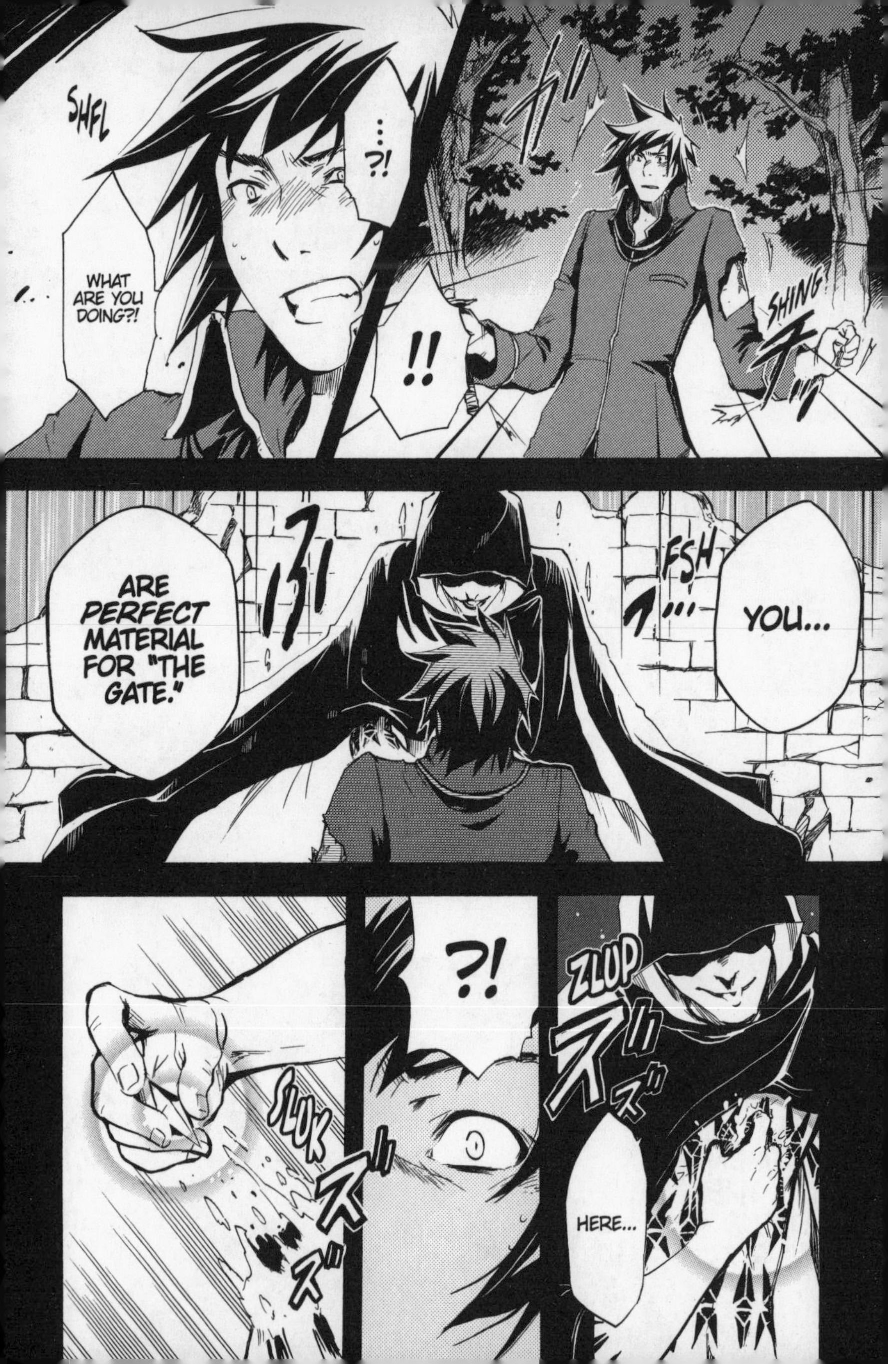
SHING
!!
...?!
WHAT ARE YOU DOING?!
SHFL
YOU...
FSH
ARE PERFECT MATERIAL FOR "THE GATE."
ZLUP
HERE...
?!
SLUK

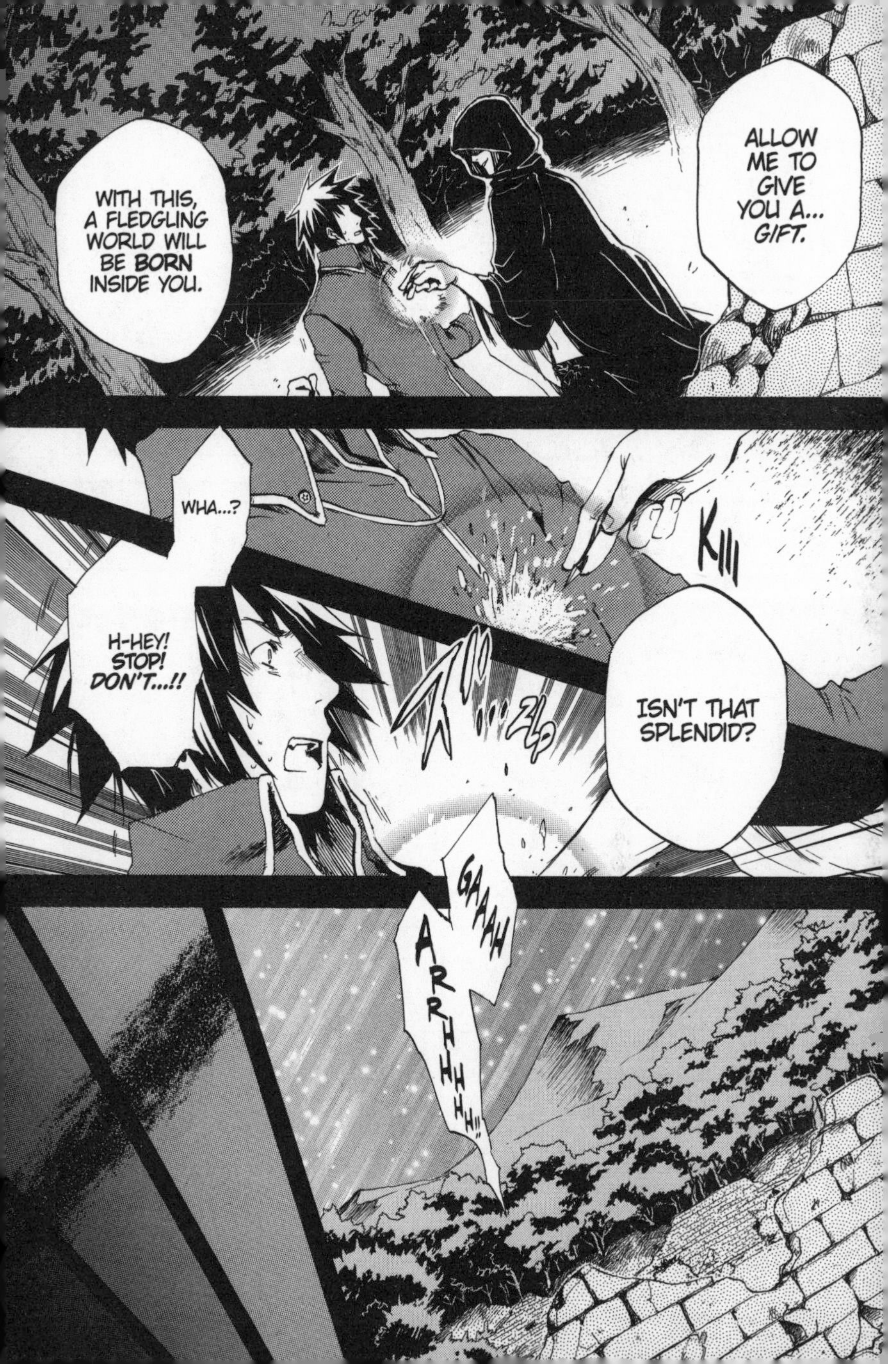
ALLOW ME TO GIVE YOU A... GIFT.
WITH THIS, A FLEDGLING WORLD WILL BE BORN INSIDE YOU.
KIII
WHA...?
ISN'T THAT SPLENDID?
...ZLP
H-HEY! STOP! DON'T...!!
GAAAAH
ARRHHHHH!!

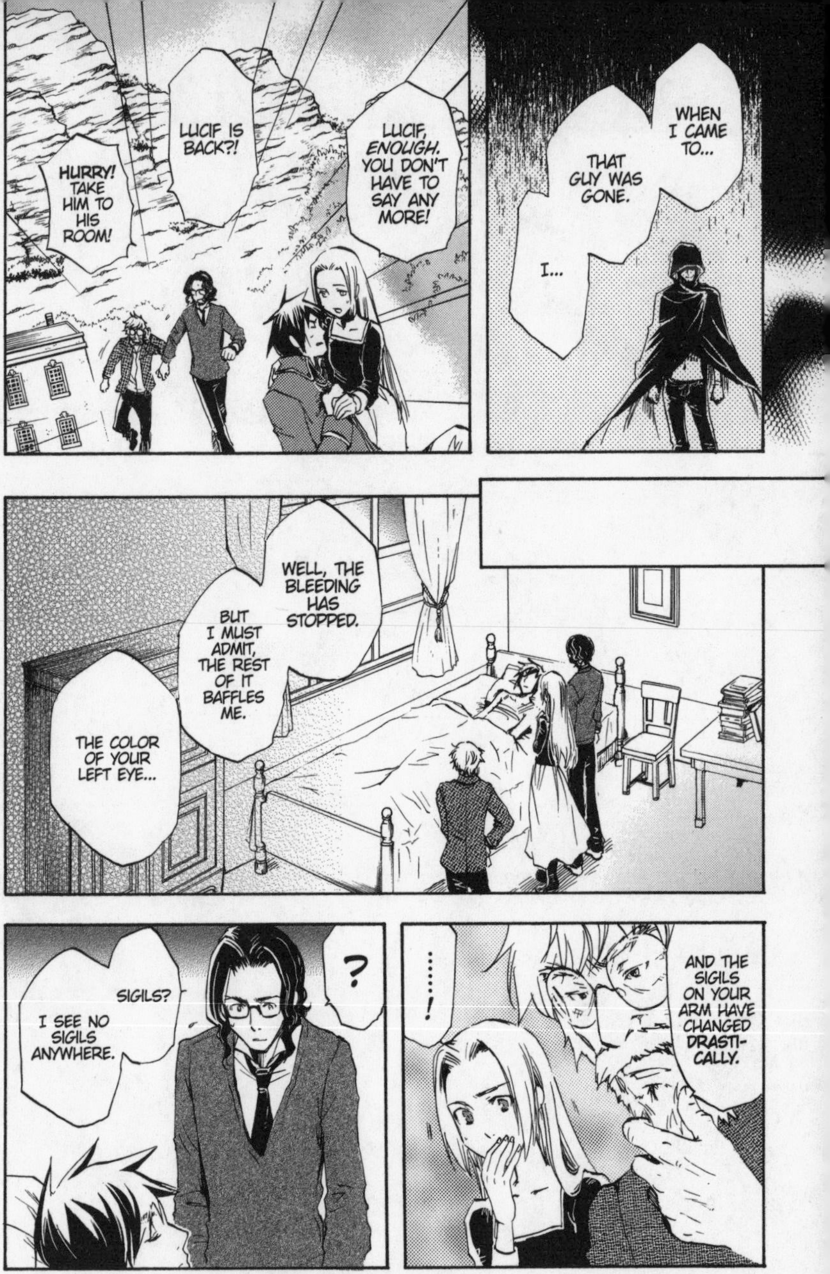
WHEN I CAME TO...
THAT GUY WAS GONE.
I...
LUCIF, *ENOUGH.* YOU DON'T HAVE TO SAY ANY MORE!
LUCIF IS BACK?!
HURRY! TAKE HIM TO HIS ROOM!
WELL, THE BLEEDING HAS STOPPED.
BUT I MUST ADMIT, THE REST OF IT BAFFLES ME.
THE COLOR OF YOUR LEFT EYE...
AND THE SIGILS ON YOUR ARM HAVE CHANGED DRASTI-CALLY.
.....!
?
SIGILS?
I SEE NO SIGILS ANYWHERE.

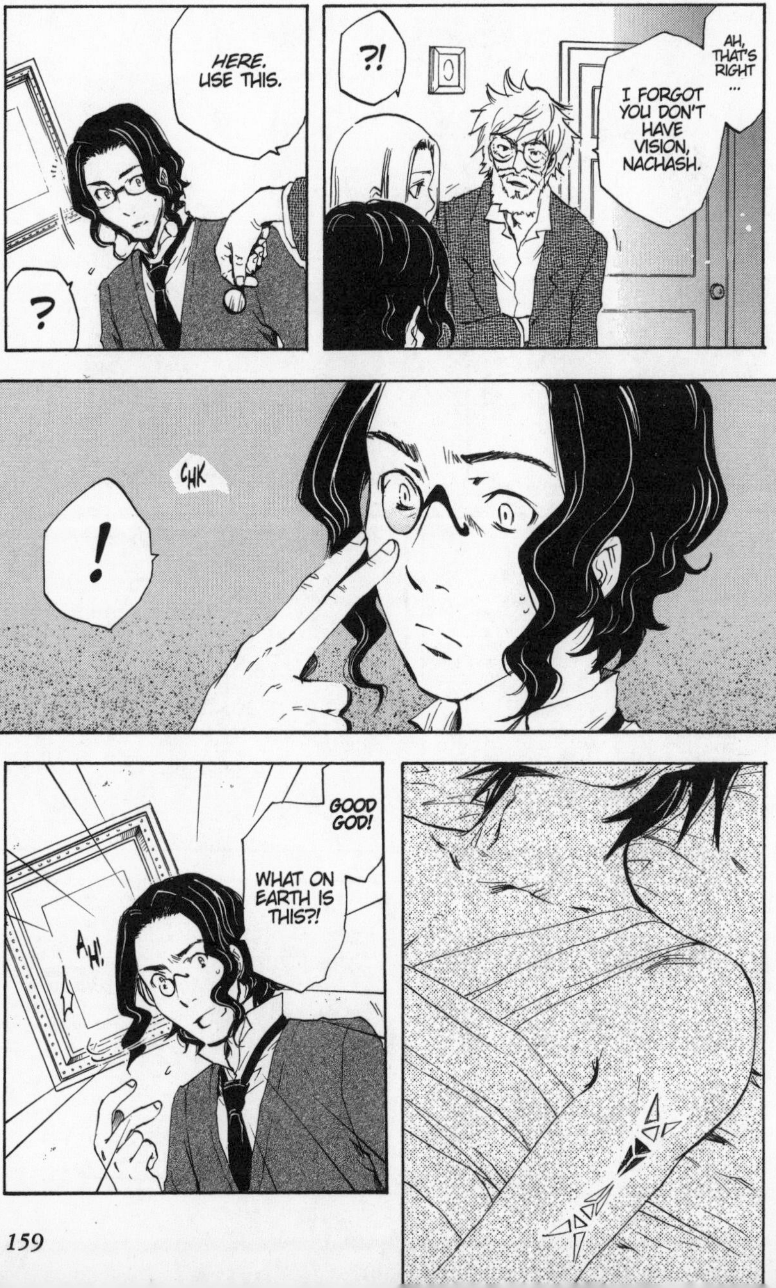
AH, THAT'S RIGHT ...
I FORGOT YOU DON'T HAVE VISION, NACHASH.
?!
HERE. USE THIS.
?
CHK
!
GOOD GOD!
WHAT ON EARTH IS THIS?!
AH!

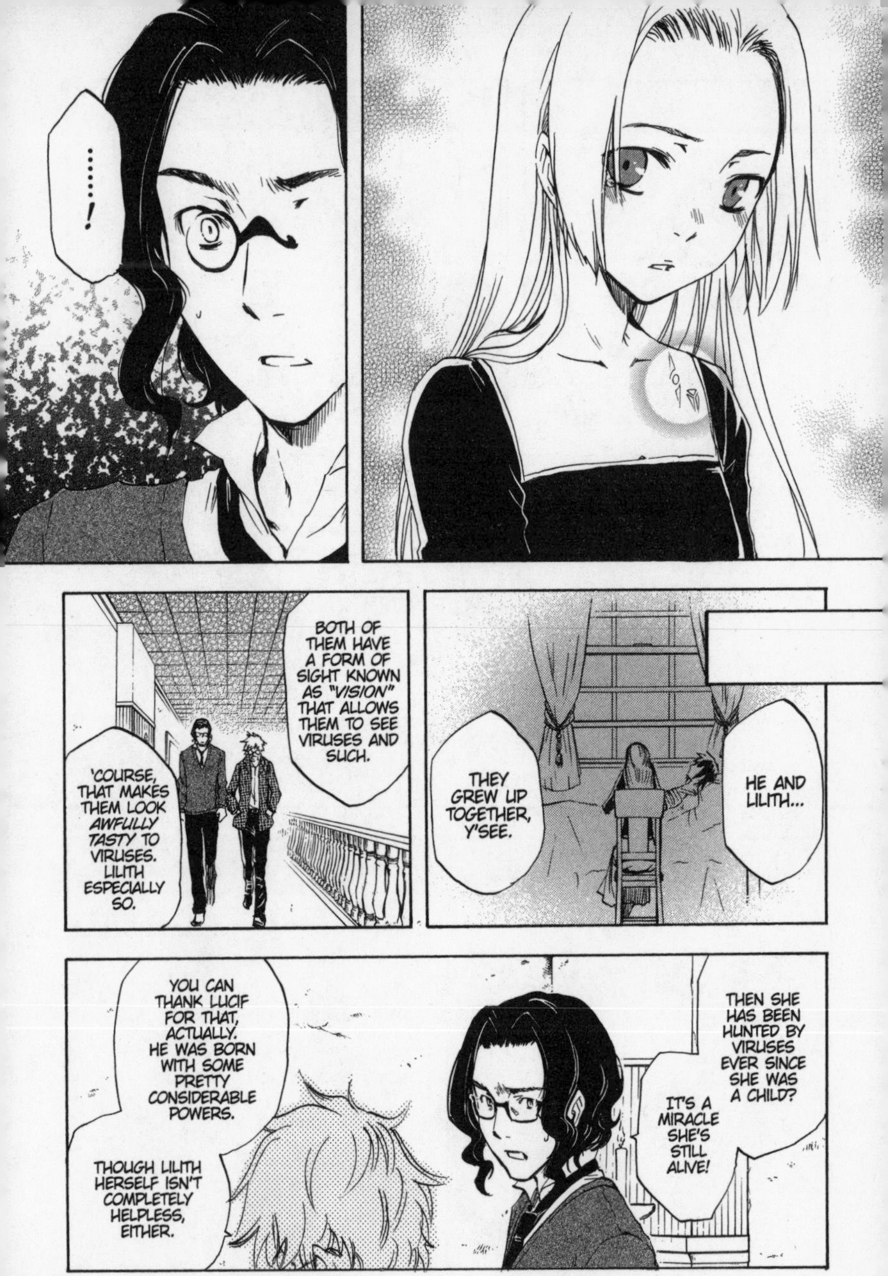
......!
HE AND LILITH...
THEY GREW UP TOGETHER, Y'SEE.
BOTH OF THEM HAVE A FORM OF SIGHT KNOWN AS "VISION" THAT ALLOWS THEM TO SEE VIRUSES AND SUCH.
'COURSE, THAT MAKES THEM LOOK AWFULLY TASTY TO VIRUSES. LILITH ESPECIALLY SO.
THEN SHE HAS BEEN HUNTED BY VIRUSES EVER SINCE SHE WAS A CHILD?
IT'S A MIRACLE SHE'S STILL ALIVE!
YOU CAN THANK LUCIF FOR THAT, ACTUALLY. HE WAS BORN WITH SOME PRETTY CONSIDERABLE POWERS.
THOUGH LILITH HERSELF ISN'T COMPLETELY HELPLESS, EITHER.

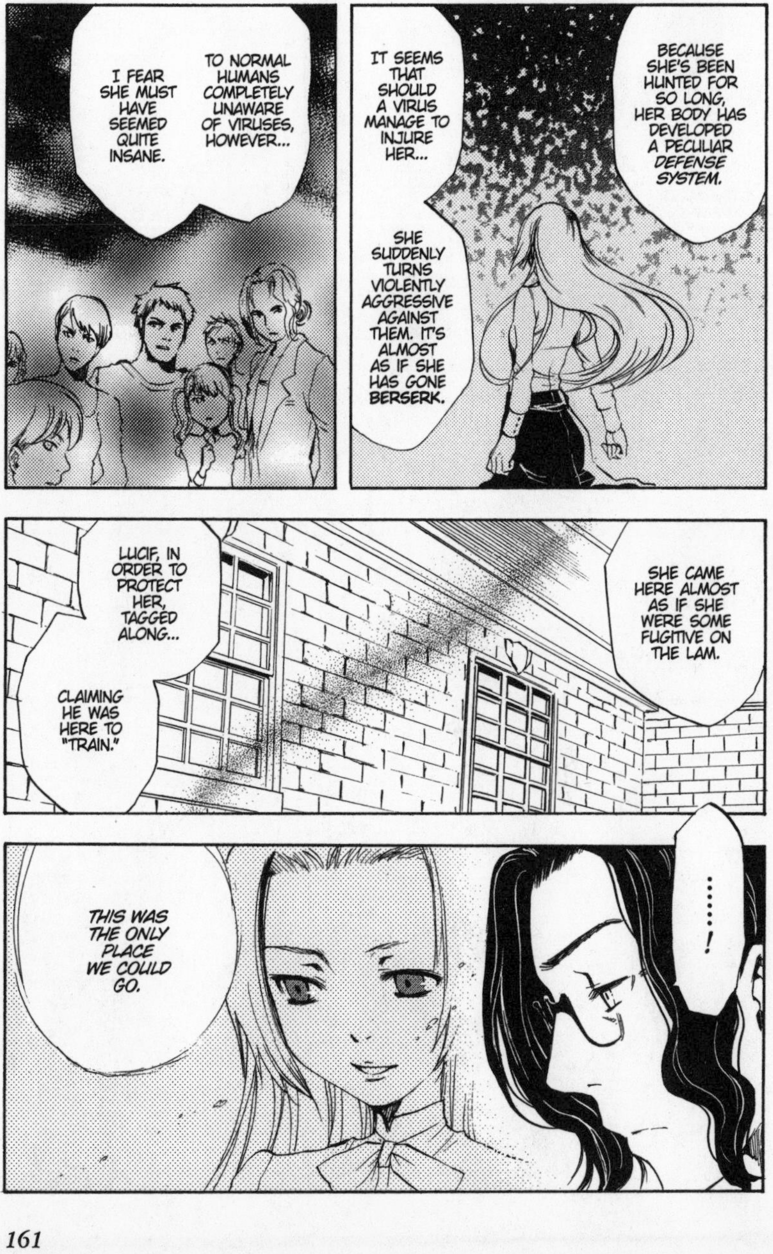
BECAUSE SHE'S BEEN HUNTED FOR SO LONG, HER BODY HAS DEVELOPED A PECULIAR *DEFENSE SYSTEM.*
IT SEEMS THAT SHOULD A VIRUS MANAGE TO INJURE HER...
SHE SUDDENLY TURNS VIOLENTLY AGGRESSIVE AGAINST THEM. IT'S ALMOST AS IF SHE HAS GONE BERSERK.
TO NORMAL HUMANS COMPLETELY UNAWARE OF VIRUSES, HOWEVER...
I FEAR SHE MUST HAVE SEEMED QUITE INSANE.
SHE CAME HERE ALMOST AS IF SHE WERE SOME FUGITIVE ON THE LAM.
LUCIF, IN ORDER TO PROTECT HER, TAGGED ALONG...
CLAIMING HE WAS HERE TO "TRAIN."
......!
THIS WAS THE ONLY PLACE WE COULD GO.

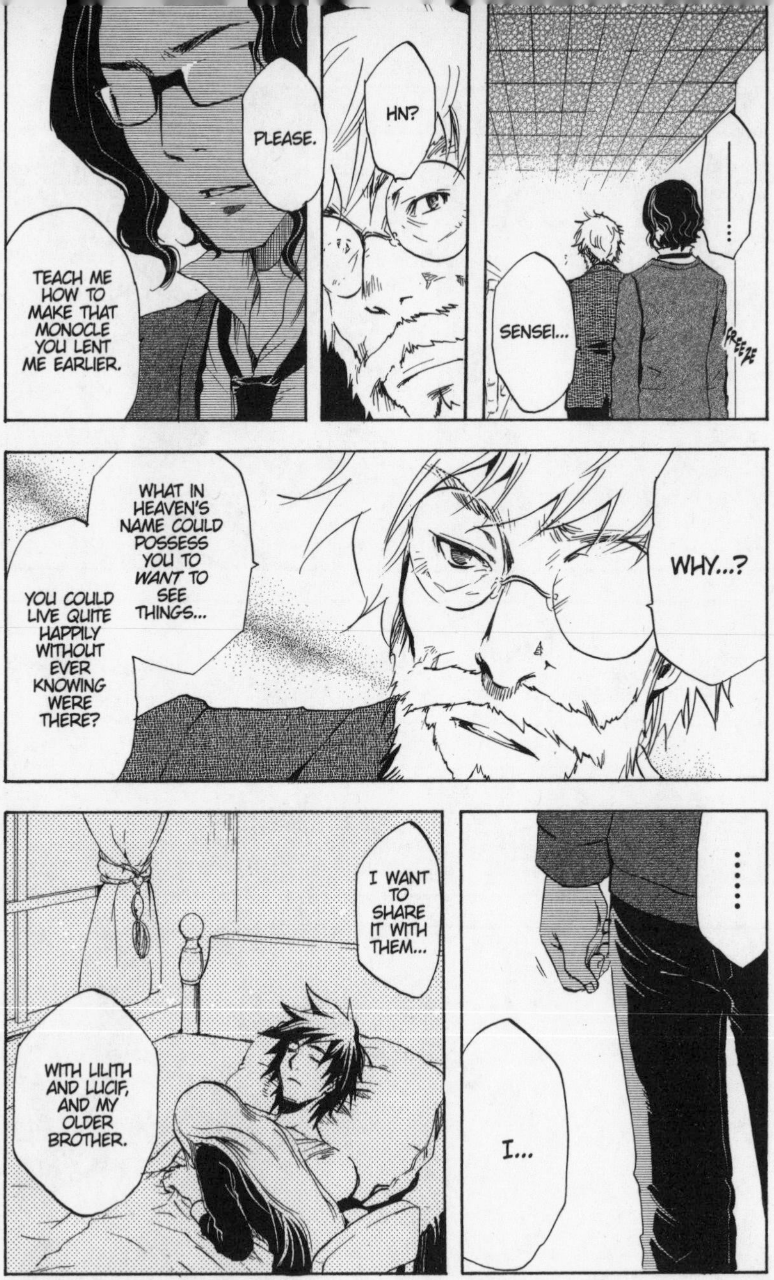
...
FREEZE
SENSEI...
HN?
PLEASE.
TEACH ME HOW TO MAKE THAT MONOCLE YOU LENT ME EARLIER.
WHY...?
WHAT IN HEAVEN'S NAME COULD POSSESS YOU TO *WANT* TO SEE THINGS...
YOU COULD LIVE QUITE HAPPILY WITHOUT EVER KNOWING WERE THERE?
......
I...
I WANT TO SHARE IT WITH THEM...
WITH LILITH AND LUCIF, AND MY OLDER BROTHER.

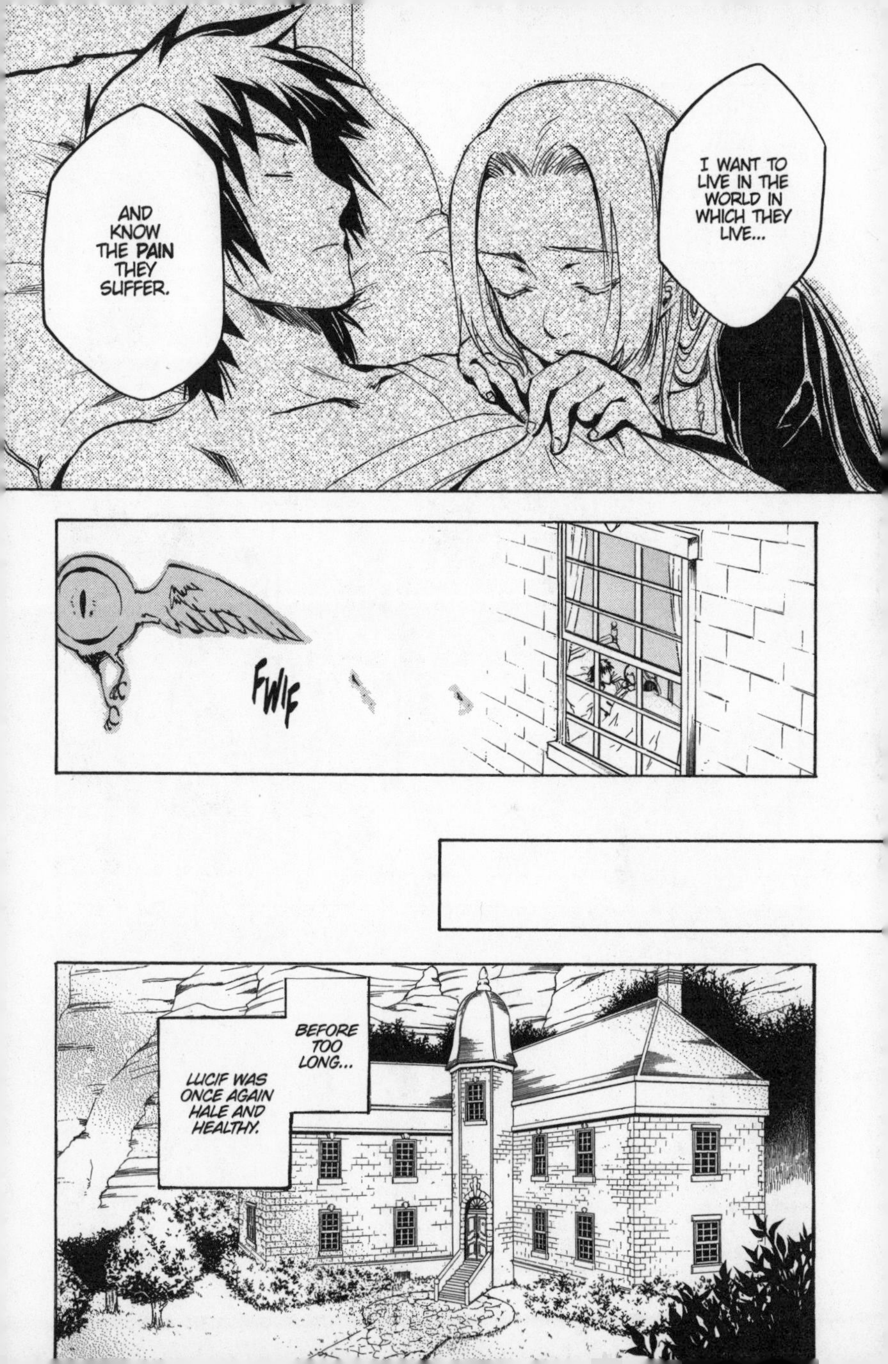
I WANT TO LIVE IN THE WORLD IN WHICH THEY LIVE...
AND KNOW THE PAIN THEY SUFFER.
FWIF
BEFORE TOO LONG...
LUCIF WAS ONCE AGAIN HALE AND HEALTHY.

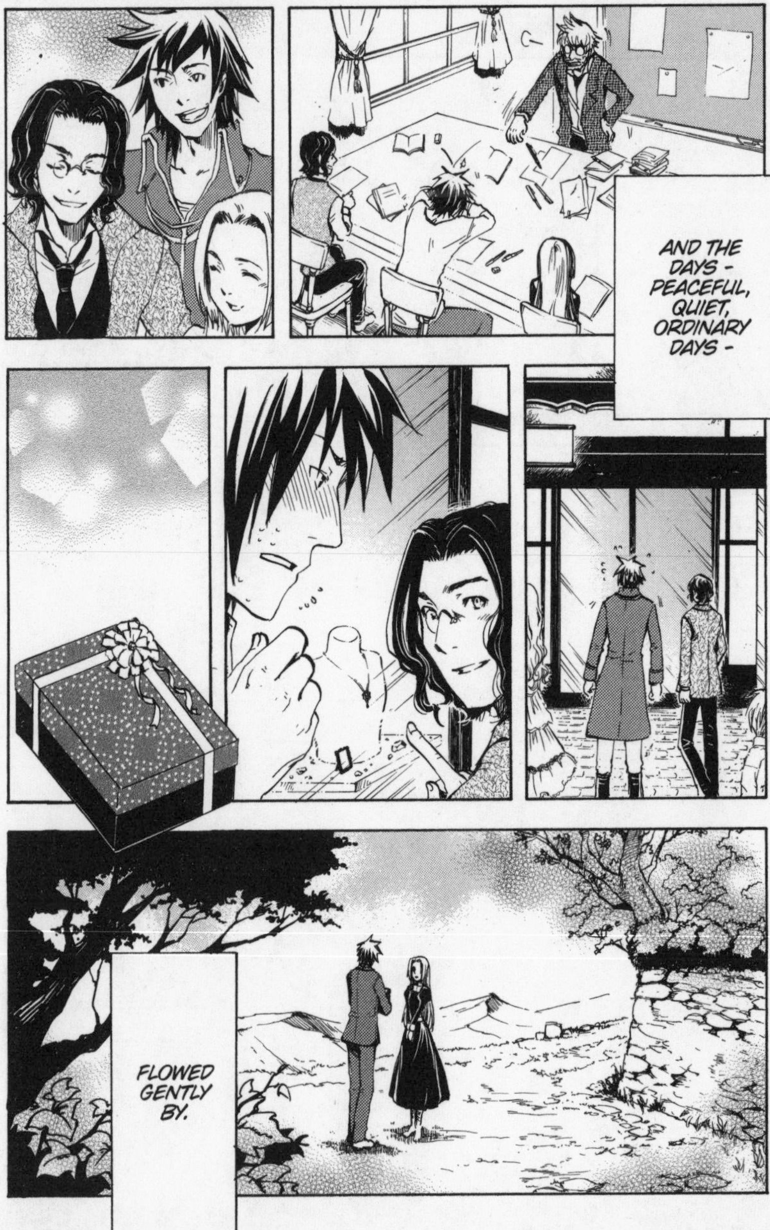
AND THE DAYS - PEACEFUL, QUIET, ORDINARY DAYS -
FLOWED GENTLY BY.

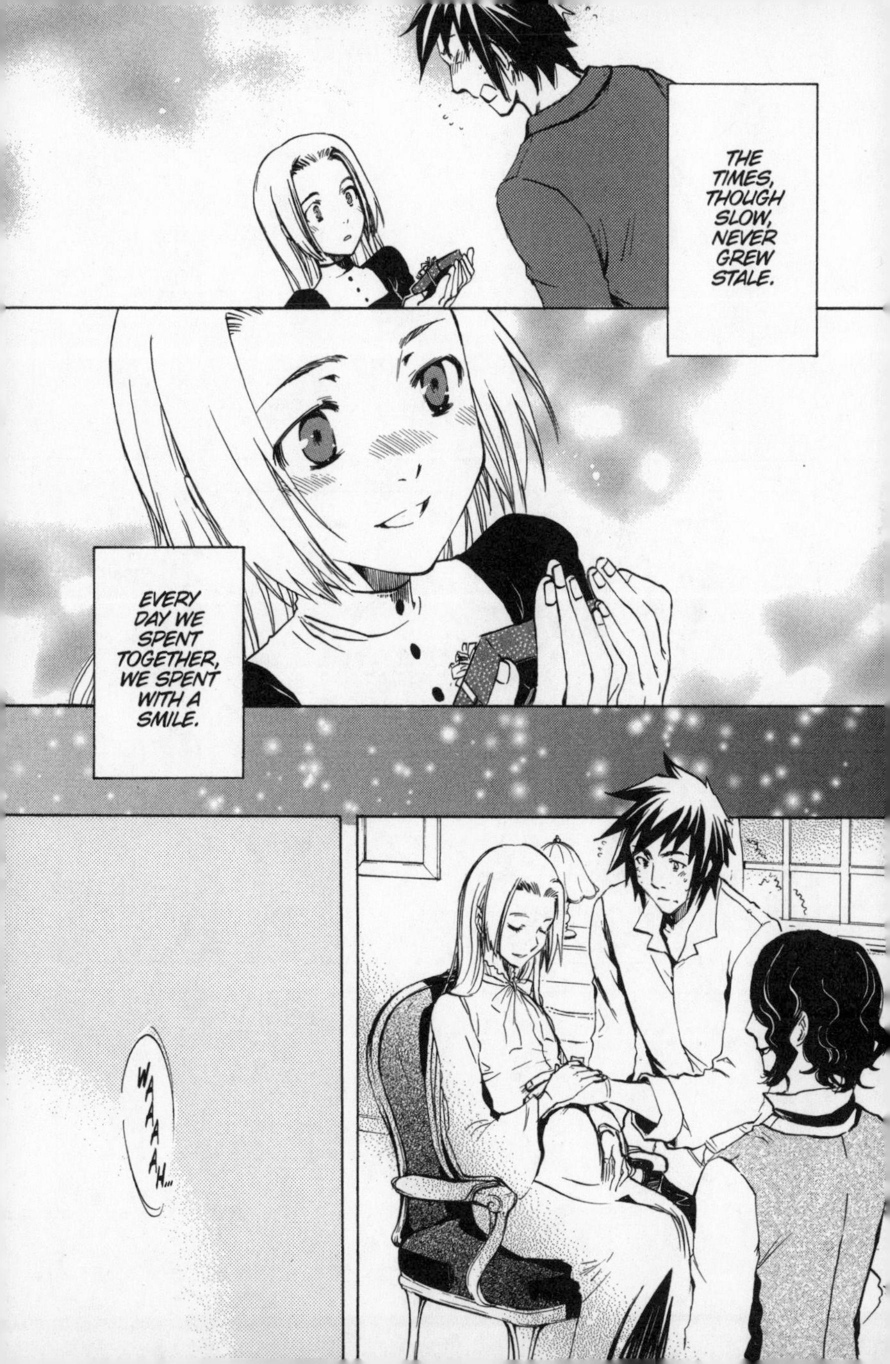
THE TIMES, THOUGH SLOW, NEVER GREW STALE.
EVERY DAY WE SPENT TOGETHER, WE SPENT WITH A SMILE.
WAAAAH...

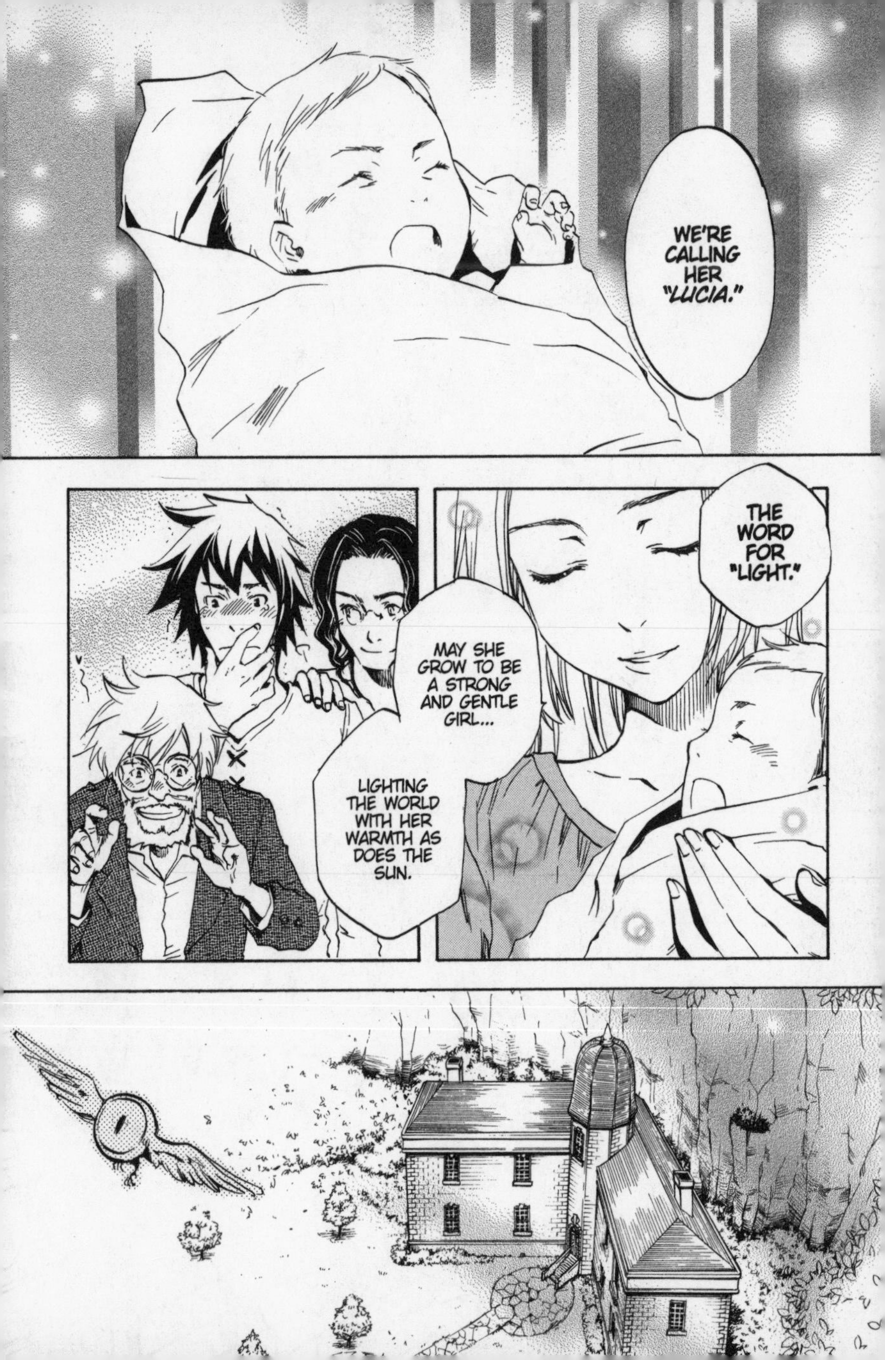
WE'RE CALLING HER "LUCIA."
THE WORD FOR "LIGHT."
MAY SHE GROW TO BE A STRONG AND GENTLE GIRL...
LIGHTING THE WORLD WITH HER WARMTH AS DOES THE SUN.

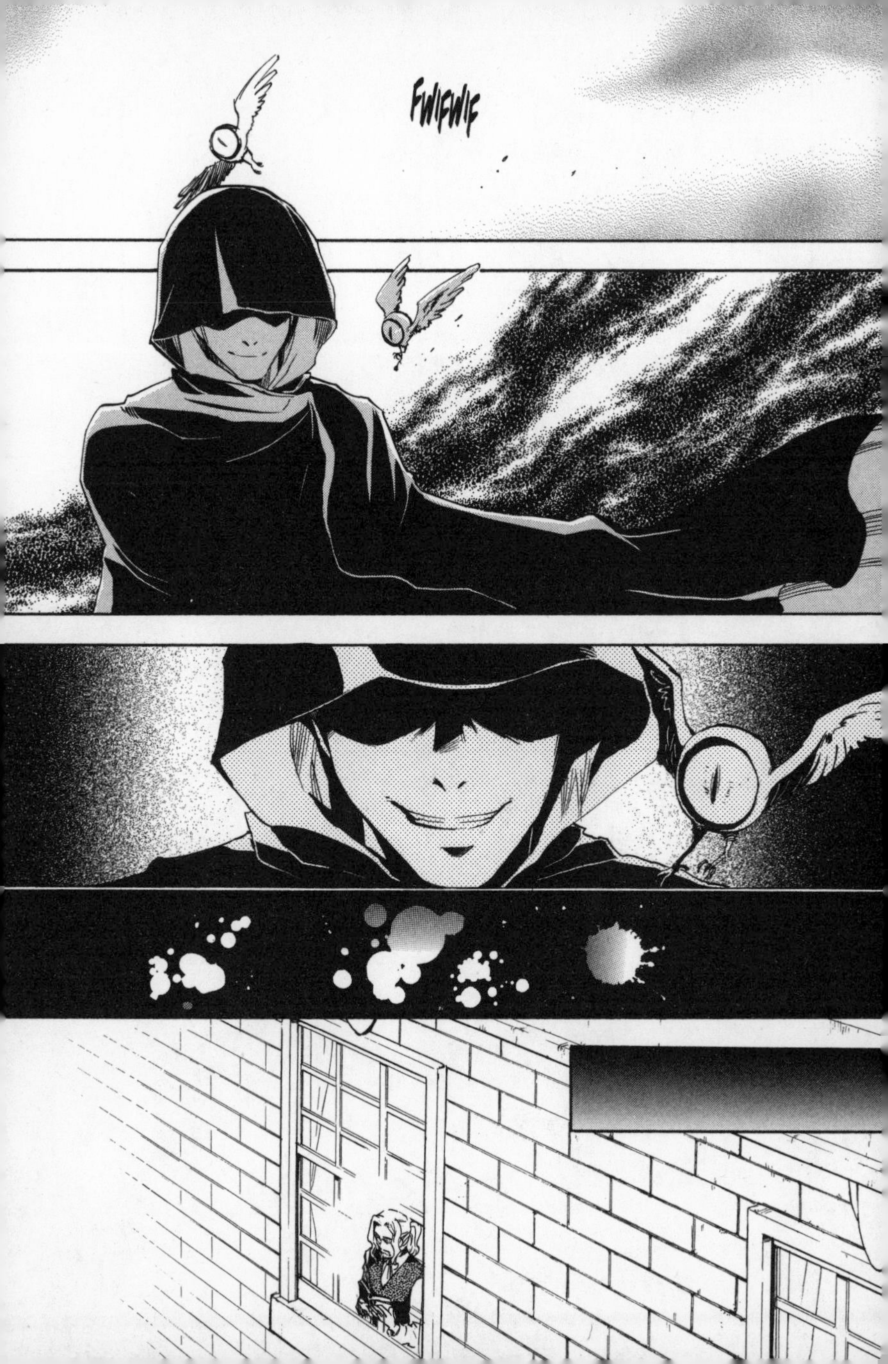
FWIFWIF

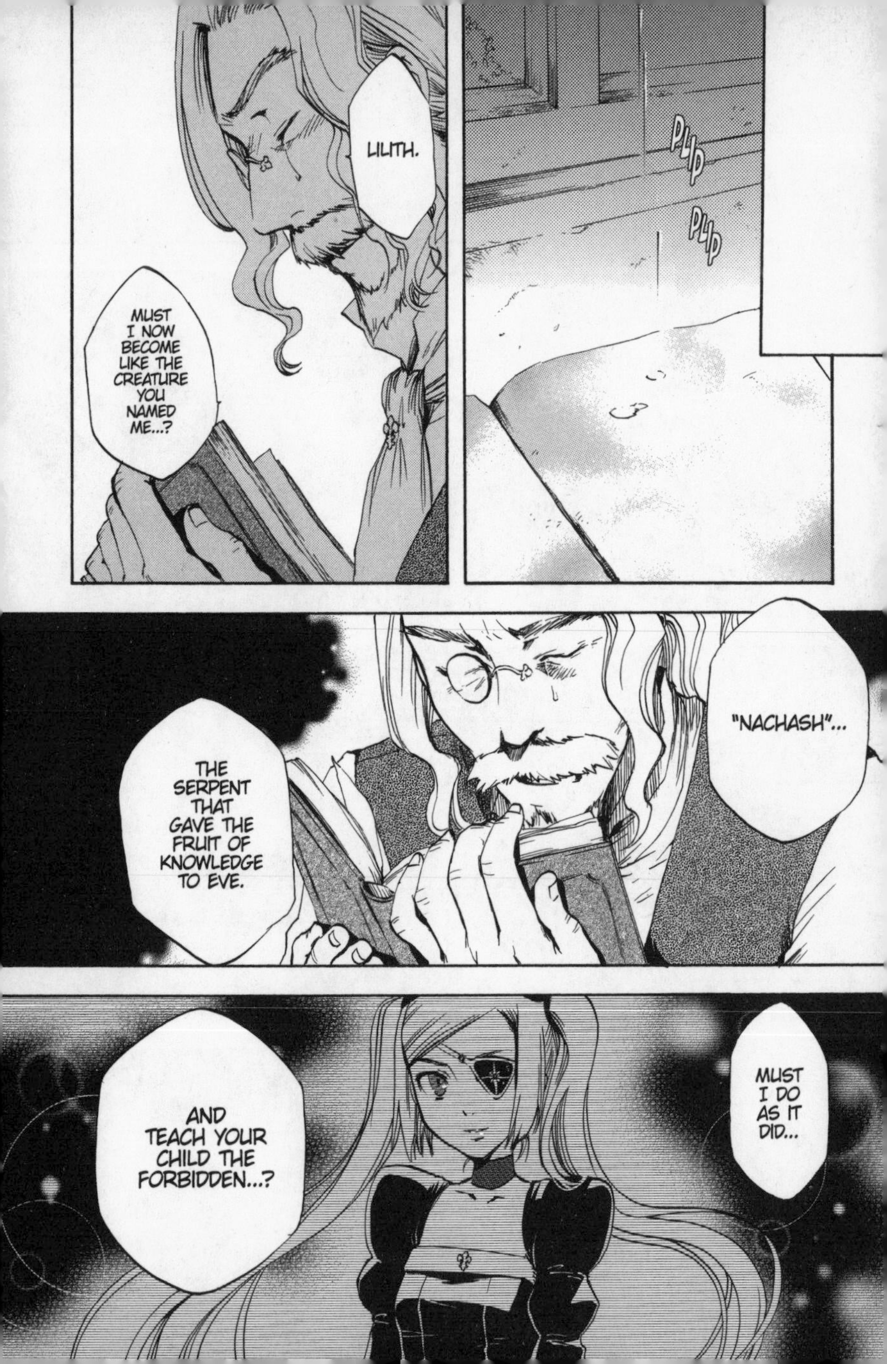
PLIP
PLIP
LILITH.
MUST I NOW BECOME LIKE THE CREATURE YOU NAMED ME...?
"NACHASH"...
THE SERPENT THAT GAVE THE FRUIT OF KNOWLEDGE TO EVE.
MUST I DO AS IT DID...
AND TEACH YOUR CHILD THE FORBIDDEN...?

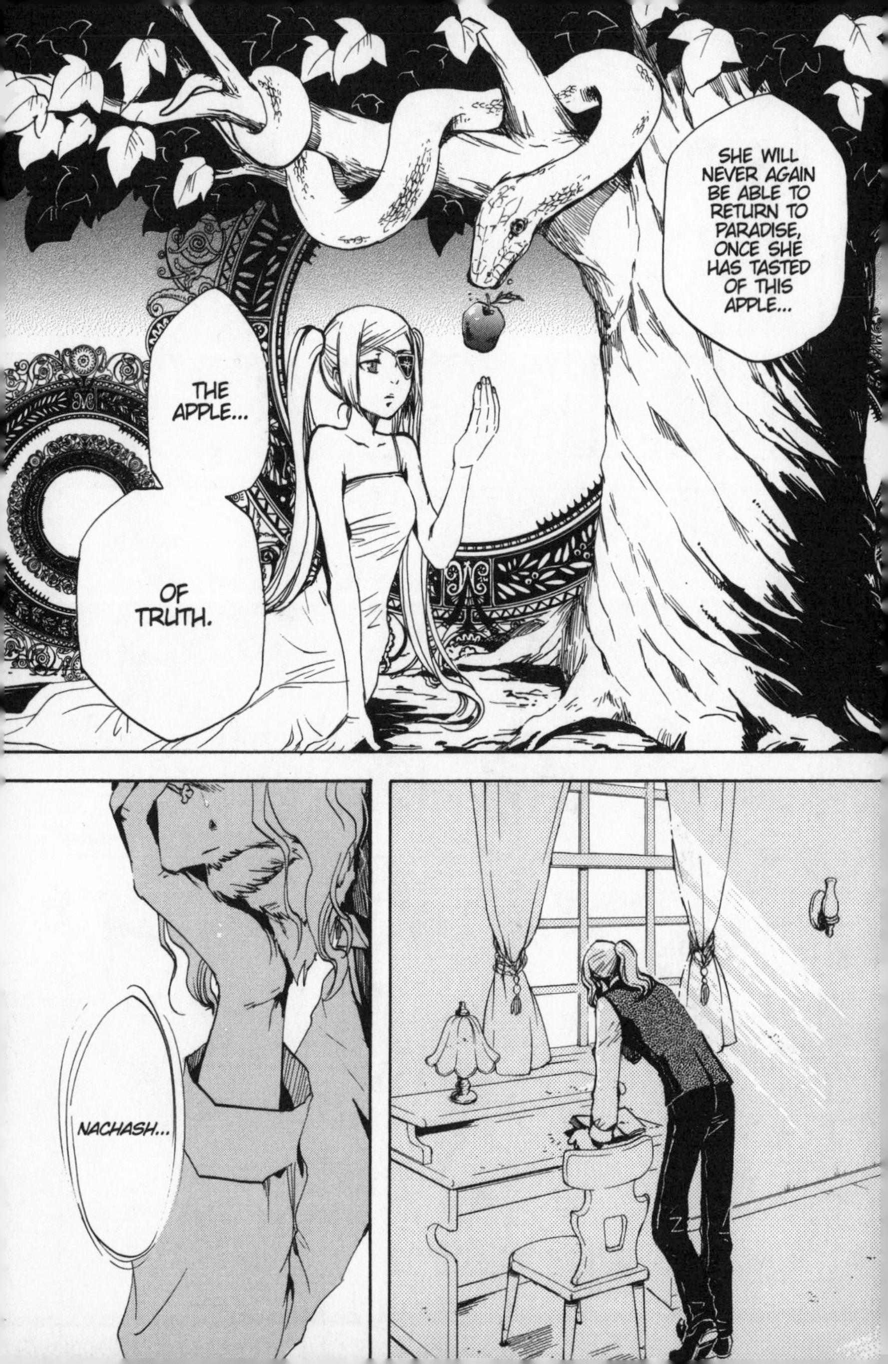
SHE WILL NEVER AGAIN BE ABLE TO RETURN TO PARADISE, ONCE SHE HAS TASTED OF THIS APPLE...
THE APPLE...
OF TRUTH.
NACHASH...

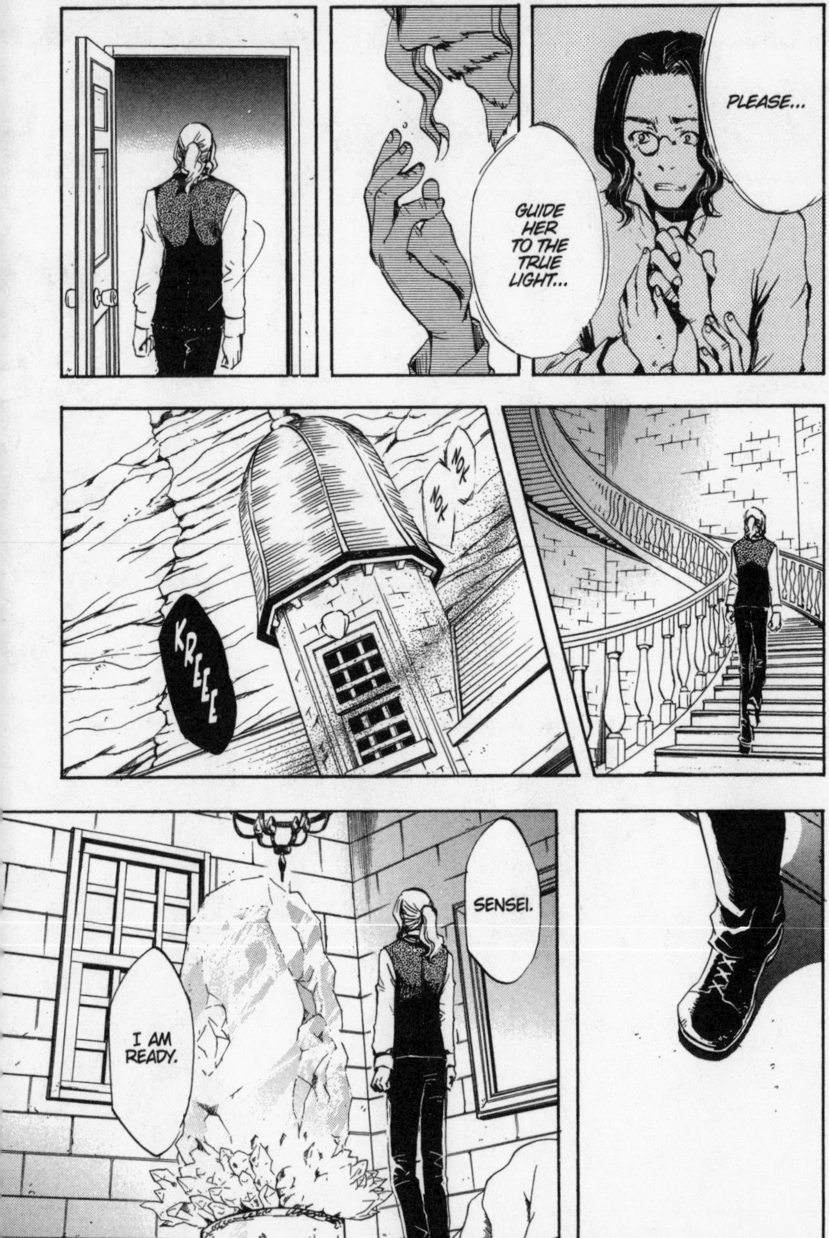

PLEASE...
GUIDE HER TO THE TRUE LIGHT...
NOK
NOK
KREEE
SENSEI.
I AM READY.

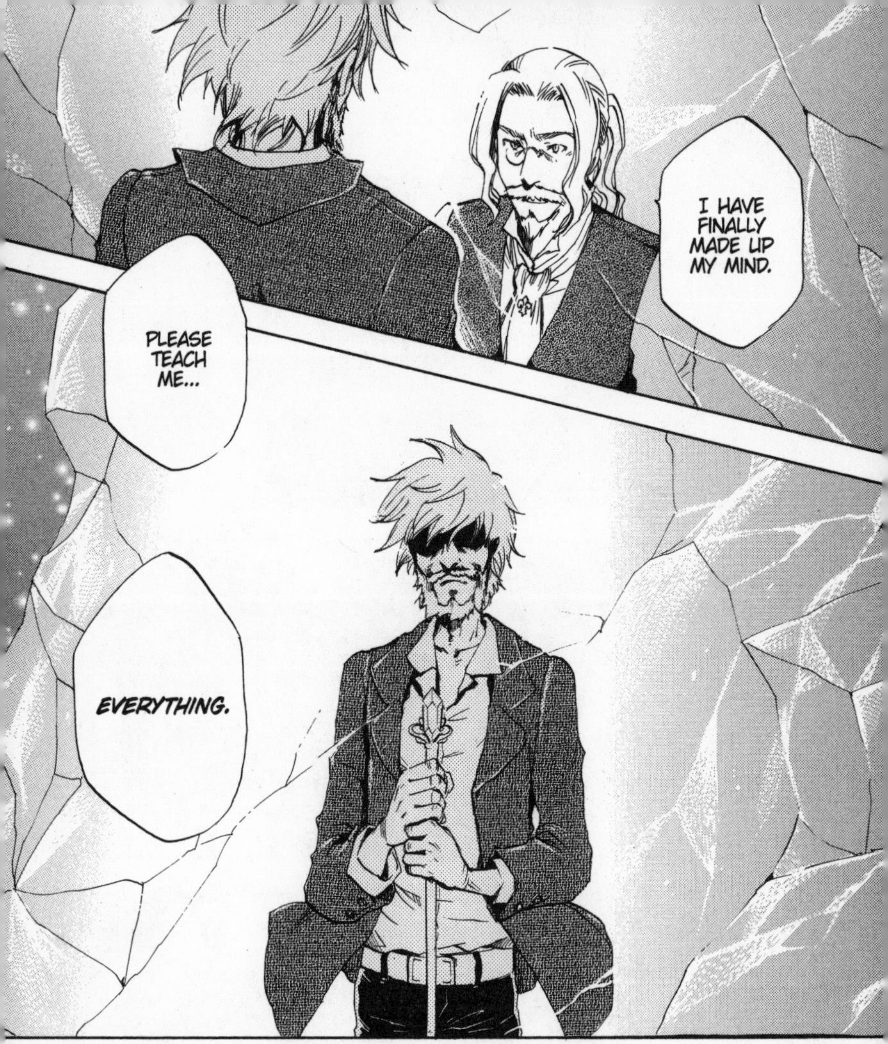
I HAVE FINALLY MADE UP MY MIND.
PLEASE TEACH ME...
EVERYTHING.

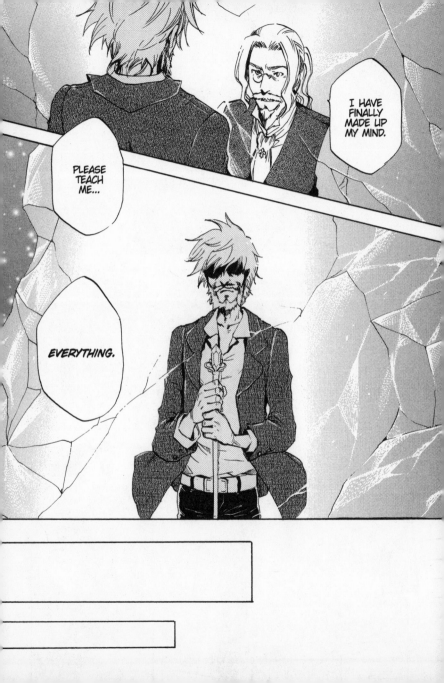

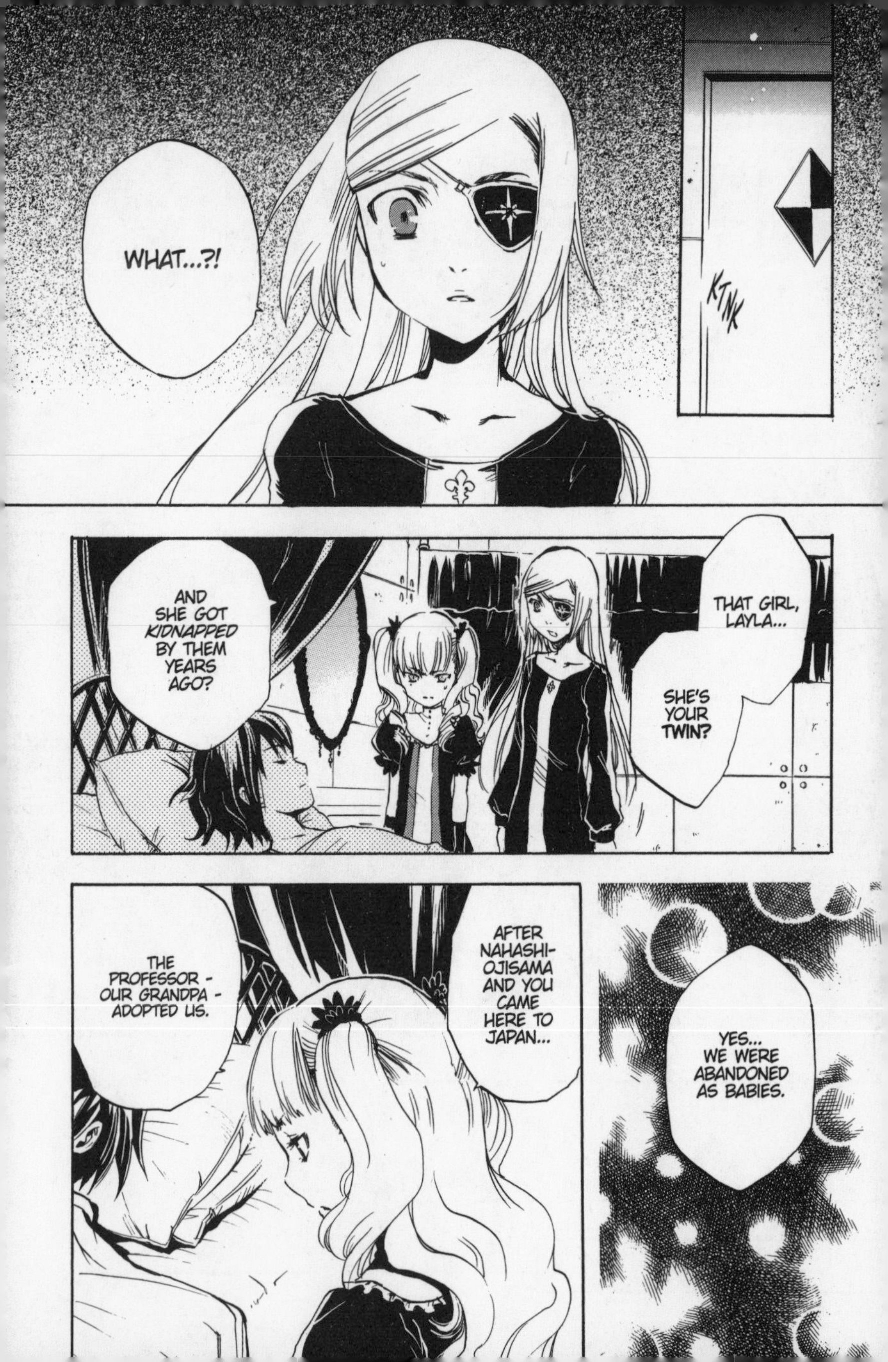
KTNK
WHAT...?!
THAT GIRL, LAYLA...
SHE'S YOUR TWIN?
AND SHE GOT KIDNAPPED BY THEM YEARS AGO?
YES... WE WERE ABANDONED AS BABIES.
AFTER NAHASHI-OJISAMA AND YOU CAME HERE TO JAPAN...
THE PROFESSOR - OUR GRANDPA - ADOPTED US.

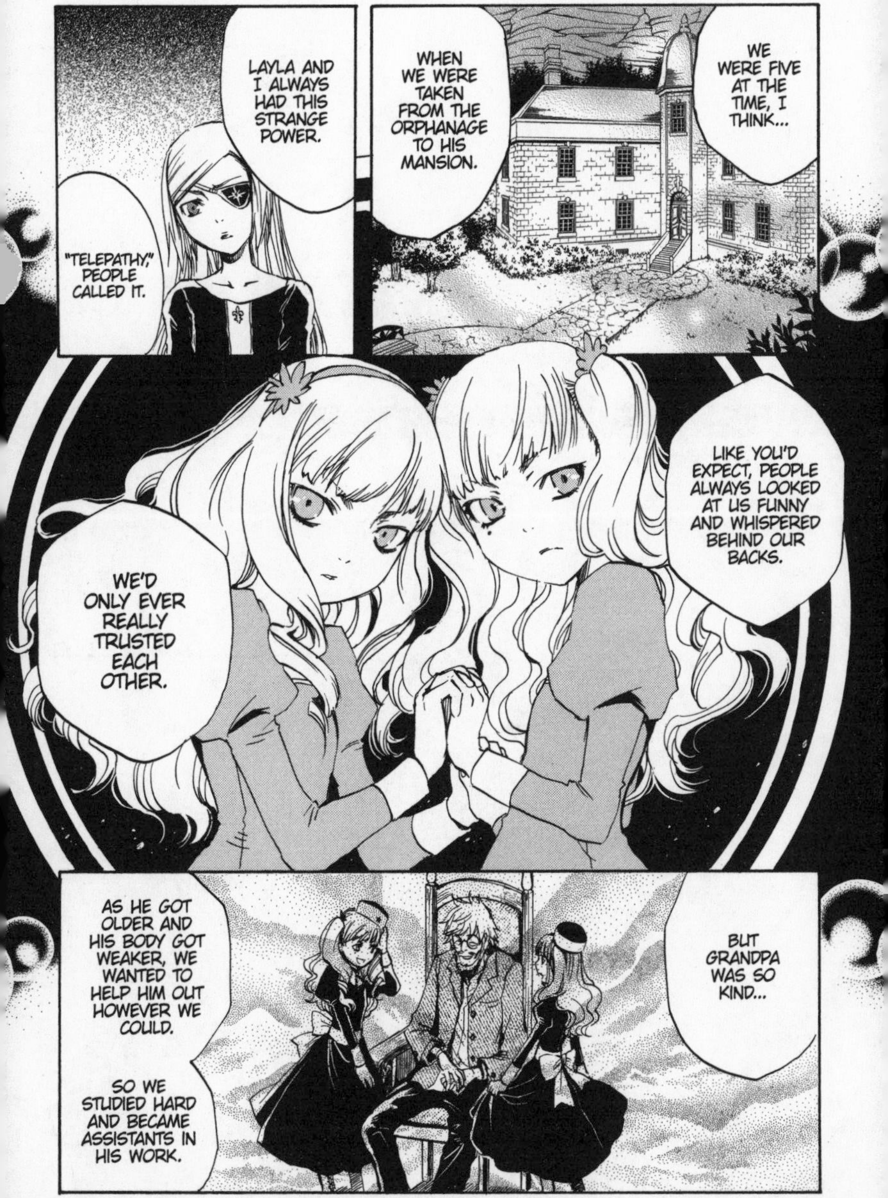
WE WERE FIVE AT THE TIME, I THINK...
WHEN WE WERE TAKEN FROM THE ORPHANAGE TO HIS MANSION.
LAYLA AND I ALWAYS HAD THIS STRANGE POWER.
"TELEPATHY," PEOPLE CALLED IT.
LIKE YOU'D EXPECT, PEOPLE ALWAYS LOOKED AT US FUNNY AND WHISPERED BEHIND OUR BACKS.
WE'D ONLY EVER REALLY TRUSTED EACH OTHER.
BUT GRANDPA WAS SO KIND...
AS HE GOT OLDER AND HIS BODY GOT WEAKER, WE WANTED TO HELP HIM OUT HOWEVER WE COULD.
SO WE STUDIED HARD AND BECAME ASSISTANTS IN HIS WORK.

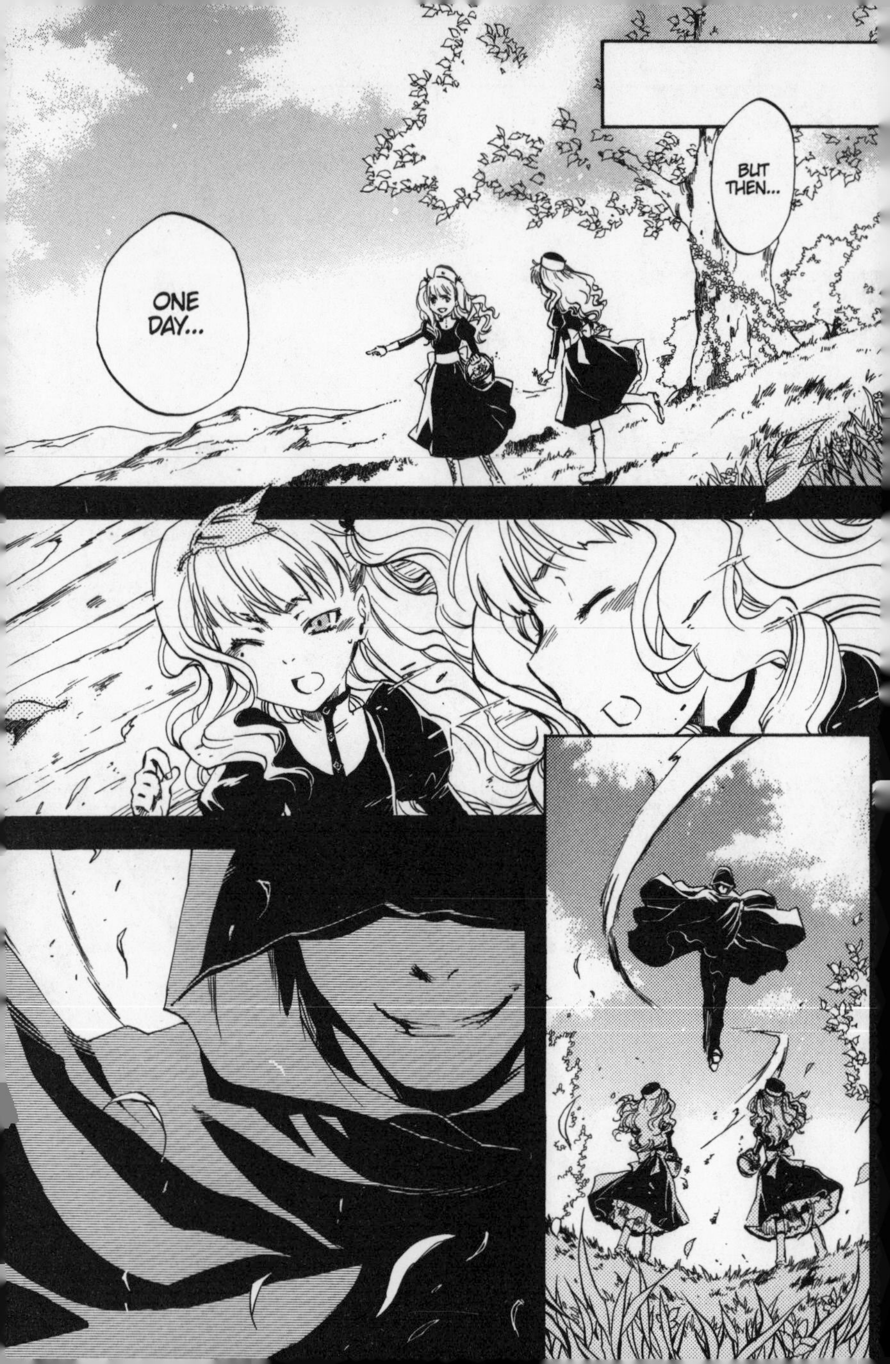
BUT THEN...
ONE DAY...

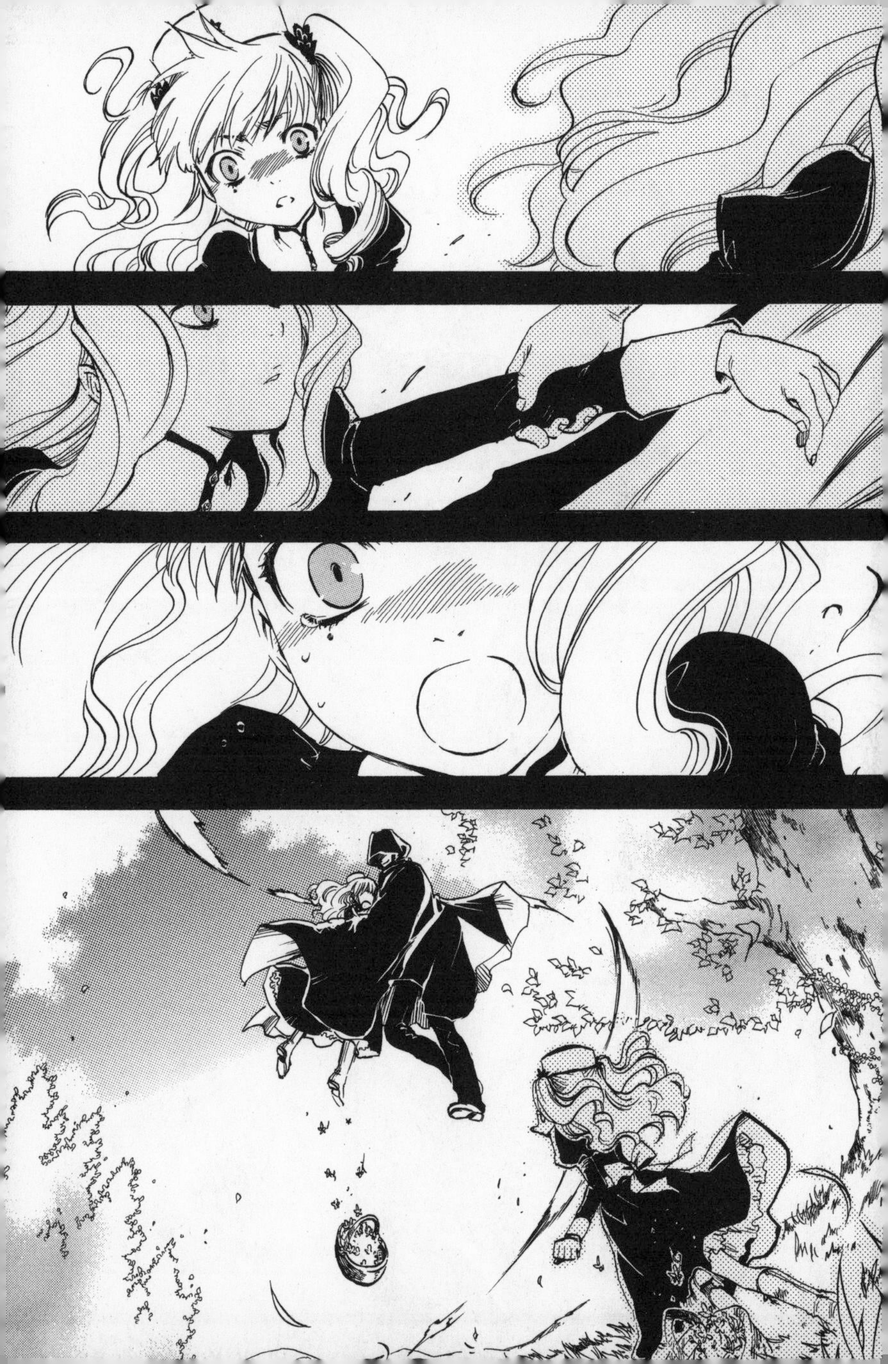

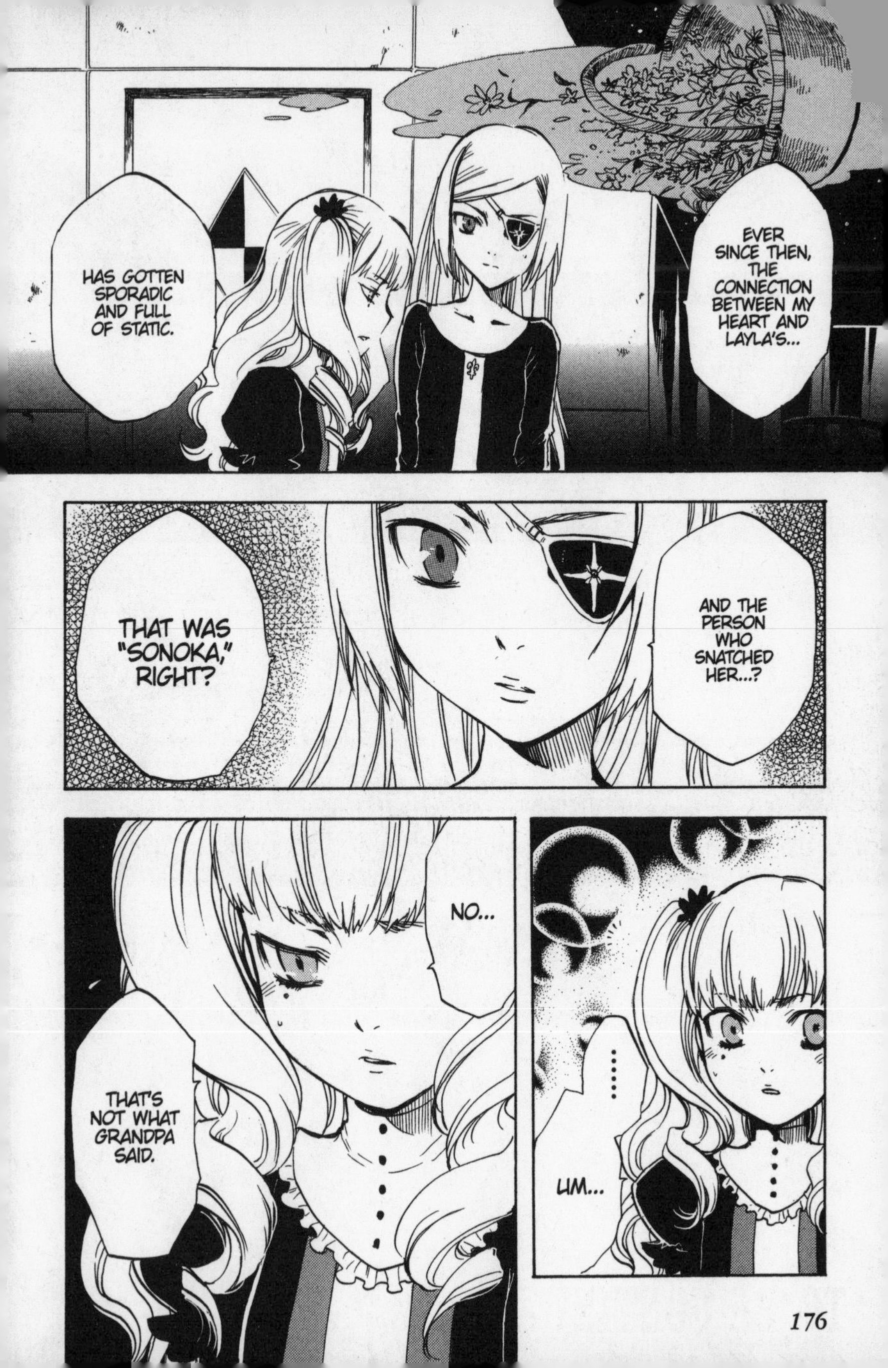
EVER SINCE THEN, THE CONNECTION BETWEEN MY HEART AND LAYLA'S...
HAS GOTTEN SPORADIC AND FULL OF STATIC.
AND THE PERSON WHO SNATCHED HER...?
THAT WAS "SONOKA," RIGHT?
......
UM...
NO...
THAT'S NOT WHAT GRANDPA SAID.

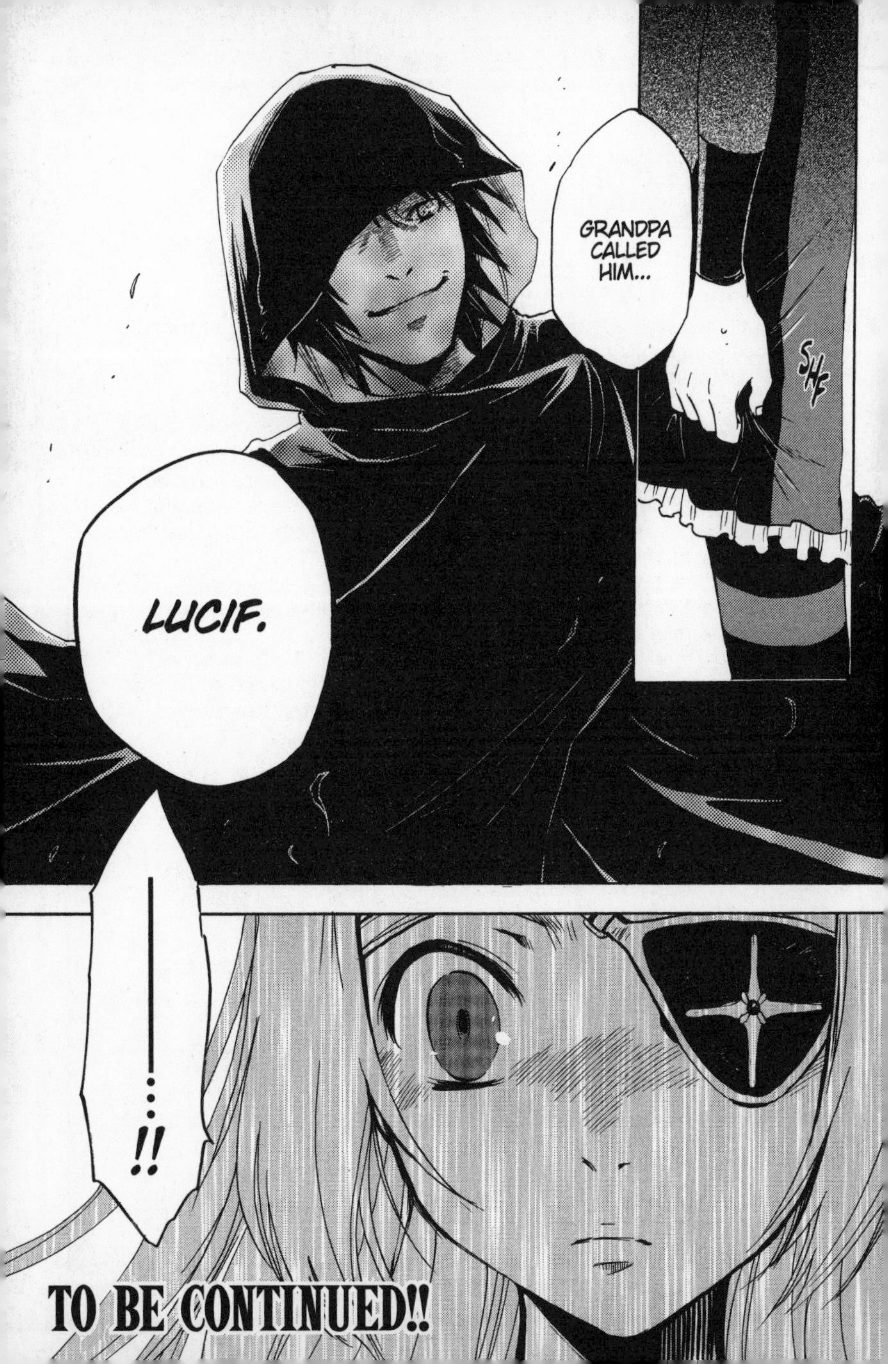
GRANDPA CALLED HIM...
SHF
LUCIF.
......!!
TO BE CONTINUED!!

JAPANESE HONORIFICS GUIDE

To ensure that all character relationships appear as they were originally intended, all character names have been kept in their original Japanese name order with family name first and given name second. For copyright reasons, creator names appear in standard English name order.

In addition to preserving the original Japanese name order, Seven Seas is committed to ensuring that honorifics—polite speech that indicates a person's status or relationship towards another individual—are retained within this book. Politeness is an integral facet of Japanese culture and we believe that maintaining honorifics in our translations helps bring out the same character nuances as seen in the original work.

The following are some of the more common honorifics you may come across while reading this and other books:

-san – The most common of all honorifics, it is an all-purpose suffix that can be used in any situation where politeness is expected. Generally seen as the equivalent to Mr., Miss, Ms., Mrs., etc.

-sama – This suffix is one level higher than "-san" and is used to confer great respect upon an individual.

-dono – Stemming from the word "tono," meaning "lord," "-dono" signifies an even higher level than "-sama," and confers the utmost respect.

-kun – This suffix is commonly used at the end of boys' names to express either familiarity or endearment. It can also be used when addressing someone younger than oneself or of a lower status.

-chan – Another common honorific. This suffix is mainly used to express endearment towards girls, but can also be used when referring to little boys or even pets. Couples are also known to use the term amongst each other to convey a sense of cuteness and intimacy.

Sempai – This title is used towards one's senior or "superior" in a particular group or organization. "Sempai" is most often used in a school setting, where underclassmen refer to upperclassmen as "sempai," though it is also commonly said by employees when addressing fellow employees who hold seniority in the workplace.

Kouhai – This is the exact opposite of "sempai," and is used to refer to underclassmen in school, junior employees at the workplace, etc.

Sensei – Literally meaning "one who has come before," this title is used for teachers, doctors, or masters of any profession or art.

Oniisan – This title literally means "big brother." First and foremost, it is used by younger siblings towards older male siblings. It can be used by itself or attached to a person's name as a suffix (niisan). It is often used by a younger person toward an older person unrelated by blood, but as a sign of respect. Other forms include the informal "oniichan" and the more respectful "oniisama."

Oneesan – This title is the opposite of "oniisan" and means "big sister." Other forms include the informal "oneechan" and the more respectful "oneesama."

TRANSLATION NOTES

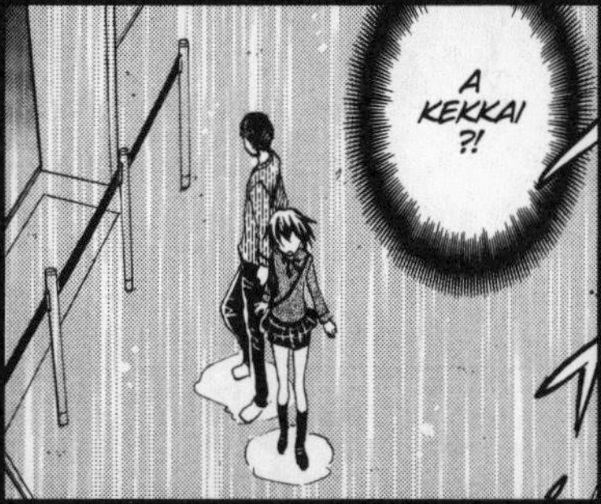
A KEKKAI ?!

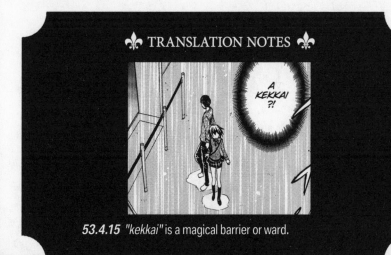

53.4.15 *"kekkai"* is a magical barrier or ward.

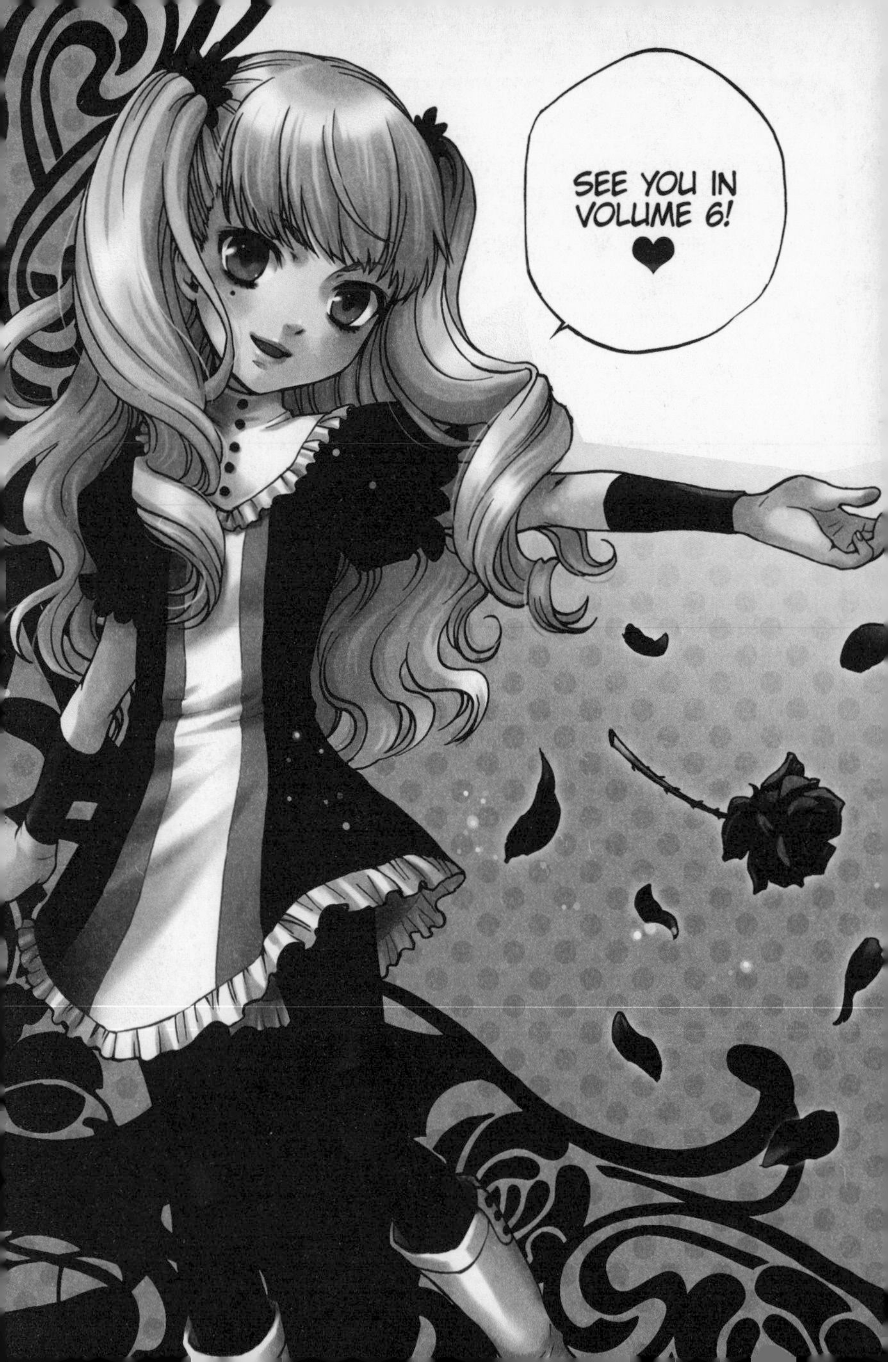
SEE YOU IN VOLUME 6! ♥

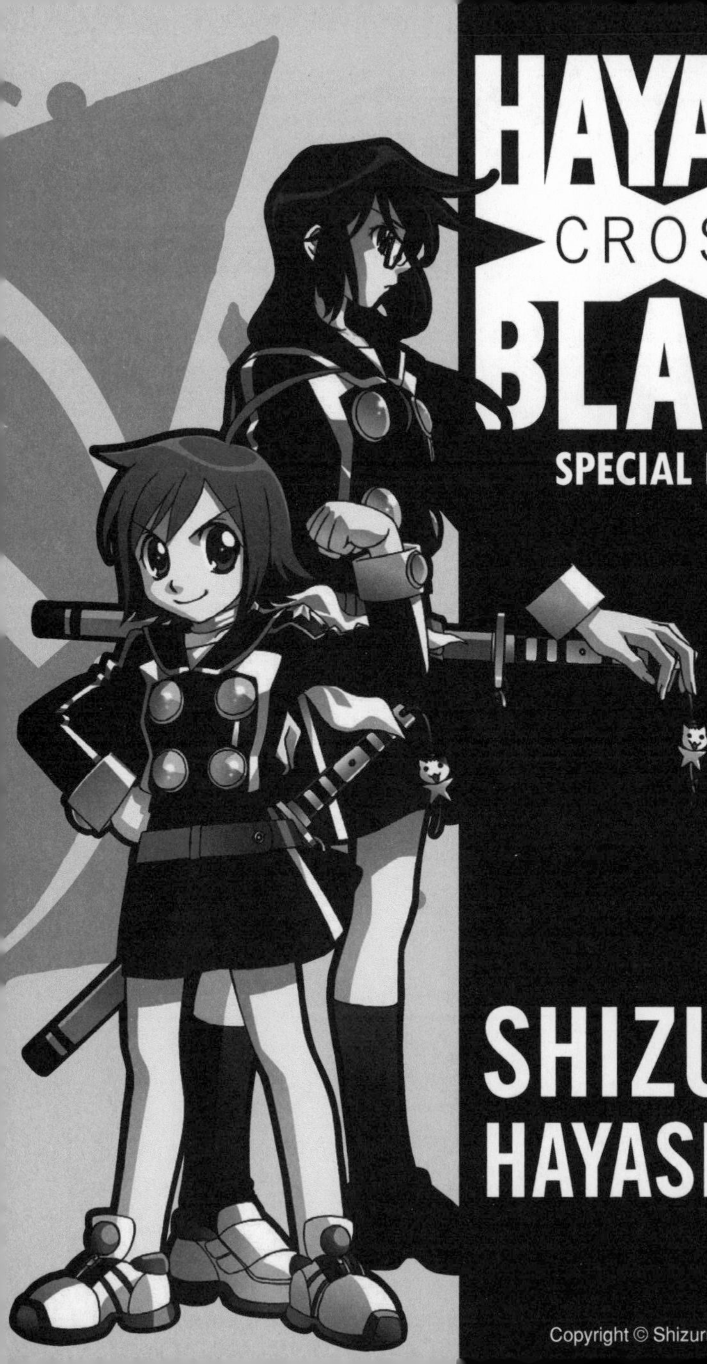

HAYATE CROSS BLADE

SPECIAL PREVIEW

SHIZURU HAYASHIYA

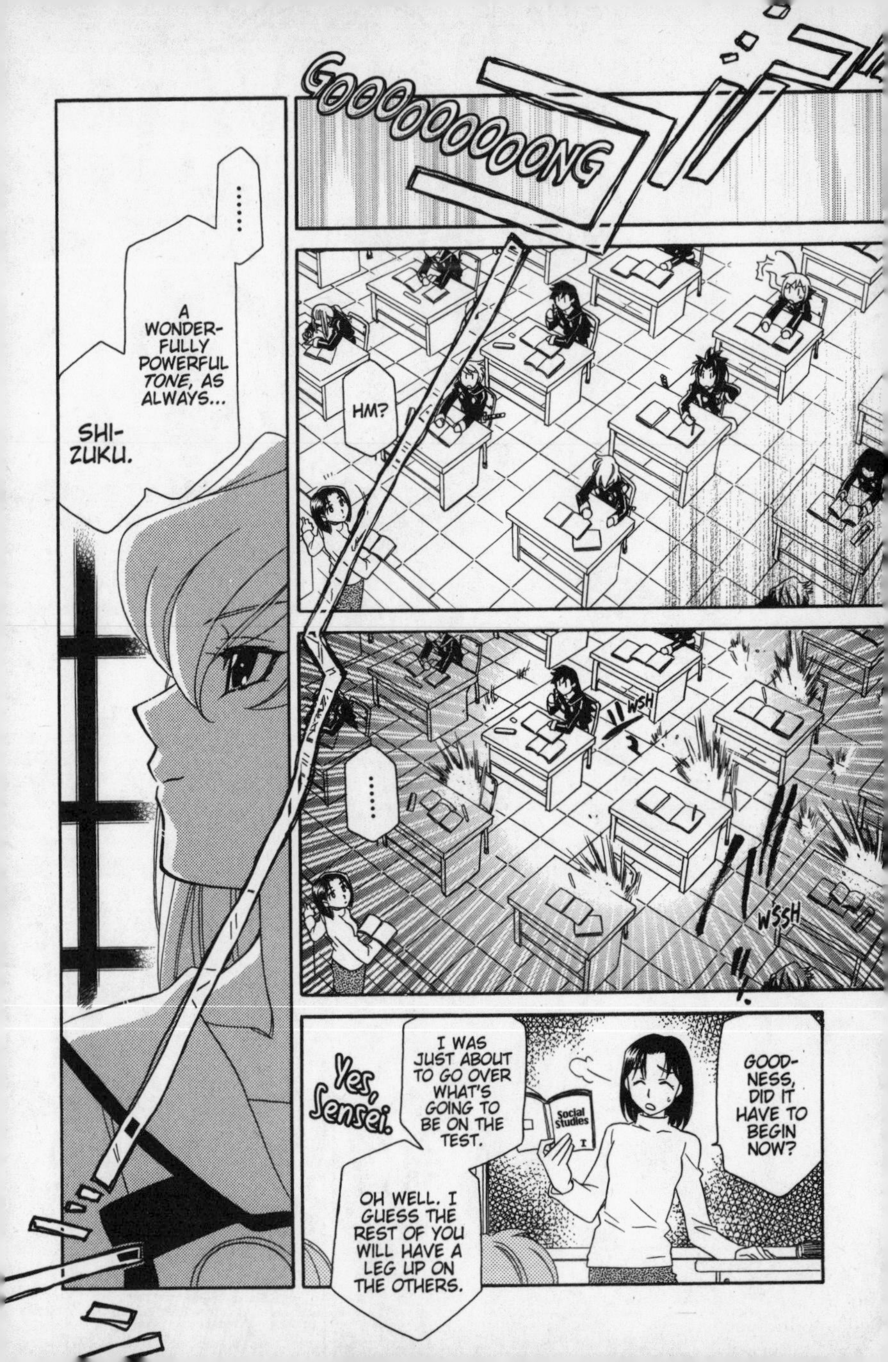
GOOOOOOOONG
HM?
......
WSH
WSSH
GOOD-NESS, DID IT HAVE TO BEGIN NOW?
I WAS JUST ABOUT TO GO OVER WHAT'S GOING TO BE ON THE TEST.
Social Studies I
Yes, Sensei.
OH WELL. I GUESS THE REST OF YOU WILL HAVE A LEG UP ON THE OTHERS.
......
A WONDER-FULLY POWERFUL TONE, AS ALWAYS...
SHI-ZUKU.

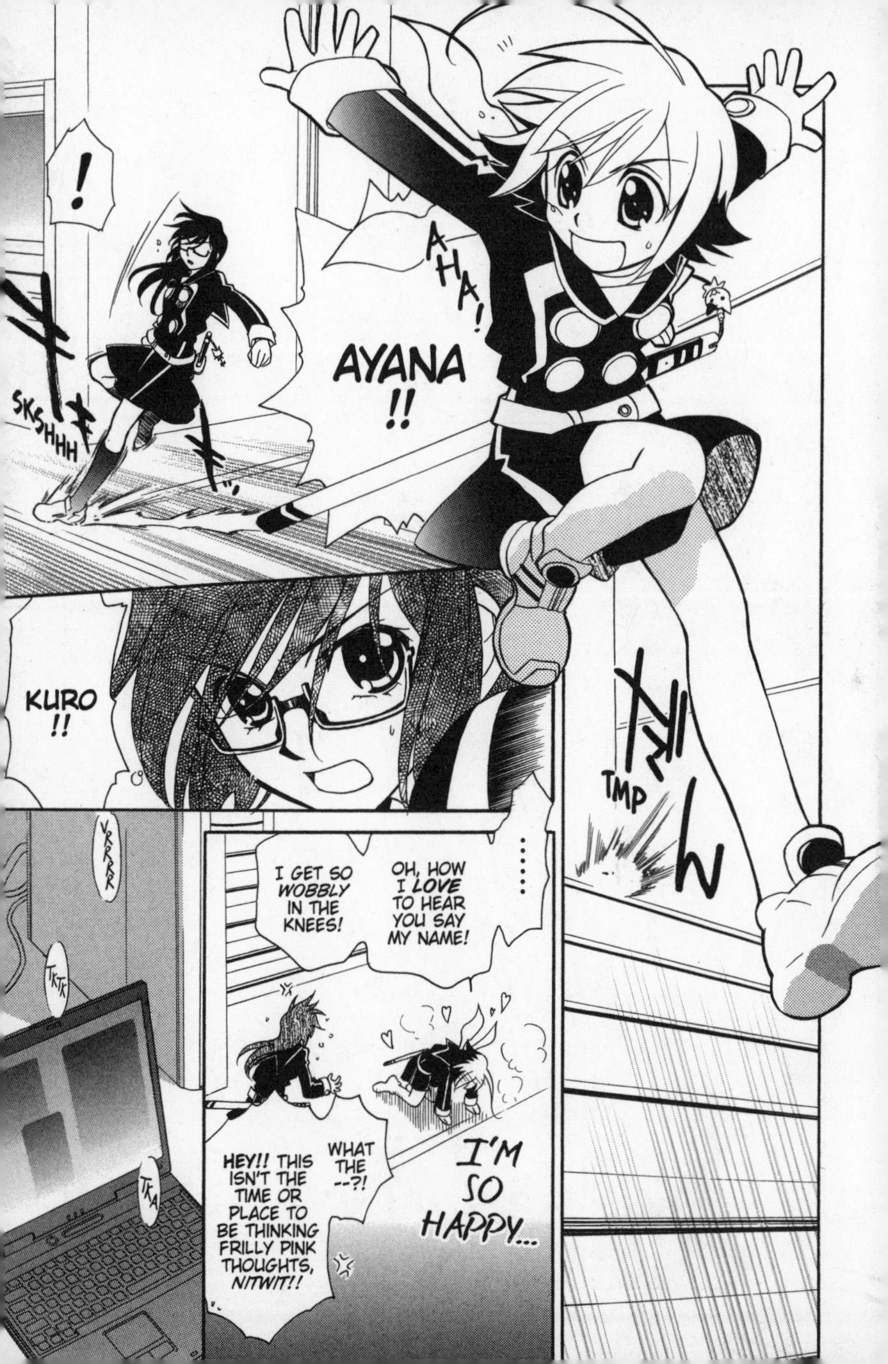
AHA!
AYANA!!
!
SKSHHH
TMP
KURO!!
......
OH, HOW I *LOVE* TO HEAR YOU SAY MY NAME!
I GET SO *WOBBLY* IN THE KNEES!
I'M SO HAPPY...
WHAT THE --?!
HEY!! THIS ISN'T THE TIME OR PLACE TO BE THINKING FRILLY PINK THOUGHTS, *NITWIT!!*
VRRRRR
TKTK
TKA

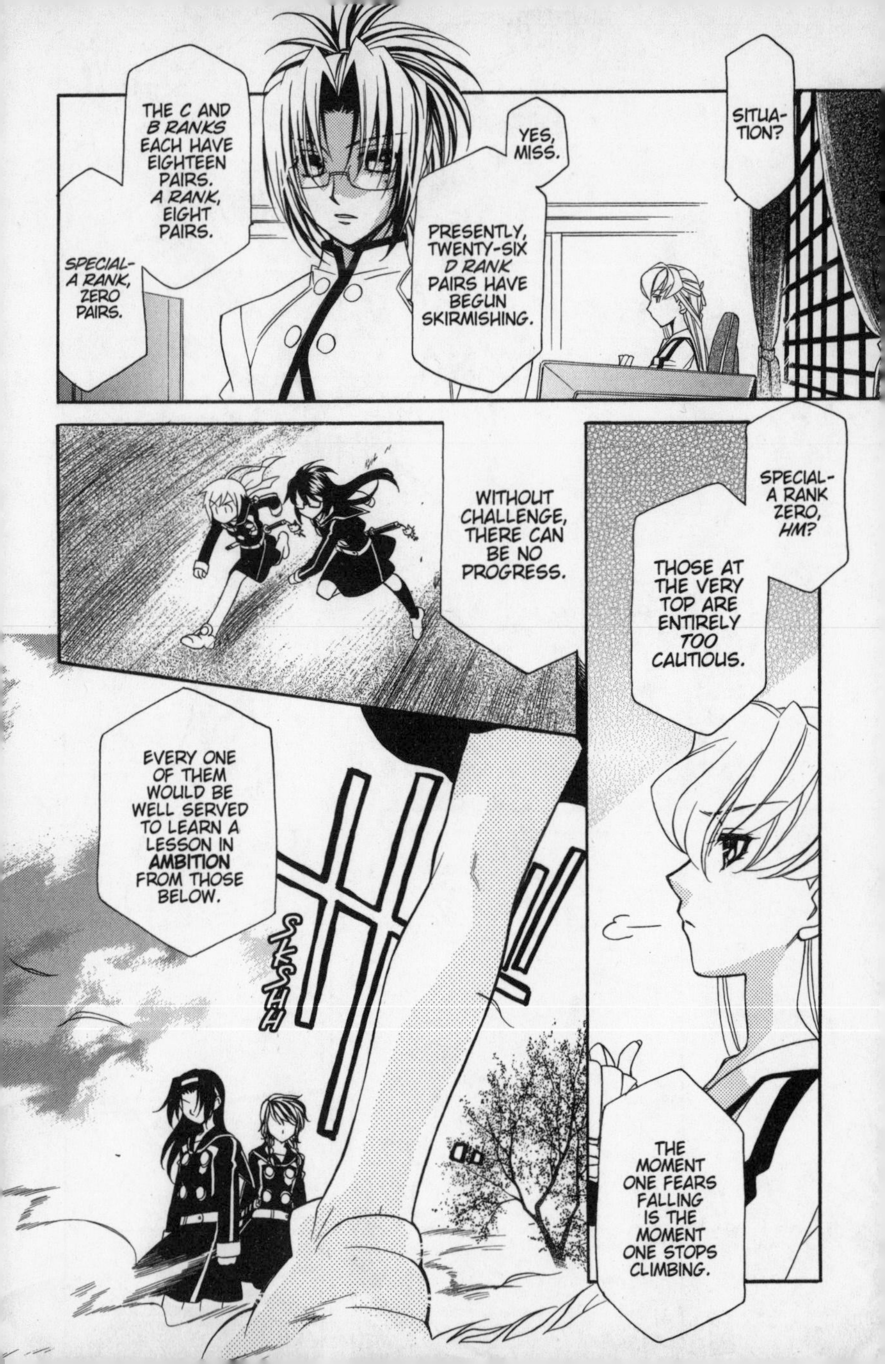
SITUA-TION?
YES, MISS.
PRESENTLY, TWENTY-SIX *D RANK* PAIRS HAVE BEGUN SKIRMISHING.
THE *C* AND *B RANKS* EACH HAVE EIGHTEEN PAIRS. *A RANK,* EIGHT PAIRS.
SPECIAL-A RANK, ZERO PAIRS.
SPECIAL-A RANK ZERO, *HM?*
THOSE AT THE VERY TOP ARE ENTIRELY *TOO* CAUTIOUS.
THE MOMENT ONE FEARS FALLING IS THE MOMENT ONE STOPS CLIMBING.
WITHOUT CHALLENGE, THERE CAN BE NO PROGRESS.
EVERY ONE OF THEM WOULD BE WELL SERVED TO LEARN A LESSON IN **AMBITION** FROM THOSE BELOW.
SKKSHH

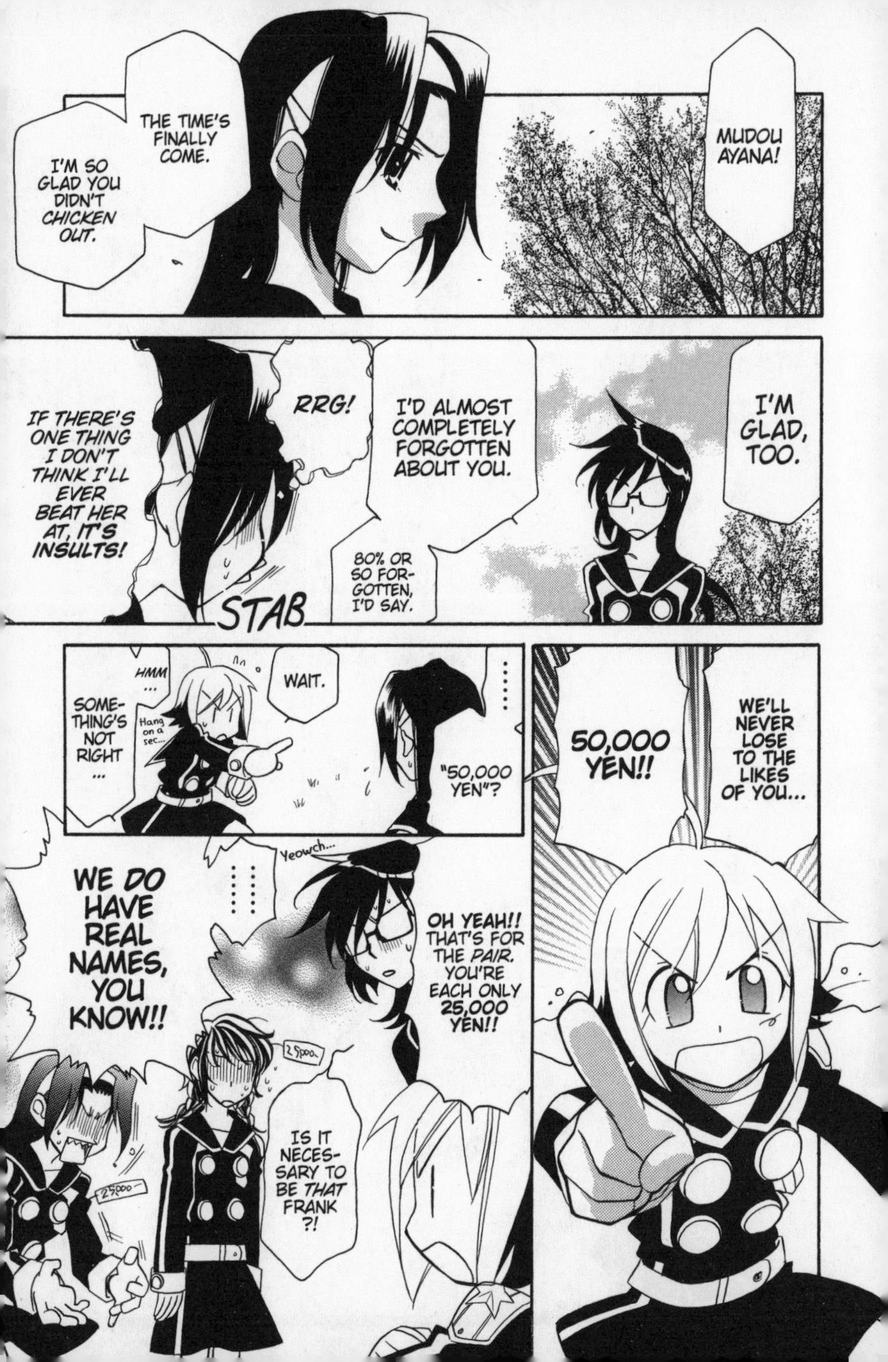
MUDOU AYANA!
THE TIME'S FINALLY COME.
I'M SO GLAD YOU DIDN'T CHICKEN OUT.
I'M GLAD, TOO.
I'D ALMOST COMPLETELY FORGOTTEN ABOUT YOU.
80% OR SO FOR-GOTTEN, I'D SAY.
RRG!
STAB
IF THERE'S ONE THING I DON'T THINK I'LL EVER BEAT HER AT, IT'S INSULTS!
WE'LL NEVER LOSE TO THE LIKES OF YOU...
50,000 YEN!!
......
"50,000 YEN"?
WAIT.
HMM...
SOME-THING'S NOT RIGHT...
Hang on a sec...
OH YEAH!! THAT'S FOR THE PAIR. YOU'RE EACH ONLY 25,000 YEN!!
Yeowch...
......
WE DO HAVE REAL NAMES, YOU KNOW!!
25,000...
IS IT NECES-SARY TO BE THAT FRANK?!
25,000—

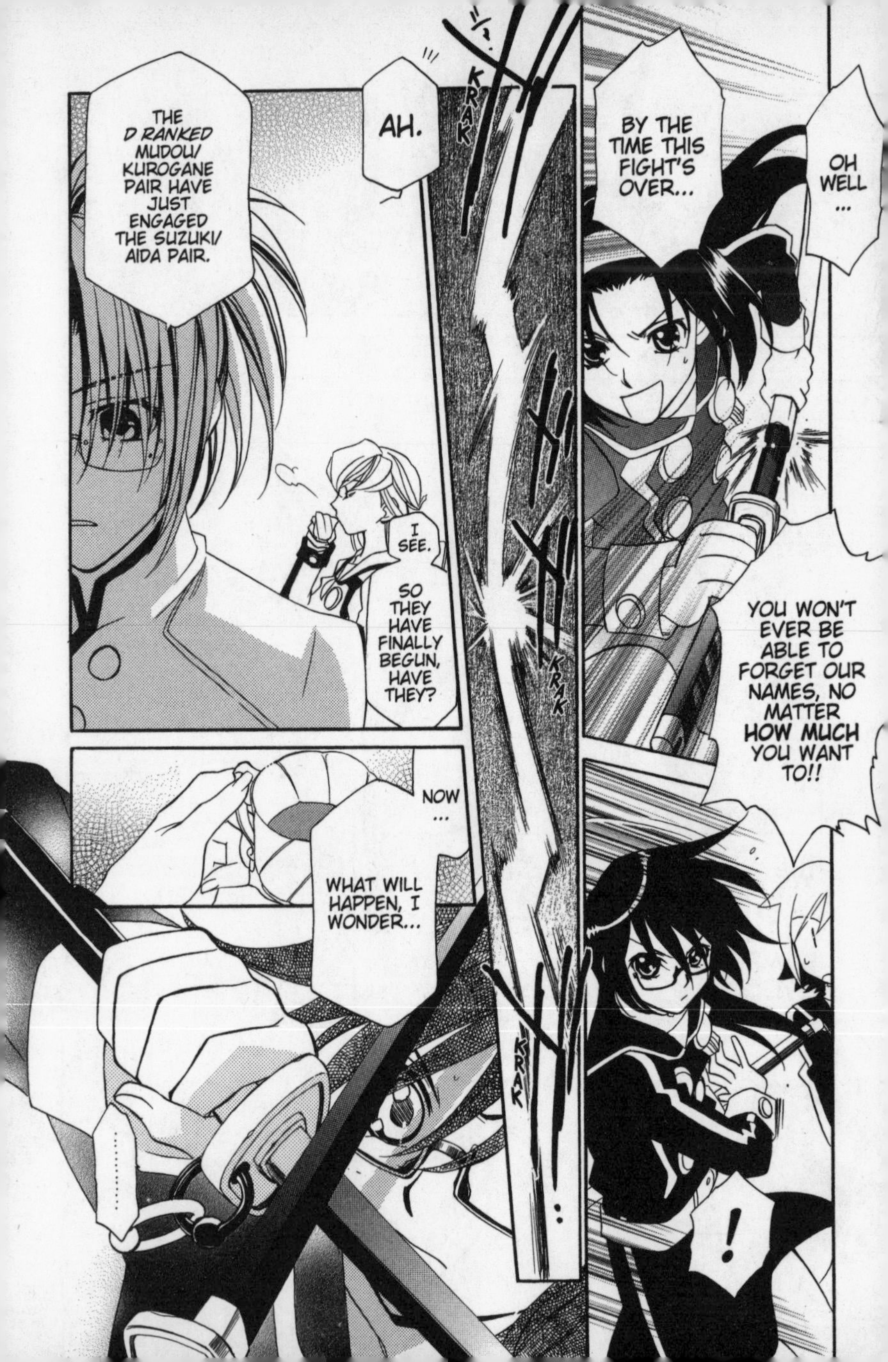

OH WELL ...
BY THE TIME THIS FIGHT'S OVER...
YOU WON'T EVER BE ABLE TO FORGET OUR NAMES, NO MATTER HOW MUCH YOU WANT TO!!
KRAK
!
KRAK
AH.
KRAK
THE D RANKED MUDOU/ KUROGANE PAIR HAVE JUST ENGAGED THE SUZUKI/ AIDA PAIR.
I SEE.
SO THEY HAVE FINALLY BEGUN, HAVE THEY?
NOW ...
WHAT WILL HAPPEN, I WONDER...
......

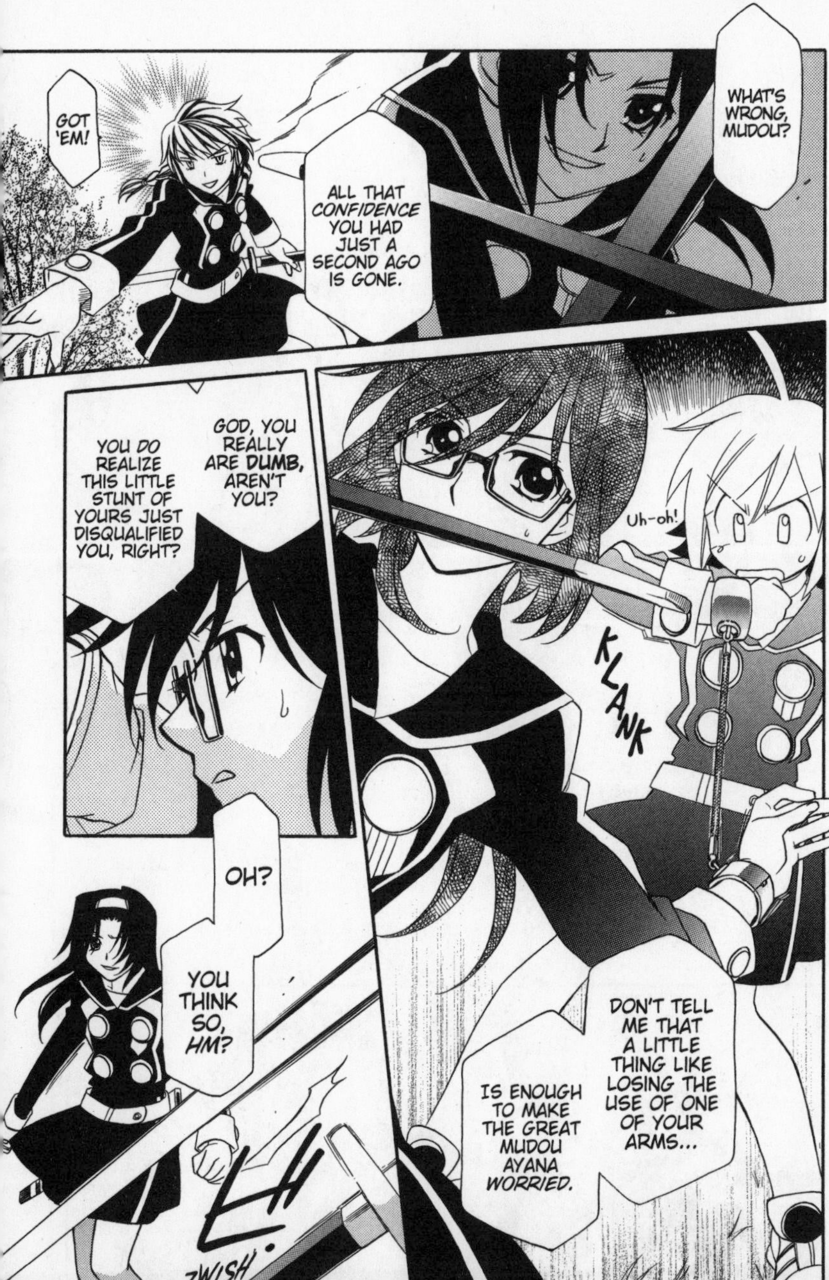
WHAT'S WRONG, MUDOU?
ALL THAT *CONFIDENCE* YOU HAD JUST A SECOND AGO IS GONE.
GOT 'EM!
Uh-oh!
KLANK
DON'T TELL ME THAT A LITTLE THING LIKE LOSING THE USE OF ONE OF YOUR ARMS...
IS ENOUGH TO MAKE THE GREAT MUDOU AYANA *WORRIED.*
GOD, YOU REALLY ARE **DUMB**, AREN'T YOU?
YOU DO REALIZE THIS LITTLE STUNT OF YOURS JUST DISQUALIFIED YOU, RIGHT?
OH?
YOU THINK SO, *HM?*
ZWISH

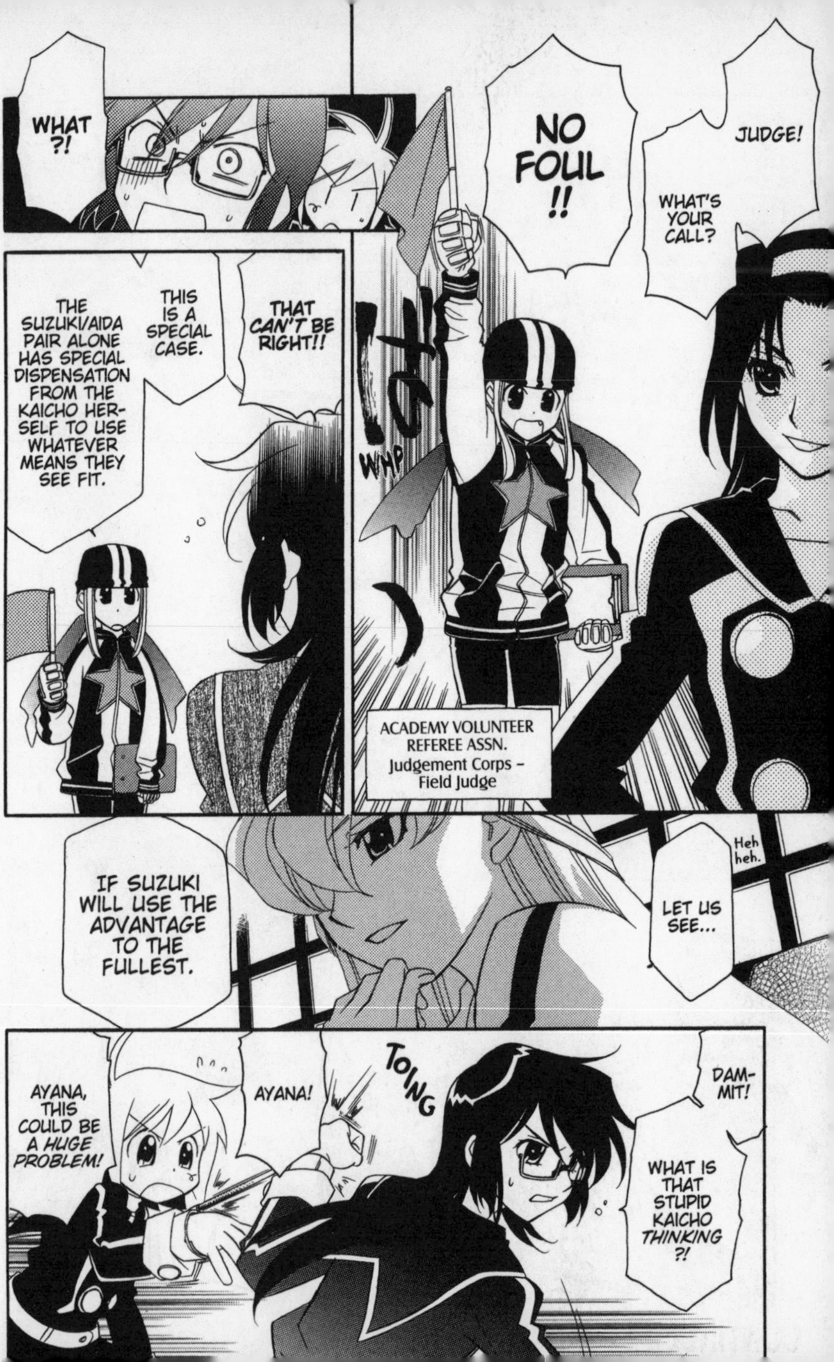

JUDGE!
WHAT'S YOUR CALL?
NO FOUL!!
WHP
ACADEMY VOLUNTEER REFEREE ASSN. Judgement Corps – Field Judge
WHAT?!
THAT *CAN'T* BE RIGHT!!
THIS IS A SPECIAL CASE.
THE SUZUKI/AIDA PAIR ALONE HAS SPECIAL DISPENSATION FROM THE KAICHO HER-SELF TO USE WHATEVER MEANS THEY SEE FIT.
Heh heh.
LET US SEE...
IF SUZUKI WILL USE THE ADVANTAGE TO THE FULLEST.
DAM-MIT!
WHAT IS THAT STUPID KAICHO *THINKING* ?!
TOING
AYANA!
AYANA, THIS COULD BE A *HUGE PROBLEM!*

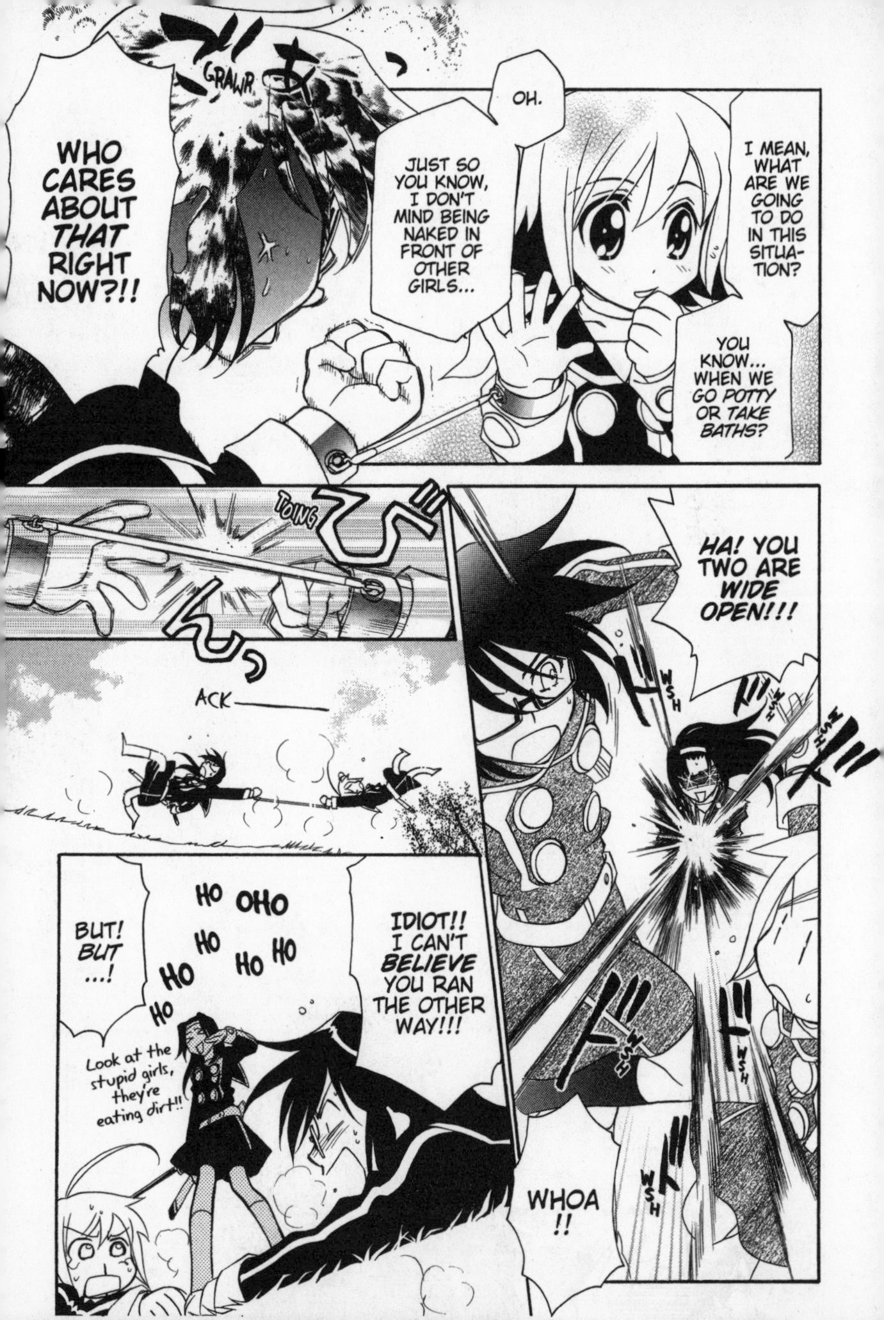
I MEAN, WHAT ARE WE GOING TO DO IN THIS SITUATION?
YOU KNOW... WHEN WE GO POTTY OR TAKE BATHS?
OH.
JUST SO YOU KNOW, I DON'T MIND BEING NAKED IN FRONT OF OTHER GIRLS...
GRAWR
WHO CARES ABOUT THAT RIGHT NOW?!!
HA! YOU TWO ARE WIDE OPEN!!!
WSH
WSH
WSH
WSH
WHOA !!
TOING
ACK——
IDIOT!! I CAN'T BELIEVE YOU RAN THE OTHER WAY!!!
HO OHO HO HO HO HO HO HO
BUT! BUT ...!
Look at the stupid girls, they're eating dirt!!

CONTINUED IN *HAYATE X BLADE* VOL.1

VOLUME 5

story & art by Atsushi Suzumi

STAFF CREDITS

translation	**Adrienne Beck**
adaptation	**Janet Houck**
cover design	**Nicky Lim**
retouch & lettering	**Roland Amago**
layout	**Bambi Eloriaga–Amago**
copy editor	**Lori Smith**
editor	**Adam Arnold**

publisher	**Jason DeAngelis**
	Seven Seas Entertainment

VENUS VERSUS VIRUS VOL. 5
© ATSUSHI SUZUMI 2007
First published in 2007 by Media Works Inc., Tokyo, Japan
English translation rights arranged with Media Works, Inc.

No portion of this book may be reproduced or transmitted in
any form without written permission from the copyright holders.

This is a work of fiction. Names, characters, places, and
incidents are the products of the author's imagination or are used
fictitiously. Any resemblance to actual events, locales, or persons,
living or dead, is entirely coincidental.

Seven Seas and the Seven Seas logo are trademarks of
Seven Seas Entertainment, LLC. All rights reserved.

Visit us online at www.gomanga.com

ISBN: 978-1-934876-17-6

Printed in Canada

First printing: October 2008

10 9 8 7 6 5 4 3 2 1

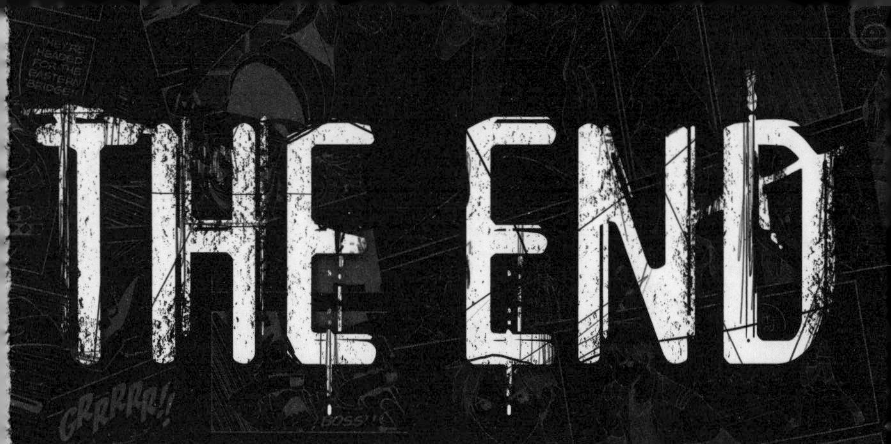
THEY'RE HEADED FOR THE EASTERN BRIDGE!
THE END
GRRRR!!

YOU'RE READING THE WRONG WAY

This is the last page of
Venus Versus Virus Volume 5

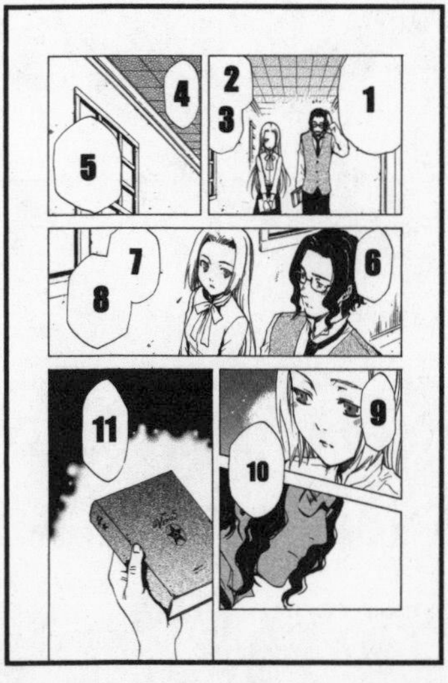
1
2
3
4
5
6
7
8
9
10
11

This book reads from right to left, Japanese style. To read from the beginning, flip the book over to the other side, start with the top right panel, and take it from there.

If this is your first time reading manga, just follow the diagram. It may seem backwards at first, but you'll get used to it! Have fun!

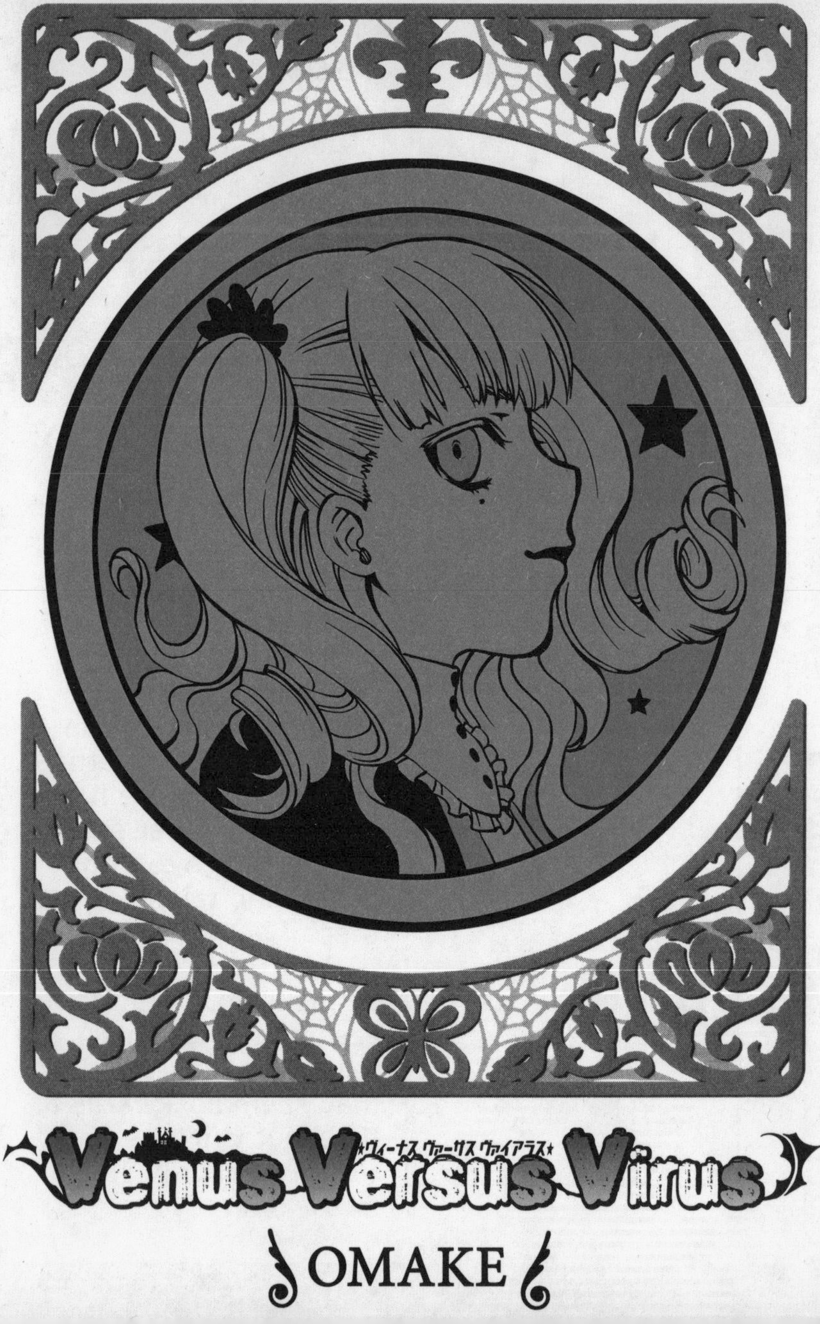

Venus Versus Virus

ヴィーナス ヴァーサス ヴァイアラス

OMAKE